From Family to Market

From Family to Market

Labor Allocation
in Contemporary China

Fei-Ling Wang

ROWMAN & LITTLEFIELD PUBLISHERS, INC.
Lanham • Boulder • New York • Oxford

ROWMAN & LITTLEFIELD PUBLISHERS, INC.

Published in the United States of America
by Rowman & Littlefield Publishers, Inc.
4720 Boston Way, Lanham, Maryland 20706

12 Hid's Copse Road
Cumnor Hill, Oxford OX2 9JJ, England

British Library Cataloguing in Publication Information Available

Library of Congress Cataloging-in-Publication Data
Wang, Fei-Ling
  From family to market : labor allocation in contemporary China /
Fei-Ling Wang
    p.   cm.
  Includes bibliographical references and index.
        ISBN 0-8476-8879-8 (cloth : alk. paper). — ISBN 0-8476-8880-1
(pbk. : alk. paper)
    1. Manpower policy—China. 2. Labor market—China. 3. labor
mobility—China. 4. China—Economic policy—1976– 5. China—Social
policy. 6. Communism—China I. Title.
HD5830.A6W357   1998
331.1'0951—dc21   98-13238

ISBN 0-8476-8879-8 (cloth : alk. paper)
ISBN 0-8476-8880-1 (pbk. : alk. paper)

Printed in the United States of America

♾™ The paper used in this publication meets the minimum requirements of American
National Standard for Information Sciences—Permanence of Paper for Printed Library
Materials, ANSI Z39.48–1984.

To the memory of my mother,

Li Zhengxiang (李征祥)

Contents

Tables and Figures

Tables

Figures

Preface

This book explores and explains institutional structures and changes in contemporary China through an investigation of the history, current forms, and new developments of Chinese labor allocation patterns (LAPs). The bulk of this study constitutes historical and statistical analyses supported by information collected from numerous field studies carried out from 1989 to 1996.

One of the main findings of the study is that China has had a highly stable and undifferentiated institutional structure centered on the family-based traditional LAP for centuries, including most of the PRC (People's Republic of China) era. However, since the mid-1980s, four LAPs have coexisted in the PRC: a restored family-based traditional LAP, an authoritarian state LAP, community-based labor markets, and a national labor market. These profound developments reflect the mixed and transitional nature of the Chinese institutional structure at the end of the twentieth century. A distorted but effective market has advanced rapidly to become the leading, if not yet dominant, institution allocating the most important resource—the labor force.

The book begins with an introduction followed by four chapters, a conclusion, and an appendix. The introduction presents the analytical approaches and framework used. The various LAPs are discussed and proposed as indicators for our observation of the institutional features and changes of a nation.

Chapter 1 examines in depth the restored family-based traditional LAP in contemporary China. The origin and evolution of this LAP, as well as its institutional impact on the Chinese organizational structure, are explored and analyzed. It is argued that the restored family-based traditional LAP, the largest of the four LAPs, has significantly reestablished China's pre-PRC institutions to the majority of the Chinese in the rural areas. The new development of this LAP in the 1990s, however, indicates its instability and stagnation—just like its predecessors. How to transfer the huge number of laborers out of this LAP without causing an institutional explosion or implosion will be a major task facing the Chinese in the twenty-first century.

The authoritarian state LAP has been the dominant LAP in urban China since the 1950s. The formal and informal institutions and mechanisms of this LAP are explored in chapter 2. Several important yet uniquely "Chinese" institutions associated with this LAP, such as household or residential registration (*hukou*), unit (*danwei*), and dossier (*dangan*), are given special attention. The chapter shows that the authoritarian state LAP is a cornerstone for the current CCP- (Chinese Communist Party) PRC authoritarian political system. We will discuss certain paradoxical advantages of this LAP in facilitating the advancement of the Chinese market institution. The current "market-oriented" reforms of this LAP pose unique opportunities and profound challenges to the whole course of Chinese modernization.

Chapter 3 investigates community-based labor markets (CLMs) as the transformed societal LAP. It begins with a brief discussion on the important role of the local communities in China. The CLMs, practiced by urban collective enterprises, many state-owned enterprises, and especially the massive and thriving township and village enterprises (TVEs), are now the second-largest LAP in China; they are growing much faster than the authoritarian state LAP, whereas the family-based traditional LAP is declining. Economically very viable and fairly efficient, while politically and socially less "threatening," the CLMs are expected to be the dominant LAP in the near future, thus producing a localized, functioning, albeit distorted market institution. The development and transformation of the CLMs appear to hold special significance for the national unity and political stability of China.

The rapidly emerging national labor market, practiced primarily by foreign-invested enterprises and native private employers, is the subject of chapter 4. How Beijing gradually gave in to the demands of foreign investors concerning the "importing" and development of this new LAP demonstrates the crucial role of external influences in Chinese modernization. As the fastest-growing LAP, though still relatively small, the national labor market has had a disproportionately great institutional impact, helping to facilitate a differentiation of the Chinese economy from the Chinese sociopolitical complex. The accommodating attitudes of Chinese political and social institutions toward foreign employment and the adaptive behaviors of foreign employers may be especially interesting for China watchers and interested foreign investors.

The conclusion summarizes and analyzes the main findings of the study. The appendices chronicle the major events in the history of the PRC's LAPs and includes background information on the individuals interviewed.

Acknowledgments

I am deeply indebted to many individuals and organizations for their assistance in the research and writing of this book. For their ideas, training, critical comments, and invaluable support and encouragement, I want to thank my mentors, colleagues, and friends at the University of Pennsylvania, the United States Military Academy (West Point), and the Georgia Institute of Technology, among other places. These individuals include Robert Barnett, Linda Brady, Peter Brecke, Thomas Callaghy, Thomas Christensen, William J. Clark, John W. Garver, Avery Goldstein, Joanne Gowa, Daniel Kaufman, Friedrich Kratochwil, Chong-Sik Lee, William Long, Arvid Lukauskas, Jack Nagel, A. Richard Norton, Daniel Papp, Stephen Wilkins, and Brian Woodall.

The Sam Nunn School of International Affairs at Georgia Tech has provided a wonderful working environment for me. The librarians and staff at the East Asian section of the Library of Congress, the Harvard-Yenching Library of Harvard University, and the East Asian Library of Columbia University have always offered great help in allowing me to use their collections. Jody Berman carefully edited the manuscript for me.

The five field trips I took to China and other East Asian countries between 1992 and 1996 were made possible with the generous support of the following sponsors: the Penfield Fellowship of the University of Pennsylvania; the Faculty Research and Development Fund of the United States Military Academy; the Center for International Business Education and Research at Georgia Tech; the Georgia Tech Foundation; the Center of International Strategy, Technology and Policy; and Cable News Network (CNN) International.

So many people helped with my field research, yet I can thank only some of them here: Chen Fei, Chen Ping, Chen Siheng, Chu Shulong, Chen Ying, Guang Li, Guo Henchui, Guo Wanqing, He Ming, Miyuki Ishii, Jung-Bock Lee, Jong-Chan Rhee, Ma Min, Yang-Ho Kim, Li Canli, Li Lei, Li Qian, Li Wei, Liu Ji, Liu Xianling, Liu Wanqing, Ming Chu-Cheng, Hakson Paik, Sheng Fumin, Sun Hui, Sun Qi, Tang Jinping, Wang Guanying, Wang Liya, Wang Subei, Wu Sou-Chang, Xu Minqi, Zhang Lanting, Zhang Nan, Zhang Xinming, Xu Yibo, Zhang Yan, Zhong Yongsan, and Zhou Renwei.

Finally, I would like to gratefully acknowledge my family, especially my wife, Yan, and children, Yvonne and Justin, for their love, patience, understanding, and support—without which I would never have been able to finish this book.

F. L. W.
Atlanta, Georgia
U.S.A.

Glossary/Abbreviations

This list contains some Chinese terms and abbreviations that are frequently used in this book. Italicized terms are phonetic translations of Chinese terms or abbreviations. To enable easier reference, the Chinese characters of most important or well-known terms, events, or authors are listed when they appear for the first time in the text, notes, or the bibliography.

CBEs (社队企业): commune and brigade enterprises.
CCP: the Chinese Communist Party.
CLMs: community-based labor markets.
CNPC or NPC: the Chinese National People's Congress.
COCs: coastal open cities.
dangan (档案): personal dossier.
danwei or *danweis* (单位): unit or units.
diannong (佃农): tenant farmers.
FDI: foreign direct investment.
FESCO: foreign enterprise service corporation.
gaogan (高干): senior cadre.
getihu (个体户): individual household (private family economy).
GMD: Gumindang, the Chinese Nationalist Party; formerly KMT, Kuomintang.
guanshang (官商): state-owned/run business.
guanxi (关系): connections.
gudinggong (固定工): permanent employees.
gunong (雇农): hired peasants.
hukou (户口): household or residential registration system.

juntian (均田) : (re)distribution of land.

LAP: labor allocation pattern.

liumin (流民): migrating and unemployed peasants.

LSEs: labor service enterprises.

mangliu (盲流): blindly (uncontrolled) floating/migrating people.

mu (亩): 0.1647 acre.

PLA: the People's Liberation Army.

PRC: the People's Republic of China.

qiye (企业): enterprise (e.g., a factory, shop or a company).

rencai jiaoliu zhongxin: talent/professional exchange center.

Renmin Ribao: People's Daily.

Renmin Ribao-Overseas: People's Daily-Overseas Edition.

rmb (人民币): renminbi—currency of the PRC.

sanzi (三资): foreign investment of three kinds (equity joint ventures, cooperative joint ventures, and wholly owned enterprises).

SEZs: special economic zones.

shiye (事业): institution (e.g., a school, hospital, or governmental agency).

SSB: the State Statistical Bureau.

TVEs (乡镇企业): township and village enterprises.

xiagang (下岗): off-duty (dismissed with minimum pay for limited time).

xiahai (下海): plunge into the sea (engage in business activities).

Xinhua: the (official) Xinhua News Agency.

yigong yinong (亦工亦农): semi-worker semi-peasant.

zhuanyehu (专业户): specialized household (a family specializing in one industry).

zigengnong (自耕农): landowning farmers.

Introduction: Labor Allocation Patterns and Institutional Structures

Since the 1970s, the People's Republic of China (PRC) has experienced profound institutional changes—especially economic. Although few question the significance of those changes, observers disagree on how to assess and interpret them.[1] Furthermore, underlying continuities have made an institutional analysis of the PRC more complex.[2]

To establish a set of indicators and as perhaps a methodological innovation, this book investigates labor allocation patterns (LAPs) in contemporary China as a tool for understanding both the Chinese institutional continuities and changes. LAPs are key components of any country's domestic institutional structure. LAPs, especially changes in them, also indicate the mechanisms, channels, and forces responsible for the endurance, structure, and evolution of the institutional fabric of a particular country.

There are two central issues in analyzing labor allocation patterns:[3] (1) how labor, as a major economic resource, is allocated and utilized; and (2) how the carriers of this economic resource—the people—are treated politically and socially. Probing these issues will reveal how political, economic, and social institutions are organized. For example, one can determine from LAPs whether the state is autonomous, effective, and participatory; whether the economy is market-oriented; and whether there is a civil society featuring functional families, voluntary associations, and individual rights (Orren 1995, 386).

Conceptualizing Labor Allocation Patterns

LAPs are defined as the ways in which the division of labor is real-ized, maintained, reproduced, and transformed.[4] They encompass the patterns and norms that guide the organization of labor in production, that is, the allocation and the reallocation of the labor force across the boundaries of professions, institutions, specific jobs, and geogra-phy. LAPs, or the ways in which the division of labor is brought about, are therefore crucial to the production, reproduction, and transformation of any human civilization. Because it is usually diffi-cult to separate people from their working abilities, patterns of allo-cating labor relate not only to the economic consideration of effi-ciency or productivity but also frequently to many other social and political concerns that motivate human behavior. LAPs thus reflect the conceptual considerations of both economic development—namely, the combination of human resources with production resour-ces ("production mode" in Marxian terms)—and sociopolitical ch-anges.[5]

Institutionally, LAPs constitute a major part of the basic frame-work in which people interact with nature and each other. Any signif-icant adjustment of the relative positions as well as the internal struc-ture of a nation's domestic institutional settings will inevitably be expressed by changes in labor allocation. For example, only when a certain LAP (i.e., a market-oriented allocation of the working abili-ties of labor) is established can a real market emerge, distinguishing the economy from politics and social activities. Only when a certain LAP (under which laborers enjoy social mobility and equality, com-prehensive political participation, and substantial economic security) is established can a civil society and democratic polity exist. There-fore, a study of LAPs becomes a reliable way to analyze social, po-litical, and economic development.

Labor historically has been allocated by the combined forces of knowledge or technology and spontaneous economic activities and the governing powers. The LAP in a nation, or even across nations, is shaped through forces of economic and political institutions, aided by a less visible but at times powerful third force of social institutions such as the family. The internalized institutions of a human grouping (the group or national culture) are also influential: traditional beliefs, religion, circumstantial convenience, moral values, codes of conduct, and customs.[6] A fourth shaping force is the interaction between the nation's domestic institutional structure and the international environment, as in FDI (foreign direct investment). The presence, function, and intensity of each force depends on numerous variables.

Empirically, there have been three major categories, or ideal types, of LAPs: (1) the traditional LAP, which features personal dependence of labor based on social or political institutions; (2) the labor market, based on the personal freedom and mobility of laborers; and (3) an authoritarian political (state) allocation of labor, which can be viewed as an extremist version of the traditional LAP by the combined forces of the state and communist ideology. The three categories reflect distinctively different types of domestic institutional structures.

The Traditional LAP

The traditional LAP has dominated most of human history. It does not differentiate the working abilities of laborers from their physical being—both are "properties" subject to full allocation and utilization by heads of families, masters, or political rulers.[7] The family-based handicraft workshops and the "self-employed" landholding peasants in nations like China belong to the traditional LAP. Traditional LAPs are found worldwide and constitute a major part of the institutional structure under which the economy, polity, and social life are organized. The traditional LAP has two variations: a societal LAP and a political LAP. They differ in their institutional basis and social status of their laborers.

The traditional societal LAP is primarily family or community based. Social institutions such as kinship are the institutional basis for this type of LAP, and universal social concerns of everyone, including the laborers, are the main concerns in the allocation and utilization of labor. In the societal LAP, laborers are confined to their social institutions—families or communities. The organization of labor is clearly hierarchical and personal, and family dependence is the norm. Labor mobility is very low, and differentiation of the working ability of the laborers is generally undeveloped. The societal LAP has been the major component of the traditional LAP through history.

The traditional political LAP is generally a slavery system organized along political institutions. Laborers, and usually their families and offspring, are virtually "owned" by their employers or masters. They have no meaningful geographical or occupational mobility, political rights, or social status. Labor is allocated by political decisions, often resulting from military actions such as conquest and war. Economic concerns such as productivity and innovation are important but by no means primary; political needs generally prevail in allocating labor. Historically the social concerns for laborers have been almost nonexistent except for "breeding" the slaves. Serfdom, a mild version of this traditional political LAP, is created by political decisions but gradually develops into more of a societal than political LAP.

The Labor Market

The second historical type of LAP is the labor market, characterized by personal freedom and mobility of labor. The working ability of laborers is traded as a commodity at a price determined by supply and demand. Personal freedom and mobility of labor across geographical, occupational, and even national boundaries are institutionalized. "Equal" contracting rather than personal dependency is the norm between labor and employer, and there is a competitive rather than monopolized supply and demand of labor (Loveridge and Mok 1979, 27; Levitan et al. 1972, 201).

Such an LAP provides the very basis for a functioning market economy. Naturally, this kind of LAP is by no means completely autonomous and is subject to several types of political and social influences. Political influences, for example, may be generated by policies adjusting wage control, the supply of labor through changes in the legal working age and/or working hours, labor demand, and most importantly, labor mobility (De Neubourg 1988, 166). Empirically, we see that a market-oriented LAP today is quite different from the pure theoretical model. There are powerful labor unions, collective (even national) bargaining practices, and labor legislation. There are tremendous barriers to labor mobility, especially on the international level, and considerable protected or privileged labor allocation practices, such as public-sector employment and government-assigned jobs. But generally, the majority of the labor force is allocated through the albeit imperfect market. The distortions of a labor market in a particular nation actually contain valuable information about the amount and effectiveness of interactions between the market economy and the polity.

Labor markets, especially at a national scale, emerged under capitalism after the sixteenth and seventeenth centuries. By the nineteenth century, the labor market became the major LAP in the West. Although there has been a close association between capitalism and the labor market, the latter is not exclusively capitalist, for it can exist even if the means of production are privately owned. This book treats the labor market as a pattern of allocating labor in which the laborers trade their working abilities/skills as their property. The participants in a labor market are legally and politically equal, and trading is protected by law—at least in theory. Outside contractual arrangements, laborers, as well as employers, are free to move geographically and occupationally. They can choose a job freely—though that is often difficult because of the transaction costs involved—and even refuse to work. Wages and other economic benefits are the only means through which the employer can control labor.

Functional labor markets tend to be nationally based because the political and social institutions of the states tend to block the free flow of labor across their boundaries. Although certain market-oriented international labor allocations exist, an integrated world labor market is probably an ideal rather than a feasible institution. Because labor has perhaps the most significant political and social implications among all economic resources, established national labor markets tend to be less free than national financial or commodity markets. Within a nation, there could be a clear historical pattern of labor market segmentation, whereby the LAP-shaping forces encourage the division of the labor market into separate, local, submarkets, or segments, with varied market orientation or distortion.

Authoritarian State Allocation

The third historical type of LAP, which may be becoming a thing of the past, is the authoritarian state allocation practiced by Leninist regimes in centrally planned economies. Study of this "socialist LAP" has been relatively limited. There are, however, some notable exceptions, such as Berliner (1957), Shirk (1981 and 1982), Oi (1985), and especially Andrew Walder's (1986) groundbreaking work on the authoritarian state LAP in China. Alec Nove (1977) discussed in detail Soviet labor policies in his classic study on socialist economy. He noted that labor in the former Soviet Union is regarded as a non-commodity and is said to be allocated according to the principle of maximizing obscure "social utility" through planning.

Under this LAP, the state allocates labor through administrative means according to various economic theories, plans, and political decisions. There is clear personal dependence of labor on the party-ruled state, economically, politically, and even socially. To a great extent, the authoritarian state LAP is like an enlarged traditional political LAP that is nationwide, agency based, and administratively operated. The state, as the central political authority, sets the basic rules and principles for labor allocation nationwide. The politicians and the state bureaucracy, rather than the supply and demand mechanism of the market, determine criteria for recruitment, pay, punishment, promotion, and dismissal. Hierarchical structures and low labor mobility are some of the defining features of an authoritarian state LAP. Rank, compensation scales, benefits, promotion, and demotion of workers are usually set nationally and scheduled routinely at a fixed pace. Job security tends to be high. Political logic and the political rationale of the ruler, ruling group, or party tend to determine the allocation and management of labor, usually at the expense of an economic or technological rationale.

The authoritarian state LAP has certain moral economy characteristics. Full employment or something close to it is the goal. Finally, a typical authoritarian state LAP generally demonstrates significantly low economic efficiency in allocating and utilizing labor resources. The authoritarian LAP organizes labor according to political logic and political organizational principles. It demonstrates the nature of a socialist institutional structure: a giant, undifferentiated complex founded on a specific political institution—the Leninist and Stalinist proletarian dictatorship. The authoritarian state LAP is the basis for the centrally planned economy. It is an important cornerstone of the whole socialist institutional structure, in which the party-ruled state tightly controls both the economy and social life.

In short, each of the three historical-type LAPs reflects a specific type of institutional structure of the state (versus its economy and society). The traditional LAP and the authoritarian state LAP provide portraits of variations in traditional institutional structures. A well-developed national labor market generally indicates differentiation and even interaction among the economy, polity, and society. In reality, of course, there are variations, distortions, and exceptions that, from an academic point of view, reveal enormously valuable information about a particular nation's institutional configuration. Although one nation may have a single type of LAP, usually there are several, with one of them being dominant.[8] However, in nations like contemporary China, there could be several major LAPs, each allocating and managing significant numbers of laborers.

Labor Allocation in China: A Short History

Throughout its long history until the early twentieth century, the Chinese LAP allocated labor essentially on the basis of the family, small community, or village. Landowning farmers (*zigengnong*) and tenant peasants (*diannong*) were the main types of employment. By the end of the nineteenth century, *zigengnongs* still owned 40 to 70 percent of the land (Huang 1986, 123). Personal dependence developed along social institutions that constituted the basic framework for an undifferentiated domestic institutional structure. The centralized and powerful imperial administration was, therefore, organized like a paternal family or clan. The cycles of the family-based LAP, from equal distribution of land (*juntian*)[9] to the land concentration and bankruptcy of the *zigengnongs,* coincided with the often bloody dynastic cycles.[10] There was a new dynasty and *juntian* at the beginning and massive migrating landless and floating, unemployed peasants (*liumin*) at the end.

The negatives of this LAP—its labor immobility, economic inefficiency, and steady population growth—led to the inevitable breakdown of the moralistic economic system. Technological and organizational innovations as well as exploration abroad were discouraged. Grain productivity per 0.1647 acre (*mu*) rose only 100 to 115 percent from the Han dynasty (third century B.C. to third century A.D.) to the Qing dynasty (seventeenth to twentieth centuries), but the grain yield decreased steadily during this period (Huang 1986, 17). Population, however, grew rapidly, leading to a steady decrease in per capita acreage of cultivated land. In the Han dynasty, per capita cultivated land was about 9.7 *mu;* by the tenth century it was less than 9 *mu;* by 1840, it fell below 2.1 *mu* (Huang 1986, 20).

Actual income of the Chinese agrarian laborers—tenant peasants and hired peasants (*gunongs*)—stagnated for centuries and began to decline significantly by the eighteenth century, when the population exploded. Archives reveal that from the first century to the twelfth, Chinese rural laborers' average income stayed roughly the same, but by the eighteenth and nineteenth centuries, this figure had declined by more than half.[11] Over time, economic disasters and famines became increasingly frequent in China.[12] Excessive taxation, war, or natural disasters were fuses to ignite the explosions of peasant revolutions and wars. The highly stable institutional structure, however, could not be changed by the political struggles, for neither a new LAP nor culture was available. The overall result was the artificial reduction of popu-

lation and a change of imperial rulers. The new dynasty usually inaugurated its rule by reallocating land and labor, thus restoring the
politically stabilizing family-/village-based LAP with some economic
viability. The corrosive forces of economic commercialization were
generally treated by the rulers with suspicion and suppression, as evidenced by the low social and political status of merchants and
craftspeople.

Under this type of institutional setting and nourished by Confucian
culture, serfdom and slavery were largely supplements to the family-
based LAP. A clear hierarchy existed in people's job selection: landholding or even tenant family-based agriculture, with the opportunity
of joining officialdom through imperial exams, were valued much
higher than commerce or handicraft industry jobs.[13] Spontaneous
commercialization of labor allocation did not evolve into a meaningful labor market, but it did produce certain market-oriented norms and
traditions of allocating labor in some areas, primarily in today's
Jiangsu and Zhejiang Provinces. The existence of local and seasonal
labor markets gradually blended into the overall institutional structure,
thus creating a certain legitimacy for market mechanisms in the
allocation of labor. The traditional Chinese institutional structure was
stable and enduring, primarily because its institutional foundation was
the family: the first, the most natural, and the most stable human
institution of all.

Changes of the Nineteenth Century

By the nineteenth century, there was an acceleration of the concentration of land ownership and the bankruptcy of millions of
zigengnong and *diannong,* a cyclic phenomenon that had served as a
major driving force for rebellions and dynastic changes in the past.
History was about to produce another bloody yet necessary dynastic
cycle. Increasing foreign factors, represented by European colonialism
and its aftereffects, however, altered the historical perpetuation of
China's highly stable institutional structure. Huge numbers of *liumin*
began flooding the country, providing sufficient fuel to revolutionary
causes and to new LAPs.

The main Chinese LAP throughout this period was still the same
family-based traditional LAP, especially in the countryside, where the
majority of Chinese lived. *Zigengnong, diannong,* and *gunong* continued to be the major work allocation patterns involving hundred of
millions of Chinese peasants until 1949. Many urban shops and enter-

prises employed their workers in roughly the same way. Meaningful alternative LAPs, however, began to develop after the mid-nineteenth century. The most significant one during this period was the emergence of a market-oriented LAP, brought in primarily by foreigners. A quasi-market allocation of labor grew in the coastal urban areas and began to acquire legitimacy from the weakening central government. In the 1840s and 1850s, the first generation of industrial labor emerged in foreign invested enterprises. The first of these was in Guangzhou in 1845 and soon afterward in Shanghai.[14] In the 1920s, it was estimated that China had about 3.8 million industrial workers, with more than half employed in a market-oriented fashion.[15] By the late 1940s, an estimated more than 8 million industrial workers were employed by a variety of enterprises (Yue 1989, 20; Wang 1987, 315).

Besides active foreign enterprises and a growing number of private employers was the development of employment in state-owned enterprises (*guanying,* or *guanshang*). Started in the late nineteenth century by some reform-minded Qing officials, the *yangwupai,* sizable state-owned enterprises were developed primarily to enhance China's national defense. Famous industrial giants of today's China such as the shipyards in Shanghai and heavy industries in cities like Wuhan, Nanjing, and Chongqing were built by the Qing or the Republic governments. Some of them later began to absorb considerable private investment (Gai 1988, 2). Labor in those enterprises consisted basically of two tiers: (1) a largely market-oriented allocation of blue- and some white-collar workers, and (2) a mostly state allocation of the majority of white-collar workers, including managerial and technical personnel. The latter was a distorted labor market that featured strong noneconomic considerations in allocating and managing labor. Personal and kinship connections, the so-called "petticoat influence," and political favoritism were the norm. In a way, it was halfway between a rather crude market-oriented LAP and the centuries-old, warm, family-based traditional LAP. It covered a very small but important portion of the Chinese labor force and thus deserves our attention. Later, it apparently provided the historical precedent for the PRC government to allocate its administrative and technical cadres, even its industrial labor force, as state employees.

By the mid-twentieth century, Chinese labor allocation continued to be largely a family-based traditional LAP. But new patterns emerged. The most important was the advancement of a labor market in the major cities and in some rural areas. Several profound distortions of the developing labor market were also identifiable. However, the serious problem of unemployment was not solved because there was no *juntian,* or land reform, to restore a stable family-based LAP for millions of unemployed peasants. From the 1920s to the 1940s, the urban unemployment rate was as high as 55 percent for males and nearly 80 percent for females (Wang 1987, 149-150). The addition of hyperinflation from 1937 to 1949 (a 368-trillionfold rise in the consumer price index) gave the former peasants who were used to the tender family-based traditional LAP enough reason and motivation to fight for changes against the existing institutional structure, including, ironically, the newly emerged labor market. The outcome of the struggle between republicans and Communists (1911-1949) thus powerfully twisted, even reversed, the institutional changes. A popular restoration of traditional institutions was accomplished in the name of new ideologies. When foreign forces were kept away, the historical trajectory of China almost predestined the emergence of a new dynasty that would restore the highly stable, traditional Chinese institutional structure as reflected in the family-based traditional LAP.

LAPs in the PRC Prior to Deng's Reform

The institutional development of the PRC under Mao shocked many as a seemingly dramatic departure from the patterns set by Chinese history. A closer look at labor allocation patterns, however, reveals that the traditional institutional setting did not change for another three decades. The Chinese Communist Party (CCP) regime first restored the traditional family-based LAP in the countryside. In the cities, for only four short years and at a dizzying speed, Mao used his sweeping political power to launch "socialist reform" campaigns throughout China. These culminated in the disastrous Great Leap Forward (1958-1961) discussed further on.[16]

Restoration of the Family-Based LAP

Even before it came to power, the CCP launched its *tugai* (land reform) campaigns in areas under its control through reallocating confiscated land and restricting rent (Bianco 1971, 150-151). In 1947, the CCP proclaimed its *tugai* guidance in the General Outline of Chinese Land Law (Huang 1986, 366-369). The CCP's land reform was received by the peasants with open arms and became a major source of strength in the CCP's bloody struggle with the GMD (Guomindang) for national political power. The restoration of family-based institutions to rural areas effectively led to the establishment of a new political regime. Mao, the son of a Hunan *zigengnong,* knew this historical secret and applied it well. His "land to the tiller" program powerfully captured the hearts of millions of Chinese peasants.[17] The CCP, a party supposedly based on the proletarian class, effectively mobilized the peasantry and won a traditional peasant war against the repressive old regimes (Johnson 1962).

Land reform was radical, thorough, and rapid. Based on the same notion of property rights that all Chinese emperors had maintained, the CCP confiscated land from the landlord class and some of the "rich peasant" class. According to the Land Law proclaimed on June 30, 1950, land and other confiscated properties were then redistributed equally among all the peasant families in the community, usually a village.[18] The PRC issued the peasants an owner's certificate for the allocated land. The redistribution took place in such an equal fashion that fertile and barren lands were carved into pieces to ensure a fair allotment. The old family structure played a great role in determining the details of this grand redistribution scheme.[19] Not only was the land thoroughly reallocated to all peasants in the village, including former landlords, but land-renting behavior was strictly forbidden. As a result, the landlord class was wiped out, sometimes physically, by humiliation, massive arrests, imprisonment, and execution.[20] Landlords and rich peasants were labeled as two of the people's enemies, and they and their families suffered extraordinary hardships until the 1980s.

By the spring of 1953, land reform was basically completed (Huang 1986, 378). After this turnover (*fanshen*), which touched almost every corner of China, millions of family-based farms were created, and the ancient family-based LAP was restored on a massive scale. A honeymoon period was thus begun between the peasants and the CCP.

Agriculture Collectivization

After land reform, most Chinese peasants became small, family-based landholding *zigengnongs.* On average, a peasant family owned 11.7 to 19 *mu* (1.93 to 3.13 acres) of land and 0.5 to 1 farm animal.[21] The long-familiar bankruptcies of *zigengnongs* and covert land transfers, however, quickly began to recur. The political implications of this inevitable development deeply worried the CCP leadership. The ambitious industrialization plans of the party demanded much greater agricultural output, which could hardly be met by the small and inefficient farms or scattered neighborhood cooperatives, despite increasingly heavy state taxation and the exploitative policy of the state monopoly purchasing and marketing grains (*tonggou tongxiao*).[22] The CCP also had a burning desire to depart from the patterns of Chinese political history so as to escape from the dynastic cycles. The party was eager to proceed along the Soviet-style fast lane of socialism, at least with the goal of safeguarding Chinese independence. Something drastic had to be done.

The CCP chose to adopt Soviet-style agriculture collectivization. Over the fairly strong resistance of some important CCP leaders, including Politburo member Deng Zhihui and Defense Minister Marshal Peng Dehuai, in 1954-1955, Mao hastily began altering the restored traditional family-based LAP and thus the overall Chinese institutional structure in the rural areas by launching "collectivization" campaigns among the peasants. With the exertion of tremendous political power, ideological agitation, and grassroots organization, the "instant" collectivization movement took off like wildfire (Friedman et al. 1991, 185). In just months, 500 million peasants were collectivized (Huang et al. 1989, 93). In Hebei Province alone, 99.4 percent of rural households were collectivized within a year.[23] Family-based landholding was a short-lived phenomenon, and the family-based LAP became a community-based authoritarian state LAP. Originally planned as a ten-year process, collectivization was completed in less than two years.[24]

The village-based collectivized Chinese peasants were pushed further at a dazzling speed to form "people's communes" during the tumultuous Great Leap Forward years. The infamous Anti-Rightists' campaign in 1957 cleared the ideological and political path for this institutional alteration; the completion of urban socialist reform (more on this later) provided further facilitation. Only two months after the CCP Politburo adopted the Resolution on Establishing People's Communes in the Countryside in August 1958, over 99 percent of the peasants were organized in communes that integrated government administration and economic management (*zhengshi heyi*) and combined industry, agriculture, military, learning, and commerce (*gongnong bingxueshang xianjihe*) (Huang 1986, 470-472).

Despite the miserable failure of the communes, the rural version of authoritarian labor allocation continued until the end of the 1970s. It was a combination of the traditional community-based LAP and heavy authoritarianism and personal dependence. The peasants were organized by geographic location and subject to the control of the cadres, some of them fellow peasants who were "developed" by the numerous "working teams" of the CCP organizations starting in the land reform era. Jobs, workload, rewards, and punishments were decided through "democratic centralism"; that is, the cadres and a few "core" peasants made decisions after consultations (often rubber-stamp exercises) with every member of the unit, excluding "class enemies" such as former landlords, rich peasants, and other "criminals." In most cases, the institution worked like an extended family-based LAP in which the cadres served as the father figure.

Moralistic concerns, traditional values, kinship considerations, and community bonds were important factors. Pay depended on the total income of the unit, usually a production team. A laborer's work was recorded daily in points (*gongfen*) determined primarily by the cadres. Labor used by the communes and the brigades was recorded as points earned by the laborer but paid later by his or her home production team. At harvest time, after paying taxes, grain and other essentials were distributed on a per capita basis to meet everyone's basic needs. The remainder was then distributed according to points accumulated. Cash was generally a very small portion of the pay. For those who lost the ability to work and had no relatives to support them, the teams provided basic supplies and service. The accounting books were open, but dishonesty, self-serving behavior, and favoritism by the cadres were common. In many ways, the system looked more like a traditional community-based LAP sprinkled with a certain communist political flavor.

Fighting Urban Unemployment

By 1949, China's urban economy was in ruins; half of its 8 million urban workers were unemployed. To consolidate its regime, the CCP used its political power to reshape labor allocation institutions in the cities, hoping to eradicate the unemployment problem. Initially, the CCP attempted to use the rural economy as a reservoir by sending large numbers of urban workers to the countryside, to "return to their villages." That move proved rather unpopular and ineffective, as land reform in the rural areas made the new *zigengnongs* reject additional people who would have to share their land. By 1952, the urban un-employment rate was still at 13.2 percent (Yuan 1990, 6).

As the new owner of the confiscated GMD-era state-owned enter-prises, the PRC assured full employment to all the employees of those enterprises other than those who had "serious historical or political problems." This wholesale approach established the first segment of the PRC's authoritarian state LAP. More than three-quarter million workers in about 2,858 enterprises and many more former civil servants and public school teachers and professors were "taken care of " by the new regime. By the end of 1950, Beijing began to put a yoke on labor allocation for substantial private enterprises. Recruitment of new workers and temporary workers was strictly monitored, and any dismissal of workers had to be approved by the authorities. Surplus labor generated by the rise of productivity in state-owned and private enterprises was "not to be dismissed." Rather, they would stay in the original unit, being paid fully to "study" or merely wait to be "reallocated."[25]

Overtime work was closely monitored and often prohibited. Hiring new workers from rural areas had to be approved by the authorities, and the CCP launched campaigns to prevent surplus rural workers from leaving their villages. Local-based rural projects were proposed as a way to absorb the abundant surplus of rural labor, and a very restricted *hukou* system began to develop to block rural workers from reaching the urban jobs. Certain socialist measures were adopted to provide unemployment relief to cover their "reasonably" sized families.[26] Enterprises were asked to provide 1 percent of salaries to the state to help the unemployed. The goal of this policy was to provide for the subsistence needs of everyone in the cities through state-organized socialist programs. Public projects were also primarily used to recruit from registered unemployed workers until the mid-1950s (Yuan 1987, 6-14).

Emergence of an Authoritarian State LAP

Several major developments directly led to the emergence of an authoritarian state LAP in urban areas. First was the institutional separation of rural from urban by the *hukou* system. Every PRC citizen was required to have identification papers for access to land, jobs, social welfare benefits, housing, education, party membership, good-character credentials, and numerous other opportunities. Without such *hukou* papers, a person was subject to arrest and investigation by the police. A most important piece of information contained in the papers was whether the holder was an urban or a rural resident. This provisional controlling measure was later built into a legal Great Wall between the majority rural population and the somewhat privileged urban dwellers. A striking dual economy was thus created in China (Xia and Dang 1991, 148).

The *hukou* system enabled the PRC government to control labor mobility geographically and created very rigid and contrasting urban-rural dual economic and social structures. Furthermore, regulation for a personal dossier (*dangan*) became the most effective administrative means to control labor mobility across professions, industries, and working units—the *danweis*. *Danweis,* including the villages (communes and brigades), shops, schools, factories, and so on, became omnipotent institutions that controlled their employees—or more appropriately their dependents—politically, economically, and socially. The personal dependence created by the *danweis* is so comprehensive and profound that Andrew Walder (1986) called it an institution of "communist neotraditionalism." To some extent, the bond between workers and their *danweis* rivaled those within the traditional Chinese family. Instead of having families as the cells of its institutional structure, the PRC gradually established the *danweis* in that role. These enlarged and distorted "families" directly contributed to the preservation of the traditional institutional setting in the PRC.

Second, the all-taking-care-of policy (*baoxialai*) outlined the goals and scope of the emerging authoritarian state LAP. This policy, aimed at "taking care of all the job seekers in a coordinated state allocation and assignment," was established between 1951 and 1952 and dominated for three decades. In the mid-1990s, it still existed in significant form (Zhang et al. 1987, 224). As mentioned previously, this policy initially aimed at taking care of the employees of the former state-owned enterprises. Later, it was greatly expanded to include all employees and managers of socialized private enterprises. Finally, all college graduates, polytechnic school graduates, discharged and demobilized military personnel, high school graduates, and even released inmates were guaranteed jobs by the state (Yuan 1987, 19). As a result, millions became permanent employees of the state; there was an increasing inflow of only such permanent employees, and no meaningful outflow of unsuitable or unnecessary workers.

Third, the labor management bureaucracy provided the organizational foundation for the authoritarian state LAP. In 1952, Beijing began to charge the labor bureaus with the responsibility and authority to monitor, allocate, and assign labor in their respective regions. No open recruitment or recruitment from rural areas was allowed without the approval of the labor bureaus. Later, no recruitment at all was allowed without that approval. Cross-regional labor allocation had to be approved by a superior labor bureau overseeing the regions involved. Only the central government, through its Labor Ministry, had the authority to allocate labor beyond a big region (*daqu*), each usually containing a few provinces. By 1957, "the labor and wage authority was already centralized in the hands of the central (government)" (Yuan 1987, 15-16, 127).

Finally, a socialist reform established the absolute dominance of the authoritarian LAP in the PRC by the mid-1950s. The PRC State Council (then called the Political Affairs Council) issued a Provisional Measure on Public-Private Joint-Management Enterprises in 1954 and started the socialist reform campaign in urban areas. Like the swiftness of the rural collectivization movement, complete socialist reform of the private urban economy took less than two years. The PRC nationally set a 5 percent fixed rate of payment (*dingxi*) for seven years for private properties that were socialized.[27] More than 810,000 payees were also assigned jobs, mostly in the enterprises they formerly owned. Those "joint-managed" enterprises began to adopt all the institutional features of state-owned enterprises and soon were virtually identical to them. The only remaining difference was that the joint-managed enterprises paid a *dingxi* to the former capitalists (Wang 1986, 128).

At roughly the same time, urban handicraft shops and commercial industries were also collectivized into similar public-private joint-managed shops. Tolerated and even encouraged before 1954, elements of the private household economy such as craftspeople and individual shopkeepers were driven into extinction. There had been 9 million such private household workers in the cities; by 1958, fewer than fifteen thousand were left (Yuan 1987, 19). The once-active labor-referring services all but vanished by 1958. Meanwhile, in the rural areas, the formerly active private handicraft shops and commercial shops were collectivized and became part and parcel of the collectives and, later, the communes. Despite the classifications "state-owned," "local state-owned" (relatively large joint-managed enterprises), "joint-managed," and "collective-owned," China's urban economy was socialized at an astonishing speed and organized in basically a uniform and centralized fashion. The authoritarian state LAP was, therefore, established as the dominant LAP in the Chinese urban areas.

In short, in just a few years (1954-1957), the CCP regime completed a major transition from multipatterned labor allocation to the establishment of an authoritarian state LAP that featured a rural-urban dual economy at the expense of eliminating the market in the economy and personal freedom and mobility in social life. For the purpose of fundamentally solving the politically undesirable unemployment problem and to develop the socialist economy along Soviet lines, the CCP suppressed the existing market-oriented LAP and attempted to transplant an authoritarian allocation pattern from its longtime military operations. Universal political management of every urban worker was institutionalized at various levels. The state-allocated workers were guaranteed lifetime jobs and related access to a variety of socialist benefits. In exchange, the workers became dependent on their superiors and lost most of their personal mobility and freedom. Workers' incomes were also held stagnant at a low level. According to Premier Zhou Enlai, a "reasonably low wage system assures enough rice to most possible people; that is what we mean by saying 'letting five people share three people's rice.' "[28]

Economic efficiency was sacrificed for political concerns such as social stability, certain ambitious or even unrealistic development plans, or some leaders' brainstorms. Labor mobility, the leading indicator for a market-oriented LAP, was systematically and institutionally abolished in the PRC through the establishment of three rare institutions serving as the backbone of the PRC's institutional structure: a national *hukou* system, a *dangan* regulation, and a *danwei* structure. The CCP literally eradicated unemployment for a time. Rural labor was effectively controlled by the CCP through the collectives and thus was no longer a threat to urban employment. The rural-urban dual structure was institutionalized, and *danweis*—including the rural collectives—finally became the family-like cells of the PRC's institutional structure. The new patterns of labor allocation that had emerged in the previous century were systematically and effectively abolished. On the macro level, Mao managed to rejuvenate the Chinese traditional institutional structure by combining economy, polity, and society into one centralized institution—the CCP-dominated state that tended to adopt a centuries-old isolationist posture. On the micro level, traditional family- or community-based institutions were restored as the basis for the PRC state.

With some minor qualifications, the authoritarian state LAP can be viewed as the ultimate form of a family-based traditional LAP in that, under Mao, the whole country was organized as a giant family. This structure had some aspects that were inherently unworkable, both technologically and practically, as well as undesirable economically and socially. The seemingly high achievement of political values, that is, order, tranquillity, and members' security, was therefore bound to be short-lived. In a nutshell, this nation-based traditional LAP restored the traditional Chinese institutional structure with a comprehensive and penetrating political power that was unprecedented for the central government, which behaved like a traditional Chinese father.[29]

General Crisis and the Remedies

Chronic shortages, massive unemployment, and especially the disaster of the Great Leap Forward soon began to threaten the CCP
regime. The decade-long Cultural Revolution (1966-1976) greatly
strengthened the PRC's authoritarian state LAP at an even greater
cost to economic development and people's standard of living. Any
experiments aimed at managerial flexibility or increased productivity
were labeled as "advocating capitalist free labor market" and zealously
fought. The monolithic and encompassing state LAP could not accommodate the new growth of the labor force even in an inefficient
way. Millions became unemployed in the cities, and millions more in
the countryside became underemployed and ready to flood the cities
at any time. Mao and his leftist followers, relying on the political
power generated by the traditional institutional setting, hoped to use
the collectivized rural areas as the outlet for surplus urban labor.

A national campaign of sending high school and middle school
graduates to the countryside to be "reeducated by the poor and lower-
middle-class peasants" was thus launched, and human tragedies on a
massive scale followed. More than 15 million young urban dwellers
were sent to the rural areas between 1967 and 1977. This policy,
however, hardly aided the worsening situation of the authoritarian
state LAP in the cities because nearly 13 million rural workers were
recruited by state-owned enterprises in urban areas through numerous
channels (Yuan 1989, 102-104). The aggravated inefficiency and increasingly unbearable burden on the state reached the point of a
general crisis. When the former urban youth returned to the cities,
gradually at first but then in massive numbers after Mao's death in
1976, unemployment in the Chinese cities exploded, with deep political implications. The monolithic authoritarian state LAP reached its
end in China's cities by the end of the 1970s, while its rural version
was at the point of total collapse.

Some remedies had to be found to compensate for the defects of
the authoritarian state LAP and the flaws of Soviet-style centrally
planned industrialization. The CCP tried to give local authorities
some flexibility in managing labor under the authoritarian state LAP.
But the result was wild cyclical swings of delegating power to the local
authorities (*fangquan*), which led to the swelling of state employment. This, in turn, caused many of the serious unemployment and
underemployment problems mentioned previously and the subsequent

centralizing power (*shouquan*), leading to tremendous economic hardships (Yuan 1989, 25-26, 134-137). To provide managerial flexibility and to combat unemployment, a community-based societal pattern was introduced as a socialist but Chinese LAP, first in urban areas and then gradually in the countryside. Later, after the 1970s, this supplementary small LAP developed spectacularly into very successful community-based labor markets. The community-based societal LAP was first adopted by those collective enterprises and the commune-brigade enterprises (CBEs), which were the predecessor of the now flourishing township-village enterprises (TVEs).

The community-based LAP allocated workers differently from the authoritarian state LAP and with little drain on the state budget for nationally provided job security, benefits, and sociopolitical status. Employees were contract workers, and no permanent employment was guaranteed. Pay was determined not by the state in a unified way but by the financial situation of employers, and only limited benefits packages were available.

Because of the lessened job security and some competition mechanisms, many of those collective enterprises actually were more profitable than state-owned businesses, and their employees' wages were sometimes higher than that of state employees. But the reduced benefits and job insecurity made collective employees socially much lower and politically less important than state employees. It combined strong social concerns of local welfare, political power, and certain market mechanisms. Social institutions such as family, neighborhood, and community were important factors affecting labor practices under this LAP. It covered only job-seekers within the community: a street, a district, a township, a village (formerly a brigade), or a city. Generally all the employees came from the community where the enterprise was located. Labor mobility was limited across communities but increased within each community. Over time, especially by the end of the 1970s, this community LAP became ready for new experiments.

Reform and the New Chinese LAPs

The year 1978 is a major turning point in PRC history. Shortly after the death of Mao Zedong on September 9, 1976, and the arrest of the Gang of Four a month later, the CCP had begun to make changes in order to survive the political, economic, social, and ideological crises created during the previous years. A very important move was to reopen the college entrance exam to every Chinese person aged sixteen to thirty-six or even older, at the end of 1977.[30] In October 1978, Beijing decided to halt "sending the youth to the countryside" and began to implement some pragmatic policies on labor allocation (Yuan 1987, 216). More importantly, desperate peasants and some sympathetic local cadres in Anhui and Sichuan Provinces, with tacit support from the reformers in Beijing, started a decollectivization effort in the rural areas. Finally, in December 1978, the CCP launched a comprehensive reform under the more pragmatic leadership of Deng Xiaoping. The Third Plenum of the Eleventh CCP Central Committee decided on a series of reform measures, formally beginning the Chinese reform that continued into the late 1990s.

Guided by Deng's pragmatism and the new "working focus," economic reforms featuring experiments based on a market orientation began. Besides state political power, other LAP-shaping and altering forces were released: spontaneous economic activities, social and cultural factors, and external influences. Very quickly, people's perceptions and popular culture adapted to the "modern" world outside China.[31] By the late 1990s, substantial liberalization took place in the rural areas, and the peasants regained substantial economic, social, and even political autonomy by the 1990s. The depth of the reform is particularly evident in the weakening of state control over the economy and the expansion of the private economy, as well as in the emergence of a commodity market, a heavily commercialized culture, and new, basically market-oriented labor allocation patterns.

By 1979, the CCP was forced to deal with a new peak of unemployment in the aftermath of the Cultural Revolution, which had deeply damaged the Party's legitimacy and prestige. This was a time when gross underemployment was already a widespread feature of labor allocation in state-owned enterprises (Yuan 1987, 206-207). The CCP Central Committee and the State Council summoned a National Labor and Employment Conference both in 1980 and 1981. Afterward, Beijing proclaimed a new Triple Combination policy to mobilize "the efforts of the state labor authority's arrangement, self-organized employment, and self-employment."[32] As a result, the traditional family-based LAP was restored through decollectivization, the community-based societal LAP flourished in both urban and rural economies, private employment greatly increased, and employment by foreign investors expanded. State-owned enterprises also began continuous reforms of their labor practices. The ideology of economic development and prosperity were emphasized and praised, and economic activities were generally granted increasing autonomy (Walder 1989, 242-243).

Structural changes soon took place in Chinese labor allocation. In 1978, for example, 72 percent of the new jobs in the cities were created through state-owned enterprises under the authoritarian state LAP, while 28 percent were created by collectives under the community-based LAP. By 1985, the authoritarian state LAP provided only 61.4 percent of the new jobs in the cities, while community-based labor markets created 25 percent and private employers created 13.6 percent (Yue 1989, 22).[33] Four distinctively different LAPs—an authoritarian state LAP, the family-based traditional LAP, community-based labor markets, and a national labor market—began to coexist in the PRC. The threatening waves of unemployment were mitigated. By 1987, the unemployment rate decreased to a safe 1.8 percent.

Chinese Labor Allocation in the 1990s

According to official statistics, the population of China in 1993 was almost 1.2 billion. The labor force—men ages 16 to 59 and women ages 16 to 54 (Yuan 1990, 6)—was more than 705.49 million, including more than 487.68 million in rural areas (separated by the *hukou* system) from the 217.8 million in urban areas.[34] The unemployment rate—the "waiting-for-job rate," as it used to be called by the Chinese government[35]—in the urban economy was about 3 percent by the end of 1990 and 2.9 percent in 1994; as many as 30 percent of rural laborers were idling or "underemployed."[36]

Objectives

By the mid-1990s, the official objective of Chinese labor and employment policies had shifted from pursuing a "socialist full employment" to the delicate goal of "considering both economic efficiency and social stability at the same time." The goal was "to expand employment at the expense of some economic efficiency when the waiting-for-job people are many and the national economy is not very good; to stress improving efficiency when the national economy is developing smoothly and the waiting-for-job people are few" (Yue 1989, 18). As the new "father," Deng Xiaoping himself posed this question as early as 1979: "Modernized production only needs fewer laborers, but we have so many people. How to consider both of these two issues at the same time?" (Deng 1985, 150). Apparently, the objective was one of developing the economy through utilizing the market while stabilizing CCP rule in the name of socialism and preserving the traditional social harmony based on an agrarian/moral, or nonmarket, economy. Distortion of the market in allocating labor by the state and societal institutions was therefore inevitable, but generally perceived to be desirable.

The Four Chinese LAPs

By the 1990s, four types of LAPs were identifiable in China, indicating that labor allocation had become diversified and was in the process of a major transformation. The Chinese labor force, the largest national labor force in the world, was allocated and arranged under four major patterns: a family-based traditional LAP, mainly in the agricultural sector in the countryside (see chapter 1); an authoritarian state allocation in the urban economy (see chapter 2); a societal LAP of community-based labor markets in local communities of rural industries and urban collective enterprises (see chapter 3); and a market-oriented LAP in foreign-invested enterprises and the private economy (see chapter 4). This typology apparently differs from Andrew Walder's categorization of the Chinese labor force (see table I.1) and will be further explored in the rest of this book.[37]

Table I.1. The Four Chinese LAPs in the 1990s

LAP	Authoritarian state LAP	Family-based LAP	Community-based labor markets	National labor market
Size	large (largest) urban LAP	largest	large & fast growing	relatively small
Primary locale	urban	rural	urban & rural	urban & rural
Primary industries	nonagricultural	agriculture, handicrafts	nonagricultural	nonagricultural
Institutional foundation	the state (polity)	family (social life)	social life & the market	the market (economy)
Historical origin	royal shops & *guanshang*	*zigengnong & diannong*	villages & CBEs	FDI & *getihu*

First there is the politically and economically predominant authoritarian state LAP. Despite attempted reforms, this LAP retains its socialist features hammered out by the PRC central-planning economic system and the CCP Leninist administration. Personal dependency, labor immobility, nonmarket management and, of course, gross inefficiency are some of the hallmarks of this LAP. In the vast Chinese countryside, there is the restored family-based traditional LAP, that is, the "family responsibility system," and specialized households (*zhuanyehu*) that practice the traditional nonmarket LAP (although those families have widely engaged in, and have been influenced by, market-oriented economic exchanges with the outside). In the cities, a substantial number of individual households (*getihus*) are practicing a family-based LAP with an increasing array of market mechanisms. Closely related to the socialist system and influenced by the traditionally local-exchange-oriented socioeconomic structures is the community-based labor markets (CLMs). Finally, there has been significant development of a genuinely market-oriented LAP—a national labor market, championed by FDI in China and accompanied by small but widespread private employment.

This typology of the four LAPs naturally has its gray areas. The typical *getihus* practice the family-based traditional LAP but increasingly hire from the outside in nonagricultural industries (Liang 1990, 14); thus we have an overlapping of the family-based LAP and the national or community-based labor markets. Many FDI and private employers are community based and appear to be practicing more of a CLM than a national labor market. Because many FDI employers get their workers from the existing state-owned *danweis,* as workers from their Chinese partners, or as moonlighters, there is institutional overlapping of the authoritarian state LAP and the national labor market. Statistics on the number of employees were collected primarily from employers; therefore, there could be substantial double counting, and the total of the four LAPs could tend to exceed 100 percent of the labor force. For example, the sizable moonlighting, or on-leave, workers in the urban areas could be reported as employees of the FDI or private employers allocated by the emerging national labor market; but officially they were still state employees, and thus counted as belonging to the authoritarian state LAP. Some of them might even be viewed as employees of private enterprises disguised as collective enterprises or TVEs and thus counted for the third time as part of the labor allocated by the CLMs. Some, conceivably, could even be counted for the fourth time as working under the family-based LAP.

Fieldwork confirmed the existence of this overlapping, but, fortunately, the potential to misinterpret the conclusions became less significant as the categorization of workers became more transparent by the late 1990s.

The four coexisting Chinese LAPs are likely to advance and sustain China's institutional structure into the twenty-first century. If the authoritarian state LAP provided the basis for a planned economic development with poor efficiency and few innovations, the restored family-based LAP reinvigorated the traditionally highly stable Chinese institutional structure that is family-like and institutionally pre-modern. On one hand, the family-based LAP clearly outperformed the state LAP, as illustrated by the impressive growth of Chinese agricultural output since 1978. But the limited economic potential of this traditional LAP became increasingly apparent by the 1990s. On the other hand, the market-oriented LAP, especially the extensive community-based labor markets, led to more efficient and more promising economic growth, with profound implications for an institutional transformation in China.

The mixed Chinese LAPs crafted a complex transformation. Scholars have suggested that China has a neotraditional society, a socialist economy in its primary stage, and a communist authoritarian polity. China, in fact, came to have all these elements, as the four different LAPs illustrated. The unique coexistence of these four LAPs demonstrates well that the Chinese institutional structure is in a period of great transition. Labor is allocated by the emerging market, however distorted, by the state, and to a lesser extent by social institutions, mainly the family.

Notes

1. Vivienne Shue, "Grasping Reform: Economic Logic, Political Logic, and the State-Society spiral," in *The China Quarterly* 144 (December 1995): 1174-1185.

2. There has been an impressive body of scholarship on the institutional analysis of the PRC. Many researchers have pursued the following angles: (1) to find a relationship between the central PRC government in Beijing and the local governments; (2) to identify the capacity of the state in regulating and even controlling the economy as demonstrated by the share of state ownership of the economy and the coverage and effectiveness of state planning; (3) to examine popular opinion as expressed through survey studies; (4) to describe the historical trend of the institutional setting in the PRC and the pre-PRC context. (The Bibliography of this book lists some of the most known works.)

3. Throughout this study, "labor" or "labor force" is defined according to the recommendation of the International Labor Office (ILO) as the "economically active

population" comprising all persons older than ten to fifteen years of age, who furnish the supply of labor for the production of economic goods and services. It consists of three major parts: employed, unemployed, and underemployed (ILO 1982; ILO 1987, 35; De Neubourg 1988, 193-201).

4. "Division of labor" or "specialization" of skills, practice, and information, as defined by Kenneth Arrow, "is a basic structural aspect, not merely of the economic world, but of all other social worlds" (Arrow 1979, 154, 156). For more discussion on the theory of labor allocation patterns, see Wang 1998, chapter 2.

5. The understanding of LAP's role is inspired by Marx's argument of "production mode." However, Marx apparently overemphasized the importance of the ownership of "production means" in his theory.

6. The debate of "moral peasants" (James Scott) vis-à-vis "rational peasants" (Samuel Popkin) illustrates how economic, political, and social forces can work together to determine the preference of the peasants and the outcome of certain ways of organizing the labor force in a rural economy. (For a summary of this debate, see Parish 1985, 13-20.)

7. This LAP alienates people differently from the capitalist alienation described by Marx. This kind of alienation goes beyond "economic bondage" and is carried out mainly through noneconomic means.

8. Even in the United States, where a national labor market has become the dominant LAP, a family-based traditional LAP exists marginally in both rural and urban areas. Even a quasi-slavery LAP can be found in the form of some slavelike seasonal workers in the agriculture industry, despite the 1984 U.S. Migrant Seasonal Agriculture Worker Protection Act. See CNN (Cable News Network): *Faces of Slavery,* a CNN Presents program, Atlanta, July 23, 1995.

9. *Juntian* (均田) was used by the Sui and Tang dynasties. It had varied names at different times. In the Han dynasty, the imperial court adopted *tuntianzhi* (屯田). In the Jin and the Southern and Northern dynasties, it was called *zhantianzhi* (占田制). The Ming dynasty had *kentianzhi* (垦田制). The Qing dynasty used *gengmingtian* (更名田).

10. Chinese historical records since Shiji have documented the correlation between political instability and the phenomenon of *liumin,* the decline of the family-based LAP. See, for example, *Hanshu* (the history of Han)—*Shihou zhi, Songshu* (the history of Song)—*Fubi zhuan,* Lu Simian 1947, 493-496; Fan 1965, 207; and Jian 1984, 29-30.

11. Liu Yonchen and Zhao Gang, "18-19 shiji Zhongguo nongye gugong de shiji gongzi biandong qushi" (The changing trend of income of the Chinese agricultural laborers during the eighteenth and nineteenth centuries), in *Mingqing dangan yu lishi yianjou* (Ming Qing records and historical research), (Beijing: Zhonghua Books, 1988), 874-875. A recent "reportage" asserted that in the Tang dynasty (seventh to tenth centuries), the Chinese passed the peak of per capita cultivated land (12.6 *mu*) and per capita grain production (500 kg). See Ma Yuejun, "Huang tudi, he tudi" (Yellow land, black land), in Liu Ying, ed., *Dangdai Zhongguo yeshenghuo—Dangdai Zhongguo redian xiezhen chongshu* (Night life in contemporary China—the series on the hot issues in contemporary China) (Beijing: Huayi Press, 1993), 4-5.

12. A study that called China "The Land of Famine." The frequency of famines increased over the centuries. There were about 69 during the first century, 171 in the

second century, 263 by the eleventh century, 391 during the fourteenth century, and 504 in the sixteenth century (Deng [1937] 1984, 1, 61, 86-126).

13. Ke Jianzhong, "Shilun Mingdai shangyi zhiben yu zhiben zhuyi menya de guangxi (On the relationship between Ming dynasty commerce and capitalist sprouts)" in *Sichuan daxue xuebao* (Sichuan University Journal), no. 3 (1957).

14. CCP Shanghai Committee, *Qinggong zhenzhi lunxun jiaocai* (Textbook for political education of the young workers) (Shanghai: Shanghai Renmin Press, 1985), 322-323; Sun Yutang, *Zhongguo jindai gongyi shi ziliao* (Historical data on Chinese modern industry), vol. 2 (Shanghai, Science Press, 1957), 1201.

15. Chen Da, *Zhongguo laogong wenti* (The issue of Chinese labor), (Shanghai: Shangwu Press, 1927), 7-20.

16. For a description of the origins of the Leap and its illustrative manifestation in one province, Henan, see Domenach 1995.

17. Mao argued in 1945 that a restoration of the *zigengnong* system was most appealing to the peasants and a major objective for the CCP. See *Maozedong xuangji* (Selected works of Mao Zedong), vol. 4 in the combined set (Beijing: Renmin Press, 1973), 1075-1076.

18. For this basic law and other *tugai*-related CCP documents, see Huang 1986, 372-376.

19. Chinese literature has many descriptions of this. See, for example, Guo Hua, *Furong zheng* (Beijing: Reminwenxue Press, 1983).

20. For a detailed description of land reform in a northern China county, see Friedman et al. 1991, 81-98. Shue 1980 also provides a general review of land reform. Because anything during the PRC era is still quite politically sensitive, Chinese scholarship on the CCP's land reform has generally been poorly developed.

21. Su Xin , *Woguo nongye de shehui zhuyi gaizhao* (The socialist reform of our country's agriculture) (Shanghai: Shanghai Renmin Press, 1977), 13.

22. At Chen Yun's suggestion, the PRC adopted this policy in the fall of 1953, setting the stage for agricultural collectivization. See *Chenyun wenxuian 1949-1956* (Selected Works of Chen Yun) (Beijing: Renmin Press, 1983), 209.

23. Shi Jingtang, ed., *Zhongguo nongye hezuohua yundong shiliao* (Historical data of Chinese agricultural collectivization) (Beijing: Sanlian Books, 1957), 1000-1019. Cited in Friedman et al. 1991, 188.

24. Deng Zihui (邓子恢), Report to the National People's Congress on Collectivization, 1956.

25. The State Council, "Guanyu laodong juye wenti de jueding" (The decision on labor and employment issues), Beijing, July 25, 1952.

26. For example, according to the 1950 PRC Provisional Measures of Unemployed Relief, an unemployed worker could get 6 to 7.5 yuan, and 1.5 to 2 yuan for each additional family member per month. But the amount was capped at 12 to 15 yuan per family per month.

27. *Renmin Ribao,* December 16, 1956, 1. Later, the payment was extended to 1965 and finally stopped in September 1966 (Xia 1991, 85).

28. Zhou Enlai (周恩来), "Guanyu laodong gongzi he laobao fuli wenti de baogao," *Xinhua yuebao* (Xinhua monthly) (September 1957).

29. This observation is quite self-evident. For a long time, Mao and the CCP were treated in the PRC's propaganda as parents of the Chinese people. For example, a very popular political song still is "I Take the Party as My Mother."

30. The 77 Ji (Class of 1977) thus became the first "genuine" college students in more than ten years. A major breakthrough was therefore achieved by the reformers. CCP Central Committee and the State Council, *"Guangyu gaige gaokao zhidu de tongzhi"* (Notice on the reform of the college entrance exam), *Hongqi* (Red flag) magazine, October 1977.

31. There is abundant evidence in the Chinese literature and popular culture that "capitalism," "getting rich," "market," "inequality," "competition," and above all, "money," have become perfectly acceptable concepts. Even in the official press, numerous comments can be found praising "new millionaires" and discussing how to "get rich first."

32. Yuan 1987, 217-219; Yuan 1990, 7.

33. At this time, employees in foreign-invested enterprises were still erroneously calculated as state employees.

34. The Labor Ministry estimated that the total labor force of China was 825 million in 1994 whereas the total number of workers was 614.69 million. See the Labor Ministry's 1994 Annual Report, cited in *Renmin Ribao,* May 11, 1995, 1. This unusually big one-year increase of the Chinese labor force may be another example of the problematic accounting of Chinese official statistics, or it may arise because of different statistical methods used by the SSB and the Labor Ministry.

35. "Employment" in China is officially defined as "people who are engaging in social laboring/working and gaining working rewards or business revenues." "Waiting-for-job" (*daiye*) is defined as "people who do not have a job, have registered in the urban local authorities, and have working abilities" (Yuan 1990, 7, and Yue 1989, 16). As perhaps a meaningful sign of rationalization, Beijing formally adopted the term "unemployment rate" in 1994 to replace the awkward "waiting-for-job rate."

36. These figures are based on governmental reports from 1989 to 1995 (*Renmin Ribao,* March 12, 1990, 2; Dec. 13, 1990, 1; Dec. 20, 1990, 1; and March 2, 1995, 2; *Zhongguo rencai bao* (Chinese professional daily), October 4, 1989; *Jingji Ribao* (Economic daily), October 24, 1989, 3; SSB 1991, 3-7; SSB 1992, 15-18; and SSB-PB 1993, 66, 88). Chinese Minister of Labor Yuang Chongwu predicted that by 1995 the real unemployment rate in Chinese urban areas could reach a high point of 4.6 percent. He said further that "based on the Chinese situation, the highest unemployment rate we can put up with should not exceed 3.5 percent" (*Renmin Ribao,* December 12, 1990, 3).

37. Walder categorized the Chinese industrial labor force in four segments, or "status groups in the labor force": state-sector permanent employees, urban collective employees, rural collective employees, and temporary urban and rural employees (1986, 39-56). His major criteria for distinguishing these four groups were the difference in receiving socialist benefits provided by the state and the differentiation of payment. David Granick discussed the various market-oriented labor practices in the PRC ("Multiple labour markets in the industrial state enterprise sector" in *The China Quarterly,* [January 1991]: 269-289).

1. The Family-Based Traditional Pattern

Before the PRC era, the family-based traditional LAP dominated Chinese labor allocation for centuries, determining much of the development of Chinese history. As a result, the family-like Chinese institutional structure continued, justifying the father-like imperial state as the almighty center of the Chinese universe.[1] The centuries-old internalization of China's institutional structure, the Confucian culture, and the natural and later self-imposed isolation of the Chinese nation contributed significantly to the stability of the institutional structure. Under such a system, a market-driven modernization could not meaningfully develop. Cyclical rebellions, famines, and other disasters could not affect the Chinese institutional system except for temporarily easing the economic and social problems accumulated at the horrendous price of destruction and loss of millions of lives.

The CCP regime, very quickly after restoring the traditional family-based LAP, forcefully built up an authoritarian state LAP in the urban areas and a "collective" LAP in the rural areas; together these can be viewed as an enlarged, distorted, and centralized "family-based" traditional LAP—a nation-based traditional LAP. The dominant LAP remained a traditional one, but instead of developing along the lines of dispersed social institutions like the family, it was organized around the centralized political institutions—the family-like PRC state. The family-like Chinese domestic institutional structure was therefore intensified and pushed to an unprecedented extreme, with an accelerated institutional explosion—another costly and more thorough dynastic cycle—looming on the horizon. Deng Xiaoping's reform started to dismantle Mao Zedong's centralized nation-based traditional LAP and restored the traditional family-based LAP in the rural areas, where most Chinese lived, and to a lesser extent in the urban areas, too. Consequently, much of the stable Chinese traditional institutions were perpetuated as much of China's pre-1950s institutional structure was restored. What was new were other competing LAPs: the remaining authoritarian state LAP, the community-based societal LAP, and the market-oriented LAP. Where and how this ancient family-based LAP moves among the four LAPs existing in the 1990s and beyond will naturally determine much of the future of China.

This chapter examines the family-based LAP in order to better understand the implications of the Chinese institutional continuities and changes. The first section begins with a discussion on the family as, primarily, a social institution and as an economic and even political institution. The second section describes the distortion and restoration of the family LAP in contemporary China and its development toward the twenty-first century. Last, we explore the implications of this family-based LAP on the Chinese institutional structure.

The Family and Family-Based LAP

The family is the oldest and most basic human institution. It has been the most important component of human social institutions to fulfill the human need for reproduction, serving also as both an economic and political institution to meet other essential human needs and desires. Before discussing the economic and political role of the family and family-based labor allocation, a brief discussion of the concept of family as a social institution is in order.

Family as a Social Institution

Social institutions are devised and maintained primarily for the purpose of human reproduction. The term "reproduction" is understood as a basic human need to extend an individual's characteristics, consciously or unconsciously, beyond the life of the individual. Sexual activities, childbearing, religious activities addressing the life beyond, personality cultivation, self-realization, and the pursuit of fame are some of the human behaviors associated with reproduction. The organizational principles of social institutions are either blood/kinship relationships or interest/geographic approximations. Genetic bonds and voluntary socialization are the main links holding people together in a social institution such as a family, church, club, or neighborhood association. Group harmony and mutual caring are valued as well as individuality; they both contribute to human reproduction. When individual desires and needs (even those as fundamental as the need for individual survival) conflict with the values needed for reproduction (such as the welfare of children), social institutions generally sanction behaviors of sacrifice for the sake of reproduction.

Going beyond Max Weber's classic work on social organizations, *Economy and Society,* this book views social institutions in terms of organizing human behavior in ways distinctively different from that of economic and political institutions.[2] Despite the fact that social institutions have hierarchical structures and authority relationships, they are mainly bonded by genetic or voluntary links rather than by ownership-based exchanges or group-based enforced participation. For one thing, interdependent and dependent behaviors are the norm in social institutions, whereas independent behavior is rare. Therefore, interactions in social institutions are distinctively different from economic or political activities, where "rationality" perhaps has a more universal meaning and people perhaps have more chance to play the "game" as independent rational actors. Furthermore, social interactions tend to be the most stable and lasting; thus cooperation, rather than competition for gain and power-seeking, has a much better chance of becoming the dominant strategy by a member of a social institution.

Institutional Characteristics of the Family

Family, or kinship, is the main component of human social institutions. To sociologists like Talcott Parsons, kinship is a major social structure or social system that "looms large in every known society," shaping people's behavior (Parsons 1951A, 153-157). The family shares many of the institutional features of social institutions. It also has some of its own institutional characteristics that deserve our particular attention.

First, the family is a human grouping and institution that exists primarily for the purpose of reproduction. Family membership, in most cases, is not by choice. As in any other human institution, transaction costs are incurred for changes of any individual membership in a family. Unlike other social institutions, family members are linked by genes, not necessarily by interest or locational approximations. Therefore, the highest transaction cost of altering human institutional membership, mainly psychological and often economic, is perhaps associated with family membership. As a result, we see family as the most stable and clear-cut of all social institutions—even of all human institutions. Great human movements such as the massive

Industrial Revolution that changed the world after the seventeenth century did not destroy the family unit; it only "indirectly" reduced its size.[3] The nearly two-decade reform and opening of China have brought a similar, though still limited, downsizing of the Chinese family without altering its basic institutional features and functions (Yan 1994, 78-83).

Time, geography, and even mutual hostility rarely destroy a family institution, especially the nuclear family. The members will almost always remain members of the same family unit. For example, even divorce cannot eliminate the unique relationship among the siblings and between the parents and the children. As one major cross-nation survey discovered, the central and traditional role of the family in society remains the same in Europe throughout the twentieth century (Moors and Palomba 1995, 248, 262).

Second, since the basic human needs of survival are logically connected to those of reproduction, people tend to be much less calculating in their social life. A functional family, therefore, strongly discourages its members from overt strategic interactions based on an individual's self-interest. Strategic behavior of the parents against the children, for example, would severely endanger reproduction of not only the genes but also the characteristics and the influence of the parents. Unconditional or maximum cooperation is usually the norm for a family institution. Hence, clearly, the application of popular rational-choice models based on microeconomics is limited in analyzing social activities in the family. In the United States, where many nontraditional family types have emerged (perhaps because of overuse or abuse of individually based and economically driven rational behavior), the basic behavioral norms within families remain centered on the need for reproduction.[4]

Third, related to the lack of strategic behavior and need for sacrifice, the family tends to produce a nearly permanent internal authority structure. The most powerful members, as in other social institutions, tend to have stable and fully recognized authority over the rest of the family. Traditionally, the physically strong and resource-providing father became the permanent head of the family. Establishing the father (or mother) as the head reinforced the stability of the authority structure and made the family perhaps the most difficult human institution to break. The authority structure is often challenged but only slowly and minimally altered. For example, despite the fact that wives have begun to gain equal economic footing with the male members of the family, one study found that, in the United States, household work still rests primarily on the shoulders of the female members (Davidson and Gordon 1979). Similar findings are seen in China and Hong Kong as well.[5] Talk about how psychologically important childhood experiences can be in affecting a person's adult life (especially popular in the United States, where a decline in the role of the family institution and a decay of the family itself are widely alleged) also illustrates a seemingly permanent authority structure of the family institution.

Finally, institutional features of the family such as stability and the discouragement of members to be too "selfish" or "calculating" tend to decrease drastically when the family is expanded beyond a nuclear family of parents and immediate offspring. An explanation may be that the nuclear family serves most of the reproductive needs and that the extended family plays a less essential role in fulfilling those needs. Therefore, the ideal of modeling other human institutions—economic, political, or social—after the family is usually unattainable, as the desirable institutional features of the family fade in proportion to the scale and complexity of the artificial family.

These generic features of the family institution apply to all families across national and historical settings. As long as a human family, including single-parent families and homosexual couples, is organized to reproduce—by birth or adoption—a family institution is established and the behavior of its members is constrained by the institution in basically the same ways. Even in the animal world, especially among those species who share many biological characteristics with humans, we see family-like institutional structures. The family can thus be viewed as the most common and stable human institution (Moors and Palomba 1995, 246) and the backbone of social institutions that serve human reproductive needs.

Family as an Economic and Political Institution

The family, though primarily organized for the purpose of social objectives, is often utilized as an economic and even political institution. Sociologists have found that in some nations, such as ancient China, "familism" became the foundation for the whole institutional structure.[6] Economists have tried to prove that family, like any other human institution, is just another economic institution. For example, Nobel Prize Laureate Gary S. Becker argues that family is just a production unit, or an "insurance company," organized primarily for the purpose of economic activities (Becker 1981). Historically, this is especially the case when technology has limited the division of labor, the need for labor mobility, the size of human grouping, and the distance of human migration. Therefore, most human groupings based on a subsistence economy tend to have the family as their social, economic, and even political institution (Nimkoff and Middleton 1960). Reproductive needs are addressed by the family institution; security needs are met by the family or clan authority structure; economic activities are also organized by the family institution, with a clear dominance of family values such as cooperation, harmony, and sacrifice in the division of labor and in the distribution of income.

The economic and political functions of the family institution have been historically integral to human civilization. Given the small size of early human groupings and a less developed division of labor due to technology limits, the family institution was actually a highly efficient and effective economic and political institution, providing needed materials and services to sustain its members and protecting them from natural or human competitors. All human nations benefit from the economic and political functions of the family institution, which, in turn, affect the family institution, even its forms. For example, a comparative study of 549 cultures found that the varied need for labor mobility, caused by the different types of economies, had a direct impact on family types. Thus, we see a dominance of nuclear families in hunting and gathering economies (as well as in modern industrialized market economies) because of the need for high labor mobility, whereas extended families are the main family type in agrarian economies in which such mobility is less important (Nimkoff and Middleton 1960, 224-225).

The historically important role of the family is alive today in every nation, including the modernized ones where families are no longer the main economic and political institutions. In the modernized nations, few families can survive as independent economic units, and few family heads can make or enforce laws upon their family members. Nevertheless, we can easily see many social and family values present in those nations' economic and political activities. Many of their economic and political activities are visibly associated with the family institution. Important public figures in the United States, such as Colin Powell, have promoted the idea "of America as a big national family" and suggested that people should behave as family members toward one another.[7] The child of the owner of an American firm may be incompetent, but still have a well-paying job in that firm, although he or she probably does not have much say in the running of that firm.

To economists like Becker (1976 and 1981), family is clearly still an important economic institution in the United States because marriage, divorce, and childbearing can all be explained by market-oriented human economic rationality on the part of individuals. Without engaging in an in-depth critique of Becker's interpretation, we need, nonetheless, to point out that to understand human social needs, behavior, and institutions in purely economic terms is useless in a practical sense.[8] The powerful rational-choice models help to explain only certain human social behaviors. But the human interest of reproduction, which dominates social behavior and social institutions, often creates a unique rationality to govern human behavior, different from other rationalities based on meeting nonreproductive needs and satisfying diverse desires. Unless we can solve the key methodological problem of ascertaining a unified human interest, thus a singular human rationality, rational-choice models borrowed from microeconomics will have only very limited utility in explaining noneconomic institutions and noneconomic behaviors.

Disadvantages of organizing economic and political activities based on the family institution are apparent. Simply because the golden rule of division of labor is not well observed, a family institution usually does a less than optimal job in these spheres. The members of the grouping (a nation, for instance) are usually poorly served because their economic and political values do not have a chance to be maximized. A family institution that emphasizes harmony and depends on cooperation can hardly promote the competitive behavior needed for economic efficiency and political equality. Furthermore, the permanent authority structure of the family is hardly conducive to the innovations and participation that are important to economic efficiency and political effectiveness. Therefore, it is no surprise to see a less developed economy in those pre-modern nations that have the family as *the institution* for their economic and political activities. Political effectiveness is generally low, and political equality is generally missing in those nations. Meanwhile, basing economic and political roles on a family-like institutional structure actually corrupts families. The political and economic activities of the family tend to overburden the family institution and make it less suitable for its primary mission: to reproduce. The social values that are supposed to be addressed by the family institution are actually compromised because the family is structurally overstretched. Chinese authors, for example, describe many depressing pictures of family life under the Chinese family-like institutional structure.[9] Even the quality of reproduction is threatened in many cases, due to politically or economically arranged marriages and numerous political and economic concerns, at the expense of self-selection by the young reproducing members of the family or the family-like nation.

The story of a famous Chinese family/clan, Qiao, in Shanxi Province may illustrate the drawbacks of having the family as an economic institution. From the mid-1700s to the 1930s, five generations of the rich Qiao family, which owned shops and banks in about a dozen major cities, lived in a huge, fortress compound in its hometown in central Shanxi. The family/clan head, usually the eldest or "most able" male of the generation, controlled the family business and income as well as the family labor division. He provided free room (one small courtyard for each nuclear family), board, and major services for everyone. In addition, the family head paid each member an equal amount of annual salary for their personal expenses such as clothing and servants. Males got about 50 percent more than females (2,400 silver yuan versus 1,600 in 1930). The problem was that the family's "public" funds became easy targets for waste and embezzlement. After a few generations, family bonds began to loosen. When the family head was caught using drugs and embezzling family funds, the family had a bitter internal "war" and eventually decided in the 1930s to split its fortune among the now rather remote nuclear families. That spelled not only the end for the Qiao economic institution—a once-mighty business empire—but also the end of the family structure.

Family-Based LAP

A family-based traditional LAP is conceptually distinguishable from and empirically identifiable among other patterns. The family-based LAP exists widely in time and space. Without attempting to exhaust the institutional characteristics of a family-based LAP, this book uses the following features to identify it:

1. *The dominance of noneconomic, mainly social, rationales in allocating labor.* The division of labor under a family-based LAP is based primarily on social and even political (or more precisely family-like political) values rather than economic ones, and seeking profit is generally secondary to the goal of feeding everyone in the human grouping. Recruitment, pay, promotion, penalties, and dismissal are based more on noneconomic concerns such as social harmony, personal relationships, ideological interests, and kinship. Thus, economically, the family-based LAP tends to be much less competitive and less innovative than a labor market.

2. *Labor immobility.* The laborers under a family-based LAP generally have a personal dependence on the employer, superior, or head of the group, rather than merely economic ties. Almost everyone is assigned a basically fixed relational role, as in a family. As a result, labor mobility is low and laborers have very limited personal freedom and individual rights.

3. *Institutionalized inequality.* Not only the economic status, but the social and political status of the laborers is lower than that of the employers, superiors, or group heads. Labor contracting of "equal" parties is rare, and bargaining is generally deemed unnecessary or unacceptable. As a result, labor protection and labor rights are generally subject to the employer's goodwill or the social and political values an individual employer/superior may have. A family-based LAP, therefore, is usually conducive to an authoritarian political system and a rigidly hierarchical social stratification.

4. *Stability and low economic performance.* Labor allocated under a family-based LAP tends to be generally small-scale and stable over time. The job turnover rate is low, if not negligible. For small groups or enterprises and in certain industries, a family-based LAP can be rather effective and even efficient, as in family farms and some family craft shops. But for most economic activities and in most industrial enterprises that require a complicated division of labor and almost constant innovation, the family-based LAP tends to perform quite poorly due to low labor mobility and the heavy influence of noneconomic considerations.

The Family-Based LAP in China

Few other nations have had such a lasting traditional institutional structure as has China.[10] This structure perpetuated itself for centuries, thanks largely to the formation and dominance of Confucian culture. People respected and obeyed, often unconditionally, their ancestors and senior family members out of a well-indoctrinated gratitude for life and a strong desire to maintain family lines. Institutional differentiation among the economy, polity, and society were not culturally acceptable or meaningfully experienced. Family thus became the institution for Chinese economy, politics, and society.[11] It was therefore the head of the family—an emperor or a ruling group/clan—who could make a difference in affecting people's behavior in modest ways. The powerful family-like institution has usually been strong enough, however, to bounce back and to overthrow the numerous top-down changes imposed by its head. Thus, the historical lessons have been: "reformers do not have a good ending,"[12] and "the doctrine of the mean" has been the golden rule for the Chinese.[13]

This family-like Chinese institutional setting is sufficiently reflected by the wide existence of a family-based LAP throughout Chinese history. Having now clarified some of the basic conceptual issues of the family-based LAP, the next section examines the status, organizational features, and institutional impacts of the family-based LAP in the PRC since 1949.

Distortion and Restoration of the Family-Based LAP

The family-based LAP existed in China for thousands of years without being seriously challenged.[14] Cycles of famine, war, and dynastic changes released the pressures and tensions that this LAP accumulated, but the family-based LAP was usually restored soon after the institutional explosions. Only in the nineteenth century was the Chinese family-like institutional setting fundamentally challenged, as Western powers approached and the market institution rapidly began to replace the family as a powerful alternative. The usual problem of the decay of the family-based LAP at the end of a dynasty was greatly worsened; the LAP was subject not only to another cyclic shake-up but, more importantly, possible institutional termination. Population pressure, heavy taxation, increasing concentration of land ownership, rent of 50 to 80 percent of output, civil wars, and the massive competition of the international market dislocated millions of Chinese peasants at a horrendous human price.[15] The Chinese were forced into rebellion or death.

For reasons that have excited scholars for decades, the CCP emerged as the new ruling group of China after the struggle between Republicans and Communists, a massive institutional explosion, in 1949. The new regime under Mao, despite its claim of being socialist and containing significant Marxist elements, soon stepped onto the traditional dynastic road by attempting to restore the Chinese family-like institutional setting by force. The traditional Chinese family-based LAP was quickly restored through bloody land reform (*tugai*) campaigns. The political benefits for the CCP were enormous, just as they were for rulers so many times in past centuries. But that was not enough to satisfy the new regime's desire to consolidate its rule. This was a changed world, in which many other sovereign nations could not possibly be incorporated into a family-like "Chinese world order," as

Mao's predecessors had tried to do. So he and his associates pushed for rapid economic development, with the clear impetus of international competition behind it. Merely returning to tradition proved to be economically discouraging and politically ineffective for the grand "socialist construction" plans in the twentieth century. But instead of establishing new institutional frameworks for the Chinese—an unknown and thus politically very risky course—Mao decided not just to restore the Chinese traditional institutions but to reform them into a new vehicle to swiftly carry the largest nation into the communists' promised land.[16]

The politically desirable family-based traditional LAP very soon became an obstacle to that dream. Despite "squeezing the peasants" to the danger point under the exploitative state policy of monopolizing the purchase and marketing of grains (*tonggou tongxiao*), the surplus grain and other goods that peasants could provide decreased rather than increased in the 1950s (Yan 1994, 18-19). The industrializing effort along Soviet lines backfired politically, as demonstrated by the heated history of 1955-1957.[17] The CCP then decided that the political beauty of the family-based LAP needed preserving, while its economic inefficiency needed correcting—not by a market institution but by further elimination of the market mechanism and creation of a giant, nationwide family.

The astonishingly speedy collectivization, one of Mao's almost romantic revolutionary ideas, soon created communes employing an authoritarian labor allocation pattern similar to the one already prevalent in the PRC's cities. Hundreds of millions of Chinese peasants were consequently "fixed to the land until death" (Wang 1994, 47-48). With such a centralized and unified family-like institution, people could be better mobilized, and organized human sacrifice could be better justified and thus better exploited (in lieu of capital and technology) to modernize China in ten years or less (Zhang 1992, 236-241).

In just a few years, a "new" traditional Chinese institutional structure was established, featuring an authoritarian state LAP in the urban areas and its twin, a collectivized LAP in the countryside. The traditional family-based LAP existed only briefly. The new PRC LAP, essentially still family-based but the size of the whole nation, replaced the relative autonomy of families with only one giant nation/family system. This new scale itself is not insignificant. By having only a single, unified, centralized family institution for everything in a nation with hundreds of millions of people, the family-like Chinese institutional structure was pushed to the extreme, resulting in gross economic inefficiency, social retardation, and political chaos. For example, the economic performance, in terms of providing surplus value of the collectivized rural LAP was much worse than that of the traditional family-based LAP (Yan 1994, 20-21). Soon, the end of this Maoist family-like institutional system was clearly in sight; Chinese reform was thus historically inevitable, or another dynasty-change style of institutional explosion would have to happen.

Displaced for more than two decades, the traditional family-based LAP was restored as the predominant LAP in the Chinese rural areas once again through nationwide decollectivization. This historical movement first took place in some of the poorest villages in the disaster-prone Huai River valley—Huaibei area (Fongyang and other counties) of Anhui Province in 1977 and 1978, initially as a desperate move by peasants to survive the drought and oncoming famine. In the winter of 1978, heads of eighteen desperate peasant families from the Xiaogang Production Team in Fongyang county held a secret meeting. They adopted then politically scorned measures of household-responsible contracts/quotas (*baochan daohu* or *baogan daohu*) and signed agreements to divide the land among them; the families would keep the extra products after providing a fixed amount to the collectives and the state. The participants of this illegal decollectivization, however, had to swear to secrecy; they signed written promises that they would take care of the family of team leader Yan Junchang in the event he was jailed for allowing them to restore the family-based economy. In one year, the grain production of Xiaogang village more than quadrupled, from less than 16,000 kg to more than 60,000 kg. The handwritten agreement, with the red fingerprints of the eighteen peasants, is now part of the collection of the Chinese Museum of History.[18]

These "two *bao*" policies, devised in the early 1960s by Liu Shaoqi and others to cope with the disastrous aftermath of the Great Leap Forward (1958-1961), proved more productive than the communes. However, they were banned during the Cultural Revolution" (1966-1976) as capitalist policies. On a very small scale in 1977 to 1978, and much more broadly a year later, peasants spontaneously picked up the two *bao* policies and carried them further by restoring the family-based traditional LAP. Pragmatic county leaders gave tacit consent to these bottom-up changes, and grain production in those counties soared by 15 to 43 percent within the same year.[19] The new "household responsibility" policy was soon adopted by then Anhui provincial leader, Wan Li, a firm supporter of Deng Xiaoping, and the party boss of Sichuan Province, Zhao Ziyang, a protégé of Deng.

By fall 1978, the real advantages of the restored family-based economy in the two major agriculture provinces of Anhui and Sichuan were already clear to Beijing. Wan and Zhao earned instant political popularity and were soon promoted to chairman of the Chinese National People's Congress (CNPC) and premier, respectively. The power struggle between Deng Xiaoping and Hua Guofeng, Mao's designated successor, facilitated this great institutional change and its justification. When Deng emerged as China's new leader, the CCP leadership issued twenty-five new policies concerning the rural economy and officially endorsed the decollectivization in 1979-1982 (Zhang 1992, 266). With the same dizzying speed that it had been eliminated two decades before, the family-based LAP reemerged, faster than bamboo shoots sprout from the ground. The traditional family-based LAP was nationally restored in less than three years.

By 1983, 98 percent of Chinese peasants were decollectivized and had adopted the household responsibility system, which divided the collectively owned land among families to use for fifteen years.[20] Later, the fifteen-year time limit was all but officially erased, the landholdings were fixed, and families were allowed to transfer land—that is, quasi-land-ownership was created. Later, in the late 1990s, there was a small-scale reallocation of land (to allow some families to move away from farming) and/or a rationalization of land division (to adjust small plots to allow more intensive use of agricultural technology) in some areas. The land the families acquired in the early 1980s, however, remained generally the same. Those reallocations were officially declared final, and both the authorities and the farmers vowed that there would be no more such actions other than the farmers' voluntary and compensated transfers of land.

In short, in the early 1980s, collective labor allocation by the communes/state was abolished and the families once again became the main institution allocating labor in the vast rural areas. The family responsibility system and the family-based LAP were finally guaranteed by the PRC Constitution in the 1980s. The economic importance of the families in the Chinese rural areas "was greatly restored and enhanced" (Liu 1993, 3, 5). In 1994, nearly two-thirds of the peasants' total income came from family-based production.[21]

Under Deng's reform policies, an increasing number of individual households (*getihu*) emerged in the urban economy and began to prosper economically. Substantial urban labor was then allocated by family institutions throughout China's cities. By 1993, in addition to about 184,000 private enterprises employing more than 3 million workers, China had nearly 15 million *getihu* with more than 22 million workers in the cities.[22] Most *getihu* and their rural twins, the specialized households (*zhuanyehu*), were soon allowed to hire help from outside the family, and thus participate in the emerging national labor market (see chapter 4) or the already strong community-based labor markets (CLMs, chapter 3). Market-oriented labor allocation, therefore, increasingly began to erode the family-based LAP from the inside. The Chinese finally completed a great historical circle, returning to the good-old family-based traditional LAP in the countryside and, to a lesser extent, in the cities as well. Only this time, the family-based LAP was in a losing competition with the newly emerged market institution.

A Statistical Analysis of the Family-Based LAP

The restored Chinese family-based LAP, though still clearly traditional, has been operating in a rather "new" environment. First, the majority of the economically more important urban labor force is not covered by this LAP. They are still under an authoritarian state LAP (to be examined in chapter 2), allocated by a societal LAP, the community-based labor markets (chapter 3), or allocated by an emerging national labor market (chapter 4). The institutional mechanism and impact of this restored family-based LAP, therefore, appear to be different from the version that existed before. More important, the restored family-based LAP is strongly influenced by the combined forces of an authoritarian state under the CCP and the increasing power of the market institution, domestic and international.[23] Traditional Chinese families have been deeply affected by more than a hundred years of revolution, wars, political turmoil, economic hardships, cultural crises, and exchanges with other nations. As a result, the Chinese family by the end of the twentieth century has acquired certain new institutional features that need to be clarified, in order to have an accurate understanding of its traditional characteristics and impacts.[24]

The Chinese Family: A Statistical Picture

Overall, there are 300.39 million Chinese families, or households (*hu*), with more than 1.17 billion people in 1992. Of these, 78.33 percent live in the rural areas (down from 82.6 percent in 1949 and 84.5 percent in 1977). In the early 1990s an interesting statistical study by Chinese scholars determined that in China's history, a total of only 5,663 surnames existed. Currently, there are 3,050 surnames in use in China, including Taiwan, but more than 90 percent of the people share fewer than 100 surnames. The top 19 surnames covered over 55.6 percent of the largest nation in the world, and over 20 percent of the Chinese carry the four most common surnames.[25]

According to a survey by the State Statistical Bureau, the average family (or household) size in China in 1993 was 3.95 members. Some 57.6 percent of the sampled households had four or more members, over 15.2 percent had more than six people, and about 5.9 percent were single-member households. Families were smaller in the major metropolitan areas such as Beijing (3.32) and Shanghai (3.05), and in the more developed provinces like Jiangsu (3.54). In predominantly rural areas, the average family size was still higher than 4.5, despite the one-child-per-family policy (SSB-PB 1993, 31-32, 399).

It must be pointed out, however, that the survey, as well as statistical reports of Chinese demography, has been methodologically biased because of an overemphasis (sometimes five to one) of samples from major urban areas such as Beijing, Tianjin, and Shanghai (SSB-PB 1993, 31). There is reason to believe that, in the vast countryside, Chinese families are larger than the statistics indicate. Furthermore, the study of rural households included only members "in residence" at the time of sampling; significant numbers of family members who were working outside might have been excluded from the reporting. If five to six members is the true average, then it may be safe to conclude that many Chinese families, especially in the rural areas, are still traditionally extended rather than "modern" nuclear families.[26] A fourteen-province field investigation revealed that, by the late 1980s, extended families still constituted nearly 25 percent of the total rural households surveyed. About 47 percent of the respondents preferred the traditional extended families second only to those who preferred the nuclear families (51 percent). The same field work found that eight out the fourteen provinces had an average rural family size larger than 4.6. In Fujian Province, the average family size was as high as 9.46 (Liu Ying 1993, 79, 86). A comparison with earlier data suggests that the size of Chinese families has been very stable since the early twentieth century.[27]

Another report by the State Statistical Bureau based on the similarly biased methodology estimated that in 1991 the average size of urban households was 3.43 (down from 4.24 in 1981) and each family had 1.96 workers employed (down from 2.39). In the rural areas, the average family size was 4.71 (down from 5.74 in 1978) and on average each family had 2.83 laborers (up from 2.27) (SSB 1992, 47, 50).

Table 1.1 shows some basic statistical information about Chinese families.

Table 1.1. Families in the PRC (Selected Years)

Year	Total (millions)	Family size			Laborers per family			% of rural population
		Average	Rural*	Urban*	Average	Rural*	Urban*	
1954	135.5	4.45	n.a	n.a	1.61	n.a	n.a	84.7
1957	144.3	4.48	n.a	n.a	1.68	n.a	n.a	83.6
1960	147.5	4.49	n.a	n.a	1.78	n.a	n.a	79.3
1965	159.5	4.55	n.a	n.a	1.80	n.a	n.a	83.3
1970	175.2	4.74	n.a	n.a	1.97	n.a	n.a	84.7
1975	193.1	4.79	n.a	n.a	1.98	n.a	n.a	84.6
1978	206.4	4.66	5.74	n.a	1.95	2.77	n.a.	84.2
1980	213.9	4.61	5.54	n.a.	1.98	2.45	n.a.	83.0
1981	220.6	4.54	n.a.	4.24	1.98	n.a.	2.39	82.6
1985	241.3	4.39	5.12	3.89	2.07	2.95	2.15	79.9
1986	249.3	4.31	4.97	n.a.	2.06	2.70	n.a.	80.6
1987	258.3	4.23	n.a.	n.a.	2.04	n.a.	n.a.	79.9
1989	278.8	4.04	4.86	3.55	1.99	2.94	2.00	78.9
1990	288.3	3.97	4.80	3.50	1.97	2.92	1.98	78.9
1991	294.6	3.93	4.71	3.43	n.a	2.83	1.96	78.7
1992	300.4	3.91	n.a.	n.a.	n.a	n.a.	n.a.	78.1
1993	n.a.	3.95	n.a.	n.a.	n.a	n.a.	n.a.	77.8

Notes: * Based on survey of sample households.
n.a.— Data not available.
Sources: SSB 1991, 45, 48; SSB 1992, 47, 50; SSB-PB 1993, 352-371; Liu 1993, 79, 101; and SSB-LM 1991, 7-8.

Historically, the male-female ratio in China has been somewhat unbalanced. The ratio was 108.2:100 in 1949, 104.9:100 by 1965, 106.2:100 in 1978, and 106.9:100 in 1992. There was one divorce per 17.9 marriages in 1993, about 5.6 percent, up from 5 percent in 1979 (with 5.55 percent in 1985 and 5.9 percent in 1990). For every one hundred marriage applications filed in 1993, 8.89 percent were divorce cases (SSB-PB 1993, 352, 399, 434-438). The urban divorce rate (9.8 percent in 1994) was much higher than the rural one (6.2

percent). In major cities like Beijing and Shanghai, the divorce rate was just over 10 percent in 1994 (up from 5 percent in 1990).[28]

Statistically, as shown in Table 1.1, changes in Chinese families are observable but small. Family size has decreased slowly over the past forty-five years, while the number of laborers per family in the rural areas remains basically the same. The downsizing of families has perhaps been a result of the strict family-planning policy that the CCP has enforced since the 1970s. The effects of a market economy and industrialization on family size, as observed in Britain and other European nations, have not been significant in China if we control for the factor of family planning. The Chinese family still demonstrates remarkable institutional stability, as reflected in the low divorce rate. A recent study by Chinese sociologists in Beijing concluded that 80 percent of two thousand people interviewed were opposed to premarital sex and three-quarters of them were against extramarital affairs. Although three-quarters of young couples in Beijing now prefer not to live with their parents, an overwhelming 97 percent believe that children should support and provide for their parents.[29] These rather traditional and conservative "family values" of Beijing residents are interesting because Beijing is considered to be one of the most modernized urban areas in China. Families in the rural and inland small urban areas undoubtedly tend to be more traditional than urban ones. It is those traditional, stable, and often extended families in the rural areas that are the institutional foundation for most of the restored family-based LAP in China.

The Rural Families: An Empirical Observation
Because the urban family-based LAP has been relatively small in China, we need to focus on the rural families in our exploration of the restored family-based traditional LAP. Chinese rural families in the 1980s and 1990s are empirically different from those before the elimination of the traditional family-based LAP in the mid-1950s.[30] There is gratitude among the rural families toward the CCP for giving them the land, similar to that felt by peasants toward the founders of new dynasties. This time, though, the rural families do not own the land on which they work. Rather, the land still belongs to the institutions that replaced the former collectives—the townships and the villages.

Historically, Chinese peasants rarely have had real ownership of their land. The ultimate ownership was always in the hands of the emperors. For a very short period, from 1949 to the mid-1950s, peasants were given ownership during the land reform campaign led by the CCP. However, after the collectivization movement in the 1950s, they were once again left with only the user's right of the land. After decollectivization, the user's right was allocated on a household basis by the townships and villages through a contract pattern—the so-called responsibility system. Legally, the families did not own the land. As Vivienne Shue concluded, the "basic human relationships and relations of production" were "changed from that of communal obligation to that of contractual agreement" (Howard 1988, 167). This figured prominently into the "rational" calculation of Chinese peasants. Short-term behavior causing the deterioration of the soil and the waste of land was widely observed among many people who were otherwise land-loving conservationists. In many places, for example, peasants competed to build spacious houses on fertile land that had already been in short supply. One study estimates that nearly three-quarters of the peasants' new investment went to housing in the early 1990s.[31] Many even built lavish tombs on the land for themselves and their children. The farmers' "user's right" of the allocated land has only recently become transferable, thus producing quasi-ownership.[32]

The return on investment from the soil is difficult to increase rapidly. Short-term behavior only undermines the long-term return. The shrinking size of family landholdings tends to reduce further the peasants' income from the land. Officially, in the early 1990s, the average size of land worked by each rural laborer was only about 2.37 *mu* (0.39 acre) including "hillside land" (SSB-RB 1992, 215). Under the principle of equality in land allocation, every family got a mixture of good and bad land that could be divided on average into nine to eleven small plots (compared to six plots per family in the 1930s) (Brugger and Reglar 1994, 128). Besides wasting precious land in ditches among the plots, the jigsawlike arrangements made agricultural machines and pest control much less effective. Such a small scale of production (only 6.71 *mu,* or 1.1 acre per family) naturally led to the stagnation of the family-based agricultural economy and the increasing need for new jobs for the underemployed rural labor force.[33]

With only 7 percent of the world's arable land to feed 22 percent of the world's population, the productivity of Chinese agriculture was indeed a vital national issue. The family-based LAP appeared to be institutionally incapable of a capital- and technology-intensive, thus more productive, agriculture. A hotbed for market-oriented labor allocation was institutionally prepared. Furthermore, among the peasant families' income sources, income from the land would be easiest to tax. Thus, rural families working on the land bore increasingly heavy tax burdens.[34] According to speeches by some CNPC deputies, the average income of many rice-growing peasants declined steadily by as much as 10 to 20 percent during 1992-1994, despite an impressive increase in per-acre output.[35] The peasants naturally started to use the land for other more lucrative purposes, such as commercial and industrial activities. Therefore, cultivated land shrank by as much as 5 percent in the 1980s: from 1.71 billion *mu* in 1979 to the lowest point of 1.3 billion *mu* in 1986. Per capita cultivated land was 2.7 *mu* in 1949 but only 1.2 *mu* by 1994.[36]

The situation was much more serious in the southern coastal areas. In Fujian Province, grain production decreased by 6.5 percent from 1992 to 1993.[37] The grain supply thus declined alarmingly in fast-growing provinces like Guangdong. The president of the Chinese Science Academy, Zhou Guangzhao, revealed that the decline of agriculture in the southeast had already altered the traditional pattern of "shipping grain from the South to the North," and a large quantity of grain now had to be freighted in the opposite direction. Serious grain shortages were thus expected, potentially requiring imports of as much as 400 million metric tons a year.[38]

A major consequence of the decline of agriculture was that the rural family-based traditional LAP fell under increasing economic pressure to change. The rural laborers by default became less land based, or land constrained, than their ancestors. Rapid development to seek jobs outside the family became a national phenomenon. In central Anhui Province, most rural families became incapable of surviving without some members working outside the family in other industries, usually as employees of other families or in the cities.[39] In the extreme case of Wuxi county in Jiangsu Province, a model of Chinese rural development, only about 11 percent of rural labor was still working in the traditional family-based agricultural sector.[40] The family-based LAP, as a consequence, generally acquired substantially more labor mobility than ever before and decreased its share of the overall Chinese labor allocation.

Another challenge to the family-based LAP came from the advancing market forces in China. Commercialization of the agricultural sector proceeded rapidly, increasing the exposure of the peasants to the national markets beyond local exchanges and even to the international market. As officially reported, monetary exchange was more than 75 percent of the overall economic transactions of Chinese peasants in 1991 (up from 52 percent in 1981). About 75.2 percent of their income was realized on a market in monetary terms (up from only 52.3 percent ten years before).[41] External commercial activities powerfully altered the minds of many peasants. Labor mobility was further encouraged by commercializing the rural economy, as seeking jobs outside the family was no longer only the desperate move of the past but a way to increase revenue and thus improve the material life of the family (Zeng 1993, 171-178). One major impact of market-oriented economic activities was that the stable family authority structure was shaken. Commercial skills and earning ability, rather than seniority alone, became the main qualifications for the family head, especially regarding financial decisions.[42] Not only was the seniority authority structure (the patriarchy tradition) weakened, its stability was affected as well. A decline in the authority of the senior family members was clearly observed in the rural areas, although males still tended to have the most authority in family decision making (Liu 1993, 15-16).

In general, however, the significant new features had not yet altered the basic institutional characteristics of the Chinese family and family-based LAP. In 1994, as one official report concluded, most peasants still lived in a subsistence economy and the rural market was still in the process of initial expansion.[43] The patriarchal structure continued to be perceived by the majority as the norm for the family institution.[44] Wage-based employment of parents by their children was still a rare, "newsworthy" event in the countryside. "Other than their normal provisional duties," reported *Renmin Ribao* in 1995, some children in a village of Shangdong Province started in 1994 to "hire their parents and pay them wages." But such a new event needed first to be "proposed and endorsed" by the unskilled but "open-minded and market-oriented" fathers.[45]

Beijing seemed to realize the danger of the destruction of the rural family-based LAP and the dismantling of the traditional families.[46] Thus, tremendous effort was made to strengthen the financial position of the peasantry and to stabilize the family-based LAP. Starting in 1993, the central government established a fund to support the price of agricultural products, and issued numerous directives and regulations to reduce the financial burdens of the land-based families.[47] But the serious and chronic government budget deficit tended to limit American-style price supports.[48] In short, Chinese families and the family-based LAP developed new features and were likely to change further but still remained largely traditional institutions with their basic characteristics intact.

The Chinese Family-Based LAP in the 1990s

By the 1990s, three types of workers in China were allocated in a basically family-based fashion. The majority was the vast number of rural families engaged in agriculture.[49] Then there were substantial numbers of *getihu* in the urban areas working in many industries ranging from commerce, service, transportation, and handicrafts to small-scale manufacturing. The rural version of *getihu* was *zhuanyehu*. They engaged in a variety of businesses including fishing, animal husbandry, handicrafts, commerce, transportation, small manufacturing, and even mining. Official statistics show that, by 1993, about 467.68 million laborers, roughly 66.3 percent of the entire Chinese labor force, worked in the rural areas as farmers, fishermen, loggers, and herdsmen. The overwhelming majority of these workers, 457.94 million, were farmers, allocated basically by the restored family-based LAP (SSB-PB 1993, 66-88).[50] The majority of nonfarming rural workers were the various types of *zhuanyehu*, which also allocated labor largely on a family basis. By 1993, China had more than 14.2 million *getihu* with 22.6 million workers in the cities.[51] In Beijing alone, there were more than 235,000 *getihu* (up from 259 in 1978).[52] Those figures show that the restored family-based traditional LAP was by far the largest LAP.

Under the family-based LAP, labor is organized around a normally paternal family based on the relationship of blood and/or marriage. The division of labor is decided by the head of the family, based on traditional principles such as holding males responsible for most heavy physical labor and business outside the local communities, and females responsible for side-line work, domestic care, and sale of certain produce in local markets. During the busiest seasons, the whole family engages in heavy labor such as planting rice or harvesting. Labor is not paid according to any preset standard established in a market or fixed by the family. Instead, payment to a laborer is determined by the size of the family income, the laborer's contribution to that income, and the laborer's needs as perceived by the head of the family. Fairness and common sense are usually important rules for the division of income. There is no contractual arrangement between the family and the laborers. Jobs are first and foremost for family members, although some workers from outside the family may be a necessary supplement.

A free exchange of labor among families is a common practice, especially when working on big projects such as house construction. In certain industries such as manufacturing, transportation, and mining, considerable outside hiring has gradually become commonplace. But both the employer and employees recognize that such employment is temporary and supplementary in nature. Payment to the outside employees, usually pre-set and negotiable, is distinguishably different from that to family members. Family members appear much like company owners who work within the company for nominal or no wages. For the majority of families, however, outside hiring is basically seasonal, temporary, and additional. Marriage and nominal kinship for the sake of business are widely practiced, to form a larger "family" of the business associates or partners.

Historically, the family-based Chinese LAP was often conditioned or modified by the clan structure. In many rural areas, a whole village may have been an extended family or clan that worshipped a common, not-so-distant ancestor.[53] The clan institution is believed to have contributed greatly to China's highly stable social structure and to overall Chinese civilization.[54] From 1949 to the early 1980s, the political power of the CCP systematically destroyed the traditional patriarchal clan institution in the rural areas, together with clan records, heads, land, rules, and ancestral temples.[55] The market economy tended to diminish further the economic importance of clans. Thus, in more recent years clan-based units became rare. Rather, there was a village-based restoration of local communities, an enlarged family institution with some of the characteristics of a clan.

As "one of the largest changes of the rural social structure," a "village community" of all villagers replaced the clan as an institution to dominate the life of many peasants beyond their families.[56] Nevertheless, in many villages, the institutional power of the clan was still clearly present in the allocation of labor for public projects, especially in the name of clan interests. Special deals were often offered to fellow clan members and some intensive farming emerged as a result. In places like Nanling county of Anhui Province, one person had less than 0.5 *mu* (about 0.08 acre) of cultivated land. Many farmers were forced to leave their villages to make a living.[57] They usually entrusted their land, dependents, and tax obligations to fellow clan members. Their cash income was shared by the family members they left behind and was often used to compensate those family/clan members who continued to work in the fields to provide food, pay taxes, and maintain the family/clan.[58]

Starting after 1985 and reaching a first peak by 1989-1990, millions of peasants began to flood Chinese cities in search of jobs and income (Zeng 1993, 172-173). By the end of 1993, more than 70 million farmers, out of an estimated 150 million surplus laborers in the rural areas, had left their villages to work outside their families/clans.[59] Hence, a significant amount of farming developed in many areas, and agriculture productivity rose tremendously. This type of agricultural development reached an impressive level in the Sunan (southern Jiangsu) area, where about 1 million farmers fed more than 9 million rural residents with only 0.8 *mu* (about 0.132 acre) per capita of arable land.[60]

The family-based LAP allows the family head to exercise a stable and often unconditional authority over the family members and employees from outside. The purpose of production can be just to feed everyone in the family, to prepare for some big events such as the wedding of a child, or to maintain a decent life among fellow villagers. Labor mobility is therefore low, and there is institutional discrimination against laborers based on their family identity and association. "Equal pay for equal work" is, as a result, systematically compromised. Clan leaders usually enjoy similar authority, which is often enhanced by the fact that they are usually CCP members and hold posts in the villages or townships. The old collective arrangement still functions in some important areas such as distributing land and "drawing up the terms of the production contracts with individual households which determine the state and local taxes." A kind of "interdependence" developed between the families and the local authorities as replacements for the former collectives (Saith 1987, 128-130). Beginning in 1991, townships were authorized by Beijing to levy their own taxes on peasant families. The clan authority structure thus acquired an additional source of power and stability. Many former collective bosses became clan leaders (Friedman et al. 1991). They had fewer obligations to the state but usually more power over their fellow villagers.

In the 1990s, more and more families became units of an emerging market economy. Profit increasingly became a legitimate purpose of production. Here, the traditional LAP began to transform as the father's authority became less permanent and family independence became threatened (Chan et al. 1992). As *Renmin Ribao* reported in a laudatory tone, since 1987 a new labor allocation pattern emerged in the agricultural sector, the so-called Rich-Poor Mutual Assistance Complex, or "the brains of the capable plus the arms of the poor." That is, rich peasant families hired labor from poor families to work on the land assigned to all families involved. The hired labor was paid in cash and bonuses while all the products were owned and disposed of by the employer. A rich peasant named Wang Xingwan in Qingan county of Jiling Province is said to have employed twenty-one such households and rid them of poverty. He was honored as a National Worker's Model (*Renmin Ribao,* February 3, 1990, 3).

Some peasant families in Jiangsu Province contracted hundreds of *mu* of land from hundreds of families and hired only a few additional workers from those families to form sizable, mechanized, and thus much more efficient and lucrative farming "big households."[61] Similar occurrences were seen in other provinces such as Beijing and Guangdong.[62] This kind of employment became rather common in the Chinese countryside, especially where there was a substantial market economy. One case study reveals that in Wenzhou county of Zhejiang Province, there were 13,121 "big labor-hiring households" employing 421,163 laborers (Chen in Nolan and Dong 1989, 140) This, in fact, was a variant of private employment in the rural areas—a quasi-market-oriented LAP. It is still empirically observed that the Chinese family-based LAP, especially in the rural areas, was not yet fundamentally altered by market forces; the quasi-market-oriented modification was nonetheless a crucial development.

Family-Based LAP in Nonfamily Institutions

It is difficult to exaggerate the influence of the family on China's institutional structure and the Chinese people. As China's most important social institution and longest-lasting institution, the family allocates labor far beyond the farming households and rural areas. The principles and practices of the family-based LAP exist in many nonfamily settings in modern China. Low labor mobility, moral economy characteristics, noneconomic considerations, clear boundaries, and the associated discrimination and stable authority structures are seen in most state-owned enterprises, the units (*danweis*). The authoritarian state LAP, in fact, shares many similarities with the family-based LAP. And to a great extent even the societal LAP, the community-based labor markets, can be understood as labor markets distorted by family institutions. Therefore, the impact of the family-based LAP is actually even greater than its role as the largest LAP in China.

A Tale of Two Villages

The following tale may help illuminate the restored family-based LAP in a typical Chinese agricultural setting.

Two villages located in central Anhui Province—Dawang (Big Wang) and Xiaowang (Small Wang)—share a common ancestor,

General Wang.[63] The general was granted many square miles of fertile land along two tributaries to the nearby Changjiang (Yangtze River), by the Ming dynasty some five hundred years ago. The population of the Wang clan increased over generations, and eventually, due to the abolition of the primogeniture system, the family-owned land was divided into small pieces in a dozen villages now located in two counties. Dawang and Xiaowang were two of those villages. In 1984, there were fewer than five hundred Wang people in the two villages. Despite the one-child-per-family policy adopted in the villages, the population continued to grow.[64] By the late 1990s, there were more than twelve hundred Wang people (one clan and about two hundred and eighty families) and fewer than two hundred people of about forty-five other families (of at least seven different surnames) living in the two villages.

The per capita arable land was only about 0.6 *mu* (0.099 acre), three-quarters of which was fertile rice fields, and farming was productive.[65] By the mid-1990s, the rice yield was about 750-1,000 kg per *mu*, worth about 1,800 rmb. After meeting the requirement to sell 175 kg of rice per *mu* to the state at a state-fixed price, the peasants could consume the rest or sell it on the local market.[66] Taxes were 350 yuan per *mu*. There were no significant woods or pastures. Almost every inch of land was used to grow crops or build houses and roads. In 1995, the per-laborer annual income was estimated at around 1,000-2,000 rmb, while some of the "richest" families earned substantially more.[67] Some men who worked outside as migratory workers could make as much as 5,000 rmb a year.

The land had been contracted through the responsibility system to the families in 1980-1981. A reallocation of land according to the existing size of the families was under way for 1995 and 1996. The reallocation was intended to stand for the next thirty years. Limited amounts of large farming equipment such as walking tractors and water buffaloes were shared and cared for by individual families. Every family, however, already owned substantial farming equipment and livestock. Some rich families had acquired their own tractors or buffaloes or even small used trucks. There was an unpaved road connecting the two villages to the paved provincial highway about two miles away. There had been electricity since the mid-1970s but no running water.[68] The supply of electricity, however, was more expensive than that in urban areas, and not very stable.

Other than the dozen "rich" families who had built two-story houses, most villagers still lived in traditional but cement and tile-roofed houses and had acquired electric fans and black-and-white televisions (some even had color sets). Eight families had refrigerators—something that was a luxury only five years before. Those eight families included among their members township cadres, state employees, TVE mangers, and business people. The richest family belonged to the CCP branch secretary of the administrative village. Together the two villages had one elementary school, two small shops, one grain processing mill, and a farmers' cooperative. The postal delivery only reached the administrative village that governed these two villages and another three. The administrative village used a wired public announcement system to alert anyone who had mail. Some villagers worked during off-season in the TVEs located in the administrative village and the township to which the two villages belong. By the Chinese standard for rural life, the two villages were just above average.

Dawang and Xiaowang had been two production teams of a brigade before decollectivization. Afterward they became natural villages (*zirancun*) belonging to a five-village administrative village (*xinzhengcun*) under a larger township (*zheng*). The administrative village had five full-time cadres provided for by all the peasants of the five villages (1.5 yuan per head annual tax) and much of the profits of the TVEs. A villagers' committee (*cunmin weiyuanhui*) was supposed to be the self-governing legislature of the administrative village.[69]

Each natural village had a head who was elected annually by the family heads of the village and then appointed by the administrative village cadres. The administrative village paid the village head an annual subsidy of only 160 yuan—too little, according to the forty-eight-year-old village head of Xiaowang.

The Wang Clan Record (*jiapu*) was last revised in the 1920s and was almost burned by the Red Guards in the 1960s. In 1994-1995, a new revision of the record was initiated by the villagers. They held a clan meeting attended by the family heads in the two villages and some who lived outside the area. The cost of the revision and printing was shared by every related Wang family in and outside the two villages (25 rmb per head and 100 rmb to include a photo).

All Wangs in the two villages were named according to a ranking order (*beifen,* 輩份) established nearly two hundred years ago. One's family ranking and status could immediately be seen through his/her fixed middle name; thus a fixed and clear family line and authority structure were maintained. Although the Wangs belonged to one common ancestor and were the majority of the two villages, they had two separate clan halls and two clan heads, a distant uncle and nephew roughly the same age. The clan head in Xiaowang village, Jisheng, was in his sixties, a party member, a former village cadre, and the head of a relatively rich Wang family of two sons. His grandfather was the eldest of six Wang brothers who constituted the first generation of Xiaowang Village when it was separated from Dawang Village more than one hundred years ago. His father had been clan head but was considered weak because of the presence of his granduncles and the CCP's campaign of eliminating the clan institution in the rural areas. Jisheng became the clan's de facto underground head around age thirty, when he became the brigade cadre in the early 1960s, despite the fact that many of his uncles and granduncles were still alive. His authority, however, was not strengthened until his generation became the highest-ranked generation in the village at the end of the 1980s.

The whole clan structure, combined with the administrative authority granted by the government, was well restored by the 1990s and functioned extensively in the two villages, especially in Xiaowang. Almost everyone in the two villages was linked to each other by family relations: any Wang might be any other Wang's brother/sister, uncle/aunt, nephew/niece, or grandnephew/niece. It would take an outsider forever to sort out exactly how one person was related to everyone else. Non-Wangs were fewer in Xiaowang and were in one way or another connected to the Wangs. In Dawang, the sizable number of non-Wangs gained a nearly equal voice with the Wangs. They, however, still had to become connected to the Wangs to acquire a sense of family.

But the formalities and the personal power of the clan head had largely been replaced by the administrative power that came from the authorization of the government and the legitimacy of the villagers' self-governing. The head of the Xiaowang village, Jiren, appeared to be not so obedient to Jisheng (his cousin) as clan head, perhaps partly because they were of the same ranking—the "Ji" generation. Families were the basic units of village life and village membership, rather than clan membership, which was considered the more important criterion in village politics. Although there was little systemic discrimination against the non-Wangs in both villages, a sense of "us" versus "them" was present when certain public issues, such as revision of the clan record and welcoming a VIP guest of the Wangs, were discussed.

This finding about the fading of the formal clan structure is similar to that of studies of some other rural areas such as Sunan and the Pearl River Delta; here, clan structures were weaker or even missing, whereas the family institution and village grouping were the primary institutions.[70] In many other areas, however, the clan structure appeared to be much stronger, more institutionalized, and much more influential than those in the two Wang villages.[71]

The clan/village head still appeared to have a significant role in deciding certain important issues such as distribution of fertilizers and pesticides, collection of family dues, assignment of public works, allocation of housing lots, distribution of taxes, arbitration of family conflicts, and organization of social and cultural events. Again, each one of those activities was organized on a family basis. Clan structure had become rather irrelevant to legal matters such as marriage certification, family planning, enforcing laws, and penalizing fellow villagers. But informally, the clan head had tremendous moral authority and power in those matters. A wedding could not be considered complete, for example, without the presence and blessing of the clan head. Despite a lack of education (Jisheng had only a fifth-grade education whereas many of the villagers had high school diplomas) and an alleged selfishness on behalf of his family, Jisheng seemed secure in his position as clan head primarily because he was the eldest grandson of the eldest of the first Wang generation of Xiaowang.

The average size of the families in both villages was about five members, with three generations usually living together in one house. Financially, however, there was often an intrafamily independence among the nuclear units (*fang,* or 房) of a couple and their children. Thus, it was common to have more than two kitchens or kitchenettes in one household. The give-and-take among the nuclear units of a family was not clearly calculated but was generally remembered so as to keep everything fair. The arbitrator was generally the family head or a senior, close male relative. Close relatives, such as those who shared a common grandfather, behaved like a looser family. Comparatively, the give-and-take among the families of a clan was generally documented with the arbitration of the clan head as a necessary aid, whereas transactions beyond the clan tended to follow the lines of signed contracts. Even those contracts were rarely enforced through the government beyond the administrative level of the village. Family/clan arbitration and negotiation over banquets were the norm.

Less transaction costs by the clan/family institutions were well illustrated by the social and economic life of the two villages (Li 1994, 3-4). Without the clan/family institutions, it would have been difficult to manage so many units of people sharing the same road and irrigation system, working on small lots of land divided like a jigsaw puzzle, and having their kids, chickens, and hogs running around all day long. Until the mid-1990s, there had been no expensive lawsuits filed by the villagers against each other, although arbitration-type conflict resolution and internal mediation were common. In the two very crowded villages, personal and property safety had never been a concern. In a case of petty theft by a juvenile, the offender's immediate relatives, fearing for the family's reputation, were actually more eager to capture and penalize the offender than to protect him. There had never been a divorce case, although there were extramarital affairs and associated quarrels.

The division of labor and income was primarily based on families and normally done along the lines of nuclear units. The exchange of labor in the family was largely free. For regular family work, however, there was generally a clear division of labor among the nuclear units, decided and managed by the family head. The real bosses of the families, however, were no longer always the senior males. Even in Jisheng's family, his eldest son, who worked part time as a construction worker, had the financial power although he was not considered a family head. The second son's wife would stop her domestic chores and go work in the family field if the second son could not get out of his sickbed to complete the work assigned to his "unit," while the grandma would take over the domestic chores with her usual complaints that the second son did not listen to her advice of staying healthy. If the work was urgent and/or the second daughter-in-law was not well either, then other family members would go to do the work originally assigned for the second son. No special negotiation or pay was needed, as long as this arrangement was not permanent. At the end of the season, family income was divided among the nuclear units according to the share of work each unit contributed and the perceived needs of each unit. The unmarried young man of the family usually, therefore, received a disproportionately large income from the family to prepare for his new nuclear unit.

A "nest" for a new couple could be very expensive. A modest, one-story house of only three rooms could run as high as 90,000 rmb— three years' total income for a young farming couple. Usually, soon after the wedding or at least after the birth of their first child, the couple would start to have a new nuclear unit within the family (*fengguo*) by having their own budget and kitchen or kitchenette. The nuclear unit occasionally would become more independent, creating a new family (*fengjia*) by having their own independent house or at least a separate entry to their quarters. New families, after ratification by the clan/village head and close relatives and a certification by the township government, would have their independent financial and labor allocations.[72] The nuclear units and the new families, however, all had basically the same obligation to support the aging parents. In many families, the nuclear units were poorly developed, and the family structure was strongly unified, even over three generations containing ten to fifteen people. Nuclear units that earned income outside the assigned family work typically kept that income, though reporting and turning over of such income was expected. Income inequality was therefore much smaller, within a family than within a clan. The key variable here is the outside family income and individual units' spending patterns.

Because of underemployment, there were no outside people employed in the two villages, except for a few persons hired temporarily to perform handicrafts such as cotton fluttering, furniture making, geomancy, and tailoring. For big projects like house construction, labor was provided first by close relatives and then by the whole clan and even non-Wangs. Other than food, drinks (tea and liquor), and cigarettes, payment was not usually required.[73] If one family had unexpected needs, such as hosting relatives from far away or the sudden death of a member, fellow clan members would customarily volunteer their time and offer household produce such as eggs and rice (but rarely money). Non-Wangs would also offer to help, though much less enthusiastically, but were usually turned down unless they were related.

Since the late 1970s, villagers began going out to look for work. By the mid-1990s, many Wang families and most non-Wang families had people working outside the two villages for at least a few months every year. Some villagers had become contractors or long-term employees working year-round in big cities such as Wuhu, Hefei, and Nanjing. Their families or relatives took over the land they left behind. Compared to the backbreaking heavy labor in the villages—averaging eight hours a day including holidays—work in the cities was considered easy money.[74] The income sent home became a major source of cash for the two villages and contributed substantially to the visible commercialization of village life.

The clan/family authority was once again compromised by the power of money, just as it had been from 1949 to the end of the 1970s due to the political power of the CCP. For example, the allocation of housing lots was strongly influenced by how much a family could contribute to the clan fund and how many favors a family could buy from fellow villagers. Another interesting development is that a couple of non-Wang families had acquired substantial influence in the two villages because they had either made a small fortune as contractors or had "back-door" access through a relative who worked in a state-owned local coal mine to a supply of cheap coal, a much-needed fuel in the two villages.

Money and labor mobility indeed caused substantial changes of the family institutions. The clan structure had apparently become increasingly outdated compared to the village grouping and the family institution. Some old Wangs were quite nostalgic, but most young ones were busily talking about making more money, in or outside the villages, and having their own new families—which would generally look like replicas of their parents' families but with a few more appliances and newer styles of furniture. Public utilities such as the village well were generally undermaintained due to the "decay of values," as remarked by the elderly. The villagers commented that Deng Xiaoping's reforms were all great, except that crimes were on the rise. In the summer of 1995, the villagers believed that their lives had improved substantially over the past decade but still asserted that "we farmers are the lowest in the nation."

The Family-Based LAP in Taiwan

A few words about the family-based LAP in contemporary Taiwan may serve as a comparison to allow a better understanding of the family-based LAP in China.

Taiwan carried out significant land reform in the 1950s, under American pressure and with American help. The success of the reform has been viewed as a major contribution to the political stability and great economic success of Taiwan in the years since. Unlike the CCP, the GMD government adopted a peaceful and gradual buying-out policy, under which landlords had to sell their property at a set price to the government, which then would be reallocated at a low price to farm families. Also unlike the CCP, the GMD did not pursue forceful collectivization of the peasants. Large numbers of farmers who owned the land they worked on (*zigengnong*) were created on the island. *Zigengnong* constituted 84.8 percent of all farming households in Taiwan in 1979 (up from 34.5 percent in 1948).[75] Within those rural families, labor allocation and income followed essentially the same rules as seen among rural families on the Chinese mainland. Traditional family values of a moral economy as well as behavioral norms were strongly present. By the 1990s, however, Taiwanese families were increasingly affected by the market institution.

A set of regulations was installed to protect the stability of the *zigengnong* institution and its family-based LAP in the rural areas of

Taiwan. Family-based land-ownership was mostly not transferable outside the family, although in order to increase productivity the land could be cultivated on a large scale, or even collectively by professional agricultural workers (who were generally still family-based). Nonfarming families were strictly prohibited from owning farm land, and nonfarming usage of the land was carefully controlled by the government.

The family-based LAP thus became the main LAP in rural areas. It was clearly visible in urban areas as well, despite the fact that the market institution had become the dominant economic institution, governing interactions among the rural families as well as the relationship between the rural and urban economic sectors. In Taiwan, which had an almost developed market economy, the role of the family still seemed very important in economic, cultural, and political activities. To a certain extent, the family played a bigger role than in the PRC, which generally had a much less developed market economy.[76] Even the average family size in modern Taiwan was larger than that in the PRC: 4.76 members versus 3.95 in 1993 and 1994.[77]

The family-based LAP, restored and secured in Taiwan, was indeed a success in that it created a rather "Chinese," thus legitimate, institution to suit market-oriented economic needs. By the efforts of a thoughtful authoritarian state and utilization of traditional Chinese culture, the family-based LAP and land ownership have been fairly stable in Taiwan's rural areas, providing great support to political and social institutions at a time when changes and shocks were numerous because of the advancement of the market. Agricultural output grew steadily since the individual *zigengnongs* desired to raise productivity while preserving the land and had the flexibility to develop marketable products. Land reform turned much of the land ownership into capital promoting Taiwan's industrialization, as illustrated by the fact that many of the business tycoons of modern Taiwan were formerly big landlords.

Taiwan has completed its transfer of rural labor to industrial and service labor. By 1994, rural labor was only 12.34 percent of the total labor force, down from 52.45 percent in 1949 and 54 percent in 1956.[78] The release of rural labor was relatively gradual and smooth under the joint force of state control and the family-based LAP. Many families simply switched to a nonagricultural business without even leaving the rural areas. The family-based LAP was so influential that one can clearly see the origin of the significant growth of the middle-sized and small enterprises that are the backbone of the Taiwanese economic "miracle."

Such a Taiwanese model of land reform and rural development has therefore been widely advocated as potentially beneficial to other developing nations, including the PRC.[79]

New Developments and Changes

The restored family-based LAP has been under increasing pressure from other LAPs in contemporary China. The Chinese family institution has been greatly challenged by the institutions of a still-formidable authoritarian state and especially by a rigorously advancing market institution. Fundamental changes are likely for the centuries-old LAP. A preliminary analysis of some of the evidence about such trends would help us to appreciate more adequately the impact of the Chinese family-based LAP.

The Small Towns as the Way Out
The decay of the family-based LAP and the instability of the family institution, intensified by the economic need for reducing rural underemployment, have inspired a few designs aimed at transforming the family-based LAP without losing its positive aspects. The central question is how to turn the family-based LAP into an economically viable institution while keeping the social and political stability it provides to hundreds of millions of underemployed people irresistibly enticed by the lifestyle of the modernized nations. A leading design has been the famous idea of "small towns," coined by Fei Xiaotong, a well-known sociologist and politician favored by the CCP leadership. Fei was educated in England and the United States before 1949 and published his early field work on the Chinese rural economy, *Jiangcun* (Jiang village), in the 1930s. In 1983, he published his *Xiao chenzhen da wenti* (Small towns, big issues), thus starting heated discussion on the virtues of small towns, rather than urbanization, for the development of the Chinese rural economy.

As a human grouping "higher" than the villages, a small town is defined as a social community composed mainly of nonagricultural families; it is different from the rural communities but keeps close ties with the surrounding villagers. It is something between the cities and the villages and has some of the main features of both (Fei 1985, 10). Very soon, this idea was adopted, and policies were made to implement it; it was perceived to be an important characteristic of Chinese-style modernization and an easy, effective way to address the problem of rural underemployment without causing too much burden on the urban population.[80]

The millions of Chinese peasants under the family-based LAP have inevitably been pushed out of their families and even their villages. This trend is likely to increase due to rural population growth, which worsens underemployment, and the increased desire for material gains inspired by the modern media and entertainment industries.[81] The "pulling" of the cities due to economic development and the relaxing of the state control over the rural-urban border have also been important.[82]

The small-town design attempts to arrange an order for such a flow of labor. Essentially, it would provide the modern lifestyle of the cities to the rural population in family-/villagelike settings. The profession of the peasants may change, but not the basic institutional framework under which they are organized. Slums, overcrowding, and other modern urban maladies could thus be avoided in the already crowded Chinese cities. If it were successfully implemented, the family-based LAP would have a conducive environment in which to perpetuate itself. The small towns would replace the villages as the groupings for the Chinese peasants. A smooth continuum, from rural villages to small towns to the urban areas, would replace the urban-rural dichotomy and become the organizational structure under which substantial economic development could be reached in both rural and urban areas without a massive, destabilizing relocation of underemployed peasants.

After more than a decade of practice, however, the small-town design has not yet fully demonstrated its viability or potential, even though it has been enthusiastically praised as "the hope for rural urbanization" and "an important deployment of the construction of socialism with Chinese characteristics."[83] A major problem has been the design's operational difficulties: what exactly is a small town? (Wang 1994, 47-49). The design often became a code name for hasty and wasteful urbanization, or for preventing peasants from leaving their homes, or for simply renaming villages and townships as towns and cities and granting their residents urban household registration (*hukou*) status.[84] According to official figures, the *hukou*-changing formal townships increased from ten thousand in 1989 to fourteen thousand in 1994 nationwide, "transferring about 120 million rural surplus laborers."[85] Meaningful small towns emerged only in relatively few areas of China, mainly Sunan (southern Jiangsu Province)—where the county-seatlike townships increased from fifty-seven in 1979 to more than seven hundred in 1995: Wenzhou (Zhejiang Province),

Mingnan (southern Fujian Province), and Ludong (eastern Shandong Province). In other areas, noticeably the Pearl River Delta, the small towns have been completely eclipsed by the near total disappearance of the differences and barriers between urban and rural areas. The sometimes striking differences between the prosperous regions and the poor (usually remote and inland) regions, still separated by the *hukou* system, became much more meaningful than the old notion of the urban-rural gaps in Guangdong Province.[86]

Transformation of the Chinese Family and Culture

Chinese families, especially those in urban and prosperous rural areas, were transformed dramatically in the 1980s and 1990s. First, as discussed earlier in this chapter, the advancing market exerted tremendous influences on the internal family structure. The size of the families declined, and substantial nuclear families replaced extended families in most urban settings and in many rural villages. The function of family economic activities was colored increasingly with market-oriented purposes, that is, to seek material gains far beyond subsistence needs. The authority structure of families was affected as money began to talk loudly. Visible labor mobility therefore become a new feature of the family-based LAP in many areas.[87]

Second, also mentioned earlier, the role of the clan institution has systematically declined in most of the countryside and almost totally disappeared in the urban areas.[88]

Third, community-based local markets have become a familiar scene to an increasing number of Chinese peasants. Within a village, or even a township (*xiang,* or *zhen*) that may include several villages, market-oriented exchange has become the norm governing people's economic activities in many areas. Sometimes, a whole village or even a township became a corporation, and every family became a shareholder living on values created primarily by workers employed from outside.[89] In a village of 561 residents located in Shenzhen of Guangdong Province, every villager on average employed or gained rent from six workers from outside. The village became one of the richest communities in China, but the villagers themselves created less than 10 percent of the total village income in 1991.[90] Such cases can be found in several other areas, according to research by Chinese scholars.[91] Internally, the village community has been organized and has functioned like a giant family with heavy moral economic behavior. But externally, these village economies have become competitive actors in the market. Some villages, via the booming township-village enterprises, have substantially reached international markets.[92] The village community may also powerfully regulate the market-oriented activities of the families—a distortion of the market by the moral economic norms within the community. An interesting example of this type of market distortion is Mao's hometown, Shaoshan, a sacred place for the CCP. There, more than fifty families established small vending shops near Mao's old house, a much-visited memorial. The location of the vendors is rearranged every week so that "everyone will have an equal chance to be at the best location (the one closest to the entrance of the Mao Memorial) for one week every fifty-some weeks."[93] Such village/community economic development further supported the development of village self-governing, which was largely restored as an important feature of the traditional Chinese family LAP.

Fourth, the restored family-based LAP, unlike in the past, has produced a variety of socioeconomic groups and even classes in the rural areas. Prior to the end of the 1970s, Chinese peasants were basically categorized into two or three groups. For centuries there were land-holding farmers, land-renting farmers (*diannong*), hired farmers (*gunong*), and landlords, with certain floating people (*liumin*), and small craftsmen and merchants as supplements. From 1956 to 1978, peasants were organized by the state as a single kind of commune member (*shiyuang*), accompanied by a few categories of class enemies, such as the former landlords under the unified leadership of the CCP, with basically the same institutional and socioeconomic conditions. The family-based LAP initially restored the *zigengnong* as the main component of the rural population with only limited diversity among them.[94] Ten years later, a multidirectional social stratification had divided the family-based peasants into a number of professions and socioeconomic groups with a variety of group interests and income capabilities. As many as ten different socioeconomic strata of the peasants have been reported, differentiated primarily by professions and the way they are allocated.[95]

The varied development of the clan institution and the increasing differences in levels of economic development further complicated the picture. Even though still family-based, Chinese rural laborers could work for different reasons, under various labor management, have divergent economic and political interests, and acquire different economic resources and sociopolitical autonomy. Through those new developments and changes, the possibility has risen that the peasants and their family-based LAP may be able to break the historical process of deteriorating from *zigengnong* to *diannong* to *liumin* and then to rebels. Yet it is still too early to assess the future and the institutional impact of a stratified family-based LAP.

Finally, the restored family-based LAP has clearly been buffeted by the winds, or even storms, of alternative cultural and ideological influences. Most of these alternative ideas, beliefs, philosophies, and even religions have come from the outside. Once again, the advancement of the market and the intensive interactions with the outside world have contributed significantly to the change of the cultural environment in which the Chinese family-based LAP operates. Related to the previously discussed rise of social associations in the countryside, increasing numbers of peasants have been converting to religions other than the traditional ancestor worship that has been a hallmark of the family-like institutional structure. The restored relative autonomy of families and the self-governing of the villagers provided the institutional possibility for such a profound change to occur. One author estimated that by 1991, there were at least 30 million Christians in rural China.[96] A field study reported that in a rather typical

Table 1.2. Rural Religious Beliefs in Quanjiao County, Anhui Province

Villages	Year	Population	Buddhism	Taoism	Islam	Protestantism
Xiaoliu	1985	94	9 (9%)	1 (1%)	no	no
	1994	88	5 (6%)	no	no	16 (18.2%)
Liuxing	1985	228	11 (5%)	4 (1.3%)	no	1 (0.004%)
	1995	232	7 (3.2%)	2 (0.9%)	no	49 (21.1%)
Dongwang	1985	170	10 (5.5%)	2 (1.2%)	no	no
	1994	187	5 (3%)	1 (0.5%)	no	33 (17.6%)
Dayang	1985	183	13 (7.1%)	2 (1%)	no	no
	1994	194	8 (4)	no	no	39 (20.1%)
Tuanji	1985	187	2 (1%)	no	153 (70 %)	no
	1994	197	1 (0.5%)	no	101 (52%)	25 (12.7%)

Note: The rest of the peasants are self-described nonreligious, that is, believers in Confucianism and ancestor worship. Many of the religious peasants, however, are observed occasionally practicing some ancestral worship activities.
Source: Yang 1994, 31-32, 34-35.

county of Anhui Province, nearly 15 percent of the peasants (48,000) had become Christians (Protestants) by the fall of 1993. "Some devoted Christians even stopped giving alms and worship to their ancestors" (Yang 1994, 31).

Several factors are responsible for the impressive advancement of Christianity. A major reason, according to the field study, is that Christianity, especially Protestantism, advocates equality between the poor and the rich and between the sexes, and discounts traditional norms and authority structure (Yang 1994, 34-35). To some observers, this trend has signaled "the sprouts of a civil society" in China.[97] Table 1.2 summarizes this belief change in five Anhui villages and reveals an interesting picture of changing religion and ideology in rural China.

The Family-Based LAP and the Chinese Institutional Structure

The institutional implication of the family-based traditional LAP in contemporary China can be seen in two ways. First, we see that this traditional LAP makes China "Chinese" in the 1990s. Namely, it reflects the fact that the PRC still remains largely a pre-modern nation. Second, this LAP may actually have some interesting impact on the advancement of the market institution in China, while producing the traditional stabilizing effect for the CCP authoritarian regime.

Ensuring the Institutional Continuities

The restored Chinese family-based LAP determines that China is still largely a traditional nation. It makes China "Chinese" by restoring the traditional Chinese institutional structure to govern the majority of the people. Powerful old norms and behavior patterns are rejuvenated, as are the central roles of the family institution and its internalization—the Confucian culture. The social control mechanism and the relationship between the state and the citizen in contemporary China appear to have been institutionally conditioned and deeply colored by the traditional Chinese families.

For centuries, the family-based LAP contributed enormously to social control mechanisms in China. The imperial courts attempted many times to gain more direct and more effective control of the people through a reduction or even a destruction of the gentry power and the clan structure.[98] No one, however, was able to replace the family—China's most important institution. Families have always been the cells of the Chinese nation whereby ruling families/groups enjoyed stable and often unquestioned power. However, "the ruler or government, as the grand family/clan head (*dajiazhang,* or 大家长), has an obligation to work for the well-being of its subordinate members. . . . [Thus, the] legitimacy of the government does not come from votes but from promoting the welfare of the people."[99]

Such a family-based and family-like social control mechanism was in place even under the considerable pressure of the market economy from 1840 to 1949.[100] During Mao's reign (1949-1976), the CCP forcefully attempted to abolish the layers of the gentry class and even the family/clans, with unprecedented success but at horrifying costs. Collectivized communes and party cadres were used to control the citizens (especially the peasants) directly, under the giant family-like state power of the CCP.[101] The only hope left for "good" rule was in refining and purifying the top leader(s) of the CCP, the family head(s), since their authority tended to be unchecked. To some, that explains Mao's constant, nearly paranoid, internal struggles aimed at producing new generations of revolutionaries to lead the nation (Wang 1994, 178-180).

Restoration of the family-based LAP, not surprisingly, also restored many traditional Chinese social relations and much of the traditional political structure. Contrary to the optimistic belief of some that agriculture decollectivization made the Chinese peasants "free,"[102] the traditionally paternal families, instead of the CCP lineage, once again became the cells of the authority relationship in Chinese politics and society.[103] A family-based "capitalist patriarchy" replaced Mao's "patriarchal socialism" to regulate basic social relations such as those between the sexes (Brugger and Reglar 1994, 304). It gave back a certain degree of economic freedom, bounded by the family institution, to the peasantry. It returned traditional sociopolitical autonomy to the villages, headed by the new gentry class that included clan heads, village and township officials (still mostly CCP members), rich peasants, and other "reputable" families.[104] Economic connections between the Chinese government and the peasants were shifted to less political and quasi-market-oriented contractual relations. Family/clan institutions rearranged social and political relations in the Chinese rural areas, and a clear and deep "familization," or "kinsfolkization" (*qinshouhua*), began taking place among the majority of the Chinese, the peasants (Wang 1994, 52). Not only were the rural social control mechanisms, social stratification, and authority structure again based on family institutions, but economic connections and property ownership were largely reorganized and redefined along family lines in the villages (Chen Junjie 1994, 57). This was especially true where the restoration of the family-based LAP was thorough and complete. For example, one case study concluded that collectivized ownership of property, even the land and state political power and social control, had all but disappeared in southern Zhejiang Province by the mid-1980s.[105]

All these changes signified the massive retreat of the CCP state from the Chinese villages. The unitary authoritarian political system was seriously weakened in the rural areas. The CCP and local governments have been experiencing a rather unpleasant and unfamiliar sense of being out of control and of losing authority in the countryside, where more than 73 percent of the Chinese population resides. In the Chinese press, especially internal publications, there have been numerous reports and complaints about the "sufferings," "hardships," "ineffectiveness," "dilemmas," "huge problems," and "the lack of controlling and regulating authority" experienced by rural CCP organizations and rural governmental cadres.[106] In fact, as one survey reveals, ever since the rural reform and the restoration of the family-based LAP, "as the economic life changed fundamentally," political life in the villages advanced ahead of that in the cities. The peasants, according to this study, became much more "democratic" in their economic, social, cultural, and political lives than their city counterparts. The advancement of the Chinese rural democratic politics on the micro level is certainly interesting and provocative, since conventional democratization theory asserts that cities offer better social and cultural conditions for micro-democracy than the countryside. In the Shijazhuang region of Hebei Province, over half the villages established a two-chamber style of assembly, the villagers' committee, to take charge of the most important issues. More than 70 percent of the villages in Hebei Province developed a variety of "mass self-governing organizations."[107] A party official reported that "democratic self-governing by the villagers" based on family representation became the major social control mechanism in the Chinese rural areas.[108]

In Jilin Province, foreign observers of village elections concluded that in rural China, "real democracy—the ability of ordinary people to affect decisions that govern their daily lives—begins at the grassroots level."[109] Empirically, the democracy in the Chinese villages was very much like the traditional village self-governing under the elite—the gentry families in the past, and later the families of cadres and clan heads, most of whom were indigenous CCP party members. Those self-governing village bodies were still basically undifferentiated economic-political-social structures with a social institution (the family and clan) as their basic organizational principle. Just like the gentry in the past, these bodies came to serve as agents of the state, which nominally had officials down to the level just below the counties—the townships. It appears clear that, once the bonds of the labor force were loosened, the state retreated and was limited while a visible independence of the economy and social institutions developed in the rural areas, based on the restored traditional family structure.[110]

In the cities, the restoration and thriving of the family-based LAP, in the form of the *getihu*, also had a clear impact on the overall institutional setting and people's behavior. There was a restoration of ancestral worship, tomb building, nominal kinship building, and concubines in some of the economically more developed areas such as the Pearl River Delta, Wenzhou of Zhejiang Province, and Shisi of Fujiang Province. Even in places like Beijing, Shanghai, Guangzhou, and inland cities such as Chengdu and Hefei, there were numerous reports of a similar restoration of the traditional social institutions as the foundation for people's social, economic, and political activities.[111] Clearly, however, the restoration of the traditional institutions in the urban areas has not been nearly as thorough as in the countryside, as the relatively small family-based LAP is only one of the LAPs in the cities. The institutions of the CCP state and other forces are much stronger there, thus effectively limiting the restored family-based LAP. Family-allocated urban laborers remained relatively few, and they were usually of low social status, including a high proportion of ex-convicts. Despite their high average incomes and usually lavish lifestyles, the *getihus* were rated the lowest social and political group in the cities by the Chinese urban residents. They actually had a "profound negative" impact, rather than an exemplary role, on the city dwellers' behaviors (Li 1993, 316-340).

Related to the restoration of the family-based LAP, a renaissance of Confucian culture took place in China. Chinese officials and intellectuals, led by influential scholars such as Liang Shuming (梁漱溟), Li Zehou (李泽厚), and Pang Po (庞朴), reassessed Confucianism with the intention of revitalizing it. The proven positives of Confucianism in and outside China were widely recognized by the official media.[112] The economic success of Korea, Taiwan, and even Japan was believed to have had direct links to Confucian culture or a "new Confucianism," which had been unfortunately almost lost in its homeland.[113] In addition to widespread commercial use of Confucius's name, a nationwide reeducation of his teachings got under way.[114] Official publications were filled with the "fine and glorious traditions" stemming from Confucianism that every "modern civilized" Chinese needed to remember and act on.[115] The government-run Readings for the Rural Press even published *Xing xiaojing* (New book on filial piety) in 1994 to educate peasants more easily and more extensively about the classic virtues of respecting ancestors and obeying the elderly. A similar publication on traditional morals and patriotism, socialist ethics, and modern civilized norms, *Xing sanzijing* (New three-word verses), edited by the Propaganda Department of the Guangdong CCP Committee, sold 10 million copies in Guangdong in 1994 alone and another 10 million in the first five months of 1995. The CCP even broadcast the new three-word verses to millions over the telephone network in some provinces.[116]

In the final analysis, perhaps paradoxically, a durable family-based LAP with its ability to absorb surplus labor tended to stabilize the power of a retreated authoritarian state in Beijing. Restoration of traditional Chinese culture also effectively served this purpose. A direct impact, in exchange for stabilization of the political regime, has been that state control, planning, and administration in the rural economy declined substantially. To the more orthodox elements of the CCP leadership, weakening party control in the rural areas was at best an obstacle to socialist construction and at worst very dangerous, considering that the CCP came to power with the strong loyalty of the rural population. They seemed to understand the negative consequences of decollectivization.

Deng Xiaoping, chief architect of China's reform, as he is officially called, repeatedly emphasized that political and social stability as well as economic development in China depends primarily on rural development and the peasants.[117] A three-stage scheme was thus planned, which entailed contracting out land to the households under the responsibility system, developing a specialized household economy and the concentration of land, and fostering a new type of cooperation among specialized households (Saith 1987, 130). To deepen rural reform and regain some control over the agricultural economy and the rural society, the CCP in 1987 decided to establish twenty-two Rural Reform Experimenting Areas in seventeen provinces to experiment with various policies, including a grain trade system, land redistribution, local cooperatives, and rural financing.[118] Whether the CCP can realize its design remains to be seen.

The Family-Based LAP and Institutional Changes

The largely restored Chinese traditional institutional structure is now in a process of transformation mainly because of the intensive interactions between the Chinese and the rest of the world. A number of issues present themselves in our observation of the family-based traditional LAP and those profound institutional changes. The most difficult yet most consequential issue has perhaps been how to transfer the massive surplus rural labor, which is key to the development of a Chinese market economy.

Employing 150 to 240 Million Surplus Labor
There is a huge number of underemployed laborers in the Chinese rural areas, institutionally stabilized by the family-based LAP.[119] According to Chinese economists, this surplus labor has had almost zero marginal productivity while consuming more than 12.2 percent of the net production of the rural economy every year (Wang 1988, 98). Estimates of the size of the surplus vary. Official statistics say 25 to 30 percent of the 487.68 million rural laborers are underemployed.[120] A study by Chinese scholars based on three econometrics models concluded that there was 10 to 16 percent "irrational or useless employment" in the Chinese agriculture sector in 1993.[121] A five-year study by the Chinese Social Sciences Academy in fifty-nine counties of eleven provinces revealed that as many as 220 million rural laborers had no meaningful work to do (Yao and Murong 1993, 34). The Ministry of Agriculture estimated in 1985 that to have full employment in the rural areas, 160 million laborers would be enough for the 140 million *mu* (about 23.06 million acres) of cultivated land. That would leave at least 240 million workers needing to find jobs outside the agricultural sector. In 1994, an article in the official *Renmin Ribao* directly stated that among the 450 million rural labor force, 250 million are surplus laborers.[122]

The population of the rural areas continues to increase at a rate of 100 million per decade. Despite the impressive growth of the township-village enterprises and the sizable absorption of rural labor by the booming urban economy, at least 100 million rural surplus laborers still need to be transferred throughout the 1990s and beyond (Zen 1993, 179-182). This will be difficult because there are more than 6.8 million unemployed urban dwellers and at least 30 million "more than needed" (*fuyu*) underemployed workers in the state-owned enterprises (Xin 1992, 39). The widespread and persistent problem of surplus

From Family to Market

labor has been one of the most important challenges to the development of the Chinese economy. The increased labor mobility of the peasants, after the family-based LAP replaced Mao's collectivized communes, led to several "rural labor tides" (*mingongchao,* or 民工潮) flooding the major cities and every transportation line. Nearly 80 million "floating people" (*liudong renkou*) have left their villages to work outside, mainly in the cities, primarily on construction projects and in service industries.[123] This has caused tremendous concerns and heated debates.[124] In Xiamen (Amoy), half of the 760,000 residents were such floating people and were believed responsible for 62 to 83 percent of all the crimes in the Special Economic Zone.[125] In Beijing, most of the criminals were also believed to be among the thousands of floating people.[126] The CCP leadership called the floating people a "major problem, directly affecting economic development and social stability."[127]

The great dilemma is that, on the one hand, there is a clear and compelling economic rationale to raise agricultural productivity by transferring rural surplus labor; yet on the other hand, large numbers of uneducated and low-skilled rural workers could cause serious economic shortages, extensive social tensions, and consequential political instability in the cities. The urban population, less buffered by family or clan, is understandably fearful of an invasion, real or imaginary, by millions of "low-class" peasants. In pure economic terms, the inflow of an almost endless supply of cheap labor could lead to structural dislocations of many of the formerly privileged city dwellers, who themselves face the increasing likelihood of unemployment. In the absence of massive emigration to other countries, antagonism, uncertainty, chaos, and even explosive events will likely dominate the scene. The traditional institutional setting, with its dual structure of rural versus urban, could collapse before any legitimate institutional framework, modern or pre-modern, can settle in. Social institutions, political stability, the emerging market institution, high hopes and tens of millions of lives would likely be the casualties. As a popular political writer put it, "the 800 million peasants are China's live volcano" that could very well destroy the relatively modernized Chinese urban sector and the whole hope of Chinese modernization.[128]

The family-based Chinese LAP has had an advantageous impact on the delicate and difficult issue of transferring rural surplus labor. This LAP has contributed immensely to the political stability of the authoritarian regime of the CCP at a time of great changes. Peasants, family/clan bounded, have earned the reputation of being most tolerant in bearing hardships, mainly economic difficulties.[129] Short of being forced by famine or by the outrageous abuse of an almost demonic ruler, they have historically been willing to die, rather than rebel, for the sake of preserving their families. The families provided perhaps the best cushion against the sufferings produced by political injustice and economic hardships, in that sacrifice is among the glorious norms a family sanctions for its members. The millions of families adequately served the purpose of diverting social pressures and energies, thus mitigating many conflicts that had potential institutional implications. The golden rule of family-based behavior, "to stay together," has a strong restrictive impact on labor mobility. Thus, a large portion of the surplus labor could be absorbed by the families before they flood the emerging Chinese market.[130]

Families are small groupings, and their abundant differences make it hard for them to form meaningful groups or become politically militant. The family/clan institution has historically played the important role of reducing social shocks through sharing, mutual assistance, and other altruistic but "rational" activities of the members and member families. Therefore, "family has been the most effective and most rational organizational structure of the traditional rural society" (Li 1994, 2). The restored family-based LAP in contemporary China is visibly less tightly controlled by Beijing, but clearly its traditional function of creating and supporting a highly stable traditional institutional structure has been achieved.

Additionally, family/clan institutions have helped soothe the emergence of the market institution and have significantly reduced the social and political costs of modernization, at the expense of distortions of the market institution. The externalities produced by the advancing market institutions can be substantially overcome by the moral economics of the family-clan institutions. An interesting "internalization" of the economic externalities by the family may take place (Li 1994, 4, 38) to minimize the negative externalities of the market economy. Thus, empirically, we often see a selfless division of labor among related peasants regarding who stays and who goes out to seek jobs. A Jiangxi peasant could easily make five times more in the cities than in his village, but he chooses to stay because his family is there.[131] Family-based villagers have so many noneconomic values and considerations that they clearly do not always pursue profits or material gains. What one's fellow family, clan, or village members will think of them tends to weigh much heavier than how much they can purchase. Consequently, the economic hardship of underemployment is more easily tolerable, compared to a breakup of the traditional family, which is often the result of seeking jobs outside.

The institutional role of the restored family-based LAP explains why it is unlikely that the 150 million to 240 million Chinese peasants will invade the cities at once, despite the fact that many are living below the poverty line with little hope of change.[132] Even in more developed areas such as Fujian Province, the transfer of rural labor has demonstrated a clear slowing trend since 1988, and there has been a sizable reverse current of peasants returning to the villages. One of the major reasons identified for this shift was the "confining" effect of the family-based LAP, which pulled many peasants back to the villages.[133] Chinese rural labor was indeed "liberalized" from the collectives—institutionalized rural authorities—and thus from the state; but under the restored family-based traditional LAP, this liberalized labor was still largely fixed to the land by the millions of stable and powerful family institutions. These traditionally paternal families, as the cells of Chinese society, came to function as millions of mini-reservoirs for rural labor. They have a remarkable ability to absorb the surplus laborers, feed them, and then turn them into reasonably satisfied underemployed rather than unemployed workers.[134] The development of the Chinese market, paradoxically, with the help of the family institution, may have acquired room and time to take its course.

Summary

After a quarter century of Mao's failed experiment in institutional revolution, the traditional Chinese family-based LAP was restored after the end of the 1970s as the largest LAP. The family became the institutional basis of labor allocation for hundreds of millions of Chinese laborers and the traditional social, mainly family-oriented, norms and considerations regained tremendous influence on the status and behavior of those people. Family, once again, became the stable and powerful social and economic and even political institution. Many of the traditional Chinese economic, social, and political relations were restored in the vast Chinese countryside and, to a lesser extent, in urban areas.

The restored family-based LAP has sufficiently provided historically effective institutional support to the rather traditional authoritarian regime in Beijing, thereby strongly perpetuating the family-like Chinese institutional structure. With its massive ability to absorb surplus or underemployed labor, this LAP has stabilized the power of the CCP state in controlling the national economy and society on the macro level, although it may lessen state control over the peasants on the micro level. The traditional authority structure and social stratification have been restored as the relative economic autonomy of the peasantry, and the limited self-governing of the villagers has been revived. This LAP contributed to chaining social institutions and the economy together with the family-like state political power, a centralized state administration, as in the past thousands of years. It has created an important basis on which a traditional moral economy can exist in the countryside, and thus limits the emancipation of the market from the traditional Chinese socioeconomic complex.

The restoration, after a failed interruption, of the family-based LAP explains why there seems to be so much continuity of history in modern China, which many scholars have considered a great enigma.[135] However, the restored Chinese family-based LAP, especially in rural areas, has demonstrated a few positive practical implications for the process of Chinese modernization. Small, stagnated family-based production should be a ready hotbed for development of a market-oriented large division of labor, utilizing the millions of cheap rural laborers. Yet the stable family/clan institution, at the cost of confining and distorting the market, has provided a much-needed cushion against the shocks of the advancing market. This is especially true in that the family-based LAP furnished precious room and time for the crucial marketization of Chinese labor allocation.

Labor mobility has increased under this restored family-based LAP but is unlikely to cause explosive labor floods that might destroy the newly emerged market institution. Furthermore, new developments of families and the relationships between them and their operational environments have produced early indications about the transformation of this LAP and its institutional impact. The authority structure of the Chinese nation, as reflected by that within and among families, has demonstrated significant changes in the direction of emphasizing "having the authority" based on resource and knowledge more than "being the authority" based on status and seniority.[136]

The formation of villages or communities as economic units and the clear erosion of Confucian culture are especially interesting and profound. The Chinese could ultimately construct an institutional structure in which the basic units are groups with clear features of social institutions—the families or reformed clans (villages/communities)—rather than individuals (Wang 1994, 57). Those economic units may actually foretell the fate and the unique nature of China's institutional structure.

Notes

1. This book uses the term "family-like" rather than the commonly used word "patriarchal" for two reasons. First, "family-like" refers primarily to a set of specific institutional structures, behavioral norms, and goals essential to a family institution, rather than just a specific father-centered authority relationship. Second, the head of the family or family-like groups may or may not be a senior male. It can even be a group of people selected through various processes.

2. Max Weber attempted to define "social action" and "social organization" in general terms to include economic and political institutions. Weber 1978, 24-25, 48-52.

3. E. A. Wrigley: "The Process of Modernization and the Industrial Revolution in England," in *Journal of Interdisciplinary History* (Cambridge, Mass.: MIT Press), vol. 3 (1972): 225-260.

4. For more information about nontraditional families, see William Dunn: "Nontraditional Lifestyles Mean More Nontraditional Families," *American Demographics* (Beijing), no. 14 (July 1992).

5. He Junfeng 1994, 49-58; Zheng Guizhen, "Dalu fugang yiming ji jiating zhuankuan diaocha" (An investigation of Chinese migration and families in Hong Kong) in *Zhongguo renkou kexue* (Chinese demographics) (Beijing), no. 1 (1993).

6. Kinship dominance in a "bureaucratic empire" empirically constituted a Chinese type of social system. See Parsons 1951A, 167-198.

7. John Stacks, "The Powell Factor," in *Time* magazine, July 10, 1995, 25-26. As its central message, the theme song of a popular public TV program, *Barney the Purple Dinosaur*, tells children every day that they are "a happy family."

8. For a recent and extended review of Becker's arguments, see Schwartz and Febrero, eds. 1996.

9. See, for example, Ba Jin's famous novel, *Jia, chun chu* (Family, spring and autumn) (Beijing: Renmin Wenxue Press, [1931], 1982), and Cao Yu's influential play, *Neiyu* (Thunderstorm) (Beijing: Renmin Wenxue Press, [1930], 1978).

10. For a case study of this institutional feature of Chinese history, see Timothy Brook, "Family Continuity and Cultural Hegemony: The Gentry of Ningbo, 1368-1911" in *Esherick and Rankin* (1990): 27-50.

11. In Max Weber's terms, China was ruled by a massive, well-educated, and organized "patrimonial bureaucracy" headed by the emperor (Weber 1978, 575, 1047-1051).

12. The famous historical case of Wang Anshi (王安石) reform and its failure in the eleventh century has been used to illustrate this point. See, for example, Ye Tan, *Chuantong jingji guan da zhenlun: Shima Guang Wang Anshi zi bijiao* (A great debate on traditional economics: A comparison of Shima Guan and Wang Anshi) (Beijing: Beijing University Press, 1990). For an interesting discussion on the major innovations and reforms in Chinese political history, see Gu Kuixiang et al., *Zhongguo gudai gaige shilun* (An annotated history of reforms in ancient China) (Shengyang: Liaoning University Press, 1991).

13. See *Zhongyong* (Doctrine of the mean), a Confucian classic.

14. There were brief periods (such as Wei and Jin) when large land-based autocrats developed to form European-style manors that reduced the family-based peasants to serfs and semi-serfs. That variation of the Chinese institutional setting was later largely controlled by the family-like centralized imperial state, especially after Ming.

15. Zhang Youyi, ed., *Zhongguo jingdai nongming shi zhiliao* (Data collections on the modern history of the Chinese peasantry), vol. 2 (Shanghai: Sanlian Press, 1957), 67, 69; Kuang Haolin, *Jiangming Zhongguo jingdai jingji shi* (A short history of modern Chinese economy) (Beijing: Mingzhu College Press, 1991), 3-9, 220-245.

16. Mao did indeed ponder the utility and possibility of using the Western, or capitalist, market mechanisms twice, in the mid-1950s and early 1960s. See Mao, "Lun shida guanxi" (On ten great relations), in Zedong 1978 and Ri 1993, 13.

17. The swell of the urban population threatened to destabilize the political regime, and the intellectuals began to seize the opportunity to demand rights and freedom under the "people's democratic dictatorship." See Wang Weili, *Zhonghuo xiandai shi* (Contemporary history of China) (Shengyan: Liaoning Renmin Press, 1984).

18. Yang Zhanghua, "Gaige, zai xiwang de tianya shang" (Reform in the hopeful fields), *Renmin Ribao*, September 21, 1994, 1; *Tianjin Ribao* (Tianjin), February 1, 1994, 7

19. Huang 1986, 554-556; Huang et al. 1989, 364-365.

20. Yan 1994, 23. By the 1990s, less than a handful of "people's communes" still existed in China, but even those had become semi-corporate, semi-local, community-type institutions.

21. Figures provided by the State Statistical Bureau's Rural Investigation Team. Xinhua News Agency, March 26, 1995.

22. *Renmin Ribao*, August 7, 1992, 1; October 30, 1992, 1; and March 10, 1994, 8.

23. For a general analysis of the impact of the international market on Chinese domestic institutions, see Wang 1994, 22-42.

24. For a collective study of Chinese families in the PRC era, see Davis and Harrell 1993.

25. Chinese Academy of Social Sciences, *Zhongguo xinshi ji* (Collection of Chinese surnames) (Beijing: Social Science Press, 1992).

26. The author's field work tends to confirm this speculation.

27. As cited in Brugger and Reglar (1994, 263), surveys found that the family size in China in the 1930s and 1940s was only four to six members, even smaller than today. However, the earlier figures may be abnormally small because the sampling years were during a period when the Chinese experienced one of their most massive population dislocations due to civil wars and the terrifying Japanese invasion.

28. He Ping, "Bejingren jiating guanglian diaocha" (An investigation on the Beijingers' family attitudes), in *Renmin Ribao*, March 4, 1995, 9. See also Zhongxin News Agency's report from Beijing, March 20, 1995.

29. Hu Ping, "Bejingren jiating guanglian diaocha" (An investigation on the Beijingers' family attitude), *Renmin Ribao*, March 4, 1995, 9.

30. For a historical examination of Chinese family institutions before the PRC, see Ebrey and Watson 1986.

31. K. C. Yeh, "Macroeconomic Issues in China in the 1990s," in *China Quarterly* no. 131 (September 1992): 535.

32. By the end of the 1980s, Beijing decided to let the peasants have de facto ownership of the land, whereby land could be contracted for much longer than fifteen years, and there would be no future changes of the size of the contracted land regardless of changes in family size. See *Zhongguo xingxi bao* (Chinese information news), December 10, 1993.

33. We need to recognize that the Chinese local leaders have a traditional incentive to "hide" certain acreage from the central government. For a vivid description of the increasingly apparent economic incentives for labor mobility out of the stagnated agricultural sector, see Ge 1990, 40-45.

34. The government acknowledges this fact openly, if apprehensively. See, for example, Jiang Zeming's speech at the Six-Province Workshop on Agriculture and Rural Works, November 24-25, 1992; *Renmin Ribao,* December 28, 1992, 1.

35. *Renmin Ribao,* March 19, 1994, 2.

36. Year-End Report by Xinhua News Agency (Beijing, Xinhua), December 19, 1994. As many other Chinese official statistics that rely on reports of the lower governments, official figures of cultivated land size may have been problematic. Significant abridgment exists due to the desires of local officials to have some flexibility in appropriating land and in reporting an increased grain production in the future. In some areas, the hidden cultivated land can be as much as 50 to 75 percent of the reported acreage. See Ma Yuejun, "Huang tudi, he tudi" (Yellow land, black land), in Liu Ying, ed., *Dangdai Zhongguo yeshenghuo—Dangdai Zhongguo redian xiezhen chongshu* (Night life in contemporary China—The series on the hot issues in contemporary China), (Beijing: Huayi Press, 1993), 8-9.

37. Zhao Bin, "Qiemu lengluo nongye" (Never ignore agriculture), in *Fangzhan yanjou* (Development studies) (Beijing), vol. 6 (1993): 25-28.

38. Undoubtedly, this could cause profound political and social problems, for being dependent on imported grain was, according to Zhou, considered "quite harmful and impractical." Zhou also asserted that the "appropriate" population that Chinese arable land could support was only 800 million to 900 million, and the maximum was 1.6 billion (it was already 1.2 billion). Zhou's interview by Xinhua reporters Jiang Guochen and Zhou Changqing, March 8, 1995, in *Renmin Ribao,* March 9, 1995, 4. For an optimistic forecast on the grain supply in China, see Agriculture Ministry, "Zhongguo yuwu nenli yanghuo ziji?" (Can China feed itself?), in *Renmin Ribao-Overseas,* June 23, 1995, 2.

39. Author's field research notes, 1992, 1993, 1995.

40. "Huaxia diyi xian" (The first county of China), in *Renmin Ribao,* December 6, 1994, 1.

41. *Renmin Ribao,* September 20, 1991, 1.

42. A glimpse at the numerous works on family life published in the 1980s and 1990s in major Chinese literature journals such as *Dangdai, Shouhuo,* and *Shiyu* yield an unmistakable impression about such social changes in the Chinese family authority structure. Official media also have noticed this trend. See, for example, the report on the so-called "science and technology heads of the family" in the villages of Sichuan Province, *Renmin Ribao-Overseas,* July 17, 1995, 3.

43. Sun Jiwei, "Nongcun xiaofei shuiping diaocha" (A study on the consumer level of the rural areas), in *Zhongguo xingxi bao,* Beijing, August 1994.

44. In a late-1980s survey, over 64 percent of the respondents hoped to live with their sons when they got old (Liu 1993, 343).

45. Ma Gaobao and Wang Keyong, "Shangdong Hengtai xinxanshi: Erzi gu laozi dagong" (Brand-new events in Hengtai of Shangdong: Sons hire fathers to work) in *Renmin Ribao-Overseas*, May 26, 1995, 2.

46. For an insider's view of the difficulties the Chinese rural farmers faced in the mid-1990s, see Zhang Luxong, "Nongchun gaige he fazhan suominnin de sida nanti" (Four major problems facing rural reform and development), in *Shehui kexue yangjou cankao ziliao* (Materials for social science studies) (Chengdu [city]), no. 21, (November 1994): 1-5.

47. "Nine Policies of Supporting Grain Production," in *Guowuyuang gongbao* (The State Council bulletin) Beijing, February 1993.

48. Except for one year (1985), Beijing had an increasing budget deficit every year in the past two decades. See SSB 1993.

49. The term "agriculture" refers to production of farm goods such as grain, meat, fish, forestry products, vegetables, and fruits. The Chinese agricultural economy is labor intensive, heavily manual, and organized on a household basis. However, there are some state-owned mechanized farms under a different LAP—an authoritarian state LAP.

50. Chinese official statistics are not always consistent. For an earlier and smaller estimate of the rural labor force (about 57.8 percent, instead of 66.3 percent), see the press conference proceedings of Chen Yaobang, Deputy Minister of Agriculture, on December 19, 1990, in *Renmin Ribao,* December 20, 1990, 1, and SSB 1992, 16-17.

51. *Renmin Ribao,* August 7, 1992,1; October 30, 1992, 1; March 10, 1994, 8.

52. *Beijing Ribao* (Beijing Daily), April 27, 1994, 1.

53. For a generic study of the clan institution in China, see Wang 1991.

54. Liu Yuangchao, "Xianjieduan nongcun de jiazhu zhuzhi" (The current rural clan organization), in *Shehuixue yanjou* (Sociology studies) (Beijing), vol. 6 (1991).

55. Yang Yabin, "Zhongguo jiachu zhidu de yangbian" (The evolution of the Chinese family institution), in *Shehui kexue zhangxian* (The front of social sciences) (Jilin), no. 4 (1993): 142-146.

56. Li Yinhe, "Lun cunlou wenhua" (On village culture), in *Zhongguo shehui kexue* (Chinese social sciences) (Beijing), vol. 5 (1993): 59-70.

57. Author's field notes 1989, 1992.

58. The official media reported an illustrative case of an Anhui woman and her two daughters who worked in Beijing as a domestic helper, cook, and sales clerk, respectively. The father worked in a construction site and the son worked in Nanjing. The family's 4 *mu* of land was "rented" to fellow villagers at a rate of 400 kg of rice per year. The forty-year-old woman made about 600-700 rmb a month and paid about 130 rmb for shabby housing and board. The purpose of her working was to "save for my son to marry a girl and to buy a house for us at home." See Ji Xiaobi, "Dao Beijing zhuozhongdiang" (Go to work in Beijing as hourly workers), in *Renmin Ribao-Overseas,* July 18, 1995, 2.

59. *Renmin Ribao,* December 16, 1993, 8.

60. *Renmin Ribao,* February 2, 1994, 1.

61. Cai Shousu et al., "Jiangsu zhongliang dahu diaocha" (An investigation of the big farming households in Jiangsu), in *Renmin Ribao,* August 21, 1995, 9.

62. See, for example: *Beijing Ribao* (Beijing daily) (Beijing), August 9, 1995, 1; *Yangchen Wangbao* (Evening News of Guangzhou) (Guangzhou), August 4, 1995, 2; and *Shenzhen Tequ Bao* (Daily of the Shenzhen SEZ) (Shenzhen), August 21, 1995, 8.

63. I visited the two villages numerous times from the 1970s to 1990s and have kept contact with the residents.

64. The one-child-per-family policy was adopted in the rural areas by the end of the 1980s. If the only child was a girl, then the couple could have another child in five years. Violators were subject to heavy fines of 3,000 rmb in this region.

65. The per capita acreage varies in different regions. In Jilin Province, for example, our field trip found that a more viable agricultural economy exists because of a substantially larger per capita acreage of 3.5 *mu* (0.58 acre) cultivated land (author's field notes, summer 1996).

66. The peasants often sold rice on the market for a higher price and then bought less expensive wheat or corn for food.

67. As a comparison, a survey reported that in 1994 the average per capita income of the Chinese peasants was 1,220 rmb (the State Statistical Bureau's Rural Investigation Team, Xinhua News Agency, March 26, 1995).

68. This was no small achievement. By 1993, according to official reports, there were more than 120 million rural people, including twenty-eight counties, without electricity in the PRC. Among the villages that had electricity, only 85 percent could have power for as much as twenty-four days every month (figures provided by the PRC Ministry of Electric Power, in *Renmin Ribao-Overseas,* July 13, 1995, 2).

69. For a general discussion on the nature and the function of these villagers' committees, see Zhao Yongxing, "Cunmin weiyuanhui xingzhi yu zhuyong de zairenshe" (A review of the nature and the role of the villagers' committees), in *Sichuan Shifang Xueyuan xuebao* (Journal of Sichuan Normal College) (Nanchong), vol. 1 (1994): 101-104.

70. Author's field notes 1992 and 1995; Zhang Yulin, "Jiangsu taichang Mabeicun diaoca" (An investigation of the Mabei Village in Taichan County of Jiangsu Province), in *Shihuixue yanjou* (Sociology studies) (Beijing), vol. 2 (1993): 1-8.

71. See, for example, Yang Yabin, "Zhongguo jiachu zhidu de yangbian" (The evolution of the Chinese family institution), in *Shehui kexue zhangxian* (The front of social sciences) (Shanghai), no. 4 (1993): 142-146, and Sun Jiaming, "Zhongqing gunagxi wang de shehui gongnen" (The social functions of the clan network), in *Shehui* (Society) (Shanghai), vol. 6 (1994): 22-24.

72. Because the land had been completely divided among the families and no redistribution was allowed or practical, the creation of a new family usually could not be completed unless the new family could either take over existing family land through renting or inheriting, or rely primarily on nonfarming income from such endeavors as handicrafts, commerce, transportation, or working outside the village. An interesting outcome was the possibility of growing incentives for young rural couples to search for jobs outside their villages in their desire to form an independent family of their own.

73. Very recently, however, some families started to hire construction teams to do such work with either cash payment or credit based on the collateral of the harvest.

74. This is comparable to the findings of a large-scale field survey. In that study, peasants were found to work on average 7.7 hours every day year-round in 1986 (11.6 hours during the busy seasons), down from 8.4 hours in 1978 (Liu 1993, 292-310).

75. Wen Guanzhong, "Nianan de tudi zhidu" (The land system on the two sides of the straits" in Wen et al., *Taiwan Mode* (New York: Oriental News Corp., 1992), 58.

76. Author's field notes in Taiwan, April 1995.

77. Figures from Table 3.1 and Taiwan's Central Academy of Economic Studies.

78. Wen et al., *Taiwan Model* (New York: Oriental News Corp., 1992), 59; author's notes of conversation with the acting director of Taiwan's Land Reform Training Institute, Taoyuan, Taiwan, April 1995.

79. For a general discussion about the Taiwanese experience of land reform and rural development and its international utility, see Wen Guanzhong et al., *Taiwan Model* (New York: Oriental News Corp., 1992); Lin Sein, ed., *Readings in Land Reform* (Taoyuan, Taiwan: Land Reform Training Institute, 1970); James R. Brown and Lin Sein, eds., *Land Reform in Developing Countries*, (Hartford, Conn.: University of Hartford Press, 1968); and A. M. Woodruff and J. R. Brown, eds., *Land for Cities of Asia* (Hartford, Conn.: University of Hartford Press, 1971).

80. Ma Rong, "Xiao chenzhen de fazhang yu Zhongguo de xiandahua" (The development of the small towns and the Chinese modernization), in *Zhongguo shehui kexue* (Chinese social sciences) (Beijing), vol. 4 (1990).

81. Qin Dewen, "Beiwang dajun xianghefang?" (Where is the million-man army heading?) in *Zhongguo nongcun jingji* (Chinese rural economy) (Beijing), vol. 10 (1993), 48.

82. Li Debin, "Dangdai Zhongguo liudong renkou de tezhe yu chenying" (The nature and causes of the floating people in contemporary China), in *Shehuixuw yanjou* (Sociology studies) (Beijing), vol. 4 (1993): 65-73.

83. Wang Qiming, "Nongcun chenshihua de xiwang" (The hope for rural urbanization), in *Renmin Ribao*, February 28, 1995, 4.

84. For some of the serious problems this design has caused in the Chinese rural areas, see Zhong Fucheng, "Xiao chengzheng jianshi jixu zhengque daoxian" (The building of small towns urgently needs the right guidance), in *Chengxian jianshi* (Urban and rural construction), no. 2 (Beijing), 1995: 21-23.

85. *Renmin Ribao*, May 8, 1995, 4.

86. Yang Yonghua, "Gunagdongsheng chenxiang jingji gunagxi de xintedian" (New features of the economic relationship between the rural and the urban areas in Guangdong Province), in *Shehuixuw yanjou* (Sociology studies) (Beijing), no. 4 (1993): 33-40.

87. Song Linfei, "Chong qingshang zhouxiang zhongshang de zhongguo shehui" (Chinese society moves from belittling commerce to worshipping it), in *Tianjin Ribao* (Tianjin Daily) (Tianjin), February 1, 1994, 7.

88. Li Yinhe, "Lun cunlou wenhua" (On village culture), in *Zhongguo shehui kexue* (Chinese social sciences) (Beijing), vol. 5 (1993): 69-70.

89. Examples are the famous national models of Chinese rural economic development: Huaxi village in Jiangsu, Daqouzhuan Xiang in Tianjin, and Liuzhuan Xiang in Henan.

90. Da Dan, "Shuiweicun gaige yilai shehui bianqin de chubu diaoca" (A preliminary investigation of social changes in Shuiwei village), in *Shehuixue yanjou* (Sociology studies) (Beijing), vol. 2 (1993): 9-16.

91. For example, see Ca Hemu et al., "Fujian sheng chunji jingji fazhang wenti tantao" (A discussion on the issue of village-level economy in Fujian Province), in *Fazhang yanjou* (Development studies) (Fuzhou), vol. 4 (1993): 28-32.

92. For example, see Zhang Yulin, "Jiangsu taichang mabeicun diaoca" (An investigation of Mabei Village in Taichan County of Jiangsu Province), in *Shihuixue yanjou* (Sociology studies) (Beijing), vol. 2 (1993): 1-8.

93. *Renmin Ribao*, December 16, 1992, 3.

94. Lu Xueyi, "Chongxin renshi nongmin wenti" (To reunderstand the peasantry issue), in *Shehuixuw yanjou* (Sociology studies) (Beijing), vol. 6 (1989).

95. CCP Central Party School, ed., *Gaigezhong de nongcun yu nongmin* (The rural area and the peasants under the reform) (Beijing: CCP Party School Press, 1992), 15, 19.

96. Chen Yaotin, ed., *Zhongguo de zhongjiao* (Religion in China), (Shanghai: Waiyu Jiaoyue Press, 1991). One external source reported that in at least one rural community, the Christian church has taken over the financially troubled public elementary schools. See *Meizhong daobao* (US-China tribune), Los Angeles, January 5, 1996, 4.

97. Anne F. Thurston, "The Search for a Civil Society," in *China Focus* (Princeton, N.J.), vol. 3, no 7 (July 1, 1995): 1.

98. For a concise but thorough review of such attempts, see Zhong 1994, 90-95.

99. Ren Xiao, "Zhenzi wenhua de fangxeng" (A reflection on political culture), in *Zhongguo shuping* (China book reviews) (Hong Kong), vol. 1 (1994): 117.

100. Wang Xianming, "Sengshi jiechen yu jingdai shituan" (Gentry class and modern social associations), in *Tianjin shehui kexue* (Tianjin social sciences), vol. 4 (1994): 81-85.

101. For case studies illustrating such efforts, see Shue 1980, Oi 1989, Friedman et al. 1991, and Chan 1992.

102. For a representative view on this point, see Ruan Min (阮铭), *Deng Xiaoping diguo* (The Deng Xiaoping empire) (Taipei: Times Newspaper Press, 1992), 76. An English translation of the book was published by Westview Press in 1994.

103. A recent semi-official publication cried out for more "social stability" through stabilizing further the "cells of the society: the families" despite the fact that even in the more open urban China "only slightly more than 10 percent of marriages were based on love" (Qiao 1994, 198-200).

104. Chinese scholars began to refer to these people as "populist ruling elite" who had become a "middle layer" between the state and the masses. See Sun Liping, "Gaige qianghou Zhongguo guojia, minjiantongzhi jingying ji minzhong jian hudong guangxi de yangbian" (The evolution of the interactive relationship among the Chinese state, populist ruling elites and the masses before and after the reform), in *Zhongguo shehui kexue jikang* (Chinese social sciences quarterly) (Beijing and Hong Kong), vol. 1 (1994).

105. Liu Xiaojing, "Jihe tizhi de songjie" (The collapse of the collective system), in *Nongcun jingji yu shehui* (Rural economy and society) (Beijing), vol. 3 (1994): 49-56.

106. See, for example, Tong Dongzhang et al., "The joys and sorrows of the party branch secretaries in the villages," in *Jingji tizhi gaige* (The reform of the Chinese economic system) an internal publication for cadres (Beijing), vol. 2 (1990): 52; Peng Xiling, "The Dual Status and Dilemmas of the Rural Cadres" in *Jianghai Xuekan* (Jianghai journal) (Nanjing), vol. 4 (1990): 40-44; and Peng Yonghong et al., "Problems and Solutions in the Construction of Rural Local Governments" in *Jianhai Xuekan* (Jianghai journal) (Nanjing), vol. 1 (1990): 43-47.

107. Wang Xiao and Hou Chouling, "Micro-Democratic Construction: The Rural is Challenging the Urban" in *Shehui kexue* (Social sciences) (Shanghai), vol. 7 (1990): 36-37.

108. Zou Heping, "Lun woguo chuanming zhizi de fanzhang tezhen" (On the development of villagers' self-governing in our country), in *Lilun yu gaige* (Theories and reform) (Chengdu), vol. 6 (1994): 33-35.

109. Anne F. Thurston, "Village Elections in Lishu County: An Eyewitness Account" in *China Focus* (Princeton, N.J.), vol. 3, no. 5 (May 1, 1995): 3, 5.

110. For an official report on the self-governing of the Chinese villagers in the 1990s, see Wang Zhongtian, "Yifa zizhi: Xinshiqi nongchun chunji zhuzhi jiangshi de xinsilu" (Self-governing by law: The new thinking of the construction of village organizations in the new era) in *Zhongguo shehui fazhan zhanlui* (Development strategy of Chinese society) (Beijing), no. 3 (1994): 14-18.

111. For some of the most vivid descriptions of these traditional institutions and behaviors in the Chinese urban areas, see Yao and Murong 1993.

112. Xin Guanjie, executive vice president of the Chinese Confucius Foundation, "Kongzi rujia xueshuo xiang shijie de chuanbuo" (The promotion of Confucianism to the world), in *Renmin Ribao,* April, 27, 1995, 3.

113. For a representative analysis on the important role played by Confucianism in the Japanese modernization, see Cui Xinjing, "Lun ruxue guanglian yu riben de xiandaihua" (On the Confucian ideas and the Japanese modernization), in *Riben Yanjou* (Japan studies) (Shengyang), no. 4 (1993): 112-119.

114. By the mid-1990s, China not only opened many tourist attractions with real or alleged association with Confucius and his famed students but also marketed his two-thousand-year-old "family wine," "family dishes," "family fashion style," and even "family medicine" (author's field notes, 1995).

115. For example, see articles in the series "Tigao quanmin shuzhi, yingji 21 shi ji" (Improve the national quality to prepare for the twenty-first century), *Renmin Ribao*, winter 1994-spring 1995. See also Fu et al., 1995, 234-252.

116. Guangdong People's Deputy Guang Shanyue spoke at the group sessions of the CNPC meeting, March 9, 1995. Also, Zhongxin News Agency news, Guangzhou, May 5, 1995.

117. *China in Brief: Factors Fueling China's Rapid Economic Development,* (Beijing: New Star Publishers, 1995), 17.

118. Xinhua News Report, Xinhua News Agency, Beijing, February 19, 1991.

119. For a discussion by Chinese economists of rural surplus labor and its transfers, see Wang 1988, 92-112, and Zhang 1988, 98-114.

120. See SSB 1991, 3-7; SSB 1992, 15-18; and SSB-PB 1993, 66, 88.

121. Niu 1993, 145-149.

122. Lu Peifa, "Xiangzhen qiye huihuang youyinian" (Another glorious year for the TVEs), in *Renmin Ribao-Overseas,* December 27, 1994, 4. As a comparison, the

total rural labor force in the fifty-two African countries in the early 1980s was only 117 million and the total rural labor force in the twenty-seven European nations was only 31.29 million (Wang 1988, 112).

123. Among which only 44 million had registered as "temporary residents." The rest were totally "black *hukou*," or illegal residents. Figures released by the National Working Conference on Floating People, reported in *Renmin Ribao*, July 10, 1995, 1.

124. Li Mengbai et al., *Liudong renkou dui dachenshi fazhang de yingxiang ji duice* (The influence of the floating people on the development of the big cities and the relevant policies) (Beijing: Jingji Ribao Press, 1991); and Liu Yanling "Dangqian woguo nongye laodongli liudong zhong de shehui wenti jiqi duice" (Social problems of the current floating peasant labor and the relevant policies), in *Shehuixue yangjou* (Sociology studies) (Beijing), no. 2 (1994): 76-82. For a vivid description of the urgency of the problem, see Wang Xiangxian et al., *Zhongguo minggong chao—"Mongliu" zhengxiang* (The tides of Chinese peasant labor—the truth of "Mongliu") (Beijing: Guoji Guangbo Press, 1990). For a more recent report on the issue, see Study Team, "Minggong liudong zhuangkuang diaocha" (An investigation of floating peasant labor) *in Zhongguo laodong bao* (Chinese labor news), March 29, 1994, 21.

125. *Renmin Ribao-Overseas*, June 16, 1995, 9.

126. Author's interview with police in Beijing, January 1995.

127. Speech by Ren Jianxin, director of the Public Security Management Commission of the CCP, Beijing, June 7, 1995.

128. See chapter 2 of Wang 1994.

129. Mao Zedong wrote about this in the 1920s. See his *Hunan   nongmin yundong kaoca baogao* (Report on the peasant movement in Hunan), 1926 in Mao, vol. 1, 1973-1978.

130. In the 1980s and 1990s, studies revealed that, even in the more "open" major cities, as many as 80 to 95 percent of parents said they would be against their children working outside their hometowns. See Mu Guanzhong, "Bei chonghuai de xiaohuangdi" (The spoiled little emperors), in *Huaxia wenzhe* (China news digest), an Internet weekly, Nos. 214 and 215, and May 5 and 12, 1995.

131. Author's field notes, 1995.

132. Among the nearly 900 million rural residents, an Yao and Murong (1993, 34) estimate that 660 million were living in absolute poverty. Official statistics were much rosier. According to Jiang Zemin, PRC president, there were more than 80 million Chinese peasants living in "poverty," defined as those who did not have enough grain to eat (*Renmin Ribao*, February, 12, 1995, 2). Some reports in 1992 and 1993 portrayed a horrifying picture of poverty in many villages in West China. See for example, "Huantudi de yangnei" (The tears of the yellow land), in *Xinhua Digest* (Beijing), no. 3 (March 1992).

133. Lin Zhenping and He Qing, "Fujian nongye laogongli zhuanyi xiangzhuan yu zhanglua tangtao" (The current situation and strategic discussion on the transfer of Fujian agricultural labor), in *Fazhang yanjou* (Development studies) (Fuzhou), vol. 1 (1993): 17-20.

134. Such a very desirable social and political role of the traditional Chinese rural economy was noticed by many long ago. It was utilized and systematically enhanced by the CCP. See Rawski 1979, 3, 131-132, especially chapter 4, and

Ullerich 1979. However, the price of this means of "absorbing" labor, especially through the collective, was also obvious. Rawski estimates that from 1957 to 1975, the productivity of Chinese peasants declined by almost one-third (1979, 128).

135. For example, see Friedman et al. 1991, Dittmer 1993B, and Dittmer, ed. 1993A.

136. Wang Xiaoyi, "Xuyuang yu diyuang" (Consanguinity and geopolitics), *Hangzhou* (Zhejiang: Renmin Press, 1993), 147. For a conceptual discussion of the notions of having authority versus being the authority, see Kratochwil 1989, 165.

2. Authoritarian State Allocation Pattern

Traditionally an agrarian nation, China nonetheless has had a long history of urban life. Cities have been the political and cultural centers of Chinese civilization and have held significant economic importance. Active commercial enterprises, impressive handicraft shops, and sophisticated city management systems can be traced to before the Warring States era (fifth to third centuries B.C.) (Hu 1979, 245-254). The Han dynasty (third century B.C. to third century A.D.) developed massive cities that rival today's major metropolitan areas. The architecture of the Tang dynasty (seventh to tenth centuries) was so well designed that it was used as a model in both Korea and Japan (Ye 1988). Economic activities in Chinese urban areas began to rival those of the countryside in the 1800s and, by the 1960s, surpassed them. Chinese urban areas by the mid-1900s—though roughly less than 22 percent of the nation's total population—produced nearly 75 percent of China's gross domestic product.[1] The cities are the political centers at the national and regional levels, and the urban areas house virtually all the media, higher education, entertainment, and health care facilities of the nation. In addition, most Sino-foreigns interactions take place in the cities where modern facilities and even luxurious amenities can be found. Throughout the past century, the urban sector has played a dominant role of leadership and innovation in China.

A leading feature of the institutional structure of the PRC since 1949 has been a centrally planned economic system, or socialism, in which the authoritarian CCP state controls and manages the nation's urban economy and, to a lesser extent, the rural economy as well. A cornerstone of that planned economy has been an encompassing authoritarian state LAP dominating labor and management, primarily in the urban areas. This LAP reached its zenith during the 1950s-1970s, when it organized and allocated peasants in a similar (though less direct, hence less effective) way through collectivized communes. A nationwide unified LAP, a giant "family," was established based on the state's political institutions. The history of the PRC, its economy, politics, and society, has evolved with this LAP as its institutional foundation.

For several generations of urban residents, the state has been the employer, thus the provider—the "father." The CCP state, through its bureaucracy, literally allocates and manages each and every urban worker. Deng Xiaoping's reform did not touch this LAP until 1984, when the CCP decided to reform the depressed Chinese urban economy after the initially impressive economic success of decollectivization in rural areas. The demise of the collectivized communes and the restoration of the family-based traditional LAP substantially weakened the position of the authoritarian state LAP, but only modestly reduced its role in Chinese economy, politics, and society. It is the advancing market institution that has posed the strongest challenge to this LAP. More than a decade after numerous additions, modifications, experiments, new names, and propositions, the reforming authoritarian state LAP still appears to be the dominant LAP in the cities, covering approximately 114 million workers in 1994 (table 2.1). This LAP also allocates and manages about 1.3 million "rural cadres," the bureaucrats staffing government offices below the county level, and many professionals including teachers and agricultural engineers working in the rural areas.[2] Given the overwhelming political, economic, and social significance of the urban sector, the authoritarian LAP, though it affects less than a quarter of the Chinese people directly, is indisputably the most important LAP in contemporary China.

To continue our examination of the Chinese LAPs, this chapter explores the status and impact of the authoritarian state LAP in the PRC. We begin with a discussion of the political institutions, the state, and the political pattern of labor allocation. The historical origins of this LAP are traced and analyzed. The second section describes the authoritarian state LAP after a decade-long reform. We conclude with an exploration of this LAP's institutional role in contemporary China.

Political Institutions and Labor Allocation

We begin this section with an examination of political institutions and their highest hierarchical form, the nation-state. Next, a brief analysis of the various organizational structures of political institutions will be presented, followed by a discussion of the role of these institutions in the economy and in society. Finally, we will inquire into the historical origins of the authoritarian state LAP.

The Nation-State as a Political Institution

Unlike the social institutions discussed in the previous chapter, a political institution is defined as a geographically confined entity that, first and foremost, has a common authority center capable of organizing and using force against anyone in or outside the grouping, for the purpose of establishing and enforcing order.[3] Humans did not have the need or desire to create political institutions before the size of a particular human grouping reached beyond the family/clan. Only in multifamily/clan groupings or where several families/clans interact constantly is a political institution necessary to meet human needs and desires: it ensures the highest possible safety/security for the people by transferring authority to a center that can then set and enforce rules that apply equally to individuals and families/clans.

Members of the political institution may or may not be genetically related. Interest or geographic approximation is not a necessary condition either. It is how far the force, more commonly known as "power," of the central authority can reach that defines the boundaries. The aggregate purpose of a human political institution is the establishment of a governing order, backed by force, to provide safety/security to the members against each other and against outsiders. The effectiveness of creating, maintaining, adjusting, and enforcing such an order is the main performance criterion separating the various types of political institutions. A hierarchical authority relationship, a clear and generally fixed group identity of the members (citizenship), the maintenance and use of armed forces, and the extraction of resources by the central authority are among the leading features of a political institution. Constant and dynamic concerns and adjustments concerning fairness in the formation and exercise of authority is essential to the operation of a political institution. Compromises and persuasion by exchange, reasoning, indoctrination, education, or force are common mechanisms of a political institution.

Human knowledge changes; thus, many human desires may fade or emerge, and human ability and technology may improve. People also move, altering the composition of the group being governed. Furthermore, no political leader, no matter how powerful or popular, can live forever to sustain a particular form of a political institution. Answers to "who is in charge?" and "what is legal?" vary over time under a particular political institution.

Nations and Nation-States

Political groupings, represented by the centralized transfer of a governing authority, have reached several levels in human history. There has been family-based political authority that uses force like a sovereign entity. There have been larger clans and tribes. The largest political grouping has been a nation, and the highest level of a human political institution has been the nation-state or, simply, the state.[4] A "nation" is commonly defined as a relatively large group of people who feel they belong together by virtue of sharing, most importantly "a common language" and "such traits as a common race, culture, history, or set of customs and traditions."[5] "Nation-state" is commonly defined as "a polity in which all citizens share a sense of common identity (nationhood) and in which sub-units, . . . are under the domain of a central government" that monopolizes the legitimate use of force (Migdal 1988, 18-19). The defining feature of a nation is a common language, a shared signal and symbol system on which a common recognition of culture, heritage, and "uniqueness" can be formed and maintained.[6] Yet other various common characteristics, interests, and experiences matter. Furthermore, one or several nations may be formed out of a human group speaking the same language.[7] Groups that speak the same language may, for historical, economic, and other reasons, prefer to form separate nations, and tend to grow further apart thereafter. The United States, which grew out of Great Britain, is a good example (Greenfield 1992, 397-484).

The defining feature of a state is its sovereignty, its independent monopoly of maintaining and using force against anyone in or outside its boundaries.[8] States historically have emerged along national lines, which provide the most enduring grouping basis for states. Nationalism, in its many varieties, has actually been a powerful and sustaining driving force, responsible for many political, social, and economic developments.[9] Empirically, however, many states are constructed by random events such as interventions by external forces. Inertia, an inherent feature of any human institution, then combines with the forces that created a state to perpetuate it, even though the state may not be a nation-based political institution. Usually, a non-nation-state is both more difficult and costly to maintain and more susceptible to destruction. Generally, a nation is the historical product of centuries, even millennia. The formation and destruction of a state, however, can be achieved in a much shorter time frame. In this book, the terms "nation" and "state" are sometimes used interchangeably, referring to the largest human grouping or the highest human political institution, respectively.

National Political Organizational Structures

Nations must have clearly established hierarchical structures to construct their political institutions. A number of national political organizational structures, or institutions (states), have been historically identified and are evident in the variety of political relationships among existing human groupings.

There may be only a single authority relationship, namely, one state governing all the people, whereby all groups and individuals are organized in a single hierarchical structure. This is the empire, or "world government," that ruled for substantial periods around the globe, unaware of the existence of similar governing hierarchies elsewhere. The Roman Empire and the Chinese World are good examples. Another type of political organizational structure has been a parallel coexistence of hierarchical authority structures, namely, the coexistence of sovereign nations/states. The collapse of the Roman Empire started a transition to this type of political structure in Europe. After a thousand years of the Dark Ages, the reconstruction of a new empire finally failed at the end of the Thirty Years War in 1648. A restoration of the Greek type of coexisting nations/states took place and the Renaissance unfolded. The nation-state international system legalized by the Treaty of Westphalia in the seventeenth century in Europe later spread throughout the globe, destroying old empires such as that of China and incorporating various institutional structures in nations that had been alone for centuries in their own "universes." Whether a state is the only known highest political institution for a people or peoples makes a profound difference in their overall institutional structure and performance. The difference is evident in the ending of the Dark Ages in Europe[10] and in the chronic backwardness of the Chinese (Wang 1995B). To some, the development of the whole capitalist world economy is inseparable from the international political system based on the coexistence of nation-states (Wallerstein 1974).

Another way to see the variety of states is through their various internal organizational features. A state may or may not be a nation-state. More important and common, states can be organized differently. How individuals are linked to the authority center and how they and subgroups are arranged against each other are among the leading factors that distinguish one state from another. There have been participatory states in which the authority center is accountable to the people, and the people have massive and meaningful participation in political decision making. The various "democracies," ranging from Athens to today's United States, belong to this category. There have been less participatory states in which decision making and the exercise of authority are subject to the input of only the minority of people. The various authoritarian or oligarchy systems, such as the CCP state in the PRC, are examples. There have been nonparticipatory states, in which there is no meaningful participation in the decision-making process by anyone other than the ruler, the ruler's family, or inner circles. Traditional, especially monarchies and totalitarian regimes like Nazi Germany can usually be described as nonparticipatory states.[11]

There seem to be links between the internal structure of a state and the performance of the state, though this issue continues to be debated. Democracies and authoritarian regimes tend to have different records of effectiveness and varied rationality in creating and maintaining order. Some have made considerable efforts to demonstrate that there may be a clear corelation between international peace and democracy.[12] More have argued that strong links exist between the internal structure of the state and the economic development of the nation. Democracy, many assert, has a positive impact on a nation's economic development and social progress. Quite a few, however, speculate that an authoritarian regime may be more conducive to the market institution in our time. There are those who believe that political democracy is a prerequisite for a market economy to thrive, while some argue just the opposite.[13] Still there are others who have argued that the political organizational structure of a nation is also subject to the impact of economic institutions (Freeman 1992; Bauzon 1992).

The States as Economic and Social Institutions

Besides the main goal of effectively creating, maintaining, and adjusting order and authority structures, political institutions have historically been used for economic and even social purposes. The Chinese Empire, for example, was thought by many to have been formed as a result of irrigation, flood control, and transportation needs.[14] Classic mercantilists advocated the role of the state in national economic development.[15] Justified and elaborated by Keynesian theories, the economic role of the state has become a household notion and a longtime practice in the West. Jobs, income, inflation, trade balance, and other economic activities have become an integral part of the activities of, for example, the U.S. government. To have a healthy economy is widely perceived as a pivotal part of the task of maintaining a just and peaceful political order. American presidential campaigns essentially became competitions to claim credit or assign blame concerning the economy in the 1990s. Similarly, the school of dependencia has argued that developing nations need the right kind of state to fight unfair practices of the developed economies on the international market (Packenham 1992). The skillful, interventionist, so-called developmental states are believed by many to have contributed decisively to the economic takeoff of East Asian economies in places like Japan, Korea, and Taiwan (Johnson 1962, Haggard 1990; Robinson 1990; Wade 1990). Similar arguments have been made about the PRC state in China.[16]

The Leninist-Stalinist states in the former Soviet Union, Eastern European nations, China, Cuba, and other places pushed the economic and social roles of the state to an extreme. Under the dictatorship of a communist party, the state became the omnipotent and omnipresent institution that regulated people's behavior in economy, politics, and society. In other words, the state became *the* institution in those nations. It was charged with the mission and authority to own, allocate, and manage almost all economic resources, including the labor force. The state also assumed the duty and power to carry out social functions, including education, parenting, sports, arts, and entertainment. Political logic, in the form of such things as hierarchical and centralized authority structures, obedience by subordinates, order, and the distribution and exercise of power based on force therefore largely replaced economic logic and social purposes of human behavior in those nations. The state bureaucracies, enterprises, and social institutions—even families—were institutionally unified and centralized, undifferentiated, in the same political fashion. An authoritarian state LAP was therefore formed in such nations.

There are certain advantages of organizing human economic activities and social behavior based on political institutions. These advantages are most clear in the case of decisive actions needed during a national emergency, such as war. During periods of crisis, states tend to draw on the strength generated by politicizing the economy and even society. Control of prices, goods, and news are some of the politicized efforts well known to Americans during World War II.[17] The seemingly impressive early economic and technological progress obtained by the Stalinist state in the USSR in the 1920s and 1930s and the Maoist regime in the PRC in the early 1950s demonstrated the strength of the state in mobilizing and allocating resources for rapid industrialization.[18]

The drawbacks of political institutions serving as economic and social institutions, however, are even more obvious and often outweigh the advantages. This is especially true when the politicizing of the economy and society lasts a long time. Over time, the Soviet style of industrialization stagnated and then increasingly fell behind the competitive and innovative, thus dynamically efficient, market economies. Political control of society inevitably led to decay of social institutions and the withering of culture and art. These failures and negative consequences in turn hurt the state, especially in a competitive international environment, causing systemic retardation and eventual degeneration of the political institution itself. External pressures and internal innovations may cause positive changes to such a stagnated institutional setting. But pressures and changes may also lead to an abrupt, total collapse of the state, together with the whole institutional setting. Such an institutional "meltdown" could result in political ineffectiveness, lawlessness, and a general decadence of the national economy and society. The dramatic fate of the former Soviet Union and the history of the post-Soviet situation in the Commonwealth of Independent States have demonstrated this point well.

Origins of the Authoritarian State LAP

As a national phenomenon, the authoritarian state LAP is a new historical pattern. Institutionally and operationally speaking, however, this LAP has been practiced widely by political authorities since ancient times, at least in partial form. State-owned slaves in ancient Egypt, Greece, Persia, and Rome were typically allocated by the political authority as laborers and as pieces of properties. More important, military forces—especially professional standing armies after the demise of knighthood—can be viewed as institutional prototypes of the authoritarian state LAP. Once soldiers are recruited, drafted, or conscripted under the authoritarian state LAP, they are assigned roles in a rigidly hierarchical military by their superiors, and no mobility is allowed without permission. Rank, position, and rewards are generally fixed and determined by the superiors. Obedience is the most important virtue in the military.

Authoritarian state allocation of labor in nonmilitary settings did not start in the West until the eighteenth to nineteenth centuries, when civil servants and state employees became significant groups of workers in Britain, France, Germany, and later the United States and Japan. Despite apparent market mechanisms in the selection, allocation, and management of these civil servants and state employees, a prevalent and powerful presence of the state left a deep imprint of political institutions and logic. In that regard, almost every nation/ state today has an authoritarian state LAP of varied size and significance.

The Bolshevik revolution in 1917 led to the first nationwide authoritarian state LAP in history. The Soviet Union actually adopted the authoritarian state LAP to cover virtually the entire labor force in that vast and diverse country. Similar experiments soon took place in the West, as state-owned enterprises emerged in Britain and France after nationalization movements in the 1920s and 1930s. More radical and thorough Western versions of the authoritarian state LAP were established in Mussolini's Italy and a little later in Nazi Germany. In those cases, the majority of workers were not directly allocated by the fascist states; they were nonetheless tightly controlled and ultimately managed under Nazi-style corporatist institutions that clearly incorporated the polity, economy, and society into a totalitarian, state-centered institution: the fascist institutional structure.[19] After World War II, less comprehensive but similar and intense corporatist policies were adopted in many northern and western European nations.[20] State employees and the state's role in overall labor allocation have become common features of those nations.

Exemplified by those developed nations and especially by the centrally planned economies, the authoritarian state LAP was soon emulated by many formerly colonized nations and has been practiced around the globe since the 1950s. In places ranging from Korea and Taiwan to Mexico and Nigeria, a substantial portion of labor was either directly allocated or strongly controlled by the state. Political institutions and concerns were often guiding principles of labor allocation and management. Results varied across the nations because the political institutions and their goals differed tremendously. Many developing nations pursued state-led modernization, as reflected by the prevalence of the authoritarian state LAP. But the degrees to which such an LAP was implemented led to different outcomes of the modernization efforts. Some nations successfully established the market institution, to the extent that it became the dominant institution in labor allocation, and thus moved significantly toward modernity. Namely, their institutional structure acquired meaningful and sustainable differentiation between at least the economy and polity/society. Korea, Taiwan, and Singapore are good examples.[21]

The Authoritarian State LAP in China

By the mid-1990s, the Chinese urban sector was indisputably the most important sector of the Chinese economy, polity, and culture. The urban population, those with an urban household or residential registration (*hukou*), was relatively small. In 1993, the urban population was 249.8 million or 21.67 percent of the total population (SSB-PB 1993, 400, 402). Those people lived in 447 cities (*chengshi*—thirty-five of them having populations over 1 million), 1,936 county towns (*xiancheng*), and between 11,000 and 23,000 "established towns" (*jianzhizheng*).[22] More than 150 million of them were workers, producing over 70 percent of the Chinese GDP.[23] From 1949 to 1995, the urban population (no more than 20 percent of the total population) elected twice as many people's deputies to the CNPC as the rural population. By 1995, as a major political and legal reform, the rural population—nearly 80 percent of the nation—was for the first time allowed to elect the same number of people's deputies as the urban residents.[24] Most Chinese urban labor was still allocated and managed by the state under the authoritarian state LAP that was established by the CCP regime under Mao in the 1950s.

The Evolution of China's Authoritarian State LAP

The authoritarian state LAP, though practiced extensively by the CCP, was not an innovation of Mao nor the CCP. Rather, it has deep historical roots. An early authoritarian state LAP in China involved the state-owned slaves (*guanglu,* or official slaves) at the direct disposal of the imperial court. China's slavery system never reached the level of ancient Greece's, but there were numerous slaves as a result of war or political persecution and criminal punishment, throughout most of the dynasties. Historically, most of the slave labor was concentrated in the imperial mines and shops—state-owned industrial enterprises producing porcelain, iron and other metals, coins, salt, arms, and silk. This was institutionalized in the early Han dynasty (second century B.C.) and was largely inherited by subsequent rulers (Fan 1953, 46). Great numbers of prison inmates and prisoners of war were also forced to work on projects such as tomb building, hydro-facilities, canal excavating, and palace construction.[25] Many registered handicrafts households were also used in those state-owned shops. Those registered households were situated between the dominant family-based traditional LAP and an imperial state LAP, and thus had some features of both. Within their families/clans, labor was allocated based on family institutions. But under the political authority of the state, labor of the families was managed and allocated by the state.

Gradually, the forcibly state-employed families replaced state-owned slaves to become the main labor force in the imperial shops and mines. Sometimes, as in the Tang dynasty (seventh to tenth centuries), persons who provided handicrafts were registered with the government and required to serve in the state shops without pay for a set number of days each year.[26] As an interesting development among the pre-industrialized nations, the Chinese imperial state always controlled most industries except cotton textiles, which was primarily sideline work of millions of peasant households. This sometimes monopolistic position of the imperial state in industries staffed by state-allocated slaves and registered families was not undermined until after the eighteenth century. Not surprisingly, the state-owned shops tended to be inefficient, largely due to the incompetence and corruption of the managers. The private shops, family-based, were more competitive, especially by the eighteenth century (Zhu 1988, 39-45).

Challenged by Western powers after the mid-nineteenth century, the Qing dynasty began to establish certain industries to strengthen its military force. A substantial number of state-owned and -managed industrial enterprises gradually emerged, with profound impacts. By the end of the nineteenth century, the imperial state employed more than one-third of the total Chinese "modern industrial workers," while foreigners employed nearly 40 percent (Wang 1987, 4). This distortion of labor allocation was significantly expanded during the Republican era, especially during and after World War II when the GMD regime controlled nearly 45.3 percent of all Chinese industries and an even higher portion of industrial workers.[27] The huge state-owned businesses were, as one might expect, very inefficient. Their productivity was, in some cases, only 15 percent of similar private enterprises and only 6 percent of foreign-invested enterprises, which generally had a much more market-oriented LAP (Wang 1986, 23).

State-owned enterprises continued to play an important role in the economic development of Taiwan after 1949, based on the authoritarian state LAP of the GMD government. In 1952, over 57 percent of Taiwan's industrial production was controlled by the GMD party-state. Such a dominant position of state capitalism visibly persisted in energy, transportation, communications, public utilities, and grain distribution into modern-day Taiwan. A "dual economy of state-owned versus private economy," therefore, existed throughout the history of Taiwan and had a great impact on Taiwan's economic development (Peng 1995, 239-240, 243-251). By the mid-1990s, a substantial portion of the Taiwanese labor force was still allocated and managed by the GMDT state. Nearly half the workers, primarily state employees in state-owned enterprises, schools, and service industries, were not even covered by the 1984 Labor Standard Law, which stipulated basic benefits, wages, working conditions, and the right to strike and unionize.[28] The Labor Commission of the government had so much power over labor issues and disputes outside the state-owned sector that some Taiwanese economists believed the GMD state was still too intrusive and had distorted the Taiwanese labor market.[29]

In the guerrilla bases of the CCP from 1927 to 1949, a substantial authoritarian LAP was institutionalized and later became the LAP for CCP-controlled industry, commerce, education, and even social services such as medical care. Starting with the famous Great Production Campaign in 1942 (from which the word "gung-ho" became famous), under pressure from both the Japanese and GMD regime, Mao led the CCP's bureaucrats and army to become self-reliant economic actors. Quotas of production, mainly of food and clothes, were set for every cadre. By the time the CCP entered the cities as China's triumphant new ruler, an authoritarian allocation of labor had become the tradition and legacy of the CCP revolution. The then-influential Soviet Union and the Stalinist central planning system offered further justification for such tradition and legacy. Very swiftly, the PRC government decided to establish an authoritarian state LAP in the cities by directly taking over the GMD state employees of the Republic era. A sizable number of employees of foreign-invested enterprises, which were quickly confiscated, were treated in the same fashion. Finally, the socialization campaigns succeeded by the mid-1950s in destroying the private economy in the urban areas, thus completing the process of creating a nationwide authoritarian state LAP.[30]

In short, the authoritarian state LAP has existed in China for a very long time and has been practiced by rulers ranging from the monarchies to the GMD and CCP. A nationally dominant authoritarian state LAP, however, was established by the CCP in the 1950s. The moralistic nature of the traditional Chinese economy and the family-like institutional setting may have been a strong basis for such an LAP to perpetuate itself. Essentially, an authoritarian state LAP may be viewed as a nationwide family-based LAP in which the state—its ruler—allocates and manages labor as a father would among his family members. The institutional legitimacy of the authoritarian state LAP is, therefore, historically and ideologically well justified in China.

A Statistical Analysis of the Authoritarian State LAP

By the mid-1990s, most of the nearly 150 million Chinese urban laborers and a small number of rural workers (mainly rural cadres and certain professionals) were still under the PRC's authoritarian allocation and management.

Size

Since its full establishment in 1957, the authoritarian state LAP has covered 11 to 19 percent of China's labor force, as shown in table 2.1. It has been the dominant LAP in the urban economy, covering two-thirds to three-quarters of urban workers for most of the PRC's history. At times, as during the Great Leap Forward years (1958-1961), the state controlled more than 80 percent of the urban labor force, including the sizable CCP-PRC bureaucracy. The authoritarian LAP allocated the majority of the most productive urban labor force and thus acquired the greatest political and economic influence in the PRC. In addition, from 1949 to 1978, the CCP state forced an estimated 10 million people to work in labor camps.[31]

Over the years, the authoritarian state LAP varied in size relative to the total labor force. The wild swings and alternations of CCP economic policies and political campaigns were responsible for the swelling and forced reduction of state employees. It became stabilized, however, after the late 1970s, and the growth pace of the total labor force and state LAP became almost synchronized during the past twenty years. The state seemed to have become either unwilling to or incapable of increasing the size of the state LAP. Yet its size relative to the total urban labor force declined steadily after the Great Leap

Forward. This may be strong evidence of the substantial growth of other types of labor allocation in the cities, especially after the reform started in 1978 (more on these other types of LAPs in the

Table 2.1. State-Allocated Labor in China

Year	Size (millions)	% total labor force	% urban labor force*	Average income (rmb)	% average urban income
1952	15.80	7.62	63.56	446	100.22
1957	24.51	10.31	76.47	637	102.08
1960	50.44	19.49	82.43	528	103.33
1965	37.38	13.04	72.75	652	110.51
1970	47.92	13.92	75.92	609	108.56
1975	64.26	16.87	78.16	613	105.69
1976	68.60	17.66	78.92	605	105.22
1978	74.51	18.56	78.32	644	104.72
1979	76.93	18.75	76.94	705	105.54
1980	80.19	18.93	76.19	803	105.38
1981	83.72	19.15	75.74	812	105.18
1982	86.30	19.05	75.52	836	104.76
1983	87.71	18.89	74.67	865	104.72
1984	86.37	17.92	70.63	1,034	106.16
1985	89.90	18.03	70.19	1,213	105.56
1986	93.33	18.20	70.22	1,414	106.40
1987	96.54	18.29	70.04	1,546	105.96
1988	99.84	18.38	69.98	1,853	106.07
1989	101.08	18.27	70.24	2,055	106.20
1990	103.46	18.23	70.24	2,284	106.73
1991	106.64	18.27	69.85	2,477	105.85
1992	108.89	18.32	69.67	2,878	106.16
1993	111.12	18.30†	69.60†	3,160	106.16†
1994	114.13	18.30†	69.50†	4,788	106.16†

Notes: In Chinese official statistics, state-allocated labor is categorized as either employees of state-owned units (*danweis*) or employees of the *danweis* owned by all of the people. In fact, the Chinese authoritarian LAP covers many workers, in urban and rural areas, outside those state-owned *danweis*.

* Urban labor force includes four components: state employees, employees of collective enterprises, private employees and businessmen, and employees of foreign-invested enterprises.

† The ratio is assumed to be the same as the year before.

Sources: Figures are based on Gao et al. 1993, 581-582, 621-622; SSB-LM 1991, 7, 12, 28, 167; Zhang 1992, 275; *Renmin Ribao,* February 3, 1990, 1; December 13, 17, 1990, 1, 3; March 1, 1991, 1; and March 2, 1995, 2.

ext two chapters). One may conclude that the large transfer of rural labor to the urban sector during the past two decades has occurred primarily outside of state allocation. Overall, the authoritarian state LAP appears to be shrinking in the Chinese urban economy.

Income

Despite the egalitarian norms in the state-owned units (*danweis*), the income gap of the employees has developed unusually. In 1995, some *danwei* bosses and a few key workers could earn many times more than ordinary workers, often at the expense of the *danwei* and thus the state. Regional variations were also growing. The largest regional workers' wage difference was only 38 percent in 1985 (between Anhui and Guangdong Provinces). By 1994, it became 118 percent (between Shanghai and Jiangxi).[32] Historically, as shown by table 2.1, workers under the authoritarian state LAP were consistently paid more than their fellow urban workers. Some observers estimated that the income gap between state and nonstate employees may have been as large as 43 percent in 1992.[33] If the difference was fairly small at the beginning, it grew to be both significant and stable. It therefore becomes a major reason for the state to attract the best urban workers and to keep them. If the state could maintain the wage difference, the authoritarian state LAP could conceivably perpetuate itself for a considerable time.

It is important to point out, however, that the government's income statistics could be misleading. My own field work yields an impression that income statistics reported by Beijing after 1984 have been significantly lower than actual figures. As will be elaborated further on, much of the urban workers' income in the 1990s was neither reported nor recorded. Nationwide in 1994, the "official" wages/salary of most workers employed by the state constituted only 68 percent of their total income. Numerous bonuses, benefits, allowances, and distribution of consumer goods made up 32 percent of a typical state employee's income.[34] From 1990 to 1993, Beijing officially concluded that state employees on average had 2,448 rmb (77.5 percent of the average wages) "nonwage" additional income. Thus, the real average annual income of a state employee in 1993, for example, would have been 5,608 instead of 3,160 rmb.[35] It was not uncommon for 60 or even 90 percent of one's total income to come from those nonwage income sources.[36] Recently, private employees and even many collective employees have been paid considerably more than state em

Table 2.2. Industrial Distribution of the State LAP (1957-1990)

Years	1957	1962	1970	1975	1978	1982	1985	1987	1989	1990
Percent in manufacturing:*	41.6	43.0	49.9	49.4	49.8	48.6	50.0	49.7	49.0	48.7
Percent of industry's total employees:†	--	--	--	--	52.5	49.5	42.7	40.4	40.9	41.1
Percent of industry's urban employees:‡	75.9	74.3	77.6	73.6	72.7	69.8	68.2	67.9	68.2	68.0
Percent in agriculture:**	4.5	10.8	11.8	11.2	11.1	9.3	8.7	8.3	7.9	7.7
Percent of industry's total employees:†	0.6	1.7	2.1	2.4	2.9	2.6	2.5	2.5	2.4	2.3
Percent of industry's urban employees:‡	96.5	95.4	96.9	97.0	93.7	93.6	93.9	94.5	94.5	94.6
Percent in transportation/communication:	6.8	7.2	8.2	6.4	6.1	6.0	6.2	6.0	5.8	5.9
Percent of industry's total employees:†	--	--	--	--	61.2	60.6	45.4	41.9	41.2	41.3
Percent of industry's urban employees:‡	58.6	60.8	58.7	67.9	68.8	70.3	72.5	73.7	75.3	76.0
Percent in retail/service:	20.0	16.2	14.0	15.3	14.2	15.1	11.6	11.7	12.2	12.3
Percent of industry's total employees:†	--	--	--	--	77.4	66.1	37.3	35.4	35.7	35.7
Percent of industry's urban employees:‡	76.0	66.1	62.3	81.6	81.9	76.1	55.4	56.5	57.7	58.0

Table 2.2. Industrial Distribution of the State LAP (1957-1990) —Continued

Years	1957	1962	1970	1975	1978	1982	1985	1987	1989	1990
Percent in education/media/culture:††	10.7	11.0	8.5	8.3	9.0	9.6	10.3	10.6	10.7	10.7
Percent of industry's total employees:†	--	--	--	--	61.7	73.1	72.7	74.5	76.2	76.2
Percent of industry's urban employees:‡	93.2	92.4	90.6	90.8	91.6	95.0	96.2	96.8	97.2	97.1
Percent in CCP/state agencies:	11.4	8.0	6.5	5.7	5.6	6.5	7.7	8.1	8.5	8.7
Percent of industry's total employees:†	--	--	--	--	89.3	92.1	86.5	84.1	84.1	83.7
Percent of industry's urban employees:‡	98.9	98.1	97.8	97.6	97.0	97.6	96.2	96.0	97.1	97.2
Percent in others:‡‡	5.0	3.8	1.1	3.7	4.2	4.9	5.5	5.6	5.9	6.0

Notes: Figures are based on SSB-LM 1991, 8-14. Totals may not be exactly 100 percent due to rounding of decimals.

* Includes construction and energy industries.

† Includes irrigation project workers, "sent-down" rural technical cadres, and employees of state-owned farms.

‡ Includes TV, filmmaking, and other entertainment industries.

** Includes scientists, bankers, health care providers, social workers, athletes, and sports managers.

†† The authoritarian state-allocated labor as the percentage of total workers in that industry. Statistically, some industries existed only in the cities until 1978.

‡‡ The authoritarian state-allocated labor as the percentage of all urban employees in that industry. Some enterprises of the industry in the cities may not have been state-owned, but the authoritarian LAP often existed, to a lesser extent, in those enterprises governing technical professionals and cadres.

ployees. Foreign-invested enterprises have been paying several times more to attract the best workers. State-owned employers, however, were not entirely losing the competition. They were still attractive to many workers because of their ability to provide cheap housing, better health insurance, other benefits, and stabler employment.

Distribution

Most workers covered by the Chinese authoritarian state LAP were in state-owned enterprises (*qiye*)—manufacturing, transportation, retailing, service, and institutions (*shiye*) such as government agencies and schools. Two-thirds to three-quarters of the urban industrial workers were allocated and managed by this LAP. It is interesting to note that the state allocated nearly all of the small number of urban dwellers working in the agricultural sector, primarily as visiting and temporary technical professionals and other rural cadres such as teachers, inspectors ("working team" members), and officials. The state clearly had firm dominance over employees in the areas of education, media, culture, and entertainment. Except in the rural elementary and middle schools, where numerous teachers and other workers might not be state employees, the PRC state employed almost all the teachers, professors, journalists, artists, entertainers, and related engineers and technicians. Although the state allocated less than one-third of retailing and service workers, it still managed more than half the retail and service employees in the cities. In the important transportation and communication industries, more than three-quarters of the workers in urban areas were state employees; but nationwide, state employees only count for less than half of the total workers in transportation and communication industries because of the many private households (*getihus*) that specialized in short-distance transportation in the rural areas.

Historically, as table 2.2 shows, the industrial composition of the state LAP changed visibly. One recent development was profound: although the state still directly allocated and managed nearly 69 percent of the urban industrial working force, it controlled less than 42 percent of the industrial employees nationwide due to the rise of rural industries or the township-village enterprises. Such a development implies that many workers of the proletarian working class, supposedly the vanguards of the CCP and ruling class of the PRC, were increasingly outside state allocation and management. On the one hand, this could cause a serious problem of justification for the existing authoritarian state LAP; on the other hand, it indicates that the nonstate LAPs have been allocating an increasing number of industrial workers who produce most of the Chinese economic output.

Another interesting finding is that the CCP state tried to penetrate the countryside by sending its employees to work in the villages (formerly the communes). During the reform years this effort decreased somewhat, but state employees working in the agricultural sector still constituted a considerable portion, almost as large as the government employees.

The authoritarian state LAP declined the most in the retail and service industries during the reform years. Its share of the labor force in those industries fell in just twelve years by more than 40 percent nationwide and 22 percent in the cities. Retailing and service have been among the industries most sensitive to the market influence. This may be a good indicator of how much ground the market institution had gained vis-à-vis the state in labor allocation in the PRC by the 1990s.

The CCP and central government have maintained absolute control over every aspect of Chinese education, the news media, and entertainment and have employed most of the workers in those industries. The presence of the state LAP actually increased from 62 to 76 percent nationwide and from 92 to 97 percent in urban areas, in twelve years. Even the number of state employees in those industries increased. Beijing apparently worked hard to maintain its control of personnel in these vital industries/professions. In the transportation and communication industries, the state LAP shrank by almost 20 percent nationwide but increased from 69 to 76 percent in the urban areas. The cause of the national shrinking was the rapid development of rural transportation run by specialized families and some private employers; the increase of the urban labor share illustrates that the PRC Government strengthened its position in the crucial communication and transportation industries during Deng Xiaoping's reform years.

Institutions

After many changes, merges, reorganizations, and re-reorganizations, by the late 1990s the PRC central government had four ministries under the State Council directly responsible for the functioning of its huge authoritarian LAP: the State Planning Commission, the State Education Commission, the Ministry of

Personnel, and the Ministry of Labor. The ultimate authority in decision making, however, clearly rested in the hands of the CCP Central Committee and its politburo.[37] Every province, metropolis, city, and county had its own bureaus or offices as branches of these four ministries and commissions. Those local offices and bureaus were "politically and organizationally led by the local party committees" of the CCP but "professionally under the guidance of " the respective commissions or ministries in Beijing (Hu et al. 1993, 939). Other government agencies—thirty-nine ministries and nearly seventy central bureaus and ministry-level agencies by the mid-1990s—had their own authority and responsibility in managing and allocating labor within their own jurisdictions.[38] Some of the agencies, such as the Ministry of Metallurgy or the Ministry of Machinery and Electronics, might make their own specific policies, based on state rules, governing millions of workers.[39]

State Planning Commission

The State Planning Commission is responsible for drawing up annual and five-year plans for state labor allocation. Considered higher than other ministries, the Planning Commission makes its plans based on past experience, requests from other ministries and provincial and local governments, and the findings of research and studies by its staff. The commission sets up national quotas and enforces them with backing of the full authority of the PRC central government. It plans the number of industries and new hires there would be in each province or metropolis every year; how many rural laborers can be hired by the state and thus be granted urban residency (the urban *hukou*) in each locality; and the pay scale and promotion schedule for all state employees; how many students will be enrolled in the colleges and professional schools; and how many graduates each province will get as state employees.[40] The commission also approves major construction projects, related state appropriations, and hiring quotas. Although there is no special bureau within the commission to plan labor allocation, thirteen of the twenty-four functional bureaus are involved in the authoritarian state LAP (Qian 1990, 154). The decisions of the State Planning Commission, once approved by the State Council, are mandatory to the state agencies and state-owned *danweis*. The commission has rather broad powers in monitoring the implementation of its plans through its local branches and ad hoc inspection teams.[41]

State Education Commission

The State Education Commission is charged with training and providing an educated labor force. The commission has managed and allocated teachers, professors, and other education employees. Since it was established, the commission's most important role concerning the authoritarian state LAP has been managing and allocating college graduates and specialists. The much larger number of middle and high school graduates have not been guaranteed a state job based on their academic credentials, thus have not been directly allocated by the Education Commission. Each year, under the guidance of the State Planning Commission, the Education Commission performs two important functions. First, it draws up and implementes a plan during the summer on recruitment to be carried out by colleges, graduate schools, and technical and professional schools (most of them owned and run by the state). The plan stipulates exactly how many students in how many majors are to be recruited by each school. All enrolled students get a basically free higher education and are virtually guaranteed state-assigned jobs after graduation.[42]

Second, the commission draws up and implements a plan, from early spring to early fall, for the number of college graduates (recently including some graduates of nonstate-owned but state-certified colleges in Beijing and other major cities) expected to be allocated by the state. Working with the Planning Commission, the Education Commission allocates those graduates according to a few politically decided principles, including "supporting the development of the remote and poor areas of the nation"; "the assigned job should be relevant to what one learned in school"; "sending more to the grassroots *danweis*"; "the graduates may have a certain career choice"; "state employers may have some choice or testing rights"; or simply, "assigning the college graduates jobs near their hometown" (Zhu 1991, 284-292).

The demands by the various ministries, local governments, and *danweis* play an important role in the formulation of assignment quotas. Quotas and allocating principles are handed down to the individual colleges and schools, and every graduate is then assigned a job by the state, through the authorities in the colleges/universities. After receiving the proper papers for the assignment and the appropriate urban *hukou* cards, the graduates then proceed to their respective *danweis* to report to work. The graduate's dossier (*dangan*) is sent through government channels from the school to the *danwei*. The new state employee is then subject to the management of the bosses at that particular *danwei*. If a graduate refuses to accept a particular job or place and fails to change the assignment through connections and back-door activities, he or she is forced to leave school within three months and cannot be hired by any state-owned *danwei* for five years.[43] In 1996, there were nearly 860,000 college graduates and postgraduates and more than 2 million professional school graduates being allocated by the Education Commission.[44]

Personnel Ministry

The Personnel Ministry of the State Council has the authority to allocate and manage the cadres and other white-collar workers, about 27 million in the late 1980s.[45] By 1991, an incomplete estimate put the size of Chinese cadres at around 35 million (SSB-LM 1991, 167-168). This ministry was established, eliminated, and reestablished in the history of the PRC because the CCP leadership had different views on the notion of cadres at different times. The Personnel Ministry establishes policies for all state-owned *danweis* to follow. Pay scales, promotion schedules, benefits, job requirements, and recruitment and dismissal of the cadres are visibly different from those rules governing blue-collar workers made by the Labor Ministry. Political loyalty and correctness, as shown by one's past record in the *dangan,* as well as personal connections, are crucial in the allocation and utilization of a cadre. "All the civil servants," stated the ministry, "are required to keep unity with the CCP central authority."[46] Together with the Foreign Experts Office of the State Council, the Personnel Ministry also has authority to recruit and manage "foreign experts," namely foreign professionals and specialists.[47]

In Chinese terminology, the term "cadre" is distinguished from four other major social groups of "the people": "workers," "peasants," "soldiers," and "students." It usually refers to two major categories of state employees: (1) politicians, government bureaucrats, administrative personnel above the rank of government clerk or military platoon leader; and (2) managerial and white-collar workers not engaged in production work in the enterprises. The other categories include specialists and professionals such as scientists, engineers, and technicians; teachers and professors; journalists, publishers, health care personnel above the rank of senior nurse; and artists, musicians, actors, and dancers (Emerson 1973, 10-11). They also include lawyers, accountants, and the "elected" people's deputies.[48] (Further on, table 2.3 provides the most recent nine categories of the cadres in the PRC.)

Almost all new hires by the state with a college education or above are considered cadres. Since the 1960s, a limited number of workers and peasants have been hired or promoted as cadres, often on a temporary and case-by-case basis (Zhang 1987, 117-118). To maintain some flexibility in the vast countryside and in the state-owned enterprises, the CCP, through the Personnel Ministry, adopts a contract (*pinyong,* 聘用) system under which the personnel bureaus hire temporary cadres to staff local government below the county level and state-owned enterprises.[49] Appointment of these *pinyong* cadres is for a fixed term, and if not renewed, they are required to return to their previous posts, *danweis,* or localities and will lose their pay and other benefits, with generally a lump sum of departing pay or pension.[50] Those hired from among the rural residents will lose their temporary urban *hukou* as well.[51]

It is indeed interesting to note that in the PRC, the boundaries between cadres and other types of state employees, mainly workers, have been clearly set and rather rigidly maintained even inside a state-owned *danwei* or within the government. In recent years a manager or supervisor of a state-owned enterprise could appoint a worker as a cadre or a professional and pay him or her accordingly; but it was still the policy that the worker's original state-assigned "status of being a worker should not be changed."[52] This was still the case in the late 1990s. Labor mobility in China, therefore, has been further lowered by this strict barrier of identification.

The appointment and assignment of leading cadres are politically sensitive and profound duties of the Personnel Ministry, and consequently are closely monitored by the CCP. The list of candidates for local officials, "elected" posts, "responsible cadres," and heads of state-owned *danweis* is generally proposed to the Personnel Ministry by the Organization Department of the CCP's Central Committee, and by organization departments of local CCP committees to the local personnel bureaus. These candidates are appointed by the personnel bureaus without any "open examination" or competition.[53] The leading cadres in the government, generally heads of agencies and local authorities, are not even subject to the PRC Civil Servants Regulation. Their allocation is, therefore, even more political and authoritarian.[54] If any state-owned *danwei* needs to recruit on a national basis to find high-level professionals to staff its key positions, it has to get approval from the National Talents Exchange Center of the Personnel Ministry before putting out ads.[55]

In short, the authoritarian nature of the Chinese state LAP and the dominance of the CCP have been most prevalent in the allocation and management of the Chinese cadres.[56]

Labor Ministry

The Labor Ministry is responsible for the demand, training, supply, allocation, and migration of blue-collar workers in state-owned enterprises and institutions, estimated at around 80 to 90 million allocated by the authoritarian state LAP in 1992 (Gao 1993, 582). As the designated governmental agency handling labor affairs, the Labor Ministry also makes policies governing nonstate employers such as urban collective enterprises, township and village enterprises, private employers, and foreign-invested enterprises. The ministry, through its local branches and offices in almost every state-owned *danwei,* decides and regulates recruitment, pay, benefits, training, promotion, reassignment, union affairs, labor protection, and dismissal of all state-employed workers. Many of its regulations and rules, such as those regarding benefits and insurance, are applicable to the cadres as well. The ministry plays an important role in deciding recruitment quotas by each and every state *danwei*. Without the approval of the labor bureaus, for example, the state-owned *danweis* cannot hire any permanent workers nor alter their pay scales.[57] Individual workers need approval of the labor bureau to change either jobs or *danweis.*

Another duty of the Labor Ministry and its local bureaus and offices was the so-called Reemployment Project implemented in thirty-two major cities in 1995, after a rather successful experiment in Shanghai in 1994. According to the PRC's Regulation on the Arrangement of Surplus Labor in State-Owned Enterprises, administrative reallocation of labor inside the enterprises would be the main solution to the problem of surplus workers.[58] Essentially, this politically motivated project called for mainly administrative and media forces to mobilize state-owned enterprises and other employers to train and hire as many as possible of newly dismissed surplus workers (the so-called *xiagang,* or "off-duty"), who numbered around 140,000 in Shanghai alone.[59] In one city, Shengyang, only about 20 percent of the 14,000 reemployed surplus workers (about 60 percent of the total *xiagang* workers) went on to the labor market as genuinely unemployed. The rest were either reallocated internally or within the same system of the original enterprises.[60]

Even after the PRC made changes to increase the autonomy of individual state-owned enterprises, hoping to encourage competition, the labor bureaus still have final authority in the dismissal of any state employees. The supposedly autonomous management of a state-owned enterprise can fine or penalize a worker, with the consent of the local labor bureau. But to dismiss a useless or even trouble-making worker is still extremely difficult, for the local labor bureaus tend to force the management to keep the workers employed to avoid the social and political problems of unemployment. Such a political rationale naturally causes big headaches for many managers. After being forced by the local labor bureau to retract his decision to dismiss two "never-working and constantly trouble-making thieves," one frustrated manager of a state-owned enterprise in Anhui Province commented in early 1995, "The labor bureau just simply wants you to keep as many people as possible [to avoid the headache of assigning jobs for those fired] now, with no regard to the issue of economic efficiency. If we cannot discipline our workers, how can we run our enterprises for profit?"[61]

Labor Union

Labor unions first emerged in China in the early twentieth century. The CCP successfully utilized the unions in its political struggles against the GMD regime until 1949. After the establishment of the PRC, a "worker's state," the unions were soon incapacitated as a political organization. Unlike in the West, labor unions have never been independent players in China's labor allocation, despite their importance asserted in the CCP's and PRC's official statements. The unions, mainly their leading cadres, participated marginally in labor management in urban China.[62] The unions were organized in a very hierarchical way and elected as a national governing body an All China Trade Union, which had by 1995 101.8 million members.[63] The headquarters of the All China Trade Union is a ministry-level government agency itself and has the responsibility of organizing workers as a "major mass organization and an important political group under the leadership of the CCP."[64] Union expenditures come primarily from government appropriations, payments of at least 2 percent of the total wages from the *danweis,* including the foreign-invested enterprises, membership dues, and other income from union activities.[65] Deng Xiaoping said illustratively about these state unions' mission back in 1978, that the "trade unions should educate all the union members to protect the highly centralized administrative authority in the enterprises."[66]

In 1983, the CCP issued an "important directive" addressing the then 270,000 union cadres. That directive called upon the union officials, based on the understanding that the unions are mass organizations led by the party, to make themselves the home of the workers.[67] In 1990, the CCP issued another major directive for Strengthening the Party's Leadership over the Works of the Trade Union, the Communist Youth League, and the Woman's Association to further incorporate those "social organizations" into the "unified leadership" of the CCP over the Chinese people.

Therefore, the Chinese trade union has been a typical state and company union with a very limited independent role. It may be viewed as an arm of the CCP's authoritarian state LAP, charged with organizing and educating workers for the state and CCP. The most the unions have done is generally welfare work—disaster relief and consolation, recreational activities, limited representation of workers in disputes, and minimal monitoring of *danwei* bosses in their dealings on labor and wage issues. The CCP often "task" the unions to help implement certain policies in the state-owned enterprises. In 1995-1996, for example, the unions were officially reported to have successfully assisted the state in turning more than two thousand enterprises from losing money to becoming profitable.[68]

Because the union bosses are state-employed cadres, the unions become an institutional part of the *danweis* rather than independent workers' organizations helping to advance their interests. In most state-owned enterprises, the full-time professional union leaders often are viewed as idlers, although they might have been officially ranked as deputy chiefs. More often than not, they are former military officers allocated to the enterprises as cadres with high ranks but with no special expertise. In many cases, semi-retired former *danwei* bosses fill the "easy" posts of union officers. In nonenterprise *danweis*, the role and position of the unions tend to be even less relevant.

Primarily among the nonstate employees and especially outside the state-owned enterprises, a genuine labor union may be in the process of being formed.[69] However, greater development of the Chinese market economy may need to occur before any genuine labor union can emerge in China. What has happened in three other Chinese environments may offer some clue to the prospect of labor unions in China. Company and state unions have become very important in both Singapore and Taiwan after decades of impressive development of the market economy. A so-called corporatist relationship among the state, employers, and unions is generally identifiable in those two places.[70] In Hong Kong, the CCP and the GMD have controlled the left and right wings of the noncompany unions. The largest independent labor union, the Hong Kong Confederation of Trade Unions (HKCTU), has been under pressure from the CCP as the future ruler of Hong Kong, as the current ruler of the British, and as a major power contender of the GMD in the territory.[71] Given that Hong Kong and Taiwan have contributed most of the foreign investment in the PRC, the experience of the labor movements in Hong Kong and Taiwan may have some deep relevance to the future of unions in China. We probably should not expect an independent labor union to play the same role as unions in countries like Argentina or Brazil, although a genuine labor movement is likely to develop and the assertiveness of some union officials may increase.

Danweis

The most peculiar institution of the Chinese authoritarian state LAP has been the unit (*danwei*) structure with its associated dossier (*dangan*) system. Functionally, *danweis* are the cells of the authoritarian state LAP and hence the major cells of China's institutional structure. Despite their importance, *danweis* have been underexposed in Western literature.[72] This section describes the *danwei* structure and its evolution under the Chinese authoritarian state LAP.

Origins
Danweis originated in the pre-PRC years. Borrowed from military techniques, they organized people into relatively independent units to carry out most of the political, economic, and social functions. China's millennia-old family-like institutional structure provided the general environment and source of legitimacy for the *danweis*. Families, clans, and villages had been the institutional structures of Chinese economic, social, and even political activities. Group identity under such structures has been largely determined by genetic bonds and geographic proximity, and social institutions served as the basis. Challenged by the imported market institution after the nineteenth century, Chinese group identity began to have new sources. One of these new sources was the development of interest similarities based on economic activities. A guild system and trade associations, as well as underground societies, developed. Another source was the politically created *danweis,* begun by the GMD and then greatly strengthened by the CCP. Over time, the *danweis* replaced clans and neighborhoods to become the primary group identity of most urban residents and substantial numbers of rural people. Virtually everyone was

organized as a stable or even permanent member of a *danwei,* which could be a factory, commune, school, college, government agency, military unit, dance troupe, street committee, shop, restaurant, or even a religious temple.[73] In modern Taiwan, *danweis* continue to have great significance.[74]

Unit membership assures roughly fair, if not always equal, treatment of everyone in the group. The CCP and PRC established a comprehensive *hukou-* and *danwei*-based supply system for urban residents over the decades, deeply reinforcing the role of *danweis* in almost every aspect of people's lives. *Danweis* effectively became small societies or even "families."[75] Differences among the *danweis* grew significantly over time, and thus unit membership became very important and increasingly rigid. *Danweis* were no longer just places to work; they became institutions that affected every member's economic well-being, political activities, social life, and even personal life. Thus, in contemporary China, people identify and evaluate each other first and foremost by what *danwei* they belong to rather than by their career or occupation, as people commonly do in the United States.

Figure 2.1. The *Danweis*: Three Types and Six Ranks

Types

1. "Institution" (*shiye,* 事业):
   Government agencies, CCP agencies, political parties, "mass organizations" such as the women's association, military, etc.
   They rely basically on state appropriations.
2. "Semi-institution and semi-enterprise" (*benshiye-benqiye,* 半事业半企业):
   Hospitals, media, museums, research institutes,* schools, temple, etc.
   They rely on state appropriations and self-created income.
3. "Enterprise" *(qiye,* 企业):
   Factories, firms, banks, research institutes,* etc.
   They rely basically on self-created income.

Notes: By 1993, an estimated 28 million workers were employed by the state in institutions and semi-institutions and more than 70 million were employed by the state in enterprises.

* By 1995, there were 13,700 various R&D *danweis* employing a total of 17.59 million technical professionals and scientists. Eight thousand were part of the enterprises and about five thousand were semi-enterprises belonging to governments above the level of counties.

Figure 2.1. The *Danweis*: Three Types and Six Ranks-Continued

---

Ranks

First: the central (*zhongyang*, 中央):
    The CCP Central Committee; the Central Military Commission; the State
    Council; and the Standing Committee of the CNPC.
Second: ministry, provincial, field army, or military region (*sheng/jun*, ,省军):
    Other examples: general or national state-owned corporations; the Chinese
    Science Academy and the Chinese Social Science Academy; a "democratic
    party's" central committee; the central bank; *Renmin Ribao;* the CCTV.†
Third: bureau, prefecture, military division (*ting/ju* or di/shi, 厅局 or 地市):
    Other examples: universities; major state-owned group corporations; major
    cities; district governments of Beijing, Shanghai, and Tianjing; state-owned
    research institutes; provincial newspapers; TV stations.‡
Fourth: division, county, military regiment (*xian/tuan*, 县团):
    Other examples: sizable state-owned factories; district governments of major
    cities; newspapers and TV stations of prefectures or major cities; smaller colleges;
    important schools.
Fifth: section, township (*ke* or *xiangzheng*, øΔ or 乡镇):
    Other examples: military battalion; factory workshops; street committees in
    major cities; county newspapers and TV/radio stations; typical schools.
Sixth: subsection (*gu*, 股):
    Administrative village, street committees, military company.
    Other examples: smaller schools; township clinics; working sections or teams
    in factories.

Notes: † Some *danweis* may have a rank that is above ministry/provincial but
lower than the central rank: e.g., the headquarters of the PLA's ground, naval and air
forces, the seven major military regions, and the Chinese People's Supreme Court.
    ‡ Some *danweis* can acquire a deputy-ministry/provincial rank. For example, there
were sixteen deputy-provincial level cities, including the famous Shenzhen SEZ, in
the late 1990s.
    Sources: CNDC 1989; Yuan 1994; Qi 1993, 234, 279, 323; Qian 1990; author's
field notes in 1989, 1992, 1993, and 1995; *Renmin Ribao-Overseas,* May 24, 1995,
1; and *Shenzhen Renshi* (Shenzhen personnel) (Shenzhen), no. 6, (1995): 17.

Functions
    Danweis have had very important functions in contemporary
China, primarily in the urban areas.
    1. *Danweis* have come to be the basic and most important eco-
nomic institution in the urban areas. A *danwei* is the employer, the
provider. Internally, an institutionalized equality and fairness exists.
Externally, however, different *danweis* provide quite differently for

their members. By the mid-1990s, Beijing categorized its *danweis* into three types (see figure 2.1): institutions, semi-institution/semi-enterprises, and enterprises. For the institutions, the state appropriates all funds for wages and has tight control over recruitment and management of employees, as well as pay scales and promotions. The semi-institution and semi-enterprises *danweis* get only part of their wage funds from state appropriation. They generally have income of their own and so have certain flexibility in making decisions on pay scales, promotion, and hiring temporary help. The enterprises *danweis* pay for their employees from their own income. State standards of pay and promotion are used only for reference, although there is still strict control over the hiring of permanent or contract state employees. The state guarantees only a very minimum wage for every employee in the state-owned or even some "large collective," or "local state-owned," enterprises.[76]

Unlike in the institution type of *danweis,* if an enterprise fell into financial difficulty, employees would get only minimum pay and benefits (usually 75 percent of their wages and no important bonuses). If an enterprise went bankrupt, the employees could theoretically become unemployed and live on pitiful unemployment benefits. Practically, however, as will be discussed later, very few state-owned enterprises are allowed to go bankrupt. They could declare themselves to be any rank and pay their employees accordingly, after their financial obligations to the state. But they remain in the same, original rank in the eyes of the state and its agencies.

Pay, under the authoritarian state LAP, may have been nationally fixed within each type of *danwei,* but actual economic benefits varied significantly. In a typical state-owned *danwei,* more than twenty different "fees" or "subsidies" could be recorded as benefits, in addition to wages that could have up to six different components (Yuan 1994, 220). The inherent differences in the nature of a *danwei* determines the members' quality of life. Dramatically different lives are offered to members allocated or assigned to different places ranging from heavy labor in dirty environments to glamorous opportunities in clean offices. Even during the most "revolutionary," thus most egalitarian, Mao era, actual monetary benefits provided by different *danweis* could vary dramatically. In the lucky *danweis,* additional financial resources were generally shared by everyone, from the directors to the janitors. Among the hundreds of government agencies in Beijing, for example, some, like the ministries of foreign trade, national security, and the arsenal, were financially well-endowed and could therefore afford to provide relatively spacious housing, generous vacations, good child care, and other benefits to their members. In many other less fortunate *danweis,* such as many universities and "nonessential" CCP offices, people's real income was substantially lower.

This *danwei*-based income discrepancy worsened drastically during the reform years as the *danweis* acquired more autonomous authority in allocating financial resources under their control.[77] Thus, today millions of Chinese urban workers essentially live in thousands of *danwei*-based small "welfare states," criticized by many reformers as grossly inefficient "enterprises-run small societies."[78]

Like families, the *danweis* generally treat their members in a more or less "fair and equal" way. In 1995, in Beijing University, for example, a professor still got exactly the same amount of fees for books and periodicals as a boiler attendant.[79] During the reform era, when wage reform was an issue in the increasingly autonomous enterprises, it sometimes took massive, *danwei*-wide participation to determine a fair pay scale for workers on each different post and shift. In one model case, all 250 posts and shifts were carefully evaluated by every one of the forty-five hundred employees on the basis of required skills, physical demands, importance to the factory, working environment, popularity of the job title, and safety risks. Then each post and shift was given a score as the basis for a pay scale.[80] Similarly, penalties were often applied to a *danwei* or sub-*danwei* as a whole, rather than to individuals. It was hoped that the internal mechanisms of the *danwei* would then mobilize everyone to respond collectively to the penalties.[81] Furthermore, as with families, the boundaries of the *danweis* were quite rigid. The fate one got when assigned to a particular *danwei* was usually permanent. The real rewards of working, therefore, depended on the *danwei* much more than on the productivity or talents of the worker. An average worker's income in two similar *danweis* in the same industry could differ by as much as ten times.[82] So "to get into a good *danwei*" has been the most important and most effective way to elevate one's economic status. This has created a great source of political power based on the manipulation of access to "good *danweis*."

2. Replacing clans and families, *danweis* have become the most important political group in urban China. Most political activities are carried out in the *danweis,* and for everyone in those units, the authority of the *danwei* bosses matters significantly more than the abstract authority of the PRC state.[83] *Danweis* also provide important political identification and protection to their members. For virtually

every Chinese urban resident, *danweis* are the only place for their political indoctrination, political bargaining and grouping, influence exertion, and formation of authority.

The political and administrative function of the *danweis* depend heavily on the *dangan* system. Each laborer, a worker or a cadre, has a permanent dossier, *dangan,* kept by his *danwei* as the basis of evaluation. A typical *dangan* collects ten kinds of materials recording personal information on everyone: a resume and updates; an autobiography and updates; regular appraisals by superiors and peers; all sorts of test results; political history and investigation into that history; party and other associations; awards and honors; penalties and confessions; professional credentials, diplomas, degrees, and certificates; and promotion or demotion records. Other materials include personal writings and reports and ultimately eulogy and death certificates.[84] Generally, the Chinese start to accumulate their *dangan* after middle/high school graduation. The content is only available to their superiors and, rarely, to peers. Only specialized *dangan* cadre(s), under authorization of the *danwei* bosses, can alter or add to the *dangan,* or remove materials. Personal revenge, false entries, and special favors are thus part of the game. Because a worker almost never gets to see his or her own *dangan,* the *danwei* bosses, through their access to it, acquire a tremendous and almost mystical power over their subordinates. Every state employee has to have a *dangan* to be employed, transferred, or promoted. If a worker resigns or is fired, his or her *dangan* would normally by transferred to the worker's street committee or township (*xiang*). Historically, the *dangan* has become a major barrier to labor mobility, for a *danwei* boss can block labor movement by simply—and easily—holding on to a worker's *dangan.*[85]

3. *Danweis* have became the cells of society and for many people are the only social institutions other than their immediate families. Over time, some *danweis* have even become a sort of family. Marriages within *danweis* are very common, especially in those *danweis* that are relatively isolated from other communities. Many families have literally every member for as many as three generations working in the same *danwei.*[86] Such inbreeding reached its peak during the 1970s and early 1980s (Zhang 1987, 149). Despite an official ban on internal recruitment (*neizhao*) in 1987, almost all state-owned enterprises (less so in government agencies) still had ways to give first consideration to job candidates from within. Child care, education, and health care are organized and provided on a *danwei* basis. Sports,

recreation, and entertainment are usually *danwei* affairs. As in the villages, weddings and funerals have to have a *danwei* presence to make them socially accepted.

The Authoritarian State LAP in the 1990s

Under the authoritarian state LAP, all employees, cadres, and workers are guaranteed lifetime jobs, making them so-called fixed/ permanent workers (*gudinggong*) (Walder 1986, 73). Resignation was almost unheard of until very recently, when studying abroad and being employed by foreign or private employers became realistic alternatives. Usually, only under state planning and with the approval of superiors and the labor or personnel bureaus could a worker be switched, reassigned, or shifted from one *danwei* or place to another, or change job or profession. Even reassigning working spouses of military officers has been considered a long-standing problem under this LAP. A special joint order from the State Council and the Central Military Commission was required for an attempt to solve the depressing problem of the separation of "thousands of families of PLA officers" in 1990.[87] Because clear and rigid barriers between the cadres and workers are basically insurmountable, regular appraisals keep employees under tight authority of superiors, and lower-ranking superiors under the power of higher bosses

To manage the laborers once they were allocated, or assigned, at the local and *danwei* levels, the authoritarian state LAP had a structure that combined three sets of hierarchically organized agencies. The cadres' section/division served as the executive office of the CCP local or *danwei* committee's personnel department, and managed the cadres and other professionals; the labor and salary section/division was the executive office of the *danwei*'s manager, taking care of labor management and salary issues; the worker's education section/ division, under the CCP committee's propaganda department, manager, or trade union, trained workers. All these agencies and offices were responsible to a unitary party leadership.[88]

Reforms

The lifetime employment system experienced changes during the two decades of the reform era. The main motivation behind the changes was to "correct" the problem of low efficiency and to create a real "socialist" labor system with superior efficiency and more human character than the capitalist one.[89] Resignation became possible and feasible due to the development of alternative LAPs. Even the *dangan* restriction could be circumvented. Determined workers could first resign from a *danwei* and have their *dangan* transferred to their street committee; then, using some connections and give-and-take, they could transfer their *dangan* to a new employer. For professionals and cadres, there came to be *danweis* called centers of talents exchange (*rencai jiaoliu zhongxin*), where for a fee between 45 rmb and 200 rmb per month in Beijing, one could "check in" his or her *dangan* while working in new places, primarily private and foreign-invested enterprises that did not care much about the *dangan*.[90] Managers of state-owned enterprises were encouraged to be market-oriented and were granted the right to recruit and even dismiss workers. Officially, they were also given the right to refuse assigned labor from the local labor bureaus if the new workers were economically unwanted (Yang 1986, 28-29). But practically, very few enterprise managers have really been able to exercise those new powers.

The year 1986 was an important one in the history of the Chinese authoritarian state LAP. The State Council issued four important though provisional directives and regulations on the reform of the labor system, followed by new regulations on managers, trade unions, and CCP organizations in the state-owned enterprises.[91] Subsequently, increasing numbers of state employees, primarily in the industrial enterprises, have become contract employees, supposedly subject to market allocation.[92] New employees were generally required to be contracted rather than permanent workers. Already employed blue-collar workers were being transferred to the contract employment system as part of an experiment of "smashing the iron rice bowl and iron chair." According to the Beijing Labor Bureau, seventeen large and medium Beijing state-owned enterprises adopted an "all contract employment" system, and fourteen thousand employees changed their permanent employee status to contract workers in 1990.[93] Workers employed under a contract system were required to sign with the *danwei* for a fixed term of six months to ten years, depending on the nature and the needs of the employer, the skills and seniority of the employees, and other state policies. Workers who had been working in the *danwei* for a very long time and/or were beyond certain ages (fifty for males, forty-five for females) might be granted a lifetime employment contract. At the end of an ordinary contract term, both sides had the right to terminate it, but the *danweis* were expected to avoid this if the worker had observed the contract and had had "no major wrongdoing" (Labor Ministry 1991, 7-8). Conflicts and disputes over a labor contract were subject to the decisions of a Labor Arbitration Commission, usually an office of the local labor bureau or civil courts. A dual employment was thus created in the state-owned enterprises, with all sorts of new issues. To implement contract employment and to deal with the increasing problem of open unemployment, a national labor security and medical insurance system was under experiment in the late 1990s.[94]

Market-oriented reforms, therefore, have begun to have a limited but lasting impact on the lifetime employment of the authoritarian state LAP. The process, however, has been slow and quickly distorted. By 1991, only 14.9 percent of state-employed workers were contract workers (Hu Ping et al. 1993, 648). In the most open and most reformed province, Guangdong, roughly half of the state-employed industrial workers had become contract workers by 1995. A national target was set to have basically all state-employed industrial workers become contract workers by the end of 1996.[95] This deadline was met only with substantial distortion of the contract employment system.

Field studies in 1995-1997 found that most of those contract employees quickly became equal members of the *danweis,* just like the permanent employees. Contract workers were paid a little higher than the permanent workers, because they could theoretically be dismissed when the contract ended. But practically, there were rarely any cases of such dismissal in the *danweis.* A "reform model," Beijing Chemical Machinery Factory, adopted "all-contract" employment in 1989. In the two years after that, only five workers out of three thousand employees had their contracts terminated (Labor Ministry 1991, 18-23). The work ethic and competitiveness of contract workers have been basically identical to those of the permanent employees. Even in *danweis* where all workers have become contract workers, one can hardly see much difference in work ethic and competitiveness, although strong resentment toward those higher-paid "pseudo-contract workers" has been interestingly detected among permanent workers.[96] Nevertheless, contract employment has provided the state, or more precisely the *danwei* bosses, with a limited legal possibility of gaining some labor mobility in the authoritarian state LAP. More important, the implementation of enterprise bankruptcy laws and relaxed state control of laborers have led to some visible increase of labor mobility in and outside the authoritarian state LAP.

The "Reformed" Authority Structure and Its Performance
By the mid-1990s, the state-owned industrial enterprises had acquired substantial autonomy in their management. The *danwei*

bosses had much more authority in allocating financial resources and could even "upgrade" their *danwei* ranks by proclaiming themselves the equivalent of a state administrative rank: ministry/province, bureau/prefecture, division/county, or section/township. They could set up new pay scales accordingly, drawing on their own funds to make up differences. Thus, a county equivalent machine-making factory upgraded itself in 1993 to the higher prefecture rank and began to pay its cadres accordingly with after-tax profits. In the eyes of the local government, labor/personnel bureaus, and the superiors, however, the official status of such self-upgraded enterprises remained the same. For example, the bureau/prefecture equivalent factory directors of that machine-maker, when reassigned to another *danwei,* were treated only as division/county equivalent cadres by the state. Furthermore, the bureau/prefecture equivalent factory managers could only have access to CCP and other internal documents and directives issued to the division/county level.[97]

The wages of state-employed labor came to be determined more by performance than before, although seniority was still a very important determinant. Managers of state-owned enterprises gained the right to penalize or to promote their employees. A worker could even be promoted temporarily to the rank of cadre, without changing his assigned permanent status as a worker. With approval, state-owned enterprises could have open recruiting outside the traditional labor bureau assignment channel, but they could hire only "eligible" unemployed people from urban areas, primarily from the city in which they were located.[98] Besides the primary type of state employees, the *gudinggong,* and the contract workers, other types developed under the authoritarian state LAP. Temporary and seasonal hiring was widely practiced. Peasant workers and rotating workers were institutionalized in 1984 and 1988.[99] Peasant workers were part-time farmers and part-time workers used by state enterprises on a short-term contract basis without their becoming city residents and thus burdening the state budget. For certain heavy labor or hazardous jobs, such as delivery and mining, state-owned enterprises hired so-called rotating workers, peasants hired to work full time on a three to five-year basis without becoming city residents.[100]

Efforts have been made to promote a national social welfare and insurance system in place of a *danwei*-based welfare provision. Due to recent practices of bankruptcy laws, there were experiments with laying off permanent employees and adopting unemployment insurance. Labor mobility increased, especially when the alternative employer was a foreign-invested enterprise.[101] As a result, labor productivity in the state-owned—but now rather autonomous—enterprises showed significant increases during the reform years.[102] By official accounts (though perhaps not entirely accurate), six thousand state-owned enterprises in Guangdong performed equally as well as or even slightly better than the six thousand foreign-invested enterprises in that province in 1994.[103]

Finally, largely due to the growth of a commodity economy and the diversity of income sources, many special benefits provided by the state could be acquired easily, though usually at a higher price, by people outside the *danwei* supply system.[104] Thus, the attractiveness of the authoritarian state LAP dwindled. The previously strong function of political indoctrination in the *danweis* also became much less enthusiastic.[105] The CCP leadership appeared to realize the danger of dismembering the authoritarian state LAP, which implied loss of control over the most productive groups of the population. Therefore, after the Tiananmen Square tragedy of June 4, 1989, Beijing began serious assistance to its major state-owned enterprises with a new policy called "inclination" and "two-way guarantee." The state would thereby guarantee subsidized raw materials, energy, and consumer goods in exchange for guaranteed product quotas and profits from state-owned enterprises. New measures were adopted to stabilize the labor force in state-owned enterprises, and political indoctrination such as "workers' education" and "ideological work" was reemphasized repeatedly, although with generally discouraging results. By the fall of 1997, the CCP decided that such assstance should be reduced to cover mainly the *danweis* of "crucial importance" to the PRC economy (Jiang 1997).

Despite the reform developments, the basic organizational principles, institutional features, and operational mechanisms of the Chinese authoritarian state LAP have remained largely intact into the 1990s. This LAP is still characterized by a tight, vertical, institutionalized, and effective control of the labor force by the state in the urban areas. An institutionalized network of patron-client relations still exists between the workers and the authority, and the labor force and families have an "organized dependence"—economically on their *danweis,* politically on the party and management, and personally on their supervisors (Walder 1986, 5-7, 13). Once assigned to a particular job, *danwei,* and place, laborers are firmly fixed to their posts, and labor mobility across occupational and geographical boundaries remained very low, if not impossible. Among the leading barriers to labor mobility created by the authoritarian state LAP, the *dangan* system is still administratively important;[106] the profound *hukou* system still functions, with some new twists; and the seniority salary system and the variety of benefits based on the whole peculiar institution of *danweis* still powerfully affects people's decisions about moving. The state-owned enterprises, primarily because of the authoritarian LAP, have been in serious financial difficulties in the 1990s. By the fall of 1996, internal estimates concluded that more than 50 percent of the state-owned enterprises were losing money.[107]

Notwithstanding the development of alternative LAPs and the decreased attractiveness of state employment, in the 1990s jobs allocated by the authoritarian state LAP, even on a contracted basis, were still considered real jobs by most urban Chinese.[108] Besides their being stable and providing benefits, the jobs at the state-owned *danweis* were still attractive because they were less demanding due to the lack of on-the-job competition. The main complaint against this LAP by those under it, therefore, was the relatively low pay and lack of opportunities. However, especially by the mid-1990s, many urban workers preferred to have a low-paid but stable and secure job in a state-owned *danwei* while openly or covertly moonlighting for a higher second income. There have been several reported cases in which workers successfully blocked the bankruptcy of state-owned enterprises. Their broken *danweis* were either merged into some financially better ones by administrative order, or kept open through reliance on government financial assistance. At the same time, the PRC state had some important economic reasons to block the market institution in the state-owned enterprises, fearing that state-owned banks would be dragged down by the bankruptcy of numerous money-losing state-owned enterprises. Thus, in the seven years after the passage of the PRC Bankruptcy Law in 1986, only about a thousand enterprises (most of which were collective enterprises) were allowed to go bust.[109] In Shanghai in 1996, among about sixty state-owned enterprises that needed to go bankrupt, the government allowed only nineteen to do so.[110] While the state had been advocating a more market-oriented employment system for its huge civil service of around 9 million workers, fewer than five hundred state employees (about eighty of them cadres ranked on or above *ke,* or section level) were dismissed each year from 1990 to 1995.[111] What the reforms accomplished was a certain decrease of central government control over the urban workers. The authoritarian state LAP borrowed some market mechanisms, such as job fairs and open examination, even for some government offices. Those new practices, though still limited, could help improve the transparency and even the efficiency of the state LAP.[112] In many cases, the developments have made the local leaders and the *danwei* bosses—instead of Beijing—the authorities controlling state employees.

Certification of Professionals

As part of the reforms of the authoritarian state LAP, by the mid-1990s the PRC had made some progress in institutionalizing its certification and management of professionals. Besides the traditional administrative ranks of cadres, now called the civil servants' system, there were eight certifications of professionals, each with five major ranks. Within each rank, there could be many "steps" and seniority differences. Those nine certifications, however, still clearly reflected the bureaucratic nature of the authoritarian state LAP, in that professionals in various fields were assigned titles that corresponded to hierarchical ranks of administrative officials and bureaucrats.

The eight professional certifications are granted for life. Even administrative ranks, supposedly only attached to the office, are practically lifetime rankings for Chinese bureaucrats. Ranks are extremely important to the authoritarian state LAP, as many nonsalary benefits are based on them. From the means of transportation, accessing state-paid residential phones, securing accommodations and health care to the privilege of visiting a foreign country, much depends on one's rank. Many state bureaucrats from minister on down actually acquired other professional ranks and put them on their official business cards.[113] The state has clear rules governing each rank of the cadres (bureaucrats) in their base salary, benefits, political rights and classification, security clearance, travel and accommodation privileges, housing allowance, health care facilities and costs, personal staff size, size and engine power of officially allocated vehicles, etc.

The base salary (or *dangan* salary) of the cadres is ranked into many, but only modestly differentiated layers, whereas many other perks and related benefits vary significantly by rank. For example, the Shenzhen SEZ government, a deputy provincial level *danwei,* had six ranks and forty-eight steps of base pay in 1995. The highest-ranked official (the deputy provincial level mayor) had a monthly base salary (630 rmb) almost three times that of the lowest ranked *gu*-level cadre with 218 rmb, whereas the lowest wage for noncadre employees in the Shenzhen government was 175 rmb. But the actual living standard of the top officials was at least ten times higher than that of the lowest-ranked cadres, although some low-ranking officials could (semi-legally or illegally) extract large sums through a variety of rent-seeking

Table 2.3. Ranks of Cadres and Professionals

Type	Entry or class I	Middle I	Middle II	High or special*	Top or national class*
Civil servants	section member	section chief	division chief	bureau chief	governor or minister
Engineers	assistant engineer	engineer	engineer	senior engineer	professorial engineer
Accountants	assistant ††	accountant	head† accountant	senior accountant	
Political‡ workers	assistant	P.W. P.W.	head†	senior P.W.	
Economic** workers	assistant	E.W. E.W.	head†	senior E.W.	
Statisticians	assistant	statistician	head† statistician	senior statistician	
Medical workers	doctor & head nurse	doctor-in-charge	head† doctor	professorial doctor	
Researchers	assistant fellow	associate fellow	research fellow	professorial fellow	
Professors	assistant professor	lecturer	associate professor	professor	Ph.D. tutor

Notes: Many other state-employed cadres, such as teachers and entertainers, have five similar ranks starting from class I to the rank of senior, or special, and national class.

  * *Gaogang* (高干): senior cadres.

  † *Zhuren* (主任).

  †† *Kuajishi* (会计师).

  ‡ *Zhenggongshi* (政工师): political ideology workers and certain managers such as dossier managers, personnel managers, and office workers.

  ** *Jingjishi* (经济师); most of the enterprise mangers outside the ideology and office management areas.

Sources: Yuan et al. 1994; author's interviews in China in 1995.

behaviors.[114] Other cadres/professionals used a similar system to make their own ranking hierarchy. It became increasingly necessary for *danweis* to treat their cadres and professionals above and beyond the basic rules of the state. For example, the state ruled that only cadres with a rank equivalent to bureau chief or higher could travel first class by train. But many unqualified *danweis,* mainly those which had their own financial resources, could send their bosses first class with bogus high ranks, as long as the *danweis* paid the difference. One provincial government, Shangxi, decided in 1995 to give all thirteen academicians of the Chinese Science Academy and the Chinese Engineering Academy in that province additional annual pay, a deputy-provincial governor level of health care privileges, and two official business passports to allow them to travel abroad more easily.[115]

Recent Legal Developments

After fourteen years and thirty versions, a PRC Labor Law, one of ten major laws proposed by Deng Xiaoping in 1978, was finally passed by the CNPC and took effect on January 1, 1995. Nine related laws and about two dozen regulations, regarding such things as wages and employment promotion, were to be made before 1999 (Yuan 1994, 397-398, 408). Beijing hailed this "great achievement" of protecting labor in a "socialist country" and published numerous explanations of its "landmark" law. It was officially viewed as a major step toward the construction of a socialist market economy, especially in the cities.

A close examination of the twelve chapters of the PRC Labor Law yields a few interesting findings.[116] Like many other PRC laws, the Labor Law only lays out some basic principles and policy preferences and leaves many crucial details and authority to the government and its offices in charge of labor affairs (clauses 9 and 11). It may be read more as a set of guidelines about workers and employment from the CCP-PRC authority's perspective than as a law governing labor allocation and management. A significant problem is that the law does not even mention some of the fundamentals regarding China's labor allocation and management. There is no mention of *hukou* or *dangan;* in fact, "every worker is entitled to an equal employment" and "shall not be discriminated against based on ethic, racial, gender and religious difference" (clauses 3 and 12). It says nothing about the barriers between urban and rural labor forces, the *danweis,* the different LAPs, and the fact that unemployment in the PRC refers only to the jobless in the cities. With those inherent problems, it will be quite difficult for the new PRC Labor Law, like many other PRC laws, to be taken very seriously and effectively implemented.

The tasks of accommodating the advancing market economy and addressing the issue of transferring millions of rural laborers, therefore, are assigned to the local governments' "detail policies," subject to the central government's approval (clauses 45, 85-87, and 106). As official explanations revealed, the main purposes of this law appeared to be for legalizing the government's power on labor issues and providing a legal basis on which to bargain with and regulate foreign investors.[117] In that regard, these recent legal efforts by the PRC government may have a profound impact on labor protection, which appears to have been jeopardized by some of the most profit-driven foreign investors, especially those from Taiwan and Hong Kong.

Although appearing to have had some intention of promoting the market institution in labor allocation and management, the PRC Labor Law works basically to institutionalize the authoritarian state LAP, mainly in urban China. It may have been a meaningful effort to legalize the authoritarian state LAP with some flavor of market mechanisms. Its provisions are applicable to all types of employment, yet it seems to be a major effort to consolidate and even expand the reformed state's authority in labor allocation and management, in the face of an advancing market, through legal means. As a general statement of the PRC's labor policy, this law adds some transparency to the state LAP, rather than changing it.

At local levels, as in the largest city, Shanghai, the authoritarian state LAP has experienced some profound legal changes. Besides legalizing unemployment and establishing an unemployment relief fund, the Shanghai government worked to legalize and institutionalize its traditional control over the labor force in a new era. Any unemployed urban *hukou* holder would become ineligible for unemployment benefits if he or she failed to take two "proper" jobs referred by the official referral service run by the labor bureaus. Starting on January 1, 1996, every Shanghai urban worker and unemployed worker was required to have a Labor Handbook to record "employment, moves, unemployment, training, and claiming of unemployment relief money." The Shanghai Labor Bureau ordered every *danwei* to use this handbook, in addition to a *dangan,* to record and report when they hired or fired anyone.[118]

Tales of the *Danweis*

To further illustrate the authoritarian state LAP in contemporary China, this section presents findings concerning labor management and wages in a few types of *danweis*. The information, except where noted, came from several of my field trips to China from 1992 to 1996. Certain names have been altered to protect the sources.

State-Owned Industrial Enterprises
Nearly 10 percent of state-owned enterprises (and thus the state treasury) lost money in 1985, the second year of urban economic reform. The situation worsened rapidly before it saw a little improvement. By 1993-1994 about two-thirds of the enterprises were losing money; by 1994-1995, half were still in the red, with an annual loss of about thirty billion rmb. By the first quarter of 1995, more than forty thousand state-owned enterprises were in deep financial trouble (an increase from thirty thousand at the end of 1994), and more than 7.43 million state employees were either dismissed or off duty.[119] The Chief Economist of the State Statistical Bureau, was reported to reveal that the situation of the state-owned enterprises worsened in 1995 with a 20 percent increase of loses.[120] The general estimate of underemployment in those enterprises has been around 30 million, or more than 30 percent.[121]

1. *An automobile factory in Hefei city of Anhui Province.* One of more than one hundred automobile makers in the PRC, the factory was listed among the top sixteen "important factories or companies" by the Hefei government for its size and profitability.[122] It had more than three thousand state employees (cadres and all contract workers who were officially viewed as the same as permanent workers) with total assets of 200 million rmb in 1994. The total population of the factory compound was around ten thousand. In 1995, the average monthly income of its employees was about 400-600 rmb (the average annual income in 1994 had been 5,670 rmb).[123] Roughly half the income was wages and the rest were bonuses and numerous subsidies on items ranging from food, transportation, haircuts, and bathing to recreation and child care. Figure 2.2 shows a typical monthly payroll statement of the factory employees. As was common in state-owned enterprises in recent years, whenever the factory was in financial difficulty, as in 1995, all scheduled raises and bonus were paid with no-interest indefinite bonds issued by the factory.[124]

Because the factory had been operating for more than three decades, there were many families with two or even three generations employed there. There was a sizable group of retired employees (nearly four hundred in 1995 including fourteen "old cadres," who enjoyed special privileges).[125] The factory leadership held the conviction that it "must give everyone in the factory a bowl of rice to eat." It had basically stopped recruiting workers from outside and had accepted a few cadres, primarily fresh college graduates or new top managers, assigned by superiors. Professionally, the factory was under the leadership of the Chinese Automobile Corporation, a ministry-level agency in Beijing. Administratively, however, it was under the Heifei city government and the Anhui provincial government. It had its own police substation and a thirty-person factory police force. It was a county- or division-level *danwei,* although it ranked itself at the prefecture or bureau level. In the fashionable trend of forming group corporations, the factory's official name had become a "group corpo-

Figure 2.2. Monthly Payroll Statement of a State Employee

Name:	
Rank:	
Income:	*Deductions:*
Base (or *dangan*) wages:*	Public funds:*
Floating wages:	Housing rents:
Occupation wages:*	Payment of debt:
Attendance pay:	Savings:
Subsidies:	Medical fees:
On-job subsidies:	Electric bills:
Special duty subsidies:*	Water bills:
Housing subsidies:	Gas bills:
Seniority subsidies:*	Sanitation fees:
Grain subsidies:*	Absence deductions:
Nonstaple food subsidies:*	Mutual assistance:
Bathing and barber fees:*	Union dues:*
Books and periodicals fees:*	Insurance:*
Bicycle (or commuting) fees:	State Treasury bills:*
Lunch subsidies	Day care fees:
Child care subsidies:	Other:
Bonuses:	
Other:	
Total income:	*Total deductions:*
Net payment:	

Notes: A Chinese state employee typically gets this type of computer-printed monthly payroll statement. Figure 2.2 is based on real payroll statements the author acquired in field studies in Anhui, Guangdong, Shanghai, and Beijing in 1992-1996.

* Items mandated by the state. The remaining items were basically dependent on individual *danweis* and/or individual employees.

ration" and all of its formal workshops and parts plant were called "companies" or "factories," respectively.

The factory had its own cable TV network, carrying nine TV channels. It invested in a nearby multishop grocery system and two open-air markets of food and vegetables. A factory-run, low-fare bus service connected the factory compound with the nearby Hefei city bus routes. There was a factory polyclinic with an in-patient facility, a complete school system (from kindergarten to middle school) and a technical school. The facilities, however, were basic. Each student had to have a valid local (Hefei) urban *hukou* or pay substantial fees after getting special permission to attend school. Middle school graduates who could not pass the entrance exam for high school could apply to the technical school. After graduating from the technical school, they were assigned jobs in the factory or in similar plants, on a swapping arrangement under which an equal number of technical school graduates from the other plants could work at the Hefei factory. Those who could not even pass the entrance exam for the technical school were allocated by the factory managers to work in the affiliated parts plant, which had about 450 employees. As a labor service enterprise, the parts plant was a collective enterprise that lived on favorable orders from the factory. The average income of those employed in the parts plant was only slightly below the factory average. They could also participate in the housing allocation and subsidized purchase of apartments offered by the factory. Still, there were drawbacks for those working in the parts plant: Their income was entirely dependent on the revenue of the plant; their health care benefits were less sufficient; there was built-in discrimination in allocating apartments; it was almost impossible to be promoted to cadre, even on a temporary basis; and, perhaps most important, the workload was heavier and the discipline much tighter.

Despite serious underemployment, the factory, like many of its type, employed nearly five hundred peasant workers on a two- to three-year contract basis. They generally worked in dirty areas and engaged in heavy labor. Their income on average was only half the factory's average. Because they did not have local urban *hukous* and were not state employees, they did not have other important benefits such as housing allocation, child care, schooling, and pensions. They were recruited primarily through referral and "guarantee" of friends and relatives who were employees in the factory. The factory deliberately tried to hire villagers from outside the surrounding rural areas for fear that local villagers might be difficult to manage. Except for sharing the workplace, those genuine contract workers from the villages were isolated from the main residential compound of the factory and thus its social and political activities.

2. *A major steel-making complex in Beijing.* This giant complex was a well-known political model in China for decades. Ranked as a bureau or prefecture level *danwei,* the complex enjoyed the privileges of a ministry- or provincial-level *danwei.* It has been a "key enterprise" of the PRC and Beijing. Its management followed Deng Xiaoping's reform closely and thus made numerous "innovations" and "breakthroughs" for Chinese economic reform. Financially, the complex has been in good shape; it had its own investment firm and invested in nearly one hundred domestic and eight foreign ventures, including some in the United States.[126] Its top manager, widely believed to be a loyal Deng follower, was finally fired in 1995 by the CCP for his family's alleged economic crimes.[127] Many began to speculate that a post-Deng power struggle had thus started.

Compared to the Anhui factory, the complex was larger and much more complicated, a city by itself. The complex-city had a fairly complete service network, entertainment facility, education system, health care system, and police and security forces. A few dozen collective enterprises, most of them so-called third industry, or service industries, were established, existing on orders from the complex to employ thousands of the complex workers' children and a sizable number of complex "surplus" workers.[128] Many peasant-workers were hired to work in the mines and in dirty posts such as the coke ovens and coal cinder processing lines.[129]

As a new-breed group corporation, the complex had nine daughter companies, mainly making steel and steel products.[130] It also sold equipment, technology, financial services, and real estate. The average income of employees varied substantially across units and positions. Senior engineers made on average 635-725 rmb per month, plus around a 200 rmb bonus. Some skilled workers in the dirty and heavy labor posts could earn 1,500 rmb a month.[131] Top managers had an average salary and a "complex average bonus" but enjoyed many perks and a significant "working expense allowance." All new employees were contract workers but were almost exactly the same as the permanent workers with lifetime employment.[132] Officially, as a reform measure in 1987, the complex did not distinguish cadres from workers—all were called "complex working persons" (*gongzuzhe,* 工作者).[133] Everyone's duty and pay were tied to their working posts, and they could apply for preferred posts through an examination by the complex management (Labor Ministry 1992, 338-340).

Every CCP member is required to wear a CCP badge at work or face punishment. The management is considered by many of its employees as "strict, inhuman, and often inefficient." Dismissal has occasionally been used in the complex, while many workers with a local (Beijing) *hukou* have left for better, "more human" and more lucrative jobs such as taxi drivers. One could ask to take a "70 percent wages vacation," an indefinite or fixed leave with partial pay to reduce the problem of underemployment.[134]

Located in the western suburbs of Beijing, the complex was granted special authority to hire nationwide the "talents" it needed. Those middle to high-level talents, mainly seasoned senior engineers and scientists, were treated the same as complex employees in almost every way, including housing allocation. But they could not have a Beijing *hukou* without going through a complicated procedure and paying as much as 100,000 rmb to the city government. Therefore, their children could not participate in the college entrance exam in Beijing, where applicants are generally granted a clear advantage in admission. Instead they had to send their children back to wherever their *hukou* was to struggle through the more competitive exam. If the children were fortunate enough to get into some college from their hometowns, they would probably be assigned back to those hometowns after graduation, not to Beijing where their parents were working and living. If they could not succeed in the college exam, they would be disqualified by their non-Beijing *hukou* from having the relatively better employment opportunities in Beijing. To compensate for that, the complex opened its own "Complex University," which admitted those workers' children who passed the college entrance exam but had a non-Beijing *hukou*. After graduation, however, those with a non-Beijing *hukou* could only be assigned to work in the complex or go back to their original hometown.

A recent case may help to illustrate labor management in this complex, one of the most reformed major Chinese industrial enterprises. The complex made a deal with Shangdong Province in 1993 to set up a joint venture with the capacity to produce 10 million tons of steel annually. The complex hired many contract workers, including many "talents" who applied through the nationwide talent exchange conferences and through word of mouth. But, unfortunately, the Shangdong provincial government changed its mind and decided to hold on to total ownership of the venture. Unhappy with the position of minor partner, the complex backed away from the deal in early

1995. Hundreds of complex workers originally hired for the joint venture were thus left useless. The complex could not dismiss them, so it took the responsibility of keeping them in the existing units in Beijing; so much for the flexibility that was supposed to be a major advantage of the contract employment system.

State-Owned Service and Trading Enterprises
1. *A long-distance bus company in Anhui Province.* A total of sixteen long-distance bus companies operated in the province of over 59 million people. By 1995, they were all either losing money or operating on a very thin margin. The largest, the Hefei Passenger Auto-Transportation Corporation (HPAC), had four thousand employees with an average monthly income of 280-300 rmb per person. It was in the red in 1994 and again in 1995. HPAC adopted a contract employment system but complained that "it was still the same," since the Hefei Labor Bureau, not the managers of HPAC, had final authority in dismissing workers. Because of an apparent under-employment problem (at least one-third of the workers were termed "surplus" by the vice general manager), it had no plans to recruit new workers. The children of HPAC employees, if they failed the college entrance exams, generally went to the technical schools at HPAC's expense. As a favor, some of them were rehired by HAPC after graduation. It did not have a complete consumer supply network or education system of its own, although it had the common offices such as family planning and "retired cadres affairs." For services, recreation, and entertainment, HAPC relied on the city of Hefei and the towns in which it operates.

Despite the almost annual doubling of the price of the bus tickets, HAPC continued to lose money and the state stopped bailing it out.[135] Nevertheless, it had to find funds to cover state-mandated base wages, benefits including 75 to 95 percent of the workers' medical bills, and a newly added 50 rmb per head monthly "vegetable basket fee" to compensate for inflation, housing costs, and other expenses.[136] Without the possibility of cutting employees, management used the now politically fashionable privatization process to sell off assets such as bus routes and vehicles to balance the books. Thus, there was not only no new investment, the existing assets were quickly being consumed. The managers acknowledged, "This is very serious but we have no choice." Many similar enterprises were doing the same in and outside the province. Essentially, the state-owned enterprises were significantly shrinking their assets. Three top HPAC managers concluded that "the reform is an enigma. It's not privatization; nor state-owning; nor stockholding. It's just a sale of state assets to pay for current accounts" (author's interview, 1986). Nationally, such behavior has been a major way of draining the PRC's state-owned assets in the reform era.[137]

The money-making part of HPAC was its bus terminal located in the heart of Hefei, the provincial capital city of about 800,000 people. The terminal had more than three hundred employees, 39.26 million rmb annual sales, and a profitable history. In addition to the usual problem of underemployment and the lack of real labor management power, the terminal had to fight HAPC management for the thin margins it made. HAPC management, in association with some terminal cadres, semi-secretly transferred a substantial portion of the terminal profits for their uses. The terminal had a rather huge but not atypical leadership of eleven members, including five deputy managers, the union chief, and the party secretary. Beneath them there were many more branch managers, foremen, and group leaders.

2. *A major group corporation in Shanghai.*[138] This group corporation was formed according to "modern enterprise principles" on the basis of the former East China Textile Administration, a bureau-level industrial agency. Group corporations are a recent type of state-owned enterprise. They are limited corporations, basically modeled after foreign-invested enterprises, with a Chinese character. In Shanghai, one of the most reformed and most open areas of China, there have been relatively few of this type of enterprise. In 1994, roughly six such group corporations were formed there. Like all other group corporations, the one that is the focus of this study had several daughter companies throughout East China and overseas. The main businesses were textile-related trade, manufacturing, technology, and finance. It was also actively involved in real estate, financial services, marketing, and investment. The headquarters and the daughter companies had their own independent pay schedules and promotion rules based on their own financial situations. Because it was still a state-owned enterprise, the corporation guaranteed the base pay and benefits for all its state employees, cadres, and workers, permanent or contracted. A substantial number of peasant workers were not included in this guarantee. Being a new breed of state-owned enterprise, the average income of its employees was roughly comparable to that of wholly owned foreign-invested firms. In 1994, the average total annual income of a state employee in Shanghai was about 7,000 rmb, whereas the average income of a worker employed by a foreign-invested enterprise was about 20,000 rmb. Employees were paid

approximately 15,000-24,000 rmb. A significant part of that income was bonuses and benefits, including numerous subsidies and fees and pension funds.

The corporation found some of its workers among employees of the previous *danweis* of the East China Textile Administration and even the old Chinese Textile Ministry; it got others through official state allocations, personal referral, quasi-job markets such as the talent exchange centers and conferences, and, rarely, media commercials. Recently, the corporation purchased a few enterprises and thus inherited most of their employees. Every new employee had to sign a one- to two-year contract, although so far the contracted workers have been treated essentially the same as those permanent employees. Like a few similar group corporations, the corporation had the authority to hire people nationwide, with much less emphasis on *hukou.* A worker hired from outside Shanghai could expect the corporation, which had to pay substantial fees, to help him or her get a temporary Shanghai Residential Permit (*zanliuzheng*), a blue card *hukou* (Permanent Resident Permit, which functions like a green card in the United States), or even a formal Shanghai *hukou.* A crucial factor was that the non-Shanghai hiree had to be a talent (*rencai*), cadre, or professional with at least a college degree and/or some special skills. Just as in Beijing, these new "immigrants" had to pay for their children to go to Shanghai schools, and the children had to return to their hometowns to take the college entrance exam, attend technical schools, and be allocated as new laborers there.[139] The corporation, however, was required to insist that workers have *dangans*; without them, no new hirees could work beyond the three- to six-month trial period or get promotions. As one senior manager commented in 1995, "Once your *dangan* is here, you can't leave at will [since most other employers would require your *dangan* to hire you];[140] without a *dangan,* it would be very difficult to manage [the workers]." The content and management of a worker's *dangan* was still basically the same as before: only the superiors and *dangan* cadres could have access to it.

Most state-owned enterprises in Shanghai were still required to hire Shanghai *hukou* holders only and were restricted from dismissing people for profit reasons. Starting in 1991, if an enterprise was about to sink, it might be allowed to persuade the least productive (often the "most difficult to manage") workers to go off duty (*xiagang*)," which is different from dismissal. After detailed "ideological work and one-on-one talks" and final approval by "collective decision," a *xiagang* worker would be paid about 160 rmb per month for one to two years.[141] The worker's *dangan* would be kept in his or her original *danwei*. The worker was encouraged to look for a new job and, after one year, if still unemployed, he or she would be dropped from the payroll of the old *danwei* and become a dismissed worker. The *dangan* would then be handed over to the worker's street committee (non-Shanghai *hukou* holders would be sent back to wherever their *hukou* was). The corporation has acquired more freedom in dismissing workers, because its rank was the equivalent of the Shanghai Labor Bureau. For new group corporations like this, there was no *xiagang* system, only the right of dismissal, which was rarely used.

The corporation reduced its social function substantially. Housing allocation changed from a benefit to a means of rewarding workers. Certain cultural and recreational activities were still organized by the company unions, and family planning was still a major task of management. The corporation had almost no consumer supply system of its own. Like almost all other Chinese state-owned enterprises, it helped its employees' children get jobs. One of its daughter companies actually opened a business that hired such young people exclusively, with the hope that someday the business might be able to stand on its own feet.

Institutions and Semi-Institutions

By the mid-1990s, China's institutions (government and party agencies, mass organizations, the military, etc., which rely on state appropriations) and semi-institutions (hospitals, museums, schools, temples, etc., which rely on state appropriations and self-created income) still had the most rigid and complete state control in their labor allocation and management. It is here one can find the authentic hierarchy and authoritarian nature of the Chinese state LAP. All employees are state-assigned permanent employees with jobs essentially for life. Benefits, promotions, and salaries are calculated based on rank and seniority. Only rarely does the state fire someone for economic reasons. Transfer is tightly controlled by superiors, thus labor mobility, both internal and external, is very low. *Hukou, dangan,* political performance, and especially networks and connections are still the key factors influencing recruitment and promotion. The traditional importance and differences of the *danweis* are still apparent. Those *danweis* have been "guaranteed" by the state with officially stipulated pay and benefits (the semi-institutions to a lesser extent). Jobs here are considered the most secure, and on-the-job competition is the least. But, accordingly, pay is also usually the lowest compared to other types of *danweis,* let alone the foreign-invested or private enterprises.

Practically, however, many institutions have very diverse and creative income sources that enable them to pay their employees significantly higher than the state standard. These include legal, semi-legal (so-called gray income, such as commissions, kickbacks, and overcharges), and even illegal sources. Almost all institutions, including many government agencies, are creating revenues (*chuangshou,* 创收) in their own ways and to the extent they could. Most semi-institutions establish profit-making enterprises such as shops, hotels, factories, and even trading companies with state funds. Some capitalize on their special connections, certain monopolies, political power, and other "resources in possession" such as state properties and unique access to certain information. Forms of extra pay are also very creative and diverse, ranging from distributing consumer goods as big as refrigerators and as basic as rice and meat, to hidden payments in the form of such things as free tours. Some institutions have the ability to promote workers and even hire some extra workers. These activities, however, are highly dependent on their function and power determined by the state. The job security, low working intensity, higher social status, and the often associated political power of those institutions still attract high-quality workers. But increasingly many employees are moonlighting, at the expense of the institutions and, ultimately, the PRC state.

The author's field notes of 1989, 1992-1993, and 1995-1996 are filled with stories of institution employees, including middle- to high-level government bureaucrats, engaging in second and even third jobs—earning substantial gray income in their working time, utilizing their *danwei*'s information and equipment, and even abusing state power. In some places like Beijing, all college professors had gray income, which often constituted 30 to 80 percent of their total income.[142] This trend continued into the late 1990s. According to an authoritative handbook, as long as it was approved by one's *danwei* leadership, practically any state employee, with the exception of government officials, judges, prosecutors, and active-duty military personnel, could have a second job.[143]

A common way of making money while keeping the secure state job has been taking leave without pay (*tingxin liuzhe,* 停薪留职). The employee, working in another job that is usually higher paying but less secure and perhaps less socially prestigious, gets to keep his original position and all related benefits, including the housing allocation, by paying his original *danwei* a fee.[144] Another way for skilled state employees to plunge into the sea of the labor market without losing the safety net of their *danweis* has been through internal early retirement (*naitui*), sometimes more than ten years before the legal retirement age.[145] The CCP regime, perhaps ironically, actually encouraged such a state-sponsored market reallocation of capable workers. The Anhui provincial government, for example, ruled that all those who wanted to leave without pay should be allowed to do so. Their state employment and associated seniority, regular pay steps, and other benefits were to be continued.[146] In some more open and reformed areas such as the Shenzhen SEZ, with the proper approval, a cadre could leave his *danwei* and job to work in nonstate sectors while maintaining his state cadre identity and status. His *dangan* salary, privileges, and regularly scheduled raises would be recorded to be used in the future if and when he decided to return to a state job.[147]

Openly having a foot in either camp, however, was not exactly popular among one's *danwei* comrades. Thus, more people began to moonlight without authorized leave, without even telling their original *danweis*. Many college professors secretly worked outside the classrooms on an almost full-time basis, making five to ten times as much money in totally unrelated jobs such as interpreting, trading, brokering, and general office work. Policemen almost openly accepted bribes and engaged in racketeering, often collectively: A station or substation might act as a group and then divide the gains. Government officials massively engaged in open or hidden business activities, preferably with foreigners. A news reporter of a major TV station in Shanghai made roughly three times as much gray income as his salary in 1994-1995, secretly and indirectly running a small state-owned trading company. Another newsman in the same institution made nearly double his salary from unspecified outside work in 1995. One high-level Shanghai official was an active and semi-open agent for two overseas investors. Some senior analysts in the Chinese central government earned nearly half of their income in 1994 through outside work such as teaching and private tutoring. In 1995 a mayor of a major city acknowledged to me in private that gray income was a common phenomenon among the government employees; he said he would not be surprised if some of his bureaucrats earned as much as 400 percent of their salary that way.

It may be ironic to note that institutions, though they still have the most authentic authoritarian state LAP, are clearly being eroded by market forces. Unlike enterprises where there might be real work to do and where many underemployed workers have only few special skills to market, the institutions provide the security, facility, time, and often names and connections for massive numbers of their employees to become a market-allocated labor force. The underemployed workers at the institutions also tend to be better educated, with more special skills and expertise. Income inequality is quietly expanding among those workers, with a profound impact on the overall authoritarian state LAP.

Such a seemingly strange marriage of the labor market and authoritarian state LAP—made possible by the increasing ineffectiveness of state authority—may demonstrate how deep the market institution has taken root in China. This "gray" advance of market-oriented labor allocation, under the paradoxical protection of the authoritarian state LAP, may be smoother and more effective, thus more enduring. It is perhaps interesting for the above-mentioned mayor to defend gray income and moonlighting of employees as a better use of resources and an effective stabilization of government employees.

The Authoritarian State LAP and the Chinese Institutional Structure

The Chinese authoritarian state LAP has been a cornerstone of the institutional structure in contemporary China. This LAP and its evolution reveal substantial information about the continuities and changes of this peculiar structure.

The Authoritarian State LAP Makes China Socialist

Though Karl Marx himself believed that comprehensive mobility of workers is necessary for the modern industry, which he believed to be the precondition for any socialist or communist system, labor mobility has been anything but certain in all Soviet-style socialist countries.[148] Labor immobility and the associated economic inefficiency and lack of personal freedom and political rights have thus become hallmarks of socialist nations, ranging from the former Soviet Union to Cuba and North Korea. The PRC has clearly been in this camp. The Chinese authoritarian state LAP may be viewed as an institutional combination of a traditional LAP, with its institutionalized personal dependence and labor immobility, and a system of authoritarian state control that allocates labor as an economic resource and controls workers as political and social actors.[149] As discussed previously, the most productive urban labor force has been largely affixed to the cells of the traditional Chinese institutional structure: the *danweis,* the equivalent of families in the rural areas. Both vertical and horizontal mobility of the urban labor force, therefore, have been very low and largely involuntary; recent reforms have only changed some of that. But for the three-quarters to two-thirds of urban laborers allocated and managed under this authoritarian state LAP, their *danweis* have remained essentially their lifetime employer and the universe of their political and social activities. Mobility is basically still a luxury for a few, and very high transaction costs are attached to it. Under this LAP, concluded one Chinese author, the "labor force basically lost its mobility."[150] Apparently, now it is the authoritarian state LAP that makes China "socialist." Combined with the family-based traditional LAP in the rural areas, the dominant authoritarian state LAP in urban areas constitutes the institutional foundation for Deng Xiaoping's "socialism with a Chinese character."

An Administrative or Bureaucratic Socialism

The authoritarian state LAP has effectively established a Chinese-style administrative or bureaucratic socialism in which people are organized in a giant, nationwide administrative or bureaucratic network.[151] As one of the "evolutionary universals," wrote Talcott Parsons, "a bureaucratic system is always characterized by an institutionalized hierarchy of authority, which is differentiated on two axes: level of authority and 'sphere' of competence."[152] Through the authoritarian state LAP, the CCP leadership externalized such a bureaucratic hierarchy of authority, at least in the urban areas. This political institution, however, tended to be incapable of governing vastly different nonpolitical behaviors. Unfortunately, the differentiation of the CCP-PRC's political authority, and even its institutionalization and thus its rationalization, have been poorly developed, perhaps due to the very fact that the authoritarian state has to serve as the basis for practically all those vastly diverse nonpolitical institutions.[153] The diversity and complexity of those institutions and the acutely felt danger to the survival of the authoritarian state's omnipresent power ironically forced the CCP state to maintain its narrow, centralized, personnel-based bureaucratic structure to fend off pressures for institutionalization and differentiation. Hence, for more than four decades the PRC institutional setting remained at the level of a centralized and narrow authoritarian political authority based on personal power, will, and revolutionary ethics.

The political institution, with its rationales and logic, has played the central role in allocating and managing labor and other resources.

Historically, economic and social desires and needs were often compromised, even replaced, by political needs and desires. Rewards and penalties were distributed through administrative channels and by administrative rank, decided by the centralized state authority. The only chance for a degree of nonpolitical rationality in this administrative socialism was that (1) the distribution of resources would be determined in a moralistic, socialist, or even democratic way with limited participation of the people, and (2) there would be a possibility of adjustment of rank, granted from above. Everyone was equal, not in terms of money or law but in terms of the superiors' authority. This LAP reflected and supported the supreme power of the political authority—the state—in controlling not only people's political activities but also the national economy and society. Things were greatly simplified and unified along the lines of the administrative bureaucrats. Everyone had a direct attachment to the state for meeting their basic needs and for the possibility of satisfying their desires. Everyone's behavior was contained, restricted, and even directed by the state authority, personified by the superiors. Political logic became the most important logic in the Chinese urban universe. The urban institutional setting was therefore an undifferentiated and state-centered complex under which people tended to be categorized and stratified into a rather rigid hierarchical order.[154]

Over time, such an organizational structure was internalized and people's behavioral norms changed accordingly. Bureaucratic ranks became basically the indicator of people's social status, power, ability, and material worth. The bureaucratic standard (*guanbenwei,* 官本位) reveals that vividly. Only recently, due primarily to the advancement of the market institution, has this begun to change. The market institution has been fundamentally challenging the bureaucratic standard as well as state-centered administrative socialism itself. But rampant corruption of officials in the government and state-owned *danweis,* beginning in the 1980s when the market began to advance in the cities, effectively reinforced China's bureaucratic standard.[155]

Empirical observation has shown that nearly every Chinese bureaucrat, including the bosses of various *danweis* (even nonstate-owned *danweis* such as the collective enterprises) are taking in gray and even "black" income on a daily basis. Some have argued that this is just a by-product of economic reform and especially of the decentralization of state authority.[156] Cultivated and justified by Chinese culture and social norms (Yang 1994) and as part of Chinese political tradition, such widespread rent-seeking based on rank and political power grossly twisted the market institution, at least for a time.[157] By the late 1990s, for most Chinese the bureaucratic standard was still the one by which everyone was to be evaluated. In most cities, public cemeteries have a specially designed, exclusive senior cadres' section fenced or walled off from the rest of the graves. Thus, senior cadres (above the rank of bureau of prefecture) kept their bureaucratic standard even after death, enjoying better-designed and exclusively maintained resting places at only a fraction (often about 10 percent) of the market price charged for a similar tomb.[158] As a sign of the continuation of bureaucratic socialism, the absolute and relative number of cadres actually grew rapidly in the reform years. From 1982 to 1990, leading cadres increased by 40 percent (from 8.1 million to 11.5 million), while clerks and low-ranking cadres increased by 61 percent (from 6.8 million to 10.9 million).[159] The new links between administrative power and wealth only enhanced the bureaucratic standard. Many newly emerged socialist millionaires, such as rich private businessmen, soon became part of the bureaucracy to acquire power and social status. In 1994, for example, the CCP approved the efforts of twenty successful businessmen to become leading cadres or bureaucrats by making them people's deputies or members of the people's consultation conference (Qiao et al. 1994, 84-89,171).

Danweis: *The Socialist Families*

The cells of the Chinese authoritarian state LAP are hundreds of thousands *danweis* with varied ranks, sizes, importance, and balance sheets. Institutionally speaking, a pure *danwei* refers to a group of people and their families, organized through the political authority of the state to engage in the provision of a product or a service. The basic scale and function of *danweis,* despite their rank, is very similar. Even religious temples are similarly organized and have various ranks just like any other *danwei.* Thus, there came to be division (*chu*)-rank temples and section (*ke*)-rank nunneries (Qiao et al. 1994, 243). Created and sustained by the authoritarian state LAP, the *danweis* have combined the three human institutions (polity, economy, and society) uniquely to define and constrain the behavior of the Chinese people. The *danweis* have evolved to be like enlarged families with comprehensive social activities and moralistic ethics. They became practically a combination of what Parsons termed "kinship structure" and "occupational structure" on the basis of political authority (Parsons 1951A 158-168). Institutionally, the *danwei* structure is directly responsible for three major forms of alleged "historical baggage" of the Chinese centrally planned economy: underemployment, debt, and the so-called "enterprise-run small societies."[160]

These socialized and politicized "families" have dominated the politics, economy, and society in urban China in recent decades. Socially, Chinese urban residents have built their personal contacts through family members and *danwei* comrades (Qiao et al. 1994, 199). Much of the historically powerful institutional impacts of the family institution in rural China has been duplicated by the *danweis* in contemporary urban China. In that regard, the organizational gap between the Chinese rural and urban sectors is more a quantitative than qualitative one. Both sectors are organized like families. The unit in the countryside is smaller (nuclear families and clans); in the urban areas it is generally much larger (the *danweis*). Urban Chinese have gone beyond family limits but have had a much tighter undifferentiation of their political, economic, and social institutions and activities. Rural Chinese have found, especially recently due to the advancement of the market, that they have a better chance to differentiate their political, economic, and social institutions outside the small shells of their families.

In short, the Chinese authoritarian state LAP enabled the state, through the managers and foremen in the *danweis,* to play a direct role in social stratification. Workers' life chances were determined by the political authority of the state under a CCP dictatorship, rather than "being determined by the conditions of labor and commodity markets" (Walder 1986, 29, 95-102). This authoritarian LAP has been one of the most important forces perpetuating China's institutional structure, for urban China carries overwhelming political, cultural, and economic weight. It has ensured firm and comprehensive control of the best educated and most productive Chinese, their families, and their social activities, and has locked the most important urban economy to the CCP polity. Any politically unwelcome political, economic, and even social activities and/or changes, therefore, cannot meaningfully take place, as the state and the CCP has tightly and effectively controlled the most important resource for all those activities and changes: the labor force.

The Authoritarian State LAP and Institutional Changes

The authoritarian state LAP has been an institutional barrier to the development of the Chinese economy, hence a major target of reform efforts. Ironically, in a rather complex way this LAP may have provided certain beneficial conditions for the development of the market.

To Transform the State LAP

The changes of the authoritarian LAP in the urban sector may be the most important indicator of institutional change in the PRC. A major impact of this authoritarian LAP was, of course, the disastrously uncertain ups and downs in China's economic development from the 1950s to the 1990s due to political problems. Contrary to the social conditions Max Weber specified as leading to the particular rationality of Western capitalism, "in China, labor is tied to the enterprise, labor and commodity markets are weakly developed, and the enterprise is a budgetary arm of the state whose existence and prosperity are linked weakly to capital and labor efficiency" (Walder 1986, 253). As the institutional basis and main component of the central planning system, the authoritarian state LAP has contributed fundamentally to the gross, chronic, and institutional economic inefficiency and lack of innovation in the PRC urban economy. An official report revealed in 1995 that employees in state-owned enterprises only worked 81.7 percent of their "working time," and as little as 40 to 60 percent of their total time was considered "effective working hours."[161] The rather impressive expansioin of China's economy over the past fifteen years apparently needs to be elevated to an intensive growth that naturally requires much higher labor mobility, both in and outside the enterprises, in urban China.

Market-oriented labor allocation has been gaining ground. The family-based traditional LAP has been somewhat weak in resisting the advancement of the market in rural areas. Social institutions, by nature, can hardly mount strong barriers against the market institution. In recent years, therefore, the family-based LAP in China has been undermined and replaced rather easily and substantially by market-oriented labor allocation, as evinced by the emergence of almost 80 million "floating people" and more than 100 million employees of the township-village enterprises. But for the majority of urban workers, the authoritarian state LAP is still a strong institutional force resisting the advancement of a labor market. In the countryside, the social institutional basis of the traditional family-based LAP is weak and divided; in the urban areas, the authoritarian state LAP, though similarly nonmarket, is based on a different noneconomic institution, the unified PRC state. The political authority of the state, unlike that of the families, has resisted the market institution more effectively. Greater distortion of the market can therefore be expected in urban economic reform. The cities may see many more political consequences and stronger social impacts from the advancement of the market. The turbulent history of the urban economic reform that started in 1984-1985 has demonstrated those politically distorting efforts and failures. The family-based LAP has been an unfriendly but fertile land for the market institution, but the authoritarian state LAP formed a mountainous roadblock that will take much more time and energy to overcome.

The bureaucratic standard caused by administrative socialism and *danwei* dominance complicates the transition to a market economy in one more way—the widespread and almost unchecked rent-seeking behaviors led by the cadres. A popular book on current affairs, published with apparent official endorsement in 1994, asserted that there was a "quasi-equal-sign" between "political power and wealth," and so corruption became common.[162] The bureaucratic standard is to be followed. Smaller cadres and even ordinary citizens thus feel compelled and even entitled to join the rent-seeking army. State ownership provides the best soil for the mushrooming of those rent-seekers, and the authoritarian state LAP is a safe base for such activities.

As an institutional barrier to the market economy and a strong support for corrupt rent-seeking activities, the authoritarian state LAP was thus understandably targeted by reformers. Chinese leaders have attempted to reform this authoritarian LAP for more than ten years, but, as reported earlier, there have been only limited achievements. The CCP leadership seemed to have decided to renovate this LAP for the sake of economic efficiency, yet has been quite reluctant to alter its basic organizational features out of political concerns. Haphazard measures and piecemeal strategies have characterized reform of Chinese urban labor allocation and management. After the political scare in 1989, the CCP made strong efforts to reemphasize the importance of the authoritarian state LAP, and the old slogan "relying on the working class with heart and soul" was once again declared state policy.[163] Official commentators asserted in 1995 that "guaranteed employment is still a goal of development."[164] Political and social stability has been more important to the CCP in the course of labor reform in urban China; economic efficiency and the structural rationality of labor allocation are clearly secondary. The still insufficient supply of consumer goods, especially grain, served as a very strong justification for sustaining the authoritarian state LAP and its associated urban supply system.[165] As previously mentioned, the labor bureaus are still granted final authority in dismissing workers and in running internal reemployment as well as reemployment projects.[166] It is expected that Beijing will adopt more new, "creative and decisive" policies aimed at "strengthening state-owned enterprises" through financial assistance and trade and tax preferences.[167] Beijing would rather hire many more productive peasant workers and put up with additional losses by its enterprises and underemployment, and even tacitly allow rent-seeking and illegal moonlighting, than let state-owned enterprises go bankrupt and have massive labor reallocation by market forces. The logic of politics is indeed powerful. The price of fighting market forces in labor allocation, however, is the continuous decline of the state-owned economy and the dwindling effectiveness of the CCP's political authority in labor allocation. By 1998 there are signs indicating that reform of the state LAP may accelerate. Yet a total marketization is still a highly risky plan and remains to be adopted.

Facilitating a Chinese and Socialist Marketization

Perhaps paradoxically, the authoritarian state LAP has had certain beneficial impacts on the development of the market economy. And it may have considerable potential to allow a smooth and effective development of market-oriented labor allocation. Essentially, this LAP contributed fundamentally to the stability and effectiveness of the CCP authoritarian regime. Despite its dismal record on individual freedom and political democracy, this regime appeared to have committed itself to developing the economy based on market principles. As long as it can provide a general political certainty and basic legal enforcement, the CCP regime seems to be the only political body that could enable a marketization of China's economy. The market hates uncertainty and chaos. An authoritarian (even dictatorial) but stable and business-friendly political regime may actually facilitate the advancement of the market economy, as demonstrated by the successes of the East Asian NICs and Chile. A CCP may, ironically, be needed by the emerging Chinese market. The authoritarian state LAP could thus indirectly and politically facilitate the market economy, even though it may itself be a barrier to the formation of a Chinese labor market.

The authoritarian state LAP, given its chronic losses and gross inefficiency, may be viewed as a state subsidy for development of a market economy. This LAP, as demonstrated earlier, combines the economic, political, and social institutions for the best educated and most skilled labor force in urban China. On the surface, it seems that, without its dissolution, this LAP would keep its grasp on the best workers and leave market forces to the mass of unskilled and poorly educated laborers. Practically, however, a huge number of workers allocated and managed by the authoritarian state LAP have joined the market in their spare time and generally at their own initiative. In all of China's major cities, as many as 26 to 70 percent of state-employed cadres and workers have become de facto workers allocated by the emerging market in the name of second jobs. The common phenomenon of moonlighting has contributed to a boom in many township and village enterprises (TVEs) and private businesses that are operated in basically a market-oriented way. In one TVE in Sichuan, 70 percent of its employees were also full-time employees of several state-owned enterprises.[168] The state and the authoritarian LAP effectively guaranteed the minimum income, benefits, and job security for those workers; thus they were willing and able to "dive into the sea" (*xiahai*) of the turbulent and risky market economy.[169] "On leave without pay," open or secret moonlighting, part-time entrepreneurship or farming, and early retirement are ways those guaranteed state employees contribute to the market economy.[170] Institutionally, there is clearly a strong incentive for the *danwei* bosses to allow their employees to be on leave or to moonlight, for the *danweis* can keep the wages of those people or use part of that money to hire much cheaper labor of the peasants. This is just another form of "eating the state" by the *danweis*. As an indication of widespread moonlighting and gray income, the CCP in 1995 ordered all cadres above the rank of county or division to report their nonsalary income to their superiors and declared that the information would be included in their *dangans*.[171] The political purpose of this directive was to enhance control over the cadres and to deter their politically damaging, corrupt activities.

The interesting practice of such a curve-ball style of market partic-ipation by secure state employees was first openly legalized in 1982 through the Han Kun case in Shanghai, but became fully legal nation-wide only in the early 1990s (Zeng 1993, 36-50). Even foreign-invested enterprises have managed to hire most of their employees, usually some of the best, from state-owned *danweis*, on a full- or part-time basis. Many urban Chinese families have adopted an even more aggressive strategy called "one family, two systems" (paralleling Deng Xiaoping's "one country, two systems" policy regarding Hong Kong and Taiwan). With this strategy, one spouse would "suffer" low wages by staying with a secure state job to keep the cheap housing and many other benefits provided by the *danwei*, while the other would "dive into the sea" to make the risky but bigger money on the market. The authoritarian state LAP, despite the CCP's politically motivated rescue efforts and economically driven reform measures, has become a state-subsidized national insurance for urban workers allocated and managed by the emerging market. This has meant tremendous savings for private and foreign employers, because the state has provided extensive socialist benefits to their employees in one way or another. The large number of those "secure" laborers has greatly increased the supply of skilled but not very demanding workers. Labor in a socialist nation has thus paradoxically become very weak in its position versus the nonstate employers on the market, as concluded by an official investigation in Guangdong province in 1993 (Qiao et al. 1994, 286-287). A boom in the market-oriented economy in the PRC thus happened ironically with significant "help" from the authoritarian state LAP but without replacing it. This is an interesting and indeed unique transformation toward market economy by default.

Summary

Since the mid-1950s, the best of the Chinese labor force, the better educated Chinese urban labor force, have been allocated and managed by the CCP-dominated PRC state in an authoritarian fashion. Political authority and logic constituted the basis of this authoritarian state LAP.[172] Political (and some social) considerations, rather than economic rationales, have dominated this LAP, and the undifferentiated institutional units of the *danweis,* the socialist families, have been its cells. The bureaucratic standard has been the organizing principle of Chinese administrative or bureaucratic socialism.

The authoritarian state LAP has been the social and political basis of the authoritarian political system in China. It shaped the urban institutional setting as a "neotraditional communist" one, or as a "socialist society at its primary stage," as the CCP termed it. Through this LAP, the CCP-ruled Chinese state gained direct and effective control over the politically and economically most important urban labor force. The state controlled the initiatives, funds, and human resources necessary for social self-governing and autonomy. Discouraging efficiency and innovation, this LAP blocked the development of a market economy by incapacitating a national labor market. The *danwei* "ownership" of laborers and the state policy against labor mobility made market operation difficult. The ultra-economic means of control and the political and personal dependence created by this LAP ensured that the CCP-ruled authoritarian state had a solid domination over the whole nation.

During the two decades of reform and opening, the authoritarian state LAP has endured tremendous pressures and competition. For economic reasons, the CCP has attempted to reform the LAP with certain market mechanisms, but political concerns have limited the scope and effectiveness of those reforms. By default, however, the authoritarian state LAP has been significantly eroded by advancing market forces. In fact, this LAP has contributed to the phenomenal development and success of the Chinese market by providing millions of willing, secure, and capable urban workers who could be allocated by the market at a low, state-subsidized, labor cost. A great differentiation of the Chinese urban organizational structure has been taking place as the *danweis* have begun losing their institutional importance while the whole authoritarian state LAP has remained a powerful politically stabilizing force. In a perhaps paradoxical way, the emerging market-oriented LAP in urban China appears to be inseparable from, and even benefiting from, the authoritarian LAP. That alone would leave us with rich information with which to speculate about the future of Chinese modernization.

Notes

1. SSB 1992, 4. The urban economy has been roughly two-thirds to three-quarters of the Chinese GDP since the 1970s. Recent urban statistics, however, often contain substantial rural industrial output that is actually part of the rural economic activity.

2. The CCP Central Organization Department and the PRC Personnel Ministry, *Gaigezhong de xiangzhen ganbu renshi zhidu* (The personnel rules of the rural cadres during the reform) (Changsha: Hunan Kexue Jishu Press, 1993), 1, 136-139.

3. "Political institution" refers to the hierarchically organized human polity. A special type of political institution—international political anarchy (IPA)—may not share some of the institutional features of the others described here. Nevertheless, even in an IPA, we see hierarchical political structures governing much of international political behavior.

4. Many states are not necessarily single nation-states because they may generally contain more than one nation; however, one of them is the dominant nation. Some other nations are divided into several states.

5. Lawson 1993, 584. For a semantic and historic examination of the notion of nation, see Greenfield 1992, 4-9.

6. "Common language" means the language in which the group members can communicate with each other. In some cases, a nation may actually have more than one common language. Canadians, for example, have two common languages: English and French.

7. Lawson 1993, 584. Liah Greenfield traced the notion of nation to its modern-day meaning of "uniqueness" (1992, 8-9). The central role of a common language

needs to be elaborated here. Max Weber argued classically that a common language is "insufficient" to the notion of a nation (1978, 395, and particularly 922-925). It is true, as the famous example of the Alsatians demonstrated (Weber 1978, 396), that a common language may not be enough to form a nation yet nonetheless necessary for a nation to exist. The Swiss nation may have two or more languages, but basically every Swiss citizen can communicate with each other in all of them.

8. This definition of the state is rather uncontroversial. See Skocpol 1979, 19; Migdal 1988, xiii, 18-19; and Weber 1978, 56, 65.

9. For an in-depth work on the roles of different types of nationalism in Western Europe and North America, see Greenfield 1992.

10. John G. Ruggie argued that the emergence of sovereign states and the interactions among them led to the changes ("Continuity and Transformation in the World Politics: Toward a Neorealist Synthesis" in *World Politics* 35, no. 2 [1983]: 261-284).

11. For a summary of the notion of democracy and other types of state, see Robert Dahl, *Democracy and Its Critics* (New Haven, Conn.: Yale University Press, 1989); Legters et al. 1994.

12. See, for example, Keisuke Iida, "When and How Do Democratic Constraints Matter? Two-Level Games with Uncertainty" in *The Journal of Conflict Resolution* 37, no. 3 (September 1993): 403-426; and Alex Mintz and Nehemia Geva, "Why Don't Democracies Fight Each Other? An Experimental Study," in *The Journal of Conflict Resolution* 37 no. 3 (September 1993): 484-503.

13. For works on the relationship between democracy and economic development in different historical and national settings, see Arat 1988, Hadenius 1992, and Robinson 1990.

14. For instance, see Weber 1978, 1047.

15. The important and influential writings of Friedrich List and Alexander Hamilton are good examples. See Jacob Cooke, ed., *The Reports of Alexander Hamilton* (New York: Harper and Row, 1964); and Friedrich List, "Political and Cosmopolitical Economy," in Augustus M. Kelly ed., *The National System of Political Economy* (New York: Economic Classics), 1966.

16. Keleinberg 1990; A. S. Bhalla, *Uneven Development in the Third World: A Study of India and China* (New York: St. Martin's Press, 1992).

17. For example, during World War II, there were 14,500 officials in the Office of Censorship, monitoring news round the clock, and they "checked every piece of mail entering or leaving the U.S." Every American got a government ration book for basic supplies such as food at a government-decided price. See Jay Lovinger et al., "Life Celebrates 1945," a *Life* magazine special issue, 1995, 79, 22.

18. For an interesting but somewhat premature assessment of such "industrialization successes" or "takeoffs" by an unexpected author, see Rostow 1969.

19. Before and after the Nazis, the Germans were believed to have a deep tradition of close relationship, even collaboration, between the state, big businesses, and union leaders. See Parnell 1994.

20. For a discussion of the once-popular notion of "corporatism" and its implementation to varied degrees in central and northern Europe, see Schmitter 1986, and Lehmbruch 1985.

21. For a general picture of labor and labor allocation in the 1960s and 1970s in Asia, primarily Southeast Asia and East Asia (excluding China), see BIAP 1979.

22. *Beijing Review* (Beijing) September 11-17, 1995, 19.

23. *Renmin Ribao,* July 4, 1990, 1; October 7, 1990, 1; March 2, 1995, 2; SSB 1992; and SSB-PB 1993.

24. A speech by Qiao Xiaoyang, deputy chairman of the Legal Committee of the NPC, at a press conference in Beijing on May 19, 1995. He further stated that "as an eventual goal, we will have the same ratio of election" in the rural and urban areas (*Xinhua Daily Telegraph)* (Beijing), May 19, 1995.

25. For an overview of China's slavery system, see Liu Weimin (刘伟民), *Zhongguo gudai lubi zhidu shi* (The history of the slavery system in ancient China) (Hong Kong: Nonmen Books, 1975).

26. *Ouyaang Xiou: Xin Tangshu* (New history of Tang), vol. 46: *Beiguangzhi 1* (Rules on officials 1) (Beijing: Zhonghuo Press, 1965).

27. Chen Zhen, ed., *Zhongguo jindai gongye shi ziliao* (Historical data on Chinese modern industry), vol. 4 (Beijing: Sanlian Books, 1961), 53.

28. Notes of conversations with the chairman of the Labor Commission of the Executive Yuan, Taipei, Taiwan, April 1995. Also see Labor Commission of the Executive Yuan, *Xingzhengyuan laogong weiyuanhui jiangjie* (A short introduction of the Labor Commission of the Executive Yuan), Taipei, Taiwan, 1993.

29. Lee Chen and Wu Hui-Ling, "Taiwande laogong faling yu cangye fazhan" (Labor laws and industrial development in Taiwan), in Yu Zong-Xian ed., *Canye fazhan yu zhengci yantaohui* (A conference on industrial development and policies) (Taipei: Chinese Economic Academy, 1993), 236.

30. Around 1957, the ending of the first Five-Year Plan and the completion of collectivization in the rural areas signified the formation of this authoritarian LAP. See Rawski 1979, 6-7.

31. *Shijie Ribao* (World journal), New York, July 18, 1995, A10.

32. State Statistical Bureau report. See "Zhegong gongzi chabie tailipu" (The wage gap of the workers is too big), in *Huaxia wenzhe* (China news digest), an Internet Weekly, at http:\\ www.cnd.org, no. 222, June 30, 1995, 14.

33. Elliott Parker, "Prospects of the State-Owned Enterprises in China's Socialist Market Economy," in *Asian Perspective* (Seoul, Korea), vol. 19-1 (spring-summer 1995), 15.

34. *Renmin Ribao,* April 28, 1995, 4. In Shanghai, wages were only 59 percent of the average state employee's total income.

35. The uncontrollable nonwage income has deeply worried Beijing, because it increases the tendency for inflation, signals the drain of state assets, and substantially evades income taxes. See State Planning Commission, "Zhongguo chengzheng jumin shouru xianzhuan fengxi" (An analysis of the current income of Chinese urban residents), in *Zhongguo shichang jingji bao* (Chinese daily on market economy) (Beijing), January 24, 1995, 7.

36. A senior official, deputy director of the State System Reform Commission, Liu Zhifong, believed that wages were less than half of the Chinese worker's total income, *Xinhua Daily Telegraph* (Beijing), May 11, 1993. Also, see Zhao et al. 1994.

37. For general information on PRC governmental institutions and agencies, see Qian 1990 and Chinese News Development Corporation ed., *Chinese Government, 2* vols. (Beijing: Xinghua Publishing House, 1989). The book was revised and republished in 1993.

38. Chen Naixing and Yang Yuexing, *Xiandai gongyie zhong de renshi guangli* (Personal management in modern industrial enterprises) (Beijing: Economic Management Press, 1988), 22-23.

39. Several PRC ministries in charge of industries such as textiles and shipbuilding were eliminated in the 1990s as a result of political reform. In their places were created "general corporations," which enjoyed identical official rank and authority as the eliminated ministries. The only change was that those general corporations were asked to get more of their budget from the state-owned enterprises under their management, rather than from state appropriations.

40. As will be described later, the PRC's central government has relinquished much of its direct control over the pay scale and promotion schedules in most state-owned industrial enterprises. But the Planning Commission's directives still serve as the basis for the individual bosses of the thousands of state-owned enterprises and units.

41. For the officially stated "missions and duties of the Planning Commission," see Qian 1990, 16-17.

42. Starting in 1985, an increasing number of colleges were granted authority to enroll a limited number of additional students who would pay for their education and look for jobs on their own. In 1989, some state-run colleges started charging tuition as a major supplement to the stagnant state funding. By 1995, a quarter of the 1,100 state-accredited colleges started to charge tuition. By 1997, all will charge tuition. See Zhou Daping, "Gaoxiao biyeshen 'fengpei' zaidanghua" (The fading of the "assignment" of college graduates), in *Liaowang* (Outlook) *Weekly* (Beijing), no. 30 (August 1995), 21-22. Also see *Beijing Review*, September 25-October 1, 1995, 15-20; *Renmin Ribao-Overseas* (Beijing), February 18, 1997, 3.

43. Zhu and Yuqun, eds. 1991, 289. This policy was still in place by the late 1990s but had become much less powerful, as alternatives to state employment had grown substantially. Even the *hukou* requirement could be largely circumvented now. Starting in 1995 and 1996, some colleges were allowed to allocate many of their state "planned" graduates through the job market rather than exclusively through state assignment. By 1998, all college graduates will have to look for jobs on their own. But the State Education Commission still guarantees every planned college graduate a state-assigned job (author's field notes, 1996-1997); *Renmin Ribao-Overseas* (Beijing) February 18, 1997, 3.

44. *Renmin Ribao-Overseas,* January 18, 1996, 3. There were 895,000 college graduates and postgraduates in 1995, the highest figure in the history of the PRC (*Xinhua Daily Telegraphy* [Beijing], March 2, 1995, 2, and June 30, 1995, 3).

45. Yue Guangzhao, ed., *Labor Policy and System in China.* (Beijing: Economic Management Press, 1989), 100. Also see Xinhua in *FBIS-China,* November 18, 1987, 17-18.

46. Personnel Ministry, ed., *Guojia gongwuyuan zhanxing tiaoli shiyi* (Explanation of state provisional regulation of civil servants) (Beijing: Renmin Press, 1993), 9.

47. Author's conversation with Sun Defu, personnel minister of the PRC, in 1995.

48. For an official description of the concept of cadres, see Zhang 1987, 115-117.

49. See the CCP Central Committee and the State Council joint directives in 1983, 1986, 1987, 1991, and 1992, in Renshibu and Zhongzhubu 1993, 131-144.

50. A joint report by the Helongjiang Province Personnel Bureau and CCP Helongjiang Provincial Committee's Organizational Department, in Renshibu and Zhongzhubu 1993, 82-83, 87-88.

51. Renshibu and Zhongzhubu 1993.

52. *Zhongguo Qiannian* (China youth) (Beijing), May, 1990, 47.

53. The heads of the *danweis* down to and including the level of section (*ke*) or township (*xiang*) were still appointed, whereas some of the deputy heads and most of the clerks could be openly recruited through "fair and open examinations." See Chen Jun, "Jing jiguan shifou duyao kaoshi?" (Must everyone take the exams to work in state agencies?") in *Hefei Wanbao* (Hefei evening news) (Hefei), August 6, 1995, 1-2.

54. Renshibu 1993, 28-29. Perhaps to institutionalize and publicize the procedures and rules governing those "leading cadres," the CCP issued Provisional Regulations on the Selection and Appointment of Leading Cadres of the Party and Government, with eleven chapters and fifty-four rules in 1995 (*Renmin Ribao,* May 17, 1995, 1).

55. See, for example, recruiting ads by the prestigious Changcun Applied Chemistry Institute, June 1995.

56. For the very extensive regulatory regime concerning the allocation and management of the Chinese cadres, see, for example, the two volumes of the *Shenzhen renshi gongzhu wenjian huibian* (Collection of documents on personnel management) vols. 1 and 2 (Shenzhen: Shenzhen Personnel Bureau, 1991 and 1994).

57. There has been some relaxation recently, whereby most state-owned enterprises can hire temporary help even from the rural areas and acquire substantial rights in deciding pay and benefits to their employees beyond state-stipulated wages—depending on the after-tax revenues of the enterprises. But the labor bureaus has still kept the authority to decide on hiring permanent workers with an urban *hukou.*

58. No. 111 Directive of the State Council, April 20, 1993. In *Guowuyuang Gonggao* (Bulletin of the State Council) (Beijing), May 1993. Not surprisingly, the LSEs (labor service enterprises) and associated tax credits were directed as the most important means of "internal reemployment."

59. Figures from the producer of a TV documentary "Zai jouye gongchen" (The reemployment project), Shanghai TV, February 1995.

60. *Renmin Ribao-Overseas,* May 24, 1994, 3.

61. Author's interview in Anhui, January 1995. Also see Wang Xinghe, "Qiye tankujing" (Enterprises are complaining), in *Xinan wanbao* (Xinan evening news) (Hefei), January 23, 1995, 3.

62. For a short history of the trade union, its "three major setbacks," and its general degeneration in the PRC, see Wang Jianchu, "Lun jianguohe gongren yundong de sanci cuozhe" (On the three setbacks of the union movement after the establishment of the PRC), in *Shiling* (The field of history) (Shanghai), no. 4 (1994): 36-42.

63. *Renmin Ribao,* Beijing, April 26, 1995, 4.

64. The opening sentence of "The General Principles" of *Zhongguo gonghui zhangchen* (The charter of the Chinese Trade Union), passed by the Tenth National Congress of the All China Trade Union in Beijing in 1983. Revised in 1988 by its Eleventh National Congress.

65. Clause 36 of the PRC Trade Union Law, passed by the CNPC in 1992.

66. Deng Xiaoping's speech at the Ninth National Congress of the All China Trade Union. In Chen 1993, 76.

67. The "Important Directives on Union Works" from the CCP Central Secretariat. March 14, 1983. In Chen 1993, 81-82.

68. Chen Jingsong, "Zhongguo gonghui bangzhu yeyi niukui" (Chinese trade unions assist the enterprises to stop losing money), in *Renmin Ribao-Overseas* (Beijing), January 15, 1996, 4.

69. For an explanation on this likely trend, see Wang 1994.

70. For this point, see Gold 1986, Haggard 1990, Wade 1990, and Peng 1995.

71. Author's interviews with Lau Chin Shek, chairman of the HKCTU and legislator, and Lee Cheuk Yan, CEO of the HKCTU, January 1995.

72. Other than some sociological investigations (a notable example is Bian 1994), there have been few focused studies on the *danweis*.

73. Author's notes on field studies in Taiwan, April 1995.

74. To move from one temple to another, for example, a Buddhist monk had to obtain an introductory letter from his old temple (his old *danwei*), in addition to the regular *hukou* documents, to have a legal residence at the new location. See Cao Jiangping ed., *Zhongda anjian zhenpou jishi (B)* (Reports on the resolution of major cases, Vol. B) (Xining: Qinghai Renmin Press, 1995), 44.

75. For a recent report on the negatives of this "*danwei* equals family" mentality of many Chinese state employees, see "Jiazi nanfang" (Hard to prevent insider thefts), in *Shenzhou Ribao* (Shenzhou daily) (New York), April 14, 1994.

76. For the historical evolution and current situation of pay and ranks in the different types of *danweis,* see Qi 1993, 234-363.

77. For two state employees with master's degrees, assigned to identical jobs in two different *danweis* by the state just six years before, their monthly income difference was nearly three times—660 rmb versus about 2,000 rmb—simply because one *danwei* had "better economic results" than the other through a monopoly on importing certain metals. The less fortunate *danwei* was "dragged down" further by a larger group of retired employees (author's notes of field studies in Beijing, January 1995).

78. For example, see Hu et al. 1993, 456.

79. Wang Xiaoson, "Shizhe rusi" (Passed just like that), in *Huaxia wenzhe* (China news digest), an Internet Weekly, no. 220, June 16, 1995, 6.

80. Labor Ministry 1991, 78-87.

81. See the interesting example reported about the famous Baoshan Steel Complex in Shanghai, Labor Ministry 1991, 116-117.

82. State Statistical Bureau report, in *Huaxia wenzhe* (China news digest), an Internet Weekly, no. 222, June 30, 1995, 14.

83. For a now-classic description of the *danwei* basis of the CCP's "communist neotraditional" political power, see Walder 1986.

84. Different *danweis* emphasized different contents of those materials. Cadres usually had more content than ordinary workers. For a general list of a typical *dangan,* see CCP Central Organization Department's "Regulations on *dangan,*" issued in 1980, in Zhang 1987, 133-134.

85. This changed in a small but profound way in the 1990s.

86. Author's notes on field studies in Anhui, Beijing, Jiansu, and Shanghai Provinces in 1989, 1992, 1993, and 1995. Also, information provided to me by correspondence from Guizhou and Sichuan, 1992-1994.

87. *Renmin Ribao,* February 12, 1991, 1.

88. Chen and Yang 1988, 22-23, 28-29. By the 1990s, the reforms had somewhat altered this managerial structure. For instance, the managers/directors, instead of the party secretaries, became the final decision makers in labor and salary issues in the state-owned enterprises. Some of the labor managing offices were eliminated or merged.

89. For an official account of alleged problems of the Chinese authoritarian LAP and suggested solutions, see Gao Keling, *Jieshi yuihua de shangping jingji* (Explaining the planned commodity economy) (Huhhot: Inner Mongolia People's Press, 1985), 113-115.

90. For example, see Beijing Rencai Jiaoliu Zhongxin's "Rules and Service Items" brochure, Beijing 1993.

91. Like numerous other "provisional" laws and regulations of the PRC, those labor regulations were still valid in 1996. For a full text of those and related regulations, see Hu 1994, 414-440. For a list of the hundreds of still-valid laws and regulations related to labor allocation and management since 1949, see Qian 1991.

92. Chen and Yuexing 1988, 28-29, 46-49; Yue 1989, 37-46. Different provinces had different practices. Some, like Guangdong, decided to employ workers (including state and private employees, and cadres) in the industrial enterprises on a contract basis. Most other provinces, however, applied the contract system only to physical laborers and a tiny group of professionals.

93. *Renmin Ribao,* December 27, 1990, 3, and March 1, 1991, 1.

94. For some of those experiments and activities, see Cao Min, "Headway Made on Labor Reform," in *China Daily* (Beijing), August 9, 1995, 1.

95. *Xinhua Daily Telegraph* (Beijing), May 15, 1995.

96. Quite a few interviewees who were permanent employees used profanity when describing the contract employment system (author's notes on field studies, 1993, 1995).

97. Author's interviews with CCP and government officials, factory managers, and corporate executives in Anhui, Guangdong, Jiangsu, and Shanghai, January, February, and August 1995.

98. This policy had several quite market-oriented exceptions. As long as an employer was willing to pay a substantial fee to the city in which it was located, it could recruit even permanent workers from outside the city. In Shanghai in 1991, such a fee was 50,000 rmb downtown, roughly fifteen to twenty times the annual wages for an average worker, and 20,000 rmb in the near suburbs (correspondence from an accountant in Shanghai on March 6, 1991).

99. Underemployment of the permanent state employees and the swollen recruitment of peasant workers could coexist largely because of the need for someone to do the heavy and dirty work, and also because of the possibility of "eating the vacancies" created by so many moonlighting or on-leave state-employees. The enterprises could then use one state employee's wages to hire two or more peasant workers, with money left over for other purposes. See "Shiye: Zhongguo kuashiji de youlu" (Unemployment: the worry of China into the new century), in *Huaxia wenzhe* (China news digest), an Internet Weekly, no. 219, June 5, 1995, 3-6.

100. For example, in the major Chinese mines, "rotating peasant workers have become the main backbone in underground excavation" (Yue 1989, 40).

101. According to much national and local legislation, if an FDI enterprise hires a worker from an existing state-owned enterprise, the enterprise should be as cooperative as possible. A worker could, in many cases, keep his or her original housing assignment, and their all-important personal dossiers might no longer be a major barrier to mobility; the dossiers could be checked in and kept by local labor bureaus serving as trustees. For subsidized benefits and consumer goods provided by the state, the foreign employer merely paid the state certain unitary fees, often waived as an incentive to foreign investors. FDI, therefore, has become a major catalyst for the increase of labor mobility, which is essential to the emergence of a labor market by eroding the authoritarian state LAP.

102. Gary H. Jefferson et al., "Growth, Efficiency, and Convergence in Chinese Industry," in *Economic Development and Cultural Change,* XL-2 (January 1992): 239-266.

103. *Renmin Ribao-Overseas,* May 3, 1995, 1.

104. For an empirical report on the development of other income by the Chinese urban labor, see Zeng 1993, 33-64.

105. For example, in the officially published *Qiye banzhuzhang bidu* (Must reading for foremen in the enterprises), the part addressing the political and moral works is only fifteen pages out of 215, roughly the same amount as the part about how to report an accident and work place safety inspections (Chinese Workers Education Society, ed., *Qiye Banzhuzhang Bidu* [Taiyuan: Shanxi Kexue Jioyu Press, 1991]).

106. Hu Jintao (胡锦涛), a top CCP leader, publicly reemphasized at the end of 1995 that the *dangan* system was very important. See *Renmin Ribao* (Beijing), December 12, 1995, 1.

107. The same figure was 80 percent in the northeast and nearly 34 percent in Shanghai (author's interviews, October 1996).

108. A report described how "80 percent to 85 percent" of unemployed and privately employed youth craved to become state employees even on a "contract" basis. Some were willing to take a pay cut, and even pay the state employer 2,500 rmb, the equivalent of nearly ten months' average wages (Xin 1992, 82-86).

109. Xu Shaowei, "Qiye pucang weihe zhiyang nang?" (Why is it so hard for enterprises to go bankrupt?), in *Xin shiji* (New era) (Guangzhou), no. 2 (1995).

110. Author's interview in Shanghai, August 1996.

111. *Renmin-Ribao,* July 17, 1995, 4; SSB-LB 1992, 179.

112. For example, in May 1995, as reported by the official Xinhua News Agency, several ministries of the central government held an open job fair to recruit a limited number of new cadres (more than fifty-eight government agencies with about ten to thirty-four openings each). But the applicants were all cadres already and were all required to have a Beijing urban *hukou.* In Henan Province, the government, after five months of open recruiting and testing of more than eight hundred applicants who were Henan cadres, selected eight new deputy bureau chiefs who were all division rank cadres already. Essentially, such open and fair competition should perhaps be better viewed as an improved way of promoting and rearranging cadres through testing and selection by the superiors (*Xinhua Daily Telegraph* [Beijing], May 26,

1995). For a similar open recruitment of cadres from cadres only in Nanjing in 1996, see *Renmon Ribao-Overseas,* January 15, 1996, 4.

113. To ensure the authenticity of the ranks and titles on one's business card, major printing firms are often required to see an official proof form of one's *danwei* to show one's "genuine" rank and title before accepting the orders of business cards (author's field notes in Shanghai, December 1995).

114. Author's field notes and interviews in Shenzhen, August 1995. Figures are from the official Table of the Salaries of the State Officials and Workers in Shenzhen SEZ, Shenzhen, 1995.

115. *Renmin Ribao-Overseas,* June 1, 1995, 3.

116. *Zhonghuo renmin gongheguo laodong fa* (The labor law of the People's Republic of China) (Beijing: Worker's Press, 1994).

117. Yuan 1994, 399-400; Li Boyong (李伯勇, the labor minister) et al., *Zhonghuo renmin gongheguo laodong fa jiangzhuo* (Forum on the PRC labor law) (Beijing: Labor Press, 1994), 5-11

118. *Xinhua Daily Telegraph,* Shanghai, May 29, 1995.

119. The Economic and Trade Commission of the PRC, *Gunagyu dangqian jingji yunxing qingkuan de huibaotigang* (An outline of a report on the current economic situation), Classified State Council document, Beijing, July 17, 1995, 10-11. The author's field work, however, found that this figure was underestimated. For example, in Shanghai, the officially reported unemployed (or *xiagang*) workers were 300,000. But the officials told the author in private that the real number was between 600,000 and 1 million (author's field notes in Shanghai, summer 1996).

120. See Meizhong Daobao (*US-China tribune*) (Los Angeles), January 12, 1996, 2.

121. The author's interviews with senior economic and labor officials in Beijing, Shanghai and Guangzhou. Similar estimates also in Xin 1993, 97-100.

122. In 1995 and 1996, however, the factory was in financial trouble due to poor sales.

123. As a comparison, in the same city of Hefei in 1995, university professors' monthly income was around 300-400 rmb; blue-collar workers' monthly income ranged from 170-450 rmb; factory managers generally made from 300-1,000 rmb; taxi drivers' net monthly income was about 1,000-2,000 rmb (author's field notes, February and August 1995). The legal minimum wage was 198 rmb in Hefei and 135-198 rmb in other Anhui cities. With approval, enterprises that were bankrupt or in financial difficulty could pay their employees less (70 percent) than the minimum wage for under a year (Anhui Provincial Government: Regulation on Minimum Wages in Anhui, in Xinan Wanbao, Hefei, June 6, 1995, 1).

124. As a comparison, the largest and oldest auto maker in China, Changchun First Auto Work (FAW), had about one hundred thousand employees in 1996, but only 30 percent were actual auto-manufacturing workers. FAW was a city of its own with more than four hundred thousand people. The average income was about 1,000 rmb per month (author's field notes, September 1996).

125. Local media praised the factory for taking care of retired workers "well." As a national rule, all retired "old cadres" (*lixiu laogangbu*—those who joined the CCP revolution before 1949) were granted special privileges including free phones, larger apartments, free use of company cars, and a special recreation center. See *Hefei jingji bao* (Hefei economic news) (Hefei) July 27, 1995, 4.

126. For a praising report on the complex, see *Renmin Ribao-Overseas,* November 4, 1992, 1.

127. CCTV Evening News, Beijing, May 5, 1995.

128. For a similar arrangement, see Chen 1992, 8.

129. As a comparison, the largest steel maker in the PRC, the Anshan Steel Group, had five hundred thousand employees (including 20 percent retirees) and nearly one million population in 1996. Only seventy-four thousand workers, however, were actually making steel. The average income was nearly 1,000 rmb per month (author's field notes, September 1996).

130. For a similar but smaller steel-making complex with fifty-three thousand employees in Anhui Province and its "overstaffing" and other problems of labor management, see Andrew Tanzer, "The China Bubble," in *Forbes,* May 8, 1995, 46-47.

131. As a comparison, in the same city of Beijing in 1995, university professors' monthly total income was about 300-500 rmb; taxi drivers' net could be as high as 3,000 rmb; central government officials (division chief level with M.A. or Ph.D. degrees) on average had incomes of 650-800 rmb; a twenty-seven-year-old middle-ranking banker in a state-owned bank earned about 1,000 rmb; a twenty-four-year-old policeman's known income was about 550 rmb; a college professor moonlighting in a foreign firm made about 3,000 rmb (author's field notes, February 1995). The legal minimum wage was set at 1.1 rmb per hour or 210 rmb per month by the Beijing municipal government, in accordance with the newly passed PRC Labor Law. See Beijing Municipal Government, "Beijingshi zuidi gongzi guiding" (The regulation on minimum wages in Beijing), in *Beijing Ribao* (Beijing daily), December 2, 1994, 1.

132. Official accounts essentially presented a similar finding about the difference between the old permanent employment and the new contract employment. Cf. Labor Ministry 1991.

133. In Liaoning Province, all cadres in state-owned enterprises (10 percent of total employees) changed their titles to either workers, technical experts, or managers in 1993 (*Renmin Ribao-Overseas,* September 9, 1993, 1). In the SEZs, all cadres in the enterprises became contracted workers. See *Shenzhen Renshi* (Shenzhen personnel), an internal monthly by the Shenzhen Personnel Bureau (Shenzhen), no. 6 (1995), 18.

134. Workers would be paid only 70 percent of their wages during this "vacation" and were not allowed to work another job other than domestic work (Chen 1992, 73). Actually, they would lose much more than 30 percent of their income, since nonwage bonuses and other benefits constituted much of total income.

135. For a general report on the fierce competition the HAPC was facing from collective and private bus operators, see Ma Yuson, "Simian cuge shepujie?" (Who'll break the siege?) in *Xinan wanbao* (Xinan evening news) (Hefei), May 28, 1995, 3.

136. Reimbursement for medical costs depended on seniority. The HAPC had to pay 100 percent for retired old cadres who had "joined the revolution" before 1949, and for work-related injuries. This rule was basically the same across the nation. See, for example, Labor Ministry 1991, 55. Like most other state-owned enterprises, the HPAC provided cheap apartments for its employees to rent. But at the time of this study it could provide housing only to those employees (85 percent) who had been

with the company for longer than ten years. Only those who had worked in HAPC for more than five years could join the waiting list.

137. Beijing estimated that such drains reached a total of over 1 trillion rmb in the past decade. In *Shengzhou Ribao* (China daily), San Gabriel, Calif., October 20, 1995, 1. For some typical Chinese discussion on this increasingly serious problem, see Wang Baoxi, "Guoyou zichang shi zhengyang liushide" (How state assets are lost) in Zhongguo gongye gingji yangjou (Studies of Chinese industrial economy) (Beijing) (May 1994): 22-26; Jiangxi Provincial Banking Institute: "Guangyu guoyou zichang liushi wenti de yangjou baogao" (A report on the study on the draining of state assets) in *Jingji yu jjingyong* (Economy and finance) (Nanchang) (September 1994), 11-21; and Tong Xin: "Guoyou zichang liushi gaikuang" (The general situation of the draining of state assets) in *Zhenfli de zhuaiqou* (Pursuit of truth) (Beijing) (July 1994): 10-16.

138. For a general picture of the Shanghai economy in the mid-1990s, see Gao Qian and Shi Donghui, "Dui 1994 nian Shanghai jingji fazhang xinshi de rugan fengxi" (An analysis of the economic situation in Shanghai in 1994), in *Chaijing yangjou* (Financial and economic studies) (Shanghai) (May 1994): 25-31.

139. These two types of nonlocal legal residence required that the holders be cadres or talents (professionals), pay an up-front and then an annual registration fee, have valid local jobs, and be reviewed annually. See Shanghai Municipal Government, *Shanghaishi nanying hukou guangli zhanxin guiding* (Provisional regulations on the management of the blue *hukou* in Shanghai) (Shanghai) 21 articles, February 1, 1994. For the detailed official policy governing these two systems in Shenzhen, see *Shenzhen renshi* (Shenzhen personnel), an internal monthly by the Shenzhen Personnel Bureau (Shenzhen), nos. 11-12, (1994): 3; no. 6, (1995): 22-24.

140. Two types of employers have made significant exceptions to this rule. Wholly owned foreign-invested enterprises and private employers usually do not require a *dangan* for hiring or promotion. But even some of them have learned to use this Chinese tool to manage the Chinese.

141. This process is apparently the same in other provinces. See Labor Ministry 1991, 54.

142. Interviews in Beijing and Hong Kong, 1995.

143. Wang Yu and Li Yuehong, eds., *Dier zheye chongye zhinan* (A guide to working in second jobs), (Beijing: Dangan Press, 1992), 2-4.

144. In Beijing, this fee could be 300 rmb per month or higher. See Chen 1992, 74-75.

145. For a vivid report on the use of this new policy and the sufferings of those who could not get a second job, see "Guoqi naitui: Yuren xihuang yuren chou" (Internal early retirement in the state-owned enterprises: Some are happy and some are sad), in *Shengzhou Ribao* (Shengzhou Daily) (New York), April 14, 1995.

146. The Organization Department of the CCP Anhui Committee and the Anhui Provincial Personnel Bureau, "Guangyu tingxin liuzhe de tongzhi" (Notice on the leave without pay) (Hefei), June 1992.

147. See the Shenzhen Personnel Bureau, *Shenzhenshi shiyedanwei zhuangye jishu renyuan he guangli renyuan cizhicitui zhangxing bangfa* (Provisional regulations on the resignation and dismissal of professional and managerial workers in the institution *danweis* in Shenzhen city), Shenzhen government document, 1994.

148. Karl Marx, *Zhiben lun* (Capital) Chinese edition, vol. 1. (Beijing: Renmin Press, 1972), 534.

149. The strong existence of labor immobility under this authoritarian state LAP is best exemplified by the sharp separation between the urban and rural economies. For instance, during 1978-1986, among new jobs created in the urban economy, only 15.31 percent were filled by laborers from rural areas (Taylor 1988, 743).

150. Yang Qinfang, in *Guangdong shehui kexuie* (Guangdong social sciences) (Guangzhou), no. 2 (1990): 140.

151. Although the words "administrative" and "bureaucratic" are used interchangeably here, by using "bureaucratic," this book does not suggest that Chinese political authority is in the hands of specialized bureaucrats who take politics as a vocation, as in Weber's terminology. Rather, in the PRC, the official, or bureaucrat (官, *guan*) means far more. Serving as a *guang* has been the best vehicle to power, wealth, and glamour in almost every profession and discipline. It is also the most common standard for measuring success, rank, and social status.

152. Parsons, 1967, 505. For a conceptual discourse on those universals, see Parsons 1967, 490-520.

153. Institutionalization and structural differentiation along the lines of rationalization of the bureaucratic system was viewed as the very process of political modernization. See Huntington 1970.

154. For some representative studies on social stratification in the PRC, see Watson 1984.

155. Corruption of CCP-PRC bureaucrats has become a major theme of the writings on current affairs in China. For example, see Zeng 1993, Yao and Qiu 1993, and the ten books of the series on "the hot issues in economic life" published by the Renmin University Press in 1992. For a foreigner's examination of this issue, see Yufan Hao and Michael Johnston, "Reform at the Crossroads: An Analysis of Chinese Corruption," in *Asian Perspective* (Seoul), vol. 19, no. 1 (spring-summer 1995): 117-149.

156. Ting Gong, *The Politics of Corruption in Contemporary China: An Analysis of Policy Outcomes* (Westport, Conn.: Praeger 1994).

157. A leading feature of the traditional Chinese bureaucratic system was that officials were generally paid by the imperial court with fixed and minimum salaries. They were therefore institutionally driven and allowed to take bribes and sell their political power to feed their staffs and families. "Clean officials" were rare exceptions in Chinese political history.

158. Author's field notes in Anhui and Jiangsu Provinces, 1995.

159. Zheng Yefu, "Shehui sengtaixue de fubai yu shehui zhuanxinqi de fubai" (The decay of social ecology and corruption during social transition), in *Zhanlui yu gunagli* (Strategy and management) (Beijing), no. 3 (1994): 100-103.

160. Bao Xiaoling, "Tangtang jingji zhengzhang de fangshi he zhiliang" (On the ways and quality of economic growth), in *Guangmin Ribao* (Guangmin daily) (Beijing), August 3, 1995, 4.

161. *Renmin Ribao-Overseas,* May 26, 1995, 2.

162. Qiao et al. 1994, 235. Published by the Central Party School of the CCP, this book was recommended to me in 1995 by a number of the Chinese elite as a "good reflection" of their thinking.

163. The CCP has reaffirmed its control over the nation's labor mobility as the key to stabilizing the authoritarian LAP. For some interesting discussions of the alleged "negative" impacts of the weakened authoritarian LAP and proposed solutions, see the articles in *Xuexi yu Yanjou* (Study and research), a monthly magazine of the Beijing Municipal CCP Committee, no. 4 (1990): 26-29, and its sister publication of the CCP Hubei Provincial Committee, *Xuexi yu shijian* (Study and practice) (Wuhan), no. 3 (1990): 16-19. Also, Lijun et al. 1994, 278-286.

164. Li Ding, "Baozhang juye renshi fazhang mubiao ziyi" (Guaranteed employment is still a goal of development), in *Renmin Ribao,* February 10, 1995, 4.

165. Barely a year after the abolishment of national grain rationing (*liangpiao*), twenty-nine out of thirty-five major cities restored this urban *hukou*-based and state-subsidized supply system in the fall of 1994 to curb the politically damaging rise of food prices when per capita production of grain in China had stayed at a low level of about 375 kg (about 827 pounds) a year (*Renmin Ribao-Overseas,* May 8, 1995, 2).

166. For such reemployment projects in one inland province, see Zhu Yin, "Shiye mushiwang" (Unemployed but not hopeless), in *Xinan sanbao* (Xinan evening news) (Hefei), January 23, 1995, 1.

167. Author's interviews with senior managers of state-owned enterprises in Beijing and Shanghai in the spring and summer of 1995.

168. Xin 1992, 28-31 and Zeng 1993, 33-64. Both reports and the author's field studies revealed that for most of those "moonlighting" state employees, their state job had become basically "rest time" while they really worked hard on their "second jobs" to make most of their total income.

169. For how active, how many, and how significant those "divers" have been to the PRC economy in the 1990s, see, for example, Zeng 1993 and the series of books on the underground economy published by the same press in 1993-1994.

170. The so-called *bingtui* (early retirement due to disease) became a convenient way for many to stay connected to the security net of the authoritarian state LAP while joining the market economy to earn more income. See, for example, Cheng Jingchan, "Bingtui xingtailu" (The mentality of the bingtui people), in *Anhui Ribao* (Anhui daily) (Hefei) August 8, 1995, 6.

171. CCP Central Committee and the State Council, *Guangyu dangzheng jiguang xian(chu) ji yishang lingdao gangbu shouru shengbao de guiding* (Regulations on income reporting of leading cadres above the rank of county [division] level) (Beijing), April 30, 1995.

172. In general, the labor force allocated and governed by the authoritarian state LAP is relatively more skilled and better educated. But the proportion of young state employees who reach high- to middle-level skills was only about 15 percent in 1994, rather low compared with developed nations, where the figure was 75 to 80 percent. See Li Zhiqian, "Qinggong, gaizenyang cencai?" (Young workers, how can you become an expert?), in *Guangmin Ribao* (Guangmin daily) (Beijing), August 2, 1995, 1.

3. Community-Based Labor Markets

Starting in 1952, a nationwide *hukou* (household or resident registration) system was implemented in China. Completed after the conclusion of agriculture collectivization in rural areas and socialist reform in the cities, this *hukou* system institutionally separated the rural and urban populations. A typical dual-economy, or more precisely a dual institutional structure, has been formed and maintained in the PRC since the late 1950s.[1] Besides the powerful measures fixing the workers to their *danweis,* or units and communes, respectively, in the cities and villages, labor mobility was further restricted because labor flow across geographic boundaries and between the two sectors was administratively controlled. Only through narrow channels, such as passing the college entrance exams, joining the military and becoming an officer (thus a cadre who was qualified to have an urban *hukou*), or some marriage schemes, were a very few laborers able to cross the boundaries between rural and urban China.[2]

The increasing gap between the rural and urban economies led to increasing disparity between living standards in the "two Chinas."[3] Political campaigns to break the barriers between the two sectors failed in the Mao era. During the ten years of the Cultural Revolution (1966-1976), the PRC recruited about 13 million workers from the rural areas, where many more people were underemployed, while it forcibly sent about 11 million young urban residents—middle and high school graduates—to work and live in the villages and to be "re-educated" by the peasants. By 1978-1979, the majority of those youths flooded back to the cities and aggravated the jobs problem in an urban economy that was already plagued by gross underemployment (Hu 1993, 452-453). Chronic underemployment and the inability of the state to create jobs in the rural and urban economies forced the CCP to tolerate limited growth of nonstate labor allocation. Political chaos and economic disasters such as the Great Leap Forward (1959-1962) and the Cultural Revolution only enhanced the urgency of such tolerance from time to time.

It is against such a background that an alternative LAP, a societal allocation in local communities, began to emerge separately in the two sectors as early as the late 1950s. Over time, the two forms of community-based societal LAPs expanded, changed, and started to have more in common. The great advancement of the market institution in China after 1978 transformed this LAP institutionally. An LAP of the community-based labor markets developed to become a nationwide alternative to the authoritarian state LAP in the cities and the family-based traditional LAP in the countryside. By the late 1990s, community-based labor markets (CLMs) had become a fast-growing major LAP while the family-based LAP declined and the authoritarian LAP stagnated. The CLMs allocated increasingly more workers and appeared to contribute profoundly to economic development, social changes, and overall Chinese modernization. CLMs are expected to be the largest Chinese LAP in the near future, uniting the rural and the urban economies and laying down a unique and deep foundation for the institutional changes in contemporary China.

To clarify the field for our exploration of CLMs, we begin this chapter with a brief discussion on the notions of community and community-based markets. This is followed by a description of the community-based LAP in contemporary China and its prospects. It will be shown that CLMs have a unique advantage to become the main LAP in China in the near future. The chapter concludes with an analysis of the institutional significance of this LAP.

Community and Community-Based Markets

The characteristics of community-based labor allocation that have made CLMs a viable alternative to the authoritarian state LAP and the family-based traditional LAP are explored in this section. A conceptual examination of CLMs may further help us to appreciate the differences and similarities between a national labor market and CLMs. Such differences and similarities, especially the former, which will be argued later, contain rich information about the nature of China's institutional structure and its future.

Communities as Human Groupings

Community, in the generic sense, refers to an identifiable human grouping commonly defined by shared location and territory. Members of a community generally have constant knowledge of each other and sustained, close interactions. Members can significantly affect each other's behavior with the extensive accessibility and knowledge acquired from community-based interactions. German sociologist F. Tenneies is believed to have been the first to explore this concept (*Gemeinschaft*). A community, defined by Talcott Parsons in a classical way, "is that collectivity the members of which share a common territorial area as their base of operations for daily activities" (Parsons 1951A, 91). The term may be used to describe a human grouping as large as the whole of humankind, as in the case of a global, or international, community in which nations and states rather than individuals are considered the primary community members.[4] It has also been used to describe a human grouping as small as a ranch that is occupied by only a few unrelated persons.

Based on Parsons's definition, the notion of communities, as presented in this book, is understood as human groupings that are beyond the family structure but do not have sovereign political authority. Those substate groups are geographically defined and historically constructed, but their members usually are not genetically related. People feel that they belong to a certain community primarily because they believe they are unique as a group in comparison to others. Geographically or politically defined social institutions form the basic organizational structure for communities. Family and clan organizations, voluntary associations, customs and traditions, shared activities and values, and self-reinforcing common behavioral norms constitute the institutional basis for communities. Over time, territory-based exclusiveness and legal barriers grow to mark communities as distinctively different from each other. In some cases, however, economic activities may serve as the initial or additional bond for a community. Communities share some basic institutional features as a layer of human grouping that may vary significantly across time and geography. Communities change their contents, boundaries, and practices. They may enlarge, shrink, or even disappear. Many of them, based on social institutions, are organized in a family-like fashion with a visibly less hierarchical authority structure. As in families, the closeness and cohesiveness of a community seem to have a reverse correlation to its size. The forces that cause changes are many. The legitimacy of

From Family to Market

the boundaries of communities, however, is ultimately upheld by the political authority of the state, which is generally and conveniently viewed as nationally based.[5]

With such an understanding, most of the Chinese *danweis* in the cities, villages, and townships may be viewed as basic communities.[6] It is here we see the most clear boundaries of communities as quasi-exclusive groupings. Village or *danwei* membership, for example, can hardly be changed by any means other than marriage, birth, or a direct political decision of the government. Some communities can be much larger with less clear and less exclusive boundaries among them. Most Chinese cities are themselves such large communities. As one study concluded, counties have been the most stable unit of communities in Chinese history, thus perhaps the appropriate unit for an "economic zoning."[7] In big cities, the districts, street committees, or residential committees may become the basis of local communities.[8] Despite the fact that many communities in contemporary China were established by political decisions and economic activities, they generally are based on social institutions and appear to be, to varying degrees, family-like. Furthermore, given the nature of Chinese administrative social-ism described in chapter 2, the administrative boundaries of the regions of the PRC state often become the boundaries of substate communities. The local CCP and government organizations often conveniently provide the political institutions for the communities. Those community-based political institutions incorporate the local economic and social institutions and thus form an undifferentiated organizational structure on the grassroots level.

Community-Based Markets

Communities are the subgroups in a nation. The political, eco-nomic, and social activities within those communities naturally vary. Because a community's political system does not have sovereign authority backed by the legitimate use of force, political authority at the community level tends to be much weaker than that of the state. The internal political activities are generally constrained fundamen-tally by the political activities of the nation. Thus, in China, local politics looks quite similar in the different communities. The deep-rooted family-like organizational structure of the communities and the powerful state authority are the two defining factors of commu-nity politics.[9] Socially, the communities also demonstrate similarities. Reproduction-based social values and behavioral norms are the same.

Political intervention and control of Chinese social activities are also similar. The power of the community-based social institutions in restricting people's behavior is not as strong as that of the family, for there are less assured mutual bonds outside the families, and members may leave a particular community for good. Furthermore, in comparison to families, it is easier for the political authority of the state to cut deeply into the power of the communities' social institutions, because the state serves as the source of legitimacy for any activity in a particular community. Therefore, social institutions, the organizational basis of communities, tend to be more susceptible to change simply because of the competition from families within and the pressure of the state from without.

The relatively weak political institutions and changeable social institutions, compared to the state and families, respectively, often lead to a soft institutional setting in communities. This structure may create an institutional possibility for the economy to acquire a certain autonomy. That is, economic activities can find significantly more flexibility within communities than in either the family structure or nation. State interventions based on political logic and values tend to be diluted, even incapacitated, by the weak position of the community political institutions vis-à-vis the social institutions. The anti-market constraints of family institutions are moderated by the multifamily community setting. The logical outcome is a relatively conducive environment for small-scale markets to develop in those communities. Even when development of a national market is difficult under the political pressure of the family-like state, substantial market institutions can grow locally in communities, outside the families, to regulate local economic activities.

The community, a human grouping that is subnational but above families, thus provides the weakest institutional constraints against the development of a market-oriented economy in a traditional nation. The power of both the state and families is somehow buffered or neutralized at the community level. Furthermore, powerful local leaders can also use their political authority to create a community-based market economy with relative ease. Starting in 1983, some innovative local cadres in the nine "reform experiment counties" designated by Beijing even used political power to forcibly turn a whole county into an integrated community, within which local resources could achieve a community-wide "free flow" and "best utilization."[10]

Historically, then, we see the flourishing of local markets in medieval Europe, ancient China, and many other pre-modern settings worldwide.[11] In fact, almost all nations had local markets to allocate economic resources in their history. Some even appeared to have quasi-national markets for a while. The difference between a national or even international market and local markets is a major indicator that separates modernized economies from pre-modern ones. In China, substantial market-based economic activities developed as early as two thousand years ago. It reached heights in the Song dynasty (tenth to thirteenth centuries) and especially in the Ming dynasty (fourteenth to seventeenth centuries). The seemingly prosperous local markets later prompted many Chinese historians to believe that China was on the eve of capitalism even earlier than Western Europeans.[12] After the seventeenth century, local markets were considerably subdued by political forces but endured until the PRC era.[13] Even during the most anti-market years under Mao, regular country-fair type local markets survived in many villages and townships. By the 1990s, active local markets, more than seventy thousand nationwide, had formed several specialized trading centers for the nation with increasingly institutionalized brokering systems.[14] Chinese scholars believe regional/community markets have become a major feature of the PRC economy in the 1990s.[15]

Local markets developed extensively in Chinese communities, mainly below the level of counties or cities. At this level, not only were the external constraints of the state and the internal bonds of families the weakest, but the inherent destructive forces of the market institution were also self-contained and mitigated by the relatively small size of the markets. The drive for efficiency, for instance, was checked because the scale of production was limited by the size of the local communities. It was usually difficult, if not impossible, for a local market to penetrate other communities meaningfully. Thus negative externalities of the market institution such as social inequality based on income were sufficiently mitigated. Moralistic principles of the communities were often protected from the erosive forces of the market institution because the market tended to be limited by the boundaries of the communities. Market-oriented economic activities were, therefore, generally not threatening to the state political authority above and the family structure within. Those limited local markets thus provided a feasible and politically and socially less costly way to increase the efficiency and innovation of the local economies to a bounded but significant—or even sufficient—extent.[16]

A monopoly or oligopoly of local markets could emerge, but neither was as economically irrational as a monopoly of a national market. Because small local markets and communities were less exclusive than national markets, they could engage in certain exchanges among themselves, especially trading the monopolized commodities. While the small scale of the local markets and sustained political and social pressures made it difficult for a firm to acquire the ability to monopolize a local market, intercommunity economic interactions also curbed the negative consequences of a monopolized local market. The well-known southern Anhui merchants (*huishang,* 徽商) played such a monopoly-breaking intercommunity commercial role within a nonmarket economy in the local markets mainly along the Yangtze River for centuries until the end of the Qing dynasty.[17]

The nature of local markets effectively prevented the emergence of a national monopoly of all local markets. On the one hand, it was difficult for one merchant to penetrate and control one industry in all communities that had relative autonomy and exclusivity. On the other hand, the political power of the state made certain that no one, other than the state itself, could enjoy a monopoly of any industry. Thus, in a very interesting way, a fragmented market could persist and operate actively in a vast number of communities, yet a national market could not meaningfully emerge. The negatives of the market institution were thus absent in the eyes of national political leaders and did not represent the same threat to every community. This arrangement seemed to meet the political needs of the dominant Chinese state for centuries. It provided an increased source of income to the state through taxation and to members of various communities who could no longer merely live off the land as families; yet it had only a minimum destabilizing effect on the family-like institutional structure of the nation.

Features of Community-Based Labor Markets

If a fragmented market (the local markets) was possible, what about the local labor markets? Historically as well as currently, the labor force is generally the most difficult economic resource to be allocated by the market institution. Even in a nation where a national market has become the undisputed main economic institution, a substantial portion of its labor allocation could still be subject to many nonmarket forces. Thus, we see empirically in today's United States, for example, that millions of workers are allocated directly or indirectly by the state through government jobs, contracts, subsidies, and welfare programs. Nevertheless, conceptually, like the commodity markets, small and locally oriented labor markets may have a chance to develop on the community level in a largely nonmarket economy.

In theory, the existence of CLMs, a fragmented labor market, may be understood better by borrowing the economics model of a "segmented labor market." Labor market segmentation is the historical process whereby political-economic forces encourage the division of the labor market into separate submarkets, or segments, distinguished by different characteristics and behavioral rules. Dual or even multiple labor markets may be viewed as the products of such a process.[18] Political forces and social institutions, usually community-based, are mainly responsible for such segmentation. The existence of different LAPs in contemporary China, the so-called multiple labor markets, may be interpreted as a deliberate political effort by the state aimed at segmentation for the purpose of perpetuating the dual rural-versus-urban organizational structure and containing the economically useful but politically challenging market institution.[19] CLMs are, therefore, essentially labor markets distorted and segmented by political and social institutions along the lines of local communities. CLMs also have several institutional features that set them apart from the family-based traditional LAP, the authoritarian state LAP, and a national labor market.

First, two essential indicators help us to identify a CLM or, more generically, a community-based LAP. One is that every member of the community is treated basically the same concerning job opportunities, pay schedules, work-related benefits and protections, and job security. In the case of CLMs, every laborer in the community would be subject to the allocation and management of the community-confined and often socially distorted local labor market. Supply and demand fundamentally determines the allocation and utilization of labor, but only within the community. The other key indicator is that community members are systematically preferred over outsiders by the employers. An institutional discrimination is practiced, even in the CLMs, against competition from outside laborers. Empirically in China, the *hukou* system has been an almost perfect tool for such labor discrimination by local communities.

Second, a CLM, by definition, is a market-oriented LAP practiced by a community within a nation. Depending on the community's size, a CLM can be quite small—as few as several hundred people—or as large as several million people, such as those in the cities in today's PRC. The cohesiveness of a CLM and the effectiveness of its institutional discrimination against outsiders, naturally, decrease as its size increases.

Third, CLMs are market-oriented LAPs and thus tend to be economically efficient and innovative. The labor allocated and managed by a CLM, within its particular community, can achieve substantially high productivity. Due to the strong influence of social institutions, competition among laborers may not be as fierce and as motivated as that in a national labor market, but limited market mechanisms are often enough to reduce or even eliminate underemployment. This is especially true when the labor force in the concerned community is the appropriate size for an efficient production scale of its particular industry or industries. The impressive growth of the Chinese "collective" economy in the rural and urban areas, where the CLMs were increasingly practiced in recent years, as shall be described later, illustrates this point.[20]

Fourth, CLMs demonstrate clear limits and rationales set by the social institutions of the community. We see, empirically, that a community that has a CLM generally has a clear emphasis on rough equality among its members. The employers are institutionally and culturally compelled to recruit community members first before even considering any outsiders, even those more qualified. When there is a need for payroll reduction, that order would be reversed. Unemployment relief, usually in hidden forms, is institutionally built in. A strong mechanism for income redistribution is therefore common for the CLMs. Those social distortions of the labor market, which stop at the boundaries of the communities, tend to reduce the efficiency of the community economies but greatly increase social harmony and stability. The redistribution scheme, however, usually does not cover outsiders who are working "temporarily" as supplements to the community labor force. Therefore, especially in prosperous communities that need outside labor and can afford it, a mini dual structure exists: a privileged and protected community labor force versus the outside workers who accepted jobs with market-oriented terms but without the socially determined and community-based benefits. The bigger the difference, the clearer the community boundaries and stronger the effort to maintain it.

Finally, a CLM may often act as single player in either the marketplace or nonmarket national economy. Seen from the outside, a CLM is organized like a combination of the market institution with an enlarged family structure that includes unrelated community members. No matter how much distortion of the market exists within it, just like the family-based LAP a CLM can engage in free-market style economic exchanges with other players as a unit. No matter how much of a market mechanism it has inside, a CLM can also survive well in a nonmarket national economy as long as the political author-ity of the state tolerates or at least restrains from eliminating the market institution in the local communities. The CLMs thus can preserve an authentic labor market with each other, or live in a non-market national economy on which they have only a limited and gradual, but perhaps persistent, eroding effect. This feature, as we shall see later, carries profound implications for the overall process of Chinese modernization.

Community-Based Labor Markets in China

Just as the community-based societal LAP has had a long history in China, so have the community-based local markets for nonlabor resources. The community-based LAP, with its deep historical and cultural roots, has acquired an apparent institutional legitimacy. In recent decades, the Chinese community-based societal LAP trans-formed itself profoundly to become the CLMs. The institutional legit-imacy of the societal LAP helped to explain this transformation and the subsequently rapid growth of the CLMs. Especially in the rural areas, CLMs became the fastest-growing LAP and had an increasingly significant impact on the Chinese institutional structure.

Origins of the Chinese CLMs

Local markets that existed widely throughout Chinese history were largely incomplete markets for the exchange of nonlabor economic resources in local communities. Unlike local markets for goods, local labor markets, though conceptually possible, did not develop mean-ingfully, mainly because the institutional barriers were very strong, that is, the state prevented labor markets from emerging even in the local communities. Almost universally, labor was politically and socially the most consequential economic resource. An undifferenti-ated Chinese institutional structure naturally could not afford to differentiate the economic role of labor (as a resource that needs to be utilized on the market for maximum economic efficiency) from the political and social roles of labor as human beings. Family institutions and the family-like state authority jointly discouraged or even eradi-cated the small local labor markets that existed sporadically in the Chinese history (Huang 1990, 93-104). Openly buying and selling the ability of every worker according to a monetary price determined by supply and demand would be understandably viewed as an unacceptable degradation by social institutions centered on the family. To the family-like state, a labor market and associated labor mobility, personal rights, and the ability to bargain would produce fundamental challenges to the clear, hierarchical, and stable political order and values. The periodical emergence of "floating people" (*liumin*) due to the slow breakdown of the family-based traditional LAP often led to the downfall of a mighty dynasty and then to total chaos (*tianxia daluan*). It was therefore not too surprising that Chinese rulers recognized the political undesirability of labor mobility that a labor market would bring. Political efforts aimed at controlling and even eliminating labor markets were thus a major tradition of Chinese politics.[21] This political suffocation of the labor market, even on the community level, was not eased until the nineteenth century, when external forces generated by the international market forced the Chinese state to adapt in order to survive. Under the same kinds of pressures, the PRC state has worked since the 1980s to introduce the market institution in China. That provided a suitable national environment for labor markets to develop, first and foremost, on the local community level.

Thus, although community-based local markets were seen in the past, Chinese labor allocation was dominated by the family-based traditional LAP and a generally smaller but occasionally sizable authoritarian state LAP, which reached its peak under Mao. Slavery or labor concentration camps, rather than sales of laborers' working ability, were needed but insignificant supplements to the dominant LAPs. In some cities, mainly in southeastern China, there were visible market-oriented labor exchanges specializing in allocating daily workers and handicraftsmen. Other than that, community-based labor markets (CLMs) did not emerge meaningfully in China until the 1980s.

Short of a local labor market, a traditional Chinese community could still have a community-based societal LAP. Beyond the families, a substantial portion of a community's labor force could be allocated and managed by neither the state nor the market. A family-friendly community became the institutional basis for such a societal LAP since, as Talcott Parsons observed, the Chinese kinship institution was "extremely closely integrated with territorial community" (1951A, 196).

Conceptually, a community-based societal LAP is based on the organizational principles of social institutions emphasizing social rather than political and economic values. Social institutions, often the enlarged family-like organizations of local communities, like the neighborhood organizations (*lingli zhuzhi*), play a major role in a community-based LAP. This LAP is primarily for projects that have community-wide implications and are beyond the scope of a family yet not handled by the state because of its unwillingness or inability to do so. Such projects could include the relief after local natural disasters, local irrigation systems, roads and other infrastructure, cultural and religious activities, security against bandits, and so on. The local gentry class usually serves as the sponsor or initiator. The labor involved is allocated and managed in a collective fashion with the principles of family-based, not individual, equality.[22] Each participant is treated roughly the same way concerning workload, provisions, and compensation. Such a collective community-based LAP served important functions in the past. Often it was mixed with clan-based or manor-organized activities. Exploitation by the gentries was naturally common, because the community-based social institutions generally set up a clear hierarchical structure determining contributions and rewards. On a smaller scale, swapping of labor and pooling of labor resources were very common among families in rural China. The historical existence of the community-based societal LAP appears evident on other continents; American Indians and ancient Russian peasants, as examples, used to have commune-style societal LAPs.

In the PRC era, starting in the late 1950s, the community-based societal LAP was allowed to develop as a politically valuable supplement to the dominant but grossly inefficient authoritarian state LAP—a help that was considered nonstate, nonmarket, and nonprivate but still socialist. The economic disasters of the Great Leap Forward and the Cultural Revolution only made such help more imperative. The result was the collective, thus socialist, employment provided by the urban collective enterprises and the commune-owned rural industrial enterprises. Both enterprises adopted a typical community-based societal LAP in that jobs were usually available only to persons officially deemed legal residents of a community, usually local *hukou* holders or direct relatives of members of the particular community. Both rural and urban versions of the PRC community-based societal LAP were heavily influenced by the nonmarket institutions of the family and state, with a major similarity of community orientation. Therefore, the Chinese community-based societal LAP empirically manifested itself into two major forms: the so-called collective enterprises in the urban areas and the township or village enterprises (TVEs, or *xiangzheng qiye*), or rural industries in the rural areas. A further description of these two versions and their marketization, and thus the emergence of the CLMs, is in order.

Urban Community-Based Societal LAP and CLMs

The urban community-based societal LAP first emerged in the mid-1950s in the PRC's urban collective enterprises. Most of these enterprises were established by local authorities or communities for the purposes of local industrialization, providing jobs for the local populace and expanding the local tax base. They practiced a community-based societal LAP with heavy influence of the authoritarian state LAP for more than two decades. Afterward, especially after 1984 when urban economic reform started, the urban collective enterprises rapidly developed market-oriented labor practices. CLMs with varying degrees of market orientation began replacing the community-based societal LAP, allocating and governing millions of workers in the urban collective enterprises. Workers were still community confined, and the authoritarian state LAP—backed by the political power of the state—still exercised great influence. But by the mid-1990s, employment and labor management of the urban collective enterprises became increasingly determined by the community-based market forces.

The urban collective enterprises have basically four origins or components.[23] The first is the small- and medium-sized private enterprises that were collectivized, or socialized, forcibly in the 1950s and 1960s through a "redemption" policy or "buying-off" scheme. Those former private and small businesses, the "national capitalist enterprises," formed the early part of the urban collective enterprises. Initially, they were called "public and private joint ventures" with the capitalist owners gradually losing control over their enterprises. Soon they were all changed into either "large collective" or "small collective" enterprises. The capitalist owners became just regular employees, with some additional income in the form of fixed interest (*dingxi*) of their formerly owned properties.[24]

The second component is the local industrial enterprises funded and owned by local governments—thus the people of the local communities—usually at or below the county level. Local political authorities funded some collective enterprises through the local government budget, usually to expand the tax base, develop the local economy, and impress their superiors. Those enterprises are divided into two types: "large collective," or "local-state owned," enterprises, and "small collective" enterprises. The large collective enterprises are relatively large, technology- or capital-intensive, in industries such as manufacturing and transportation. They enjoy almost the same benefits as state-owned enterprises under similar state control. The LAP in these enterprises gradually became an authoritarian state LAP similar to those in state-owned enterprises, but usually less rigid and less comprehensive (Chen and Yang 1988, 48). A crucial difference is that new workers are typically recruited only from the local community. The small collective enterprises are generally small and in the service and retailing industries.[25] They are essentially financially independent from the local governments once they are created. Employing more people than the large collective enterprises, they have a quasi-contract-based LAP limited to the members of the local community.[26] The authenticity of those labor contracts in the small collective enterprises has depended greatly on the overall political environment. In recent years, such labor contracts have become much more institutionalized as the basis for CLMs due to the tolerance of the market institution by the PRC state.

The third component is the more authentic community-owned enterprises. They are similarly called "small collective enterprises" but are founded by urban communities, usually the "residents committees" or "street authorities," often through the truly collective effort of community members. Private contributions are financially important. They typically have the same LAP as the small collective enterprises owned by the local political authorities, but they limit employment to the community in which they are located. Those genuine collective enterprises grew rapidly after 1978. A considerable number are actually private enterprises under the "red hats" of societal names.[27] Their labor practices, therefore, have been the most market-oriented among all the urban collective enterprises. In most communities, many of these enterprises have followed more market-oriented than community-based policies in recruiting and managing their workers.

Finally, the fourth component of the urban collective enterprises is the "labor service enterprises" (LSEs) created by local communities after 1978 with state help—usually through existing state-owned enterprises and other *danweis*. The LSEs were a major effort to cope with the increasing problem of so many "waiting-for-job" people during the reform years.[28] They have been praised as "a new type of societal labor organization that fits into the Chinese national conditions of a huge population," and a "special product" of China in dealing with the chronic problem of surplus labor.[29] LSEs are founded with government funds and/or through state-owned enterprises, as branches of their parent enterprises, and later are encouraged to become financially independent. Some LSEs have turned out to be a major source of income for their parent state-owned *danweis*.[30] In 1988, the majority of LSEs were sponsored by various *danweis* such as factories, social mass organizations, schools, and hospitals. Local authorities and neighborhood communities operated 18.6 percent of them. Only 8.3 percent were run by state labor agencies.[31] The LSEs' main purpose was to employ as many "job-waiters" of the local community as possible, most of them engaged in commercial and service businesses. By the end of 1990, greater than 230,000 LSEs were established in urban China. They employed 16 million people with a gross product value of 76.2 billion rmb, and had absorbed about 20 percent of the urban job-waiters in the 1980s.[32] It was normal for many LSEs to operate without a profit, although as a whole they were in the black. LSEs were practicing a typical Chinese societal labor allocation pattern in various urban communities. Except for the heads and a few technical specialists, most LSE workers were temporary, flexible, and contracted employees from local communities. LSE employment was still considered just temporary work, not a real job, by numerous young job-waiters, although many had stayed more than ten years. In terms of the number of employees, LSEs have become the largest component of the Chinese societal LAP in urban areas. Inevitably, in order to survive in an advancing market economy, they have become market-oriented to varying degrees in their labor recruiting and especially their labor management.

Related to the LSEs, other collective enterprises have been created mainly to employ retired workers. According to PRC labor laws, there is a mandatory retirement age for workers (fifty-five for males and fifty for females) and low- to middle-ranked cadres (sixty for males and fifty-five for females). But, especially in the collective enterprises, not every retired worker gets a pension. More importantly, when there is a pension its value tends to evaporate during an era of considerable inflation. The communities therefore are compelled to do something to help these people.[33] In Shanghai, for example, the city-based Shanghai Retired Workers Management Authority established forty-eight hundred collective enterprises since 1986 to hire more than 100,000 retired workers; revenues from their earnings provided on average 160 rmb annually for about 66 percent of the more than 1.47 million retired urban workers needing financial assistance. Because "there is no way for the government to guarantee the provision for every urban worker," such a "mobilization of social forces" in the community is therefore deemed necessary.[34]

TVEs, or Rural Industries

The majority of community-based socially allocated Chinese labor is in the rural areas, in the TVEs (township-village enterprises), or rural industries. These enterprises emerged in the mid-1950s as a part of collectivized agriculture but did not start expanding until 1963, right after the miserable failure of the Great Leap Forward (Rawski 1979, 4, 60). Then called communes and brigade-run enterprises (CBEs), they benefited from a relaxation of Beijing's control of the rural areas and the massive inflow of "sent-down" urban youth and other counterrevolutionary urban intellectuals from the early 1960s to the end of the 1970s. The gross inefficiency and inability of the state-owned enterprises in meeting the growing demand for consumer goods and services provided opportunities for steady growth of the CBEs even before the reform started.[35]

In 1975, 14.2 million laborers were employed by CBEs. By 1977, at the end of the Cultural Revolution and before Deng's reforms, more than 17 million people worked in CBEs (Rawski 1979, 38).[36] By 1978, 1.52 million CBEs employed about 28.26 million workers, roughly 9 percent of the total rural labor force at that time (Zhang 1992, 65). By 1991, more than 19 million TVEs (the overwhelming majority of them below the village level) were operating.[37] They provided 60 percent of the gross product in the rural areas, or 30 percent of total Chinese industrial output, or 25.5 percent of the combined output of Chinese industry and agriculture.[38] By 1995, TVEs employed more than 120 million former peasants and roughly 2.5 million professionals. More than 46 million of those employees were engaged in manufacturing and construction. Quite a few TVEs were joint ventures between townships/villages and foreign investors.[39]

Most TVEs are funded and owned by townships and villages, formerly collectivized communes and brigades. Compared to collective enterprises in urban areas, TVEs enjoy fewer state benefits but more management freedom. They employ mostly local peasants, though in many cases they recruit workers from outside the area, even from other provinces. This is especially the case in those more open provinces such as Guangdong. Many TVEs there have close to half of their employees from outside their local communities. In one toy factory in Guangdong, half the employees (more than one thousand) came from at least thirty counties of seven other provinces in 1990.[40] Another successful TVE in Zhejiang Province, the largest manufacturer of electrical timers in China, employed 85 percent of its nearly one thousand workers from the rural areas of other "remote" provinces in the mid-1990s.[41] This kind of outside hiring was due partly to a shortage of local young female workers, who were preferred because many TVEs were labor-intensive assembly-line factories producing electronics and plastic goods for export. Key technical positions were commonly filled by recruits from urban areas and by many moonlighting urban workers from state-owned *danweis.*

TVEs were generally more community-based than the urban collective enterprises, and recently have become more market-oriented in their labor allocation and management. On-the-job competition and performance have become the main criteria for pay, promotion, and even dismissal. But community boundaries were clearly maintained along township or village lines. Employees from outside, if hired, were typically treated quite differently from local residents. In the most prosperous areas of Sunan, for example, outside workers were commonly paid only half the locals' wages and had almost no access to the substantial community-based benefits.[42] They could be recognized as community members and thus have the same rights and treatment only through marriage or legal change of *hukou,* or after a number of years of continuous residency as good workers.[43] The internal division of labor among the community members, increasingly market-oriented, was still strongly influenced by social institutions and values. Important considerations were community welfare, local employment, and neighborhood harmony.[44]

It is worth noting that there are two types of TVEs, each practicing a somewhat different labor management. One is called "left the soil but not the rural," referring to TVEs with very close relationships—economically, politically, and socially—with their local townships/villages. Workers still belong to the township/village administration, and economically they were under a unified distribution framework just like other members in the township or village. TVEs of this kind are still part of the local economic community, and community confinement is strong and deep. Most rural CLM-allocated workers are in this type of TVE. The other type of TVE is called "left the soil and the rural," which means the TVEs are quite independent from their parent townships or villages. Many of these TVEs are actually private-owned enterprises in disguise. They continue their economic obligation to the townships or villages basically through taxes, donations, employment, expenditures, and other economic means. They acquire their supply of food, materials, and energy mainly through market exchange rather than through local community distribution. The employees are much less exclusively local recruits. In fact, with their strongly local-oriented but clearly mobile and contractual labor management, those TVEs practice an LAP that is much more a typical labor market than a community-based societal allocation.

In short, despite the fact that there had never been any meaningful national market in China, the Chinese did have a rich tradition of fragmented and limited market economy at the community level: the local markets. Besides the dominant family-based traditional LAP and the authoritarian state LAP, China has had a substantial community-based societal LAP, especially during the PRC era. Unlike the local markets for commodities, labor was never significantly allocated by the market institution. The historical community-based LAP was generally based on community-confined social institutions rather than the market, until the 1980s. By the late 1990s, the community-based societal LAP had largely become CLMs to varying extents in Chinese rural and urban communities.

A Statistical Analysis of Chinese CLMs

In the PRC, the community-based societal LAP emerged in the rural and urban areas almost simultaneously. By the mid-1990s, however, there was a tendency of convergence as they increasingly became CLMs. The statistical analysis on the Chinese societal LAP and the CLMs presented here will first treat the history of the societal LAP and the CLMs in the urban areas because of the unavailability of comparable data about the CBEs and the TVEs. The rural-urban dual economy and the strong bias against rural communities in general, and the CBEs/TVEs in particular by the Chinese State Statistical Bureau in the pre-reform decades, make it difficult to gather systematic information about the rural CLMs before the 1980s. Table 3.2 shows the Chinese CLMs, including TVE employment, in the reform era.

Size
As tables 3.1 and 3.2 demonstrate, the community-based societal LAP became an important Chinese LAP by the beginning of the 1960s. It used to cover from 15 to nearly 25 percent of the urban workers before the reform. By 1978, the rural societal LAP affected only about 10 percent of the rural labor force. The growth of the CLMs has been clearly steady in both rural and urban areas since then. We see big surges in 1984-1985 due to the start of urban economic reforms. We also see slight stagnation around 1989 when the political environment was temporarily quite unfriendly to reformers. By 1994, the urban societal LAP, now more appropriately the urban CLMs, held its share of the urban labor force in approximately a quarter of the total urban labor force. The growth of the urban societal LAP/

CLMs should be considered still impressive given the following facts: (1) the urban labor force grew by over 55.7 percent from 1978 to 1992 (Gao 1993, 581), and urban CLMs apparently grew faster than the growth of the urban labor force; (2) the share of the authoritarian

Table 3.1. Community-Based Labor Allocation in Urban China

Year	Size (thousands)	% of urban labor force*	Average income (rmb)	% of average urban income	% of state worker income
1952	230	0.9	348	78.2	78.0
1957	6,500	2.1	571	91.5	89.6
1960	9,250	15.1	409	80.0	77.5
1965	12,270	23.9	398	67.5	61.1
1970	14,240	22.6	405	72.2	66.5
1975	17,720	21.6	453	78.1	73.9
1976	18,130	21.0	464	80.7	76.7
1978	20,480	22.4	506	82.3	78.6
1979	22,740	22.7	542	81.1	81.1
1980	24,250	23.1	623	81.8	77.6
1981	25,680	23.2	642	83.2	79.1
1982	26,510	23.2	671	84.1	80.3
1983	27,440	23.4	689	84.5	80.7
1984	32,160	26.4	811	83.3	78.4
1985	33,240	26.0	967	84.2	79.8
1986	34,210	25.7	1,092	82.2	77.2
1987	34,880	25.3	1,207	70.4	78.1
1988	35,270	24.7	1,426	81.6	77.0
1989	35,020	24.3	1,557	80.4	75.8
1990	35,490	24.1	1,681	78.6	73.6
1991	36,280	23.8	1,866	79.8	75.3
1992	36,210	23.2	2,109	77.8	73.3
1993	37,041	23.2†	2,323	78.0†	n.a
1994	38,099	23.2†	3,518	78.0†	n.a.

Notes: In official Chinese statistics, community-based socially allocated urban labor is categorized as either employees of the urban collective enterprises or employees of the *danweis* owned by local governments, including the residential committees.

  * Urban labor force includes four components: state employees, employees of the collective enterprises, private employees and businessmen, and employees of foreign-invested enterprises.

  † The ratio is assumed to be the same as the year before.

  Sources: Figures are based on Gao 1993, 582, 621-622; SSB-LM 1991, 7, 12, 15, 28; and *Renmin Ribao-Overseas,* March 2, 1995, 2.

From Family to Market

Table 3.2. TVE Employment in Rural China and Size of CLMs

Year	TVE employees (millions)*	% of rural labor force‡		Size of CLMs (rural & urban) (millions)	% of total labor force
		data 1†	data 2		
1978	22.24	31.50	10.28	51.98	13.00
1979	22.53	31.90	10.28	54.65	13.32
1980	25.37	35.02	11.00	59.27	13.99
1981	25.89	n.a	7.92**	51.55**	11.79**
1982	28.04	n.a.	8.30**	54.55**	12.04**
1983	31.22	43.40	12.51	70.84	15.26
1984	42.09	58.88	16.37	91.04	18.89
1985	49.92	67.13			
		(69.79)	18.82	103.03	20.66
1986	57.52	75.22	19.79	109.43	21.34
1987	61.78	81.30	20.85	116.18	22.01
1988	64.99	86.11	21.49	121.38	22.34
1989	63.28	84.98	20.76	120.00	21.69
1990	63.39	86.74			
		(92.65)	22.05	128.14	22.58
1991	65.01	(96.09)	22.30	132.37	22.68
1992	n.a.	(105.81)	24.16	142.02	23.90
1993	n.a.	(112.78)	24.66‡	149.82	24.50‡
1994	n.a.	(120.00)	26.69	158.10	25.10‡

Notes: In official Chinese statistics, community-based socially allocated rural labor is categorized as people working collectively in rural industries of manufacturing, construction, transportation, and services. But there is clear evidence showing substantial private business may have been included in the official statistics on the CBEs and especially the TVEs.

* It is difficult to find complete and reliable historical data about employment at the CBEs/TVEs. The total number of the rural labor force, for example, has shown up differently in different official statistics. For the year 1982, the error was estimated by Chinese economists to be about 74 million people (Zhang 1988, 99-100). Figures in this column are based on SSB-LM 1991, 21; SSB 1992, 53, 67; and the survey findings of Liu 1993, 104-107.

† Figures in this column came from SSB-PB 1993, 316-317. Figures inside the parentheses are those officially recorded as employees of the TVEs in Gao 1993, 604; and the State Statistical Bureau's reports in *Renmin Ribao-Overseas,* March 2, 1995, 2.

‡ Based on data 2 (or the figures inside the parentheses when available), SSB-LM 1991, 7; and Gao 1993, 581. The ratio is assumed to grow at roughly the same speed as the previous three years.

** Based on data 1 or data 2, SSB-LM 1991, 7; and Gao 1993, 581.

state LAP shrank by more than ten percentage points from 1978 to 1992 (see table 2.1 in the previous chapter of this book); and (3) private employment and employment of foreign-invested enterprises both increased several-fold in those fifteen years (see table 4.1 in chapter 4 below).

The fastest growth of the societal LAP/CLMs has been in rural areas. The rural community-based societal LAP started in 1978 at essentially the same size as the urban societal LAP. The rural societal LAP/CLMs more than tripled from 1978 to 1992 and more than doubled its share of the allocation of rural labor. Given the absolute size of the rural CLMs, such a growth rate was indeed remarkable. The lessening of the PRC state's political control in the countryside, accompanied by the restoration of the economically unstable family-based LAP, may be the most important factor causing this phenomenal growth. By the mid-1990s, Chinese CLMs, with varied degrees of market-orientation in the rural and urban communities, had emerged to become the second largest LAP (nearly 160 million employees in 1995) after the family-based traditional LAP, surpassing the authoritarian state LAP (112 million workers) by more than 47 million people.

Despite its being the largest, the family-based LAP was primarily in agriculture and had little technical or productivity edge to dominate Chinese labor allocation. CLMs were prospering in almost all industrial and service sectors, thus had the potential to surpass the dominating authoritarian state LAP economically, technologically, and eventually politically. On the one hand, CLMs were growing much faster than the authoritarian state LAP. On the other hand, unlike the state-owned enterprises, more than half of which were still losing money, the collective enterprises and especially the massive TVEs tended to be financially healthy and growing.

Income

Historically, as shown in table 3.1, urban workers under the community-based societal LAP were paid much less than employees under the authoritarian state LAP. The income gap between the two, sometimes nearly 40 percent, may have contributed significantly to the maintenance of the generally inefficient authoritarian state LAP. The gap continued at 25 percent into the late 1990s. In addition, state employees enjoyed much better nonwage benefits, labor protection, and job security. Workers under the authoritarian state LAP had a much higher per capita investment and technological sophistication. During the Seventh Five-Year Plan period (1986-1990), for example, every state employee got on average about 12,639 rmb worth of new investment while the same figures for the urban collective enterprises was only 2,664 rmb and for the TVEs only 2,164 rmb.[45] The attractiveness and dominance of the authoritarian state LAP is thus further illustrated.

Data on the income of the rural CLM workers are scarce. Sporadic reports and empirical findings from field studies reveal that the average income of rural industrial workers has been significantly lower than even that of urban collective enterprise workers. Beijing officially reported that the average annual income of urban workers was 4,338 rmb in 1994.[46] Based on the ratio (78 percent) in column five of table 3.1, the average annual income of the urban CLM-allocated workers would have been about 3,383 rmb that year. The average income of TVE employees in 1994, according to the official Xinhua New Agency, was only 2,892 rmb, despite a nearly 25 percent increase over 1993.[47] But compared to family-based agricultural laborers, whose average income was estimated to be 38 to 40 percent of the urban worker's average income (thus roughly 1,758 rmb in 1994), it is quite evident that the wage income of rural industrial workers was much higher than that of the farmers.[48] Another study reported that the average annual income of TVE workers in the agriculturally most developed Sunan area was about four times that of the best farmer in 1990 (2,000 rmb versus about 500) (Ge 1990, 41).

Adding in the benefits of labor protection and a better working environment, the rural CLMs have become understandably attractive to the peasants. In most rural communities with a CLM, however, the real income difference between the industrial workers and the farmers has become less shocking because of the existence of community-based income redistribution, the practice called "using rural industry to feed the farming." The TVEs nevertheless have a much higher potential of increasing cash income than the farm fields. It is estimated that from 1989 to 1994, 65 percent of the increase of the cash income of the Chinese rural population came from TVE wages.[49]

Distribution

Like the authoritarian state LAP, the community-based societal LAP and the CLMs allocated and managed workers in basically every industry and profession and in almost every urban *danwei* and rural township, if not in every village. In the CCP and PRC state agencies, for example, many noncadre employees, including some that still had a rural *hukou,* were allocated and managed by a community-based societal LAP or a CLM. Almost all state-owned *danweis* had an LSE or the like to employ their workers' children and surplus workers. It became almost unthinkable for any rural township to survive economically, let alone prosper, without a TVE of some sort. Most villages have already developed their TVEs, especially so in the more prosperous southern and southeastern China. Incomplete data from field trips suggest that the rural CLMs were heavily concentrated in manufacturing, construction, local transportation, retailing, and other services. Rural CLMs played only a limited role in allocating professionals and urban *hukou* holders. By 1994, there were about 3 million urban *hukou* holders working in the TVEs, yet a vast majority of those city dwellers appeared to be more like moonlighting urban professionals than full-time TVE employees.[50]

Due to the unavailability of rural data, table 3.3 describes the industrial distribution of the societal LAP/CLMs in urban areas. A few interesting findings about the CLMs are worth further attention here. First, it appears that urban collective enterprises, primarily the LSEs, do hire a certain number of workers with a rural *hukou,* as the figures in rows eleven, twelve, fourteen, and fifteen demonstrate. Empirically, this finding is supported with the observation that many urban collective enterprises, especially the LSEs, often employ some rural residents who are close relatives of the members of the particular urban community. Here, the CLMs interestingly cut the employment barriers between rural and urban along the lines of family institutions. Social institutions and values are clearly important even in the 1990s when most societal LAPs have become CLMs. Similarly, rows seventeen and eighteen report that among government employees, a considerable number of CLM-allocated workers have a rural *hukou.* This may be because, besides LSEs run by government agencies, local governments hired some rural residents to work in their offices in the countryside.

Second, the urban CLMs have a sizable and increasing presence in the industries of manufacturing, retailing, and service. They are losing ground in transportation, interestingly not so much to the still dominant authoritarian state LAP, as row nine shows, but to competition from rural-based enterprises, as row eight shows. In highway and waterway transportation, especially the local and short haul of goods and passengers, the CLMs have emerged to be almost the main LAP.

Table 3.3. Industrial Distribution of the Urban Societal LAP/CLMs (1957-1990)

Years	1957	1962	1970	1975	1978	1982	1985	1987	1989	1990	# of Rows
Percent in manufacturing:*	49.7	47.7	48.4	68.2	67.9	68.5	62.0	63.3	62.9	63.0	1
Percent of industry's total employees:†	--	--	--	--	19.7	21.4	17.2	18.6	18.2	18.2	2
Percent of industry's urban employees:‡‡	24.1	26.3	22.3	26.5	26.6	27.3	27.9	29.6	29.1	29.4	3
Percent in agriculture:‡	0.6	1.7	1.7	1.2	2.7	2.1	1.5	1.3	1.3	1.2	4
Percent of industry's total employees:†	--	--	--	negligible		--	--	--	--	--	5
Percent of industry's urban employees:‡‡	3.4	4.5	3.0	2.9	5.8	6.1	5.9	5.4	5.5	5.3	6
Percent in transportation/ communication:	18.3	12.5	14.6	10.7	10.0	8.2	6.3	5.8	5.5	5.3	7
Percent of industry's total employees:†	--	--	--	--	27.8	25.6	17.1	14.9	13.4	12.9	8
Percent of industry's urban employees:‡‡	42.1	39.1	41.0	31.9	31.2	29.7	27.4	26.1	24.3	23.9	9
Percent in retail/service:	23.8	27.3	28.4	12.5	11.4	15.4	25.1	24.6	25.3	25.4	10
Percent of industry's total employees:†	--	--	--	--	18.2	24.1	44.8	43.4	42.3	42.0	11
Percent of industry's urban employees:‡‡	24.0	32.9	36.7	18.4	18.1	23.9	44.3	42.8	41.5	41.0	12

Table 3.3. Industrial Distribution of the Urban Societal LAP/CLMs (1957-1990)—Continued

Years	1957	1962	1970	1975	1978	1982	1985	1987	1989	1990	# of Rows
Percent in education/ media/culture:**	6.0	6.1	6.3	6.2	6.2	4.1	3.2	3.0	2.9	2.8	13
Percent of industry's total employees:†	—	—	—	—	8.7	7.1	6.1	5.5	5.1	5.1	14
Percent of industry's urban employees:‡‡	6.8	7.6	9.4	9.2	8.4	5.0	3.9	3.2	2.8	2.9	15
Percent in CCP/state agencies: ††	0.5	0.5	0.5	0.5	0.6	0.5	0.8	0.7	0.7	0.7	16
Percent of industry's total employees:†	—	—	—	—	2.5	2.3	3.4	2.9	2.5	2.4	17
Percent of industry's urban employees:‡‡	0.1	0.2	0.2	0.2	0.3	0.2	0.4	0.4	0.3	0.3	18
Percent in others:	1.1	4.2	0.1	0.7	1.2	1.2	1.1	1.3	1.4	1.6	19

Notes: Figures are based on SSB-LM 1991, 7-9, 12-15. Totals may not be exactly 100 percent due to the rounding of decimals.

* Includes construction and energy industries.

† The labor allocated by urban community-based societal LAP/CLMs as a percentage of the total workers in that industry. Statistically, some industries existed only in the cities until 1978.

‡ Includes irrigation project workers, "sent-down" rural technicians.

** Includes TV, film-making, and other entertainment industries.

†† Includes scientists, bankers, health care providers, social workers, athletes, and sports managers.

‡‡ The labor allocated by urban community-based societal LAP/CLMs as a percentage of the total urban employees in that industry. In the state-owned *danweis*, the urban community-based societal LAP/CLMs often exists, to a lesser extent, to govern blue-collar workers and LSE employees.

The authoritarian state LAP dominates air and railway transportation, as the state still has a monopoly on those industries. But a great number of hard-labor workers in railway stations and docks, such as porters and loaders, have been allocated and managed by the CLMs.

Third, the urban CLMs have only a marginal and decreasing presence in the industries of education, media, and culture (down from 9.4 percent to 2.8 percent in 1975-1990). CLM presence in governmental agencies is even smaller. The urban societal LAP and the CLMs since the 1950s never exceeded 0.5 percent of the government's workers with an urban *hukou* and 3 percent of the total government employees. Other than the small number of contract (*pinyong*) cadres in rural government offices, the CLMs apparently have had only minimal influence on cadres and professionals. An important exception is the sizable number (estimated at about 2.3 million in 1995) of peasants-run (*minban*) or non-state-employed teachers in rural elementary and middle schools. Those quasi-professionals are largely rural *hukou* holders certified or approved by state educational agencies to staff the rural schools. They do essentially the same work as state-employed (*gongban*) teachers but are paid much less.[51] The state pays them a minimum salary (45 to 70 rmb per month in 1993-1994, usually one-third to half their total income), with the majority of their income provided by the communities in which their schools are located.[52] Those *minban* teachers have thus become the largest group of professionals allocated and governed by the CLMs.

The smaller but more powerful group of local cadres at the township and the administrative villages was also basically governed by the CLMs. They were generally full-time administrators but not state-employed cadres, and thus were largely paid for by the economy of their townships and villages through the peasants' taxes and profits of the TVEs. The CLMs may gain more influence with white-collar workers in the future as the TVEs and urban collective enterprises produce their own professionals and managerial cadres, and increasing numbers of college graduates become willing to work in the better-paid nonstate enterprises while keeping their official state cadre status.

Finally, some recent studies by Chinese scholars have reported interesting findings on the extremely uneven geographic distribution of TVEs. In 1990, 80 percent (mostly the small enterprises below the village level) were located in natural villages, 7 percent were located in administrative villages, 12 percent were located in townships, and only 1 percent were in county seats or above. The TVEs, due to the low levels of technology and dispersed location, used three times as much land per worker as urban industries. This is indeed a major drawback of TVEs in a country that faces serious diminution of arable land.[53] More importantly, in 1993, eastern China had 63.9 percent of TVE assets and 65.8 percent of TVE output. The central provinces had 27.4 percent of TVE assets, whereas western China had only 8.6 percent of TVE assets and 7.6 percent of TVE output.

In some areas, a rural community could have as many as twenty TVEs, including small ones below the village level, while in some other places in the northwest, the figure could be less than one (sometimes a township would share a TVE with another township or with several villages).[54] Among the 365 TVEs that had over 100 million rmb production in 1993, 93.2 percent were located in the east while the western provinces had none.[55] Such an uneven distribution of TVEs, plus the already highly uneven development of the urban economy, has made the rapid-developing CLMs an additional cause for the massive west-to-east flow of job-seeking rural laborers. The increasingly uneven distribution of the CLMs, especially the TVEs, has prompted the CCP to act.[56] The role of the CLMs on the uneven development of the Chinese economy will be visited again later.

Institutions

The LAP-related PRC governmental agencies, outlined in chapter 2, have regulatory power over the CLMs, especially those in urban areas. Among the agencies, the Labor Ministry and its local bureaus and offices are perhaps the most important affecting the CLMs. Usually, the community-based features of the CLMs are monitored and maintained through the labor bureaus' efforts. Although the urban collective enterprises under a CLM can hire and fire workers as they think economically appropriate, the local labor bureaus often intervene to encourage more hiring, thus causing underemployment in these enterprises. The labor bureaus can often use "sticks" such as labor arbitration committees and the distorted enforcement of labor protection codes to control the collective enterprises. They sometimes require the enterprises to implement some of the same state hiring quotas as the state-owned enterprises.[57] More importantly, the labor bureaus enforce rather strictly the *hukou* requirement, hence effectively maintaining the community confinement of the CLMs, especially in urban areas. A collective enterprise that hired from outside the local community without approval could be fined heavily or its managing cadres could be penalized and even fired. This is especially true for the large collective enterprises in the cities. The TVEs generally have more flexibility in employing outside workers with different terms. In general, the PRC labor laws and regulations applicable to the authoritarian state LAP are also the legal basis for the CLMs. Local governments are tasked to "register, monitor, manage, and guide" the CLMs closely.[58]

Because many CLMs are located in rural areas and relatively concentrated in commercial retailing, construction, services, and local transportation, several ministries of the PRC state have jurisdiction or regulatory power over them. The Agriculture Ministry, for example, has substantial authority through its TVE Bureau, which has authority regarding data collecting and "macromanaging" the TVEs. The State Bureau of Industry and Commerce Management has the authority of "approving, monitoring, and suspending" collective enterprises in urban and rural areas. The Domestic Commerce Ministry regulates the retailing industry, while the Transportation Ministry oversees highway and waterway transportation industries, in which CLMs are soon likely to become the main LAP. From the mid-1980s to the early 1990s, more than half a dozen ministries have issued dozens of regulations and directives affecting CLMs and the overall operation of the collective enterprises (State Council 1993, 299-411).

Starting in the late 1980s, the TVE Bureau of the Agriculture Ministry became the central authority regulating and governing the massive TVEs outside any ministry's clear jurisdiction. Though still just a bureau under a ministry, the TVE Bureau has acquired deputy ministry status and authority and has branches down to the levels of province, prefecture, county, and even large townships. On the provincial and metropolis level, the TVE bureaus (officially termed TVE Management Bureau) have acquired the status and authority of a prefecture/bureau, just like any other provincial bureaus (Cai 1994, 579-590). An interesting finding is that the bureaus appeared to function as monitoring agencies representing the TVEs in the government, rather than directly managing them. The TVEs generally need the bureaus to assist and approve their external activities, such as setting up joint ventures with foreign investors, acquiring credits, passing product quality inspections, and meeting labor and environmental standards.[59] For such managerial services, the TVEs have to pay the bureaus from their profits.[60] In some areas, such fees accounted for half the employees salaries at the local TVE bureaus (Cai 1994, 10). The TVE bureaus are also responsible for the organizational activities of the CCP, Communist Youth League, and unions in the large TVEs, as well as the maintenance of the dossiers (*dangans*) of the cadres who work in the TVEs or TVE-related *danweis*.[61] Other than that, however, the TVE bureaus generally do not have the authorization, willingness, or ability to affect the labor allocation and management aspects of TVE operations. This is clearly reflected by the local TVE bureau's routine activities and their annual reports.[62]

Local governmental and social institutions such as residential committees and villagers' committees, are legally the owners of the collective enterprises.[63] Significant policies and changes of a CLM must usually be approved by those semi-political and semi-social institutions. National regulations on the TVEs and the urban collective enterprises stipulate clearly that local governments above the county or city level may make their own regulations and policies concerning the operations of the collective enterprises (State Council 1993, 38). Local legislation appears to have been very important in the formation and maintenance of the communities.[64] In some rare cases, the local government could even nationalize some TVEs to make them cash cows for the local government instead of property of the rural communities.[65] Given the variety of collective enterprises and the communities they are located in, ostensibly uniform government policies tend to be twisted and greatly distorted by local officials, especially in rural areas. Field studies reveal that community constraints typically are much more important than the central government's regulations in the practices of the CLMs. In the same region of southern Jiangsu Province, for example, CLMs in different communities vary significantly on the issues of treating outside workers, income composition, and hiring procedures.[66]

CLM Danweis

In the eyes of the PRC government, both the urban collective enterprises, large and small, and the TVEs are "part and parcel of our nation's socialist public-owned economy."[67] In urban areas, the collective *danweis,* modeled after the state-owned ones, are the cells of the CLM-style labor allocation and management in a particular community. Sometimes those *danweis*, as well as many state-owned *danweis,* are the communities on which CLMs are based. Internal structures and operational mechanisms of the collective enterprises are often modeled after those of the state-owned *danweis* described in chapter 2. Political organizations such as CCP branches and the Communist Youth League are required for the collective *danweis* as in the state-owned ones. It may be appropriate to understand urban collective *danweis* as cells of labor allocation and management similar to those in state-owned *danweis,* but with a much higher flexibility due to the influence of the market institution, a greater distance between them and the CCP political authority, and a smaller community-defined operational space. Many *danweis* practicing the CLMs, such as the LSEs, are often just extensions of the state-owned mother *danweis.* In such situations, the market influence would be naturally weaker and the mother *danwei*'s culture would have a stronger presence, although the community-based features would be the same as most other CLMs. In most cases, therefore, the role of the *danwei* institution under a CLM is less significant than that under the authoritarian state LAP, as the economic and political cohesiveness of the communities tends to be weaker and less stable than that in the typical state-owned *danweis,* whereas social institutions tend to be stronger.

Many collective enterprises labeled themselves with various ranks like "division or section ranking" as the state-owned *danweis* would do, in the hope of being treated as such by the government and the media. For state employees, usually cadres, who worked in those self-ranked and often self-promoted collective *danweis,* this probably meant a raise in salary but not a real promotion in rank.[68] Very few collective enterprises or TVEs, no matter what rank they claim and how big their business, are officially recognized as *danweis* of or above the equivalent of a division/county by the government. Their political participation is therefore institutionally minimized.[69] As a result, influence-buying through donations, charity, and widespread bribery has become an important tool helping the collective enterprises, especially TVEs, to deal with the PRC state on issues such as taxation, environmental protection, labor protection, consumer rights, and other law enforcement matters.

In rural areas, the structure of the CLM-practicing *danweis* would be even less well constructed and functionally unimportant. Other than the hidden private enterprises that began coming out of the closet recently as the market advanced rapidly in the PRC, TVEs were organized and owned collectively by rural communities: a village, an administrative village that may include a few villages, a township, or even just a neighborhood association or a subvillage (*zhu,* or team). In 1991, there were 225.7 million rural households, 430.93 million rural laborers, and a total of about 905.25 million rural people living in

55,542 townships and 804,153 villagers' committees, or administrative villages. Those communities had a total of 1.44 million TVEs in 1991 directly employing 47.67 million workers, and another 17.64 million small enterprises below the village level employing 48.42 million people (SSB-RB 1992, 39, 47). Those TVEs were not very independent from their communities and were often still just part of their communities, even though economically they may have appeared to be separate entities. In these cases, the communities and their social institutions, rather than the economic institution of the TVEs, functioned similarly to state-owned *danweis*. It is here, especially in those well-developed CLMs that tended to be more market-oriented than community-confined, that the traditional PRC *danwei* institutional structure has been transformed.

Chinese CLMs in the 1990s

By the late 1990s, the community-based societal LAP in contemporary China was rapidly becoming a market-oriented LAP limited to the members of local communities—urban residents of a particular district of a particular city, or residents of a particular village or township. Led by the TVEs (which grew at a remarkable rate of 33 to 36 percent between 1981 and 1993 and are expected to grow above 30 percent annually into the next century), the CLMs emerged as the second largest Chinese LAP and continued to grow very rapidly.[70] In 1991, on average, each rural community (township or village) had about 1.7 TVEs and 20.5 small enterprises employing about 112 TVE workers (SSB-RB 1992, 39-47). By 1994, the figures were estimated to be about 2.1 TVEs and 23.3 small enterprises employing 140 workers. If the CLMs kept the same growth rate, roughly 7 million new workers each year, they could become the largest Chinese LAP within fifteen years, surpassing the family-based traditional LAP.[71] By 2010, CLMs would be about twice as large as the now dominant authoritarian state LAP, assuming the latter maintains its current growth rate.

In a typical CLM in the 1990s, all eligible community members, such as the legal residents of an urban district, township, or sizable *danwei*, had more or less equal access to jobs. In many cases, the direct relatives (spouses and children) of the members of a community were treated the same. This was especially true when the community was a state-owned *danwei*. Recruitment was generally open and competitive. An examination or the like was usually required to screen potential new hires and "fairly" reject those less qualified. The LSEs, given their job-creating missions, tended to hire almost every jobless laborer in the particular community. Recently, facing increased pressure to be financially self-sustaining, the LSEs have become more selective in their hiring. Despite a clear market orientation in recruitment, the CLMs were under heavy influence of the political and social institutions in the communities. So-called connections (*guanxi*) of candidates and their families and friends sometimes had more effect in hiring and in job assignments than the quality of the candidates.[72] Generally, such influential connections were developed based on social institutions and through interactive social cultivation. With few exceptions, relatives of local VIPs and respected families tended to get the best jobs in the community. An unwritten and even unspoken code of conduct worked in the minds of the recruiting administrators.

Naturally, different CLMs had drastically varying degrees of social and political distortion of the local labor markets. In some cases, connections have been observed to be almost irrelevant, with hiring and assignment based primarily on economic considerations. But almost all the CLMs, with the exception of some hidden private enterprises in the more open southeastern coastal regions and especially in the rural areas of Guangdong Province, practiced a rather strict community-based discrimination against competition from outside. A local *hukou* has usually been the number-one recruiting requirement in most CLMs.[73]

Once hired, laborers are subject to the authority of the bosses of the collective *danweis*. Those bosses have increasingly become professional managers but are still frequently appointed to their positions through political and social connections. Some had been state cadres who volunteered or were assigned to serve in the collective enterprises. Except for state cadres and the few state-employed workers whose minimum wages and benefits as well as their jobs are guaranteed by the state, employees are managed in a market-oriented way. Productivity and contribution to the enterprise are the main criteria for pay, promotion, demotion, and even dismissal. The wages are in cash and generally consist of two parts. One portion is the scheduled on-the-job wage paid upon full attendance. The other portion is the bonus; it is usually bigger than the wage but is subject to the superior's evaluation of the employee's performance and the profitability of the employer. Piecework wages and part-time employment, especially in the TVEs, are very common. Some enterprises short on cash might occasionally pay their employees with their products—watches, radios, food, furniture, and even numerous canned "tonic fluids" containing often questionable ingredients.

Underemployment continues in many enterprises under a CLM because of the still-powerful political and social distortion of the market mechanism, but it is much less serious in the urban collective enterprises than in state-owned enterprises. Community-defined noneconomic concerns are important. As one TVE manager in Jiangsu Province told me in 1995, "We are all fellow townsmen and we must give everyone a bowl of rice to eat." As a result, certain underemployment exists even in those TVEs. Often some TVE managers have to find some outsiders to do the dirty jobs because they can't fire their fellow townspeople even though those local workers may have refused to work on jobs. And the TVEs' managerial posts, as we found in Sunan, are often rotated every three to four years among the township or village leaders and their relatives or friends to allow the local elite to share the lucrative "gray income" associated with those offices.[74]

For most TVEs, however, underemployment has been largely replaced with a community-based welfare-like structure in which the surplus laborers are paid, albeit usually less, to do other things deemed good for the whole community, like street cleaning. Within an enterprise, the workers' pay might vary significantly, especially in the TVEs and some small collective enterprises where managers have more autonomy. As a rule, the same jobs in a given CLM have roughly the same pay. In a recent trend, nonlocal employees have started to get nearly the same pay as locals who work in the same jobs, though not participating in the more significant community-based benefits distribution. Similar jobs in different CLMs, however, have carried drastically different pay and benefits. Furthermore, many TVEs and urban collective enterprises have become sort of "stock-company" establishments open to individual investors, instead of establishments collectively owned by local communities.[75] In those cases, labor allocation and management became more genuinely market-oriented, as recruitment often moved beyond the local boundaries and became more open and more competitive. Some communities, in order to have their own permanent talents from the locality, spent substantial funds to send a few dozen local high school graduates who had narrowly failed the national college entrance exam to be trained at well-known colleges, with contracts stipulating that they would return to their CLMs after their graduation. This was praised as an intellectual investment for the future by and for the local communities.[76]

Workers under a CLM acquired substantial labor mobility within the community. Allocation and utilization of the labor resource generally achieved a community-defined high efficiency. This was especially apparent in rural communities, where the most able laborers were generally allocated to work in the TVEs, which have the best economic efficiency. The land (or at least the user's right to it) was then largely redistributed to old and unskilled members. This practice has contributed to the recent decline of agriculture in the southern and southeastern China.[77] Many prosperous communities even started to hire strong but cheap outsiders to work in their low-yielding fields. Some outsiders began to work in the fast-growing TVEs as well.

Hiring outsiders as better qualified workers or, more frequently, as supplemental labor for expansion, has contributed to increasing inter-community labor mobility, which is still institutionally limited by the community boundaries. *Hukou*-related community identification remains the main institutional barrier against national labor mobility among the CLMs. Unable to absorb the massive number of job-seekers and unwilling to replace the authoritarian state LAP with a national labor market, the CCP seemed to have decided to use the limited labor mobility generated by the CLMs as the main vehicle to solve unemployment and underemployment in the form of a socialist public economy. The TVEs have been especially praised by the PRC experts and scholars as "the must route to the rural prosperity and the main avenue to the solution of employing the rural surplus labor force."[78]

Urban CLMs

Chinese urban communities such as the cities, towns, districts, and *danweis* continue to hold socialist full employment as their major employment objective. Led by local labor bureaus, community-based political and social institutions generally view urban unemployment as something destabilizing, abnormal, and even immoral. "Everyone needs to have a bowl of rice to eat" and "everyone needs to work somewhere" have been the predominant beliefs in urban communities. Because the family-based LAP exists only marginally in the cities, the PRC state is unable to create new jobs through its authoritarian state LAP, and the emerging national labor market has yet to absorb the millions of unskilled laborers, the socially and politically desirable "full employment" task is left largely to the communities, controlled by social institutions and values. Workers dismissed or laid off due to bankruptcy of their employers are generally reallocated within the community with the help of the local labor bureaus.[79] To PRC local leaders, the collective enterprises benefit communities' economies tremendously through their local employment, taxation by the local government, donations, sponsorship, and other activities. To the fiscally burdened PRC central government, the financially better off but politically weaker collective enterprises are good sources of additional income. Thus, starting in 1993, the collective enterprises, together with the TVEs, have been charged at least two new taxes that do not apply to the state-owned enterprises.[80]

By the 1990s, all PRC cities had city-based CLMs. In small and middle-sized cities, there might be only one meaningful CLM, even though there could be many collective enterprises participating in it. In large cities such as Beijing and Shanghai, the huge size of the community (from 2 million to nearly 10 million people) would have made a single city-based CLM less cohesive and quite ineffective. Instead, smaller but more genuine CLMs emerged on the basis of districts, streets, *danweis,* and even neighborhoods.[81] Nearly all job advertisements ask specifically for the applicants to bring their *hukou* or personal identification cards clearly showing their detailed legal residence and *hukou* type (rural or urban). Many jobs are open only to local residents of a particular district of the city or to members of a particular *danwei.* It is, therefore, easy to imagine why it became common to seek "illegal" alterations of one's *hukou* through connections to the *hukou* police in order to be considered a member of a "good" community.

New Developments

Many reformed aspects of the authoritarian state LAP in the state-owned enterprises increasingly reflected the spirit of the CLMs. As a result of "enterprise autonomy" and the political decision to construct a socialist market economy, the state-owned *danweis* generally adopted significant CLM-style labor practices.[82] Looking beyond the minimum wages, benefits, and job security guaranteed by the state, the *danweis* are trying their own ways to raise the employee productivity and increase the income and benefits for basically everyone. The financial source for such *danwei*-based community distribution has been the various types of legal or, more often, illegal small "gold boxes" (*xiao jingku*), the term used for *danweis*'s hidden funds gained through tax evasion, additional created income, or even illegal activities such as corruption and double bookkeeping.[83]

Market mechanisms have been tried internally, and the emerging national market has been utilized externally. Traditionally nonprofit state-owned colleges such as the famous Beijing University have started to develop their own *danwei*-owned businesses to use commerce to support education and research for its community members: the underpaid and dispirited poor faculty.[84] Gradually, as chapter 2 described, many state-owned *danweis* have become rather similar to CLM-practicing communities. An internal quasi-labor market and external exclusivity have developed considerably in those state-owned *danweis*. Certain internal mobility of employees has become widely practiced by many state-owned enterprises.[85] Even state-assigned new workers are often subject to the acceptance of state-owned *danweis*, especially the enterprises. This may be a rather "Chinese" way of profoundly converting the authoritarian state LAP to CLMs. CLMs have also grown in the form of directly taking in former state employees though mergers with depressed state-owned *danweis*. In Shengyang, Liaoning Province, a collective (district-owned) small factory of ninety employees that produced bellows grew into a group corporation of more than three thousand workers in four years, annexing ten bankrupt state-owned factories along the way.[86]

Another new development has been that the LSEs have become much more market-oriented than they were in the 1980s. The original primary purpose of the LSEs was to employ as many job-seekers in a local community as possible. The social distortion of the market in LSEs was thus far more abundant than in other collective enterprises. Empirically, we can see that the LSEs often became a charity-like employment agency for jobless and unskilled urban youth. By the mid-1990s, however, the LSEs had undergone tremendous transformation. Recruitment had become a competitive process in most cases, and underemployment was reduced. The wages and benefits of the LSE employees tended to be determined by the community-wide supply and demand of the job-waiters, rather than by the founders of the LSEs.

TVEs

The most impressive and institutionally profound development of the Chinese CLMs was the astonishing development of the TVEs in the 1990s. The collective enterprises with practicing CLMs came to employ about 27 percent of the total rural labor force, but they provided more than 67 percent of gross rural production and about 40 percent of the gross national product.[87] A surprisingly large number of TVEs became sizable, high-tech enterprises and even joint ventures between the townships/villages and foreign investors. More than four hundred had established branches in foreign countries, including the

United States.[88] In 1989, TVEs had employed about 17.6 percent of the entire Chinese labor force, compared to the authoritarian state LAP, which covered 18.2 percent.[89] By 1994, TVEs employed 120 million people, compared to only 106 million by the authoritarian state LAP (table 2.1 in the previous chapter and table 3.2 below).

TVEs were officially viewed as an efficient and important way to provide jobs for the rural laborers. Beijing concluded that "if the state were to supply so many (92 million in 1990) jobs in the state-owned enterprises, over 3 trillion rmb (investment) would be needed. But the TVEs provided that many jobs with less than 200 billion rmb."[90] So the senior officials in charge of TVE affairs decided in 1994 that, contrary to some economists' call for a "proper" (meaning slower) growth of the TVEs, out of concern for environmental pollution (Ma et al. 1994, 314), the TVEs should have an even faster development—aimed at producing half the Chinese GNP (gross national product) and employing an additional 60 million rural residents by the year 2000.[91]

In some areas such as Sunan (southern Jiangsu Province), Guangong, and Zhejiang Provinces and Jiaodong (eastern Sangdong Province), the TVE style of CLMs employed about two-thirds of the rural labor force. A few rural communities (mostly townships and villages) had multiple TVEs and had ascended to the level of mid-sized cities in terms of gross product and per capita income. Additionally, foreign investors have come in. In Jiangsu Province alone, there were more than ten thousand TVE-foreign investment joint ventures in 1994.[92] The famous examples of Huaxi village (township) in Jiangyin county and Shengze township in Suzhou city (both in Sunan), Dachu township in Tianjin metropolis, and Fuchang township in Hubei Province all had reached the edge of economic modernization according to the PRC's official standard.[93] Some of them started to employ outsiders on a large scale. In 1995, for instance, 40 percent of the 100,000 people of the prosperous Shengze township of Suzhou city (the so-called number-one township of the PRC) were nonlocal *hukou* holders. [94] The main TVE of the township, the Yinong Group, hired half of its sixty-two hundred workers from eighteen other provinces (primarily Anhui and Henan).[95] Huaxi village of Jiangyin, (the so-called number-one village of the PRC), had two-thirds of its working force from outside the community. About one-third of those employees had an urban *hukou.* Such news appeared to have inspired the reemployment project of the State Labor Ministry to enlist TVEs as a "golden key" to the "solution of the difficult employment problem in the urban areas," where more than 68 million new job-seekers were expected to enter the scene in the 1990s.[96] Developments of rural CLMs like these naturally prompted many to speculate that the small towns design may, after all, be a valid future for China's rural population.[97]

Since "the sky is high and the emperor is far away" (*tiangao huangdi yuang*), the numerous TVEs (about 1.8 million in 1994, with around 20 million small enterprises below the village level) have developed a much larger and more complex variety than the urban collective enterprises. Many were actually private or semiprivate enterprises.[98] Some have become fairly technology- and capital-intensive enterprises with foreign investment, and more than a hundred had annual sales of more than 200 million rmb. In Jiangsu Province, by 1995, more than 1,043 TVEs each had assets over 32 million rmb and annual sales over 50 million rmb.[99] In Changzhou, some TVEs have become leading producers of products such as refrigerators, cash registers, and air conditioners. Some had as many as a few thousand employees. Most, however, were small, technically backward and highly labor intensive. On average in 1993, a TVE had thirty-four employees, 31,000 rmb in assets, and 1.21 million rmb annual output.[100] But the numerically more important small enterprises had on average as few as about three employees that year. In one county in Hunan Province, 12,623 TVEs had only 60,166 employees (4.7 workers per TVE) in 1993. Only 1.1 percent were "skilled workers" and only 0.6 percent had a college-level education.[101] Despite the great variety and the generally small size, however, almost all of the TVEs demonstrated stronger features of CLMs than their urban cousins.

TVEs generally remain an inherent part of their local community. Like the urban nonstate-owned enterprises, TVEs are charged additional taxes by the government.[102] Interestingly, they are required to pay their communities 10 percent of their profits before taxes as a so-called social expenses fund; 5 to 10 percent of their profits as a constructing agriculture fund; and 0.6 percent of their total sales as grain or education fees. Those and many other local taxes and fees constitute the financial basis for the substantial community-based income redistribution in townships or villages.[103] Local (below the county level) governments and officials have become increasingly dependent on TVE taxes. In one prefecture in 1993, 57 percent of local fiscal income came from TVEs, which accounted for 92 percent of the increase in income of the rural population during the previous fourteen years.[104] Such a financial burden has naturally constrained the development of TVEs but reflects the nature of the CLMs in which they have operated. As a kind of exchange, TVEs have been allowed to practice rather flexible and market-oriented labor policies within the confines of the local communities. When orders are down or during slow seasons, many TVEs would just ask most of their workers to go home with minimum or no pay and would call them back when either new orders came, the busy season arrived, or management decided to make a new product.[105] To strengthen the CLMs, the community-based social and political authorities in some places have made efforts to consolidate the community-confinement of the TVEs further. For example, in Zhejiang Province, many TVE employees were given "false stocks" amounting to as much as 20 percent of the total assets of their TVEs. They could get dividends from these stocks but could not sell them or take them away. The purpose of this scheme was to "tie down the skilled workers" in the community.[106]

In short, CLMs achieved great success in the PRC by the end of the twentieth century and continued developing rapidly, in contrast to the stagnation of the authoritarian state LAP and decline of the family-based traditional LAP. The institutional confinement of the communities still appeared strong, but the market orientation of the CLMs was growing. This was especially evident as many urban collective enterprises and TVEs increasingly undertook the trendy option of privatization of the 1990s to become openly private or public stockholding enterprises.[107] One report estimated that by 1994 the stockholding TVEs were already more than 10 percent of all TVEs in China.[108] A direct result of the privatization has been the visible relaxation of the community confinement of many CLMs. Even though privatization of the socially owned enterprises has been slow and often superficial due to strong resistance of the community-based nonmarket institutions, more market orientation of the CLMs and more convergence between urban and rural CLMs is expected.[109] CLMs are likely to overtake the authoritarian state LAP as the most important LAP in China and may also replace the family-based traditional LAP as the largest LAP. In speculating on the future of Chinese labor allocation and China's overall institutional structure, the CLMs clearly deserve attention.

Tales from the Communities

This section describes one urban CLM, as reflected in the operations of two urban collective enterprises, and two rural CLMs. Except where noted, the source of information is my five field studies in China from 1989 to 1996.

Urban Collective Enterprises

  1. *A home appliance manufacturer in Anhui Province.* This highly successful group corporation used to be a large collective enterprise owned by the Second Light Industry Bureau (now the Second Light Industry Corporation, or SLIC) of Hefei city, which had about 700,000 people at the time of this research. The company and the Weida Factory, described further on, were two collective enterprises belonging to Hefei city, more precisely the SLIC community. After three company names and four brands, the company had become prosperous by making nationally best-selling washing machines. It was expanding and had elevated itself to the equivalent of bureau, or prefecture, level but was still under the leadership of the division or county-level SLIC. Frequent and interesting conflicts between the company and the SLIC were thus inevitable. Often, the company resorted to the superiors above the SLIC and to local media for help in its struggle against the SLIC, the representative of the community where the company is located.[110]

  In 1994 there were fifteen hundred employees in the company. Their average monthly income was about 1,000 rmb, significantly higher than similar enterprises in the city.[111] Starting in 1995, as the company acquired joint venture status with Hong Kong and Japanese investors, the average monthly wages of its employees were expected to double, far exceeding the limits set by the now-weakened SLIC. Despite active and varied rent-seeking by the SLIC, its own office employees by this time made less than those in the company, which adversely affected the morale within the SLIC.

  All the company's employees were Hefei urban residents, except for several temporary peasant workers working in heavy labor and staffing dirty and hazardous positions. There has clearly been preferential treatment of job applicants from the SLIC community. All new hires and especially dismissals had to be approved by the Hefei Labor Bureau and the SLIC. But pay schedules and promotions were largely decided by the company management through the demoralized SLIC. The company, as one of the few successful collective enterprises in the community, was struggling to gain more independence from the SLIC and the community at large. Thus, some of its new employees, mainly technical talents and marketing experts, had been hired from outside the community with special approval of the Hefei Labor Bureau.[112] A substantial number of its employees, including the top managers, were formerly allocated by the authoritarian state LAP and were still considered state cadres/ employees.

Because of its financial strength, marketing success, and newly boosted status brought by foreign investors, the company essentially had the same internal labor management as a major state-owned *danwei* regarding job security and nonwage benefits. The remaining differences between the CLM-allocated workers and those state cadres/employees, however, were significant. First, the company essentially had two groups of employees in regard to job security. For most workers, job security still depended on the financial situation of the company, whereas the state cadres/employees, who had higher than average pay, were guaranteed a job by the state even if the company's luck changed. There was also a difference in nonwage benefits. State employees enjoyed 100 percent health care benefits for themselves plus 50 percent of medical bills for their dependents and unemployed parents—the "big protection" (*dalaobao*). The CLM-allocated workers and new hires had benefits, usually reduced, for themselves only—the "small protection" (*xiaolaobao*).

Despite the market-oriented independence it had struggled for and its new joint-venture status, the company still appeared to be affected by strong community confinement. The company donated huge funds to local courses and pledged to help several other local enterprises in financial trouble. In a number of instances, the company used lesser-known local suppliers to replace brand-name suppliers from other cities to help home industries. One example of such community orientation was that the company publicly reported an impressive 80 million rmb profit in 1994—but that figure had been deliberately reduced by the company's management, with the consent of the SLIC, "to prevent the Hong Kong investors (who own 24 percent of the stock) from taking away too much in dividends."[113] Another Hefei-based major home appliance maker, the number-three refrigerator maker in China, had roughly the same situation as the company. As a community-confined large collective enterprise, it also sought more market orientation and independence through turning itself into a joint venture with foreign investors.

2. *An electric motor factory in Hefei.* Weida Factory used to be a collective enterprise funded by the SLIC. It has changed its name twice and its product lines many times, from electronics, portable radios, electric shavers, and electrical wire to washer motors. In 1994, Weida had five hundred "formal employees," including some "state employees" and mostly CLM-allocated workers. The average monthly income was only 300-350 rmb that year. It also had about 170

temporary peasant workers with an average monthly income of 150-230 rmb and no health care benefits beyond the pitiful 15 rmb per month "health fee." The factory director's monthly salary was the highest, but only about 430 rmb a month. As I detected, however, the top managers, all state cadres, had apparently substantial gray income in the form of gifts from employees and prospective job applicants. "Basically most of the Hefei's large collective enterprises are like us," asserted the director.

Weida Factory had been in good financial shape for more than ten years. It had never fired any employees despite some financial difficulties. Other than temporary peasant workers, who generally had one-year renewable contracts, very few employees ever left the factory. Many of its workers were formerly residents of the land that was used by the factory; because they lost their land and houses, they were taken care of by the city. The factory allocated limited housing only to its male employees, who formed a very long waiting list; at the time of this research, only 25 percent of employees had been allocated apartments.

After a better-than-average performance record, Weida was forced by the SLIC in 1994 to merge with two small collective enterprises: a defunct umbrella plant and a bankrupt water-heater plant. Right away, Weida lost about 2 million rmb in 1994 and increased the number of its retired workers to three hundred. The burden of paying the pensions and especially the medical bills of these workers, according to the factory director, would force the factory into the red for the foreseeable future. The rationale for the forced merger was strictly to "take care" of the employees of the two small plants that were part of the same community. It was also alleged that the bosses of the two bankrupt plants were related to some important officials in the Hefei local government. (This is quite similar to what happened in Beijing's Dongchen district in 1993. Two small collective plants there were taken over by the Dongchen District Labor Bureau because they were bankrupt. A total of 478 workers and 849 retired workers were paid by the community to cover their minimum expenses and were "introduced" and "reallocated" to other community-based enterprises. The district and its Street Administrative Offices have relied on two enterprises created in 1988 as "self-help bases" to provide funds and temporary jobs for similar tasks.)[114]

To save itself, Weida actively sought a marriage with its now more prosperous big brother and business partner, the washing machine-making company. The SLIC, mostly out of fear of the "too big" washing machine maker and based on its own community economic planning, obstructed the deal until the two partners obtained the help of social opinion and eventually the support of the Hefei city government. Starting in 1995, Weida became a part of the washer company as an independent accounting unit. The managers were reassigned, and the average income of all workers was expected to rise to 50 to 70 percent of the company's average income. A major and interesting condition for the SLIC and thus the community to approve the merger was that, among the five hundred formal employees and three hundred retired workers of Weida, none would be dismissed by the company once it took over.

Rural CLMs

1. *A prosperous township (xiang) in Zhejiang Province.*[115] This township is located in northern Zhejiang Province, which is part of the region where the rural economy led by the TVEs had very impressive development in the past two decades. The region had a rich history of local markets and highly developed agriculture. In the 1960s and 1970s, the township already had a sizable number of CBEs. In 1992, the township had 12,092 laborers, nearly 40 percent (4,782) employed by the TVEs. Most of the TVEs, including the small enterprises below the village level, were located in the township seat, with smaller enterprises spread out in the villages. The TVEs were in the industries of construction, automobile-related machinery, textiles, transportation, chemicals, food processing, and services. As in most other rural communities, many were technologically backward workshops. The majority (92 percent) of the 3,376 industrial workers in the community were employed by the township- or village-level TVEs; only 0.75 percent (256) were employed by small enterprises below the village level. Income figures were not consistently available.[116] But by the Chinese standard, the township had achieved substantial economic success. People's living standards appeared to be significantly higher than those in the two Anhui villages discussed in chapter 1 of this book.

Most TVE employees were basically "adjunct workers," in that almost all still had to work in their family fields on a regular basis even though most of their income came from their TVE jobs. Unskilled, weak, and old people tended to work more in the fields, helped financially by their TVE-employed family members. Some families had become "pure farmers," subsidized to varying degrees by the township and their villages. Those "losers" had all but lost their political influence in the community even though many of them had socially respected seniority. The TVE managers, as expected, had the highest social status and political influence. Their control of the financial resources and access to TVE jobs made them and their families the most important social group in the community.

The full-time township and administrative village cadres still had formidable power, backed by the county government above, and frequently used their political power to interfere in community affairs. The township authority strictly enforced certain nationally mandated policies such as family planning. It used methods like imposing fines, dismissing of employees, demolishing houses, and freezing bank accounts to implement the policy of one child per couple. But its authority had been clearly circumscribed by the market-driven shift of power in the community.[117] Numerous cadres had a variety of gray income from the TVEs, and many of their personal expenses, including extravagant banquets, were paid for by the TVEs.

Labor management in the TVEs appeared to be a typical combination of the market mechanism and community confinement. Workers were paid and promoted or penalized basically according to their on-the-job performance. A TVE's profitability was the bottom line for employees' income and job security. But numerous exceptions existed. For example, especially during the planting or harvesting seasons, the TVEs were generally forced to tolerate their employees' tardiness or leaving early. Contracts had become the basis for intra-community economic transactions between the employer and the employees, but enforcement of contracts was often compromised by the prevalent human feelings (*renqing*, 人情) and connections (*guanxi*). To be socially judged "appropriate and humane" was far more important than contract bidding or economic rationality.

As in almost all other TVEs in China, there were no trade unions nor management-sanctioned "political studies."[118] There were few outsiders working in the community on a long-term basis. When a TVE was losing money, the managers usually closed it down before new orders came in. During the closure time, employees became full-time farmers working in their families, with only a meager allowance from their TVEs. Nonlocals were sent back to their hometowns with the possibility of being rehired later. To most workers, the TVE jobs had not yet become secure enough to be their livelihood.

A curious development was the seemingly intensified conflicts between community confinement and the market mechanism. Several community-based protectionist policies of township government were almost openly defied by the profit-driven peasants. For instance, since the mid-1980s, the township tried every year to keep all the locally produced silkworm cocoons for the local TVEs to process, thus to increase the total financial gains for the community. The government issued orders prohibiting selling of raw silk materials to any outside buyers. Cadres and local police were mobilized to establish barricades and checkpoints every year during the season. But lured by the much higher price for the cocoons on the national market, many peasants "betrayed" their community. They even resorted to some "quasi-guerrilla tactics" to get the cocoons out of the community. Similar conflicts between TVE managers and the township government were identified on issues such as hiring more workers, budgets, and expansions. Because most TVE managers were appointed by the township cadres in a collective fashion, the market-conscious TVE managers often had to bend to the demands of the cadres, who might have political and social desire for more hiring and prudent expansion beyond the community.

Finally, similar to developments in the rural communities discussed in chapter 1, advancement of the market institution caused certain erosion of the traditional family institution and the old family-based Chinese culture. Alternative cultures and religions, as internalized alternative institutions, began to develop quietly. There was substantial advancement of Protestantism in the township, as a supplement to still dominant family-based religious activities such as ancestor worship.

2. *A plastics plant in Guangdong.* This small-scale TVE, located right outside the Shenzhen Special Economic Zone (SEZ), had thirty-four workers in 1995 (down from fifty-seven in 1992), two cadres, and three professionals. The plant is a joint venture between a Hong Kong plastics marketing firm (30 percent of shares) and the local township. The township has a financial and technical partnership with a county-owned corporation—the famous Baoan Corporation—which issued the first stocks in the history of the PRC in 1983.[119] The Hong Kong investors put in 2.61 million Hong Kong dollars (about 3 million rmb in 1995) in assets. Making plastic foam as packaging materials to be used by the Hong Kong firm, the plant had annual sales of more than 8 million rmb in 1992 and more than 10 million rmb in 1995.

Being a joint venture and located in one of the most open areas of China, the plant got to hire workers from outside the local community. Due to its low wages and poor working conditions, the plant eventually started to hire all its workers, except for the two cadres and one of the professionals, from outside the prosperous local county. The workers were all young former peasants from other counties and other provinces. The manager could hire and fire work-ers with easy approval from the local labor bureau and his bosses at the Baoan Corporation. But the plant also needed to get sometimes difficult approval from the local labor bureau for hiring from outside the community.

Job applicants from outside needed to have at least one local resident as a "guarantor" in order to be hired. They also had to produce their *hukou* and personal ID and their family planning ID, which stated whether they had fulfilled the birth quota of one child per couple. The plant sponsored an employment-related temporary resident permit (*zanjuzheng*) for its employees at an annual fee of 400-500 rmb. To prevent workers from leaving the plant and "illegally staying" in the township, the plant offered these *zanjuzheng* for only three months at a time. Because all employees were tempo-rary residents of the local township, they did not participate in the community-based distribution of nonwage benefits such as housing and low-cost stocks of the county and township corporations.[120] A two-bedroom apartment was priced at 30,000 rmb for local residents, but would cost over 200,000 rmb for temporary residents.

In 1992, average wages were 300-400 rmb per month for the nonlocal workers and 1,000 rmb for the cadres and professionals. By 1995, the wages for the workers were increased only to 400-500 rmb, with the foremen's wages about 1,000 rmb. The cadres, however, made 3,000-10,000 rmb, which was comparable to the average wages for similarly ranked state employees in the Shenzhen SEZ.[121] There were no other benefits, and the workers took care of their own health insurance.

The manager, however, could share an unknown portion of the profits with the township and Hong Kong owners through the "responsibility" system. He was given full responsibility for and bene-fited from running the plant, on the condition he send a negotiated amount of profit to the two owners annually (about 800,000 rmb in 1995). The profit margin was recorded differently in the two sets of books the plant kept for its owners and the government taxation officials, respectively. The manager, a friend of mine, revealed in pri-vate that the real profit was at least twice as big as the figure shown to government officials. For his good work, the manager was invited on a vacation to Singapore and Thailand, paid for by the satisfied Hong Kong investor. The Hong Kong firm also give the plant a used Dodge minivan, which was still quite fashionable in Guangdong at that time. For the apparent financial contribution to the local community from the plant, the township also rewarded a subsidized apartment to the manager, who was still a state cadre that had been assigned to work in the county some eight years before by the authoritarian state LAP.

The plant was a typical example of the TVEs, and small joint ventures, flourishing in the Pearl River Delta. Both its equipment and technology were fairly primitive. There were only three plastic foam shaping machines, all made in Japan, in the 1960s and used by the Hong Kong investor for two decades. The working conditions and environment were reminiscent of a workshop in a Charles Dickens novel or a Charlie Chaplin movie. The workers, in the words of the manager, had "no rights and no labor protection." Injured workers usually would leave the plant and return home with only a small compensation. The workers, most of them single women between sixteen and twenty-two years old, lived in the plant's free but very crowded dormitory, with eight people per room. The turnover rate was high, and dismissal was quite common. There were no CCP or union organizations. The required labor contract did not even specify working hours, pay, or working conditions. Although Beijing legislated the five-day workweek for the PRC in May 1995, the plant, like most other TVEs and small joint ventures, was still on a six-day workweek in the fall of that year. The work required little skill other than simple repetition of physical labor. It appeared to be a market-oriented revenue generator for the local community, the manager, and the Hong Kong investor, at the expense of the nonlocal laborers.

Institutional Role of the CLMs

The second largest and still fast-growing LAP, the CLMs reflect much of contemporary China's institutional structure and have a profound impact on the evolution of that structure. The CLMs seem to be crucial to the emergence of a "Chinese" and "socialist" market institution in the PRC.

Continuing a "Chinese" Socialism

Given its ability to create new jobs with minimum drain on the state's budget, the community-based societal LAP clearly contributed to political order and social stability in the PRC's history. It created room under the authoritarian state LAP for social institutions to survive and function and thus to mediate between the authoritarian state and the traditional families, or between the CCP dictatorship and the individual's rights and demands. If the authoritarian state LAP made the PRC a socialist nation, the societal LAP colored that socialism with a hue of traditional "Chineseness." Labor acquired economically important mobility within the communities, greatly enhancing the economic viability of those communities. But across the communities, the flow of labor was still institutionally restricted. Even by the late 1990s, intercommunity labor mobility was still essentially a supplement to the intracommunity labor allocation. To belong to a "good" community, or *danwei,* was as crucial as belonging to a good family. Group identity and the related, almost predetermined, position in the Chinese institutional setting were still far more important than an individual's quality, ability, or effort. The rise of labor productivity in the CLMs thus had not yet institutionalized individualism significantly in China. Under the CLMs, therefore, the institutionally and functionally undifferentiated families, groups, and communities continued to be the basis for the traditional institutional structure, despite the visible increase of labor mobility and productivity within the communities. Even the most open Special Economic Zones (SEZs) needed to use the community structure to control the massive inflow and increasing presence of the *hukou*-less floating people.[122]

The traditional role of communities was brought back under CCP national rule, and limited but significant autonomy was acquired by the economy and society on the community level. The localistic, dispersed, and stable Chinese culture and ethics thus survived in Mao's era when the authoritarian state LAP threatened to institutionally transform Chinese culture. The existence and operation of the societal LAP may have, therefore, greatly alleviated the negatives of the failure of Mao's bold but misguided revolution carried out on the basis of the authoritarian state LAP. Furthermore, in the rigidly maintained dual economy of the rural-versus-urban system, the community-based societal LAP (especially the CLMs) eased conflicts and confrontations considerably between the urban and rural populations by creating urban-style industrial and cash employment in the countryside. Certain urban jobs were also made available to rural residents through the societal LAP/CLMs. The fast-growing CLMs, with their tolerable political and social challenges have not yet affected the fabric of the Chinese and socialist institutional structure. In fact, the CLMs contributed to the stabilization and continuation of that structure in the reform era with only a minimum amount of institutional adjustment.

Linking the State and the Families

The community-based societal LAP and the CLMs have been important to the undifferentiated organizational structure on the community level, effectively connecting the PRC state and families as the institutional framework for Chinese economic, political, and social activities. Chapter 2 discussed the profound role of the *danweis*. Because the *danweis* became the most important form of urban communities, the institutional role of the societal LAP and CLMs in urban China would be understood if we appreciate the institutional functions of those *danweis*.

In rural areas, the societal LAP and the CLMs also contributed to the maintenance of the undifferentiated institutional setting. Unlike the urban areas, where the state's political institutions may be the most important basis for the organizational structure, the rural organizational structure may have been based more on family-centered social institutions that are community confined. How to solve the gradual breakdown of the family-based traditional LAP has been a key to the preservation of the family-based Chinese culture, and thus the family-like institutional system. Cyclical dynasty changes were basically the results of the inherent difficulty of this task. Mao's collectivization and authoritarian state LAP may have helped to forestall that problem but ruined the development of the Chinese economy. The community-based societal LAP, as spontaneous as it was initially, consolidated the social institutions on the community level in the face of an intrusive and active PRC state. The stability and continuity of the Chinese institutions (rather than its radical version advocated by Mao) thus were maintained, at least in the local communities. The social harmony and equality maintained by the societal LAP and the flexibility and diversity provided by the coexistence of large numbers of communities are two of the leading institutional advantages the societal LAP/CLMs have generated for the Chinese.

The institutionally stabilizing role of the societal LAP in rural China is illustrated by its capacity to meet the basic needs of everyone in the community. The advantages in providing important social services by the collective Chinese communities have been recognized in the West (Brugger and Reglar 1994, 126-130). In rural areas, about 3 million families in the early 1990s could not support themselves, primarily because of their lack of young laborers. As many as 74 percent of them had their basic needs provided for by their local communities in the form of five protection families (*wubaohu*). The societal LAP made such collective support of the *wubaohus* possible through allocating the labor needed to care for those families. The rest (about 25 percent) of those needy families were provided for by the state only because they did not belong to any specific community. Among the 4.2-6 million rural households below the poverty line in the early 1990s, the rural communities helped 60 to 64 percent (SSB-RB 1992, 316-321). In total, about 2 to 3 percent of Chinese rural households (5.25 million in 1991) were provided for by their local communities.

Similar community-based poverty-relief activities can also be seen in the urban areas where the polarization of income has accelerated lately.[123] Such an institutional structure, unlike charity or government relief, appears to have strengthened the communities. It may also help to explain the implementation of some harsh policies such as family planning and birth control measures in a culture that traditionally valued more offspring—primarily because of concern for providing for the elderly. Another, perhaps more important function of the rather effective community structure has been its ability to control inflation and fight crime. It was reported that local community organizations could have a very effective role in reducing the chaos and crimes associated with floating people by joining hands and institutionalizing neighborhood watches.[124] Almost all major cities and even small towns passed "anti-inappropriately high profit" laws as the basis for community-centered efforts to control the socially and politically undesirable inflation. The localities then set up their own "fair profitability" standards for common commodities (Beijing decided how many kinds of commodities nationally, and the local governments could add many more) and then published the price ceiling for each type and brand. Every community member was mobilized to report any violation.[125]

Furthermore, the institutionally significant stabilization of rural communities is well reflected by the maintenance of the typical hierarchical order of families/individuals and the related values and status, often under new names, in the rural areas. This continuation, closely related to the community-based societal LAP and the CLMs, was usually done in the name of preserving community values and tradition and with strong help from the legitimization provided by the political authorities. In Henan Province, a county developed a system of three kinds of families (*sanhu*) to categorize each rural family according to its economic and social achievements, judged against community-based traditional values. Community authorities established detailed criteria for the categorization. The villagers then got together to make self-nominations and mutual evaluations, and the families were categorized into three ranks, each of which was signified by a plaque affixed to their doors. The first was "comfortable family" (*xiaokanhu,*小康户), with the honor of having their plaque installed by the county's leading cadres. Such families were generally rich and socially well considered in the community. The second was "five-good family" (*wuhaohu,*五好户) whose plaque was put up by the townships' leading cadres. These families were socially well regarded but not necessarily rich or "capable." The third and largest group was the "law-abiding family" (*shoufahu,*守法户), whose official honors were done only by the villages' leading cadres. As the name suggested, these were common families that had no legal or disciplinary problems with the government or community authorities. Interestingly enough, at least in one village, every family got a plaque, hence a position, in this simplistic but effective formal ranking.[126] The rural communities, equipped with the family-based traditional LAP and the economically more advantageous CLMs, seem to have the potential to provide a paradise for the Chinese institutional structure and CCP regime.

Having a "Chinese" and "Socialist" Labor Market

In a way, the CLM form of the Chinese societal LAP is a clearly distorted "Chinese style" market-oriented LAP that combines the economic utility of the market, yet preserves the cultural essence of Chinese tradition. As unique Chinese and also perhaps socialist labor markets, CLMs came to have some features that separate them from the family-based traditional LAP, the authoritarian state LAP, and a national labor market. Unlike the family-based LAP, laborers in a CLM were recruited and managed in a market fashion. Productivity was the basis for recruiting, promotion, or dismissal, although it was often concealed under moralistic notions such as being good or bad for the community. Employees were paid scheduled cash wages related to an enterprise's profits and workers' performance. Employees basically worked in industrial enterprises with a substantial, coordinated division of labor. As a result, the labor force of a community, under a CLM, achieved significant mobility and contractual relations, no matter how informal. Economic concerns often replaced social or even political concerns as the foremost values in the CLMs. Their greater efficiency and innovation, compared to the family-based traditional LAP, should therefore not be a surprise.

Unlike a national labor market, CLMs were community-based; thus, there were substantial community-based barriers against a national labor mobility. The outsiders, that is, the nonlocal *hukou* holders, were systematically discriminated against by the CLMs. A college graduate with no local *hukou,* for example, even after using several connections, could only get a temporary job as a blue-collar worker in a collective enterprise at half the wages.[127] Community-based welfare concerns such as security and equality were valued, and giving every community member a job often took precedence over the pursuit of profits. Consequently labor mobility and productivity were both likely to be significantly lower than that in a national labor market. Considerable room existed in the CLMs for increasing efficiency of the allocation and utilization of labor resources. One way to do that would be to open up the CLMs and merge them to form a genuine national labor market. For that purpose, the fashionable idea of privatizing the urban collective enterprises and TVEs may have been viewed by many as a major vehicle.[128] A prominent proponent of the now infamous "shock therapy," Harvard economist Jeffery Sachs, was invited by some government officials to promote the idea of TVE privatization forcefully in the PRC in 1994.[129] But the Chinese may find that such a prescription is sound only to economists, who perhaps are more "rational" than ordinary Chinese peasants. The political and social prices of a complete privatization plan would deem it almost completely not feasible in the PRC. A quiet and widespread clanization or familization of the TVEs may have been more effective in adding more market mechanisms to the existing CLMs.[130]

Unlike in the authoritarian state LAP, the working conditions, employment terms, and pay in the CLMs have been largely market-determined and have varied significantly across communities. Employment did not guarantee a local *hukou,* so there tended to be a quasi-permanent division of the privileged local residents and the outsiders among the employees in a CLM. Social institutions and values, rather than nationalism and statehood or political values, affected labor allocation and utilization in a particular CLM. Wages and benefits were determined by distorted market mechanisms based on community-wide supply and demand of labor. The state, as the centralized political authority of the nation, did not have nearly as much control of the labor in the CLMs as it has had in the authoritarian state LAP.

Establishing the Chinese Market Through the CLMs

Despite the social distortions—which may actually be necessary modifications—the community-based societal LAP and especially the fast-growing CLMs have become effective avenues for the Chinese market to grow in a nonmarket Chinese economy, allocating and managing the most consequential economic resource—the labor. The predominant family institution and the family-like Chinese state have been linked to the market institution via the dispersed, diverse, and small CLMs. As perhaps one of the most important and most stable socialist practices in China, CLMs may have represented an effective, smooth way to utilize the market institution without eradicating the long-existing, thus quite legitimate, social, and political institutions. More interestingly, the deep legitimacy of the preexisting social and political institutions may have effectively legitimized the newly introduced market institution, therefore greatly facilitating the rather smooth progress of marketization of labor allocation. If all the Chinese communities had developed well institutionalized CLMs, then nearly the entire labor force would be allocated and managed by the market institution. A Chinese market would then be established in allocating the labor force through the CLMs, suboptimal but nonetheless truly feasible labor markets. It would be a great achievement if the Chinese could have a market-oriented LAP, perhaps fragmented by community-based social institutions, with the help rather than obstruction or even destruction from powerful social and political institutions.

A few scholars have expressed admiration for and even fascination with the Chinese societal LAP.[131] A major reason is perhaps their hope that the societal LAP and the CLMs might promote significant economic development and reach full employment with low labor mobility at the same time, thereby maintaining social and economic equality, at least in the local communities. It would indeed be consequential if somehow the Chinese could have the market institution established as their main economic institution while safeguarding the humane, deeply legitimate social institutions. Differentiation could develop among the economic, political, and social institutions in the communities. A balance could be struck on the community level leading to a Chinese style of modernity. Following that logic, "the ownership of modern corporations is in essence a collective one," therefore, an employee ownership and management like the CLMs could be a viable alternative to the socialist reforms tried by Eastern Europeans.[132]

The market institution practiced by the Chinese CLMs, has, however, been fragmented, distorted, and incomplete, one that has not come close to reaching the potential of efficiently utilizing the Chinese labor force. Waste, irrational labor decisions, underemployment, and especially unfair labor practices have continued in the CLMs. At the small scale of community economies, substantial efficiency may have been reached. But beyond the hundreds of thousands of local communities, the national economy of the PRC still desperately needs a market-oriented labor allocation pattern. Local social institutions, though they have facilitated the labor market on the community level, may prove to be some of the strongest barriers to the emergence of a national labor market. Despite impressive achievements and great potential, we should be aware of the limits of the CLMs in promoting a national labor market in China. Should the CLMs become the main LAP in China, as recent trends suggest is possible, we probably could not expect a genuine national labor market in China.[133] What is more, the community structure has given the market institution an easy time to develop quietly. The same structure may also give nonmarket institutions an easy time to "roll back" the market institution in labor allocation. A politically motivated and powerful state could mobilize local political institutions to break the market institution one community at a time, in that CLMs tend to be vulnerable due to their small size and close ties to local political authorities.

In recent years, the growth of the societal LAP and especially the development of the CLMs has reduced the CCP state's role in allocating labor and in managing the entire Chinese economy. The process has been slow, and the guise of collective ownership has been comforting to CCP leaders who have been gradually losing control. However, that reduction of control reached a critical mass by the late 1990s in both cities and rural areas. In Beijing, for example, local party officials were alarmed to find that among 485 local state-owned and small collective enterprises that were leased out to their managers through public bidding in 1990, 50 percent were leased to non-CCP members, 35.9 percent did not have a single CCP member, and 41.2 percent had only one CCP member.[134]

The CCP's leadership in the CLMs has indeed fallen into jeopardy, especially in the countryside. Foreign media have reported about the growing political autonomy of Chinese villages since the 1980s. The family/clan heads, the TVE managers—the financially "capables"— and the community-based CCP cadres have formed a new trinity replacing the CCP authority from above in the local communities. In some areas, the election of local CCP cadres was even subject to the approval of all the villagers, party members or not.[135] A "civil society" could even emerge strongly in the PRC as a result of the development of the CLMs.[136] The new development of "rich" villages/TVE corporations "annexing poor villages," first reported in 1995, has caught the "watchful attention of the government."[137] The further growth of CLMs, and the conversion of many state-owned *danweis* to CLMs as mentioned previously, could likely cause more alarm and some political responses from the state to set yet additional limits on them. Preventing CLMs from generating too much alienating social force appears to have been a worrisome and serious political task for the CCP leadership.[138]

CLMs and Regionalism

Perhaps more interesting to China observers, a major institutional impact of the rapid CLM development may be facilitating the increase of regionalism as a result of unevenly accelerating development of China's economy in the past two decades. Despite the concentrated efforts of Beijing toward more balanced development between the booming east and the slow central and western provinces, the gap of investment, growth, and technology levels between the two regions and among the provinces has continued to grow.[139] The six provinces/metropolises in eastern China received 54 percent of total Chinese R&D investment in 1994; the eighteen provinces in central and western China got only 35.9 percent.[140] All top ten provinces/ metropolises in economic development and income were on the east coast, while the growth rate of the six to ten central and western provinces was declining in the early 1990s.[141]

The economic growth gap between east and west expanded in the reform years. The share of the eastern region (36.7 percent of total population and 10.7 percent of territory) in the Chinese GNP rose from 52.3 percent in 1980 to 60.1 percent in 1993, while the share of the west (25.2 percent of the total population and 69.1 percent of the land) declined from 16.5 percent to 13.1 percent. Among the one hundred most "prosperous counties" in 1993, ninety-one were located in the east whereas the western provinces had none. Ninety percent of the 592 "poor counties" were in the west. Prosperous areas like Sunan (Jiangsu Province) in the east had a per capita income nearly six times that of poor areas like Simao (Yunnan Province) and Biji (Guizhou Province) in the west.[142] Official statistics showed that in the first half of 1995, the average wage level in the eastern coastal provinces was 2,702 rmb, 35 percent (up from 29.2 percent in 1994) higher than that in the central and western areas. The average wage in the same period in the more open coastal province of Guangdong was more than twice that in neighboring Jiangxi Province (3,595 versus 1,713 rmb).[143] Other figures estimated that the east-west income gap grew from 48 percent in 1986 to 52 percent in 1991 (2,283 rmb in the east and 1,095 rmb in the west).[144] The government-mandated minimum wage in the PRC also varies drastically across regions, separated by *hukou* and other community barriers (see table 3.4). It appears that the dominance of the CLMs may generate some institutional hazards for the unity of the Chinese nation. The CLMs, by definition, tend to encourage and promote divisive regionalism in a vast and diversified nation like China. Apparently, scholars have not yet included the impact of the CLMs in their discussion on the uneven development of the Chinese economy.[145]

Table 3.4. Minimum Monthly Wages in Selected Areas (1995)

Places	rmb	Region
Shenzhen SEZ	420	East
Zhuhai SEZ	380	East
Guangzhou	320	East
Xiamen SEZ	280	East
Shanghai	220	East
Fuzhou	225	East
Beijing	210	East
Tianjin	210	East
Ninbo	210	East
Zhejiang Province	200	East
Hefei	198	Central
Wuhu	180	Central
Nanchang	170	Central
Huaibei	165	Central
Deyang	141	Central
Dangshan	135	Central
Jingzai	135	Central

Sources: Beijing Ribao (Beijing Daily), December 2, 1994, 1; *Xinmin wanbao* (Xinmin evening news) (Shanghai), March 3, 1995, 3; and *Xinan wanbao* (Xinan evening news) (Hefei), June 6, 1995, 1.

In short, the CLMs have been largely beneficial to the quiet but extensive growth of the market institution in China. The advantages and achievements of the CLMs are likely to make this LAP a dominant Chinese LAP in the near future. While promoting the market institution, the CLMs may have only limited effect on the differentiation of the Chinese institutional structure beyond the community level. A resilient, but nonetheless distorted, even controlled local market may survive and develop in the local communities, leading to visible and consequential differentiation of the economic, political, and social institutions in those communities. Beyond the communities, CLMs may actually help consolidate the national institutional changes by limiting the development of a national labor market. Or maybe a community-based institutional structure would be the future of China? What would that imply about the future of Chinese politics and Chinese foreign policy?

Summary

The community-based societal LAP and the CLMs historically have provided substantial breathing space for the Chinese economy. Active and widespread, this LAP functioned as a giant buffer between the authoritarian state and socialist planning on one side and a freer and more dynamic Chinese economy on the other. This was especially true during the reform years after 1978. Practically, the CLMs helped solve the problem of unemployment at the end of the 1970s and throughout the 1980s. As a community-based, semi-market-oriented and semi-socialist LAP, CLMs have become an alternative to the authoritarian state LAP in the cities and to the family-based traditional LAP in the countryside, representing progress in both cases.

CLMs have had enormous importance concerning the issue of unemployment, which has been economically, socially, and politically profound in the largest nation on earth. Having demonstrated the ability to absorb large numbers of laborers in fairly efficient urban collective enterprises and especially in the TVEs, CLMs have become a pivotal part of the PRC's job-creation strategy. As cited earlier, CLMs were more than ten times as efficient in creating jobs than the authoritarian state LAP in the 1980s and 1990s.[146] The TVEs alone already accounted for 47 percent of the Chinese economy and a quarter of rural employment in 1995, up from only 9 percent thirteen years before.[147] In a nation of more than 200 million surplus labor in the rural areas and more than 30 million underemployed urban laborers, the fast-growing, job-generating CLMs have naturally become the great hope. The government has estimated that more than 100 million rural laborers will need to be employed by the year 2000, not even counting the 10 million annual growth in the rural population.

The TVEs have been the only reliable relief, absorbing roughly 7 million new workers a year.[148]

CLMs break away from both the confines of the family and the control of the state in a way quite acceptable to most Chinese, who are influenced by the harmony-valuing localistic culture. CLMs permit the existence of variety, diversity, and competition, yet do not cause much breakdown in the Chinese institutional structure, which still appears to have deep legitimacy. This LAP calls for efficiency and optimal management while incorporating the local community-based socialist style of welfare, or "moral economy" characteristics in Chinese economy and society. CLMs substantially promote a quasi-market economy with only limited political "damage" as viewed by the neotraditional communist Chinese state, in that the production means are still owned by the collectives rather than by individual capitalists. Though not as spectacular and clear as a total and sudden privatization to many Western observers, CLMs, as a distorted or Chinese style market-oriented LAP, have the realistic potential to function as the new fabric of the Chinese institutional structure in the near future. Further study of CLMs and their operations, therefore, should be a requisite for those wanting to understand the future and the nature of institutional changes in contemporary China.

Notes

1. The PRC NPC passed the PRC *Hukou* Registration Regulations in 1958 and institutionalized the national *hukou* system and the rural-urban dual economy. These regulations were reaffirmed in 1985 by the NPC.

2. Despite some development and modifications, the *hukou* system was still firmly in place in the 1990s. Beijing publicly stated that the rural-urban division would continue for a "very long" time, and thus the national laws on labor protection and insurance would not be applicable to the "vast rural areas" (*Renmin Ribao-Overseas*, December 7, 1993, 1).

3. The income gap between urban and rural residents grew, for example, from 2.2 times in 1964 (2.5 times in 1978) to about 4 times in 1991-1993. See Zhong Yicai, "Chengxiang eyuan shehui de yonghe yu yingnong jingcheng" (The merging of the dual urban-rural societies and the pulling of the peasants into the cities) in *Shehui kexue* (Social sciences) (Shanghai), no. 1 (1995): 55-58.

4. Many influential theories are based on the notion of a "human community" or a community of the earth, for example, the "global commons" argument for the protection of earth's ecology. See Marvin S. Soroos, "The Tragedy of the Commons in Global Perspective," in Charles W. Kegley Jr. and Eugene R. Wittkopf, eds., *The Global Agenda*, 4th edition (New York: McGraw-Hill, 1995), 422-435.

5. For further discussions on the notion of community, see Allen D. Edward, *Types of Rural Community, Community Structure and Analysis* (New York: Crowell, 1959); Jessie Bernard, *The Sociology of Community* (Glenview Ill.: Scott

Foresman, 1973); and Colin Bell et al., *Community Studies* (New York: Praeger, 1972).

6. For a Chinese view on the concept of community in contemporary China, see Sun Fonghua and Tang Mingda, "Shiqu jiqi yanju tujing" (Community and the ways to study it), in *Xinjiang Daxue xuebao* (Xinjiang University journal) (Urumqi), no. 4 (1993): 56. See also Li Jiangmin, "Shiqu fazhang" (Community development), in *Zhongguo renkou kexue* (Chinese demographics) (Beijing), no. 1 (1994): 21-24.

7. Lu Dazhuan, "Zhongguo xinzhengqu, jingjiqu fazhan de huigu he zhanwang" (A review and the prospects of China's administrative and economic zones), in *Zhongguo Renmin Daxue xuebao* (Journal of the Chinese Renmin University) (Beijing), no. 6 (1994): 1-6.

8. For the currently more humane role of "linking government policies to the daily life of the people" played by those urban "residential committees," see Fan Ping, "Heli, ruer, tiexin" (Reasonable, penetrating, thoughtful), in *Renmin Ribao,* February 26, 1994, 9.

9. For an interesting discussion on the interactions between the state, family, and community in the Chinese rural areas, see Chen Junji and Mu Guanzong, "Nongchun shiqu erchongxin yu nongmin shengyu juece" (The duality of the rural communities and the peasants' reproduction decisions), in *Zhongguo renkou kexue* (Chinese demographics) (Beijing), no. 6 (1994): 43-48.

10. For a summary of this nationwide community-based marketization of the Chinese local economy, the so-called government sets up the stage and the market puts on the show, see Lu Rizhou, "Shehui zhuyi shichang jingji yu nongchun gaige" (Socialist market economy and rural reform), in *Ri Shan* (1993): 259-264.

11. For this, we only have to recall the vivid descriptions of local markets in premodern nations in classic literature such as Homer's *Odyssey,* Dante's *The Divine Comedy,* Shakespeare's *The Merchant of Venice,* the famous Arabic stories in *One Thousand and One Nights* and Cao Xueqin's *Dreams of the Red Chamber.*

12. Lishisou 1963-1965 contains rather rich material on the "sprouts of capitalism" represented by local markets, primarily in the southeastern provinces. For a treatment of local markets, especially the market-oriented commercial activities in the Song dynasty, see Hua 1982. Hu 1979 did some systematic examination on "emerging capitalism" in China. For a Western account, see the multivolume series *The Cambridge History of China* (Cambridge, N.Y.: Cambridge University Press, 1930-present).

13. For an authoritative discussion on the development of Chinese local markets in this period, see Huang 1990.

14. *Renmijn Ribao-Overseas,* June 7, 1995, 2. For a general discussion about Chinese local and regional markets in the 1990s, see Hu 1993, 725-733, and Yan 1994, 131-151.

15. Ding Xianhao and Gu Decheng, "Lun quyu tici shichang de hongguan tiaokong" (On the macro regulation of regionally layered markets) in *Dangdai jingji kexue* (Contemporary economics) (Xian) (March 1994): 42-47.

16. Based on roughly the same logic, some reform-minded Chinese scholars have contended that a major reason for the great success of the Japanese economy was that it was based on the "self-interests of the firms/companies" or groups rather than on the self-interests of individuals, as in the West. See Wang Lina, "Dongxifang hanxuejia xinmuzhong de Zhongguo chuantong wenhua" (Chinese traditional

culture in the eyes of Oriental and Occidental Sinologists) in *Renmin Ribao-Overseas,* May 29, 1995, 3.

17. For a recent comment on the historically positive role played by the merchants from Anhui, see Sheng Yuju, "Chong rushang shuo hui shang" (From Confucian merchants to Anhui merchants), in *Renmin Ribao-Overseas,* June 23, 1995, 2. For extensive information about this merchant group, see Zhang Haipeng and Wang Tiangyuan, eds., *Mingqing huishang ziliao xuanbian* (Selected materials on southern Anhui merchants in the Ming and Qing dynasties) (Hefei: Huangshan Press, 1985).

18. Cf. Reich, Gordon, and Edwards 1973, and Loveridge and Mok 1979 for further theoretical analysis of the segmentation of labor market within a nation.

19. David Granick, "Multiple Labor Markets in the Industrial State Enterprise Sector" in *The China Quarterly* (January 1991): 269-289.

20. TVEs, for example, have significantly outperformed the state-owned enterprises throughout the past decade. One authoritative Chinese study concluded that, clearly, the lack of market mechanisms in allocating and managing labor was the major reason for the unimpressive record of the state-owned enterprises (Ma and Sun, eds., 1994, 310).

21. Although small-scale slave trade was never fully banned, a market-oriented transaction of the labor force was generally deemed unfit to the pre-modern Chinese domestic organizational structure, which was centered on the family.

22. We can still observe this type of family-based, not individual-based, equality in community works and projects in Chinese villages. For example, a family of four capable laborers would send just one—the same as a neighboring family that had only one able laborer—to work on the village well or village roads (author's field notes, 1992-1995).

23. For the history of the first two components of the urban collective enterprises, see Wang 1986.

24. Payment of fixed interest was terminated in 1965 on the assumption that owners had redeemed all of their properties. After 1978, however, most former owners of those enterprises, the "national capitalists" who supposedly were a part of the "united front" led by the CCP, were paid a lump sum to settle their ownership in a so-called implementing policy campaign as a correction to the radical policies during the Cultural Revolution.

25. The criterion is mainly the size of the enterprises and the products. As with many other issues in the PRC's political economy, the definition of "large" versus "small" has been greatly influenced by informal networking and personal decisions of local government officials.

26. However, those enterprises hire people from outside to fill special positions such as technicians, accountants, managers, etc.

27. *Renmin Ribao-Overseas,* April 15, 1994, 2. Some estimate that such pseudo-collective enterprises may make up as many as 30 percent of all Chinese collective or societal enterprises. See Liang 1990.

28. Chinese official statistics recorded the urban "waiting-for-job rate" in 1978 as 5.3 percent, the highest in the decade. See *Xinhua wenzhai* (Xinhua digest) (Beijing), September 7, 1990, and Yue 1989, 23.

29. Yuan 1990, 8; *Xinhua Daily Telegraph* (Beijing) February 18, 1991.

30. For example, see Zhao Huanxin, "Education Profits from School-Run Firm," in *China Daily-Business Weekly* (Beijing), vol. 15, no. 4535 (August 13-19, 1995): 7.

31. Yuan 1990, 8; *Shengyang Ribao* (Shengyang daily), December 15, 1993.

32. Chinese Labor Ministry figures in *Renmin Ribao*, March 12, 1993, 3, and December 12, 1990, 3.

33. The retirees, therefore, are generally allowed to find a job on the urban CLMs, get a *getihu* (individual household) commercial license (Wang 1992, 13), or work part-time in the TVEs.

34. Speech by Chen Peiying, deputy secretary general of the Shanghai Retired Workers Management Authority in *Renmin Ribao-Overseas*, June 6, 1995, 4.

35. For a history of the TVEs, see Byrd and Lin 1990, and Zhang 1992, 65-68.

36. The CBEs provided myriad jobs in the rural areas and were considered one of the three major factors that eliminated Chinese rural unemployment. (The other two were collectivized agricultural underemployment and the large-scale rural capital projects sponsored by the state.) See Rawski 1979, chapter 4, and Ullerich 1979, 115.

37. Zhang Sai 1992, 67, and SSB-RB 1992, 45-47. "Enterprises below the village level" were about 17.63 million in 1991, compared to 1.45 million true TVEs. The former, despite their massive number, only employed roughly half of the total labor force allocated in the rural CLMs in 1991 (about 48.4 million people). Many appeared to be actually private enterprises.

38. In Jiangsu Province, which has had the biggest economy among all the PRC's thirty provinces for several years, TVEs produced half of that province's output (*Renimn Ribao-Overseas*, January 3, 1991, 3).

39. For instance, as early as 1990, there were seven hundred such foreign-invested TVEs in eastern China's six provinces. In Quanzhou city of Fujian Province, more than four hundred TVEs were either foreign-invested or connected to foreign enterprises. Nationwide, about five thousand TVEs have joint ventures or cooperative contracts with FDI. In Zhejiang Province, 40 to 70 percent of FDI enterprises are TVE enterprises (*Renmin Ribao-Overseas*, March 8, 1990, 5; November 23, 1990, 3; January 3, 1991, 3; and March 2, 1991, 1).

40. *Renmin Ribao*, February 24, 1990, 3.

41. Li Lin, "Zhaizhao xiangzhen qiye xinxiang" (Remake the image of the TVEs), in *Renmin Ribao-Overseas*, April 10, 1995, 3.

42. Author's interview in Wuxi, Jiangsu Province, August 12, 1995.

43. As will be elaborated later, in some areas such as the famous Shengze township of Jiangsu Province, the community boundaries had faded somewhat under the pressure of market forces by the mid-1990s (author's interviews in Shengze, August 18, 1995).

44. A successful TVE is usually encouraged or compelled to support those fellow peasants still working in the field. This is called "using industry to support agriculture." The government tends to take a local community, TVEs, and other aspects of economic activities as a single taxation unit.

45. Figures are calculated based on tables 3.1 and 3.2 and Gao 1993, 584-585.

46. State Statistical Bureau, *1994 nian guomin jingji he shehui fazhang de tongji baogao* (A statistical communiqué on national economic and social development in 1994) (Beijing), February 28, 1995, chapter 9.

47. *Xinhua Daily Telegraph* (Beijing), May 30, 1995.

48. State Statistical Bureau: *1994 nian guomin jingji he shehui fazhang de tongji baogao* (A statistical communiqué on national economic and social development in 1994) (Beijing), February 28, 1995, chapter 9.

49. *Xinhua Daily Telegraph* (Beijing), May 30, 1995.

50. Xiao Hangping, "Dao xiangzhen qiye qu" (Go to the TVEs), in *Renmin Ribao-Overseas,* August 15, 1994, 4.

51. One effective means the PRC state has employed to "correct" the gross economic, social, and political unfairness in treating people-run (*minban*) teachers has been to grant recruitment quotas to local communities to enable them to transfer some *minban* teachers into state-employed positions. But such efforts have been minimal at best. In 1995, for example, the Personnel Ministry and the State Commission of Education, with a "special effort," only arranged to transfer one 150,000 out of the total of 2.3 million *minban* teachers. See *Shenzhen renshi* (Shenzhen personnel), an internal monthly by the Shenzhen Personnel Bureau (Shenzhen), no. 6 (1995): 25.

52. Such community-based provision for *minban* teachers has caused widespread mistreatment and underpayment. See, for example, "Jiaoshi dataowang" (The great exodus of the teachers," in *Huaxia wenzhe* (China news digest), an Internet Weekly, no. 201, February 23, 1995.

53. Gao Xincai, "Dangqian xiangzhen qiye fazhang zhongde zhuyao wenti fengxi" (An analysis of the main problems in the current development of the TVEs), in *Zhuze renshixue yanju* (Organization and personnel sciences) (Lanzhou), no. 6 (1994): 44.

54. Yang Xianzhen and Chen Naixin, "Joushi niandai xinagzhen qiye de tedian he qushi" (Features and trends of the TVEs in the 1990s), in *Zhonghua gongshan shibao* (China business times) (Beijing), November 4, 1994, 5. Similar figures appeared again in *Zhonghua gongshan shibao* (China business times) (Beijing), January 16, 1995, 5.

55. Interestingly, the largest known Chinese private enterprise (annual sales exceeded 1 billion rmb in 1993) is located in Chengdu in the western province of Sichuan. In *Zhonghua gongshan shibao* (China business times) (Beijing), January 16, 1995, 5.

56. In February 1993, Beijing issued its resolution on accelerating the development of the TVEs in central and western China, aimed at a more even development of the economically vibrant TVEs. Cf., the speech by Chen Junsheng, commissioner of the State Council, at the PRC TVE Work Conference on September 18, 1993, in Cai 1994, 11-15.

57. For example, the Guangdong provincial government ordered in 1995 that every *danwei* and enterprise, including the collective enterprises and TVEs, must hire no fewer than 1.5 percent of its workers from among handicapped people. See He Huifei, "Guangdong anbili anpai cangjiren jouye" (Guangdong arranges jobs for the handicapped according to a quota), in *Renmin Ribao-Overseas,* February 16, 1995, 4.

58. For example, see State Council 1993, 24-25, 38-40.

59. As part of the CCP's effort to fight inflation, TVE bureaus were tasked with the authority of approving TVEs' capital expansion. In Anhui Province in the mid-1990s, any TVE new investment above 3 million rmb had to be approved by the county TVE bureau; investments between 3 million and 5 million by the prefecture

TVE bureau; and above 5 million by the provincial TVE bureau. (author's interviews with officials at the Anhui TVE Management Bureau, August 1995).

60. Most local TVE bureaus have acquired regular financial contributions from the TVEs and some even directly tax the TVEs for part of their operating budgets. In Anhui, for example, the Provincial TVE Management Bureau gets an annual 0.08 percent of TVEs' profits as a management fee (author's interviews in Anhui and Jiangsu Provinces, summer 1995).

61. Author's interviews in Changzhou and Suzhou, two star regions of Chinese TVE development, in Jiangsu Province, summer 1995. Also see the articles in *Anhui xiangzhen qiye* (Anhui TVEs), a monthly of the Anhui TVE Management Bureau (Hefei), no. 6, 1995.

62. See for example, "Anhui xiangzhen qiye guangliju 1994 niandu baogao" (The 1994 annual report of the Anhui TVE Management Bureau), *Anhui xiangzhen qiye guangliju wenjian* (Documents of the Anhui TVE Management Bureau) (Hefei), no. 25 (1995).

63. Article 18 of the PRC Regulations on the Rural Collective Enterprises (June 1990) and Article 4 of the PRC Regulations on the Urban Collective Enterprises (September 1991) in State Council 1993, 21, 28.

64. For example, Guangzhou city adopted at least eleven local laws by the mid-1990s to create a localized market-oriented economy. See *Renmin Ribao-Overseas,* June 5, 1995, 4.

65. See the report of how a TVE Bureau chief in a county of Guizhou Province fought the county government's attempt at "nationalizing" tens of peasant-owned small hydro-power stations in 1994. The county government eventually was defeated in the prefectural court. *Baokan wenzhai* (Digest of the periodicals) (Shanghai), June 29, 1995, 2.

66. In Suzhou and Wuxi, one would find much stronger influence of the market on those issues than in Changzhou and Zhenjiang (author's field notes, summer 1995).

67. Article 3 of both the PRC Regulations on the Rural Collective Enterprises (June 1990) and the PRC Regulations on the Urban Collective Enterprises (September 1991) in State Council 1993, 19, 28.

68. In Hefei, for example, a fairly successful and sizable urban collective enterprise promoted itself to the rank of division or county level. But it was still under the leadership of a county-level state-owned corporation. It is indeed confusing (author's field notes, January-February 1995).

69. A financially shaky state-owned but genuine division- or county-level *danwei,* therefore, can legitimately have access to the "appropriate" CCP documents and meetings, while a TVE five times as big and ten times as strong financially could only have access to party documents and meetings at the level of township, or *gu,* two levels lower.

70. Yang Xianzhen and Chen Naixin, "Joushi niandai xinagzhen qiye de tedian he qushi" (Features and trends of the TVEs in the 1990s), *Zhonghua gongshan shibao* (China business times) (Beijing), November 4, 1994, 5.

71. There have been signs of a modest decrease in the growth rate of the CLMs in rural China. In the early 1980s, every 6,700 rmb in new sales would create a job in the TVEs. By the 1990s, it took as much as 73,000 rmb in new sales to generate a new job (Ma and Sun, eds. 1994, 28-29).

72. The official *Renmin Ribao* reported that a jobless urban youth without the right connections, despite high marks in the community-based recruiting exams, could still "wait-for-job" for several years (*Overseas* edition, August 15, 1994, 4).

73. Author's field notes in Anhui, Beijing, Gunagdong, Jiansu, Shanghai, and Sichuan, 1989, 1992, 1993, and 1995.

74. Author's interviews and field notes in Changzhou, Wuxi, and Suzhou, summer 1995.

75. As will be addressed later, the shares of stocks issued by the collective enterprises, especially the TVEs, are often available exclusively to members of the local communities. The owners cannot freely trade their shares (author's interviews and field notes in Anhui, Guangdong, and Jiangsu Provinces, 1992, 1995).

76. Xue Tao, "Xiangzhen qiye kuashu fazhang de aumi" (The secret of the rapid development of the TVEs), in *Xiandai qiye daokan* (Forum on modern enterprises) (Beijing) (September 1994): 27-29.

77. For a field observation on this economic optimization of the labor force, see Ge 1990, 41-42. One study estimated that the average productivity of TVE employees was five times that of average farmers in the 1980s. See Huang Jizhong, "Lun xinagzhen qiye yu shehui zhiyuan de youxiao peizhi he chongfeng liyong" (On the TVEs and the efficient allocation and full utilization of social resources), in *Liaoning Daxue xuebao* (Journal of the Laioning University), no. 29 (May 1994): 29.

78. Lu Peifa, "Xiangzhen qiye huihuang youyinian" (Another glorious year for the TVEs), in *Renmin Ribao-Overseas,* December 27, 1994, 4. Also see Ma and Sun, eds. 1994, 310-315.

79. For two cases of such community-based labor reallocation, see Gao 1993, 222-226.

80. The two taxes are the Energy and Transportation Adjustment Tax and the Budget Adjustment Funds Tax. See Cai 1994, 6.

81. For a study on such district-based CLMs in Beijing's Dongchen district, see Zhang Shuhua and Liu Xian, "Daiye baoxian gongzu de diaocha yu sikao" (An investigation and consideration of waiting for jobs and insurance services), in *Shehuixue yanju* (Sociological studies) (Beijing), no. 6, (1993): 53-55.

82. For an early discussion on the development of enterprise autonomy, see Lee 1990.

83. The PRC central government, naturally, has been working hard to gain access to these small "gold-boxes," which could, in fact, contain substantial sums. In 1994-1995, the first step of a cleanup campaign of the gold-boxes in 1.15 million *danweis* produced more than 1.47 billion rmb for the state treasury of the PRC. See *Anhui Ribao* (Anhui daily) (Hefei), August 9, 1995, 4.

84. See the report titled "Xiahai yu shangsan" (Diving into the seas and climbing the mountains), in *Huaxia wenzhe* (China news digest), an Internet Weekly, no. 221, June 23, 1995.

85. A famous enterprise, the Baoshan Steel Complex in Shanghai, transferred as many as twelve thousand workers in six years (1986-1992), mostly to low-paying jobs in its newly created "third industries," such as service and retailing, to increase its steel-making productivity. See Gao 1993, 334-335. In the summer of 1996, I discovered, however, that the Baoshan Complex was still responsible for most of the income of those transferred workers. Thus, the overall efficiency of the complex was not significantly affected although the steel-making branches had achieved a big

improvement in its efficiency because of the reduced steel-making employment. Similarly, a state-owned enterprise in Anhui Province transferred one thousand of its three thousand workers to its third industries in 1994-1995. See *Anhui Ribao* (Anhui daily) (Hefei), May 4, 1995, 2.

86. *Renmin Ribao-Overseas,* May 23, 1995, 2.

87. *Renmin Ribao-Overseas,* December 20, 1994, 1, and December 27, 1994, 4.

88. Nationwide, about thirty-five thousand TVEs have joint ventures or cooperative contracts with FDI. In Zhejiang Province, 40 to 70 percent of FDI enterprises are TVE enterprises (*Xinhua Daily Telegraph* [Beijing], March 2, 1991, 1, and December 27, 1994, 4).

89. *Jingji Ribao* (Economic daily) (Beijing), October 24, 1989, 3.

90. *Xinhua Daily Telegraph* (Beijing), February 18, 1991.

91. The workshop of TVE bureau chiefs from ten provinces and municipal cities, summoned by the Agriculture Ministry, August 1994. For details of this meeting, see *Hongcun jingji daokan* (Journal on rural economy) (Hongzhou), no. 10 (1994): 24-25.

The problem of environmental pollution has become a major by-product of the community-based TVEs that commonly are focused on short-term gains for small local communities. The discharge of heavily polluted water to the rivers by the TVEs, estimated to be as much as 4.3 billion tons in 1994, was something the TVEs could afford to ignore simply because their small community orientation. See Cai Tongchen, "Nongchun gongyi ruhe zhouchu wurang guaiquan" (Rural industries how to walk out the strange cycles of pollution), in *Guangmin Ribao* (Guangmin daily) (Beijing), November 8, 1995, 4.

92. *Renmin Ribao-Overseas,* December 12, 1994, 4.

93. As frequently reported in praising terms, these rural communities have generally had community-wide labor and health insurance, family housing units, running water, telephone service, parks, cable TV, entertainment troupes, and cinemas. Most of the laborers are "off the soil," working in the numerous TVEs. For example, see *Renmin Ribao-Overseas,* August 15, 1994, 4; June 1, 1995, 8; and June 2, 1995, 3. Also, author's field notes, 1992-1995.

94. For a general picture of the prosperous economy in Suzhou, see *Beijing Review* (Beijing), September 25-October 1, 1995, 26.

95. This township has eliminated unemployment since 1983. Every nonlocal resident needs to pay 3,000-5,000 rmb fees to acquire a temporary *hukou*. Outside workers are generally paid less than local employees, although some gradually can become skilled workers and have roughly equal wages. They have to pay more for housing than local residents (author's interviews with the leading cadres of Shengze township and the Yinong Group, August 18, 1995).

96. Xiao Hangping, "Dao xiangzhen qiye qu" (Go to the TVEs), in *Renmin Ribao-Overseas,* August 15, 1994, 4.

97. For more on this influential idea, see "The Authoritarian State LAP and the Chinese Institutional Structure" in chapter 2 of this book.

98. In Hebei Province, surrounding Beijing, 51.4 percent of the small TVEs were identified as privately owned in 1994. But the private TVEs generally employed much fewer workers. See Sun Baocun and Li Jianguo, "Hebei xiangzhen qiye changquan zhidu" (Property ownership of TVEs in Hebei), in *Jingji luntan* (Forum of the economy) (Shijiazhuang), no. 19 (1994): 15.

99. These large TVEs had 30 percent of the total Jiangsu TVE assets and 20 percent of the total Jiangsu TVE output in 1994 (*Renmin Ribao-Overseas*, June 10, 1995, 1).

100. In 1978, the same figures were 19.5 employees, 15,600 rmb assets, and 22,300 rmb sales, respectively. Yang Xianzhen and Chen Naixin, "Joushi niandai xinagzhen qiye de tedian he qushi" (Features and trends of the TVEs in the 1990s), *Zhonghua gongshan shibao* (China business times) (Beijing), November 4, 1994, 5.

101. Author's field notes in Anhui, Guangdong, and Jiangsu Provinces, 1992-1995. Wang Huihuang, "Hengdongxian xiangzhen qiye de diaocha" (An investigation of the TVEs in Hengdong county), in *Hunan jingji* (Hunan economy) (Changsha) (October 1994): 50-51.

102. Despite the fact that the TVEs and all other nonstate-owned enterprises are charged higher state taxes, the actual collection of taxes from the TVEs has been very small. Some estimate that TVEs pay only about 10 percent of their scheduled taxes. See Yu Xinan, "Xiangzhen qiye ying jiji shiying xinshuizhi" (The TVEs should actively adapt to the new taxation codes), in *Guangmin Ribao* (Guangmin Daily) (Beijing), August 2, 1995, 5.

103. He Rongfei, "Zhejiang xiangzhen qiye fazhang de zhuyao jingyan, wenti, duice" (The main lessons, problems, and solutions in the development of TVEs in Zhejiang), in *Nongchun jingji daokan* (Forum on the rural economy) (Hongzhou) (September 1994): 11.

104. Song Zhaoshou et al., "Qiangxin fumin de biyu zhilu" (The only way to have a strong county and rich people), *Zhongguo xiangzhen qiye bao* (Chinese TVE news) (Beijing), no. 10 (1994): 1.

105. Seasonal employment is common even in prosperous areas like Sunan, where the TVEs have had substantial institutionalization. A famous star TVE in Changzhou, for example, would temporarily lay off 95 percent of its workers to cut labor costs for three months each fall—the season when orders for air conditioners and refrigerators are low. Naturally, outside employees usually got no pay for such leaves, while local employees got on average 136 rmb a month (about 65 percent of the Changzhou legal minimum wage in 1995). Their average monthly wage was about 600-800 rmb (author's field notes in Changzhou, Wuxi, and Suzhou, summer 1995).

106. He Rongfei, "Zhejiang xiangzhen qiye fazhang de zhuyao jingyan, wenti, duice" (The main lessons, problems, and solutions in the development of TVEs in Zhejiang), in *Nongchun jingji daokan* (Forum on the rural economy) (Hongzhou) (September 1994): 11.

107. There have been numerous empirical reports on this powerful trend. For examples, see Wang Shouwen, "Dui Shandong xiangzhen qiye gufeng hezuzhi de sukao" (Thoughts on the stockholding TVEs in Shangdong), in *Zhongguo gongye jingji yanju* (Studies on Chinese industrial economy), (Beijing), no. 11 (1993): 19-21; Cao Weisong, "Cunji qiyehua guangli" (Village-level enterprise management) in *Fengjin* (Rushing forward) (Zhengzhou) (November 1994): 37-38; Yu Huamao and Lu Weifong, "Shaoxing tujing gufengzhi" (Shaoxing promotes stock-holding system), in *Zhejiang jingji* (Zhejiang economy) (September 1994): 21-22; Sun Baocun and Li Jianguo, "Hebei xiangzhen qiye changquan zhidu" (Property ownership of TVEs in Hebei), in *Jingji luntan* (Forum of the economy) (Shijiazhuang), no. 19 (1994): 15-18; Zhou Huanmin, "Yuxian shenghua xiangcun jiti qiye gaige de zhoufa yu qishi" (Measures and hints from Yu County's deepened reform of the TVEs), in

Huxian luntan (Huxian forum) (Changsha), no. 5 (1994): 87-89; He Rongfei, "Zhe-jiang xiangzhen qiye fazhang de zhuyao jingyan, wenti, duice" (The main lessons, problems, and solutions in the development of TVEs in Zhejiang), in *Nongchun jingji daokan* (Forum on the rural economy), (Hongzhou) (September 1994): 10-11.

108. Zhu Xianchun and Chen Hongyu, "Zhongguo xiangzhen qiye beiwanglu" (A memo on the Chinese TVEs), in *Zhongguo Nongmin* (Chinese peasants) (Beijing), no. 1 (1994): 10.

109. For example, as a result of reform and advancement of the market institution, the communities are taking over from the *danweis* and the state in providing increasingly burdensome health care benefits to all laborers. See reports on such new measures employed by the Xichen District of Beijing. See Wu Tao, "Zhongguo tesi de shehui baoxiang zhidu" (Social insurance system with a Chinese character), in *Beijing qingnian* (Beijing youth), December 1994.

110. In 1994, for example, the company relied on the help of a sympathetic reporter in the local *Xinan wanbao* (Xinan evening news) to defeat the "irrational" decision the SLIC made against a merger the company planned with another "large collective enterprise," the Weida Factory. For a praising report on the economic development in Hefei in the 1990s, see *Renmin Ribao-Overseas* (Beijing), January 25, 1996, 1, 4.

111. As a comparison, in the same city of Hefei in 1995, the legal minimum wage set by the labor bureau was 150 rmb per month. University professors' income was around 300-400 rmb; most workers in the collective enterprises had an average income of about 170-300 rmb. For the state-owned enterprises, average monthly income was about 400-600 rmb in 1994 (author's field notes, January-February 1995).

112. There were rumors about how the top managers had bought critical connections to the local authorities of the city and provincial officials.

113. Author's interview with a company insider, a state cadre working in management, February 1995.

114. Zhang Shuhua and Liu Xian, "Daiye baoxian gongzu de diaocha yu sikao" (An investigation and consideration of waiting for jobs and insurance services), in *Shehuixue yanju* (Sociological studies) (Beijing), no. 6 (1993): 53-55.

115. Most of the statistical information on this township was adopted from Zhang Nutian, "Yi zhebei nongcun weili de diaocha" (An investigation of the rural areas in northern Zhejiang), in *Zhannue yu guangli* (Strategy and management) (Beijing), no. 4 (1994): 91-96. Information I acquired about other similar rural communities in the region has been added to make this township a representative case.

116. TVE workers tend to be much more secretive about their real income for fear of being viewed as "unduly rich." Most TVEs also tend to have a poorly managed bookkeeping system. In Wujiang of Suzhou, a "good" TVE generally pays its workers on average 8,000-10,000 rmb a year, with entry-level wages at about 5,000 rmb and top wages at about 16,000-20,000 rmb. The TVE bosses have at least two to three times that amount of income (author's interviews in Suzhou, August 1995).

117. For a general discussion on the role of the local government in relation to the TVEs, see Wang Hansheng, "Nongchun gongyehua guochengzhong de shiqu zhengfu: Quanli yu liyi de fenghua" (The community government in the process of rural industrialization: The divergence of authority and interests), in *Beijing Daxue xuebao* (Journal of Beijing University) (Beijing), no. 4 (1994).

118. By 1993, among the millions of the Chinese TVEs and nearly 100 million TVE employees, there were only twenty thousand company unions and about 2 million union members. See Hu Hanchang, "Xiangzhen qiye yu eryuan jingji jigou" (TVEs and the dual economic structure), in *Jueci yu xinxi* (Decisions and information) (Wuhan), no. 11 (1993): 11.

119. It was listed as one of the seventeen joint ventures of the Baoan Corporation. See *Zhongguo Baoan Jituan* (Chinese Baoan Corporation), a handbook by the Baoan Corporation, Baoan, Guangdong, 1994, 12-13.

120. Later, the price of those stocks soared in the Shenzhen Securities Exchange and made many of the township residents millionaires.

121. As the manager of the plant frankly told me, the rather brutal exploitation of the workers, most of them nonlocal *hukou* holders, was "the secret of the success" of the Shenzhen SEZ economy. In 1995, the legal minimum wage in Shenzhen was 1.8 rmb per hour, or 345 rmb per month. The minimum income required for a three-person family to survive in Shenzhen in the mid-1990s was "at least 1,500-2,000 rmb per month" (author's field notes in Shenzhen, summer 1995).

122. The Xiamen (Amoy) SEZ, for example, passed a local law requiring that employers and landlords be responsible for the actions of their "floating" employees and tenants, respectively. See Zhang Nanan, "Chong wuxu zhouxian yuxu" (From disorder to order), in *Renmin Ribao-Overseas,* June 16, 1995, 9.

123. For an official report on such a "Warming Project" in Shengyang, a major city in the Northeast, see *Xinhua Daily Telegraph* (Beijing), January, 12, 1996, 3.

124. For two examples, see *Xinmin wanbao* (Xinmin evening news) (Shanghai), February 13, 1995, 2, and August 19, 1995, 3.

125. See Liu Zhongyu, "Fang baoli, Yige changju de huati" (Anti-unfair high profits: A continuing subject), in *Maimei shijie* (Business world) (Shanghai), vol. 25, no. 4 (July 1995): 36-38. In Hefei, for example, the "fair profitability" of cold soft drinks and ice cream products in the summer of 1995 was set at 15 percent for wholesale and 30 percent for retail. In *Xinan wanbao* (Xinan evening news) (Hefei), August 2, 1995, 2, and *Hefei wanbao* (Hefei evening news) (Hefei), August 3, 1995, 3.

126. Wen Weiping, "Nongjia yuangli kang minzhu" (Talking about democracy in the peasants' yards), in *Renmin Ribao-Overseas,* June 9, 1995, 8.

127. The enterprise was a joint venture between a state-owned enterprise in Hebei Province (in which the person's parents had some power) and a street committee-owned Beijing company. This person, of legal Hebei residence, had no chance to become a permanent employee of that enterprise located in Beijing—unlike her co-workers who had only high school diplomas but held a local *hukou.* Thus, no community-based benefits were available to her. After about two years, she left for Shanghai as the new secretary to a Hong Kong investor (author's field notes in Beijing, 1993, 1995).

128. For a recent discussion on this topic by Chinese scholars, see Xiao Zhongmin, "Xiangzhen qiye canquan zhidu gaige de lilun yu shijian" (The theory and practice of ownership reform in the TVEs), in *Xinhua Ribao* (Xinhua daily) (Nanjing), August 11, 1995, 8.

129. See his article, "Xiangzhen qiye de shuoyuzhi gaige" (To reform the ownership of the TVEs), in *Zhongguo nongcun jingji* (Chinese rural economy) (Beijing), no. 10 (1994): 42-45.

130. In one rural community in Zhejiang province, family-owned private industrial enterprises employment has reached one-third of the total TVE employees. See Chen Junji, "Jiazhu chuantong yu nongcun qiye de jiazhuhua" (Family tradition and the familization of rural enterprises), in Shehuixue yu shehui diaocha (Sociology and social investigation) (Beijing), no. 2 (1994): 57-59.

131. See, for example, Rawski 1979; Ullerich 1979; and Howard 1987.

132. Zhi-yuan Cui, "Marx, Theories of the Firm, and the Socialist Reform," in *China Report* (Washington, D.C.) (July 1990): 1.

133. On this note, a valid question may be asked: By the end of the twentieth century, how many nations, modernized or pre-modern, have a "genuine" national labor market anyway?

134. In *Xuexi yu yanju* (Study and research), a journal of the CCP Committee of the Beijing Municipality, no. 4 (1990): 28.

135. *Shijie Ribao* (World journal), New York, July 18, 1995, A11.

136. Primarily in the cases of the TVEs in the rural communities. See Brugger and Reglar 1994, 173-174.

137. In Shangdong Province, there were more than three hundred "poor villages" annexed by the rich villages and/or TVEs by 1995. See *Wanhue Pao* (Wenhui daily) (Hong Kong), December 12, 1995, 2. This extremely significant development of the expansion of the rural CLMs through the expansion of the local communities, though still limited, may signal a new avenue for a national labor market to form in the rural areas.

138. The author's impression from interviews with CCP officials in 1993 and 1995.

139. Officially, the PRC calls all twelve provinces/metropolises along the Chinese coast "eastern China": Beijing, Fujian, Guangdong, Guangxi, Hainan, Hebei, Jiangsu, Liaoning, Shandong, Shanghai, Tianjin, and Zhejiang. See *Anhui Provincial Government: 1995 Anhui Shengqing Shouce* (Official Handbook of Anhui, 1995), an internal publication by the CCP, Hefei, 1995, 93.

140. Guo Tong, "Keji touru: Dongzhongxibu bupingheng" (R&D investment: Uneven among the east, central, and west), in *Zhongguo xinxibao* (China information) (Beijing), SSB, August 3, 1995, 1.

141. SSB, "1993 shehui fazhan shuiping baogao" (Report on social development in 1993), in *Liaowang* (Outlook) (Beijing), February 10, 1995, 10-11.

142. Observations revealed that technological levels were much lower in the western provinces and income inequality there was also larger than in the east. Figures and speculations in Xu Fongxian and Wang Zhengzhong, "Jingti: Quyu fazhan chaju zhubu kuoda" (Warning: The regional gap of development is gradually enlarging), in *Zhonghua gongshan shibao* (China business times) (Beijing), January 16, 1995, 5; and January 23, 1995, 5.

143. State Statistical Bureau data, in *Zhongguo xinxibao* (Chinese journal of information) (Beijing), SSB, August 1, 1995, 1.

144. State Planning Commission figures, in *Jingji gongzhuzhe xuexi ziliao* (Studying materials for economic workers) (Beijing), no. 68 (1994): 7.

145. For example, see Yu Zhongxian, "Shilun Zhongguo daludiqu jingji zhi bu junheng fazhang" (On the uneven development of the economy on the Chinese mainland), in *Jingji xuejia* (Economist) (Chengdu) (May 1994): 16-23.

146. *Xinhua Daily Telegraph* (Beijing), February 18, 1991.

147. *Renmin Ribao,* March 2, 1995, 2.

148. Lu Peifa, "Xiangzhen qiye huihuang youyinian" (Another glorious year for the TVEs), in *Renmin Ribao-Overseas,* December 27, 1994, 4.

4. An Emerging National Labor Market

China's traditional institutional structure has demonstrated an impressive super-stability, reinforced by that nation's enduring natural and human-made international isolation. For the Chinese, a centralized authoritarian "world" government and a family-like hierarchical "world" political order were established as early as the third century B.C., when the Han dynasty inherited the Qin empire. Afterward, all of China's political activities, including some of the bloodiest revolutions, coups, revolts, civil wars, and ethnic wars in human history, had a clear and fully legitimized goal of restoring or maintaining that world government. Division of the Chinese polity, although it existed for about 20 to 25 percent of the more than twenty-two hundred years since the Qin dynasty, was viewed essentially as an abnormality. Divided Chinese regimes, therefore, would literally fight to their deaths to reunite the nation and reestablish the "world" hierarchy.

For the past millennium, one cannot identify a single decade of peaceful division of the Chinese polity. Those who tried to legitimize political division were viewed as national traitors, traitors to tradition, or immoral "son-emperors," or puppet emperors (*erhuangdi*).[1] Confucian culture, this deeply legitimized and cherished political order modeled after the family institution and its internalized version, has been the institutional framework for Chinese economic, political, and social behaviors. This highly stable institutional framework has thus perpetuated itself at the gross price of economic and social stagnation and, as the bottom line, loss of millions of lives.

Chances for the market institution to grow (other than in marginally existing local markets) were institutionally eliminated under this family-like, centralized, extraordinarily stable and static political power. The institutionally differentiating power of the market was largely contained or even annihilated by the dominant family institution expressed in the political power of the state. Market allocation of the labor force was never a historical or cultural phenomenon to the Chinese. It was only when the Chinese world order collapsed and the family-like state was forced to face the reality of an anarchic international political order that the market, as an "imported" institution, began to develop as a national phenomenon. By the mid-twentieth century, the labor market had emerged as a viable LAP. But then, because of the political power of a new but institutionally traditional state—the CCP—and the intentional or given isolation of the PRC after 1950, the market institution, especially the national labor market, was effectively abolished by the mid-1950s.

As a major result of the "opening" policy adopted in 1978, China restarted its economic and cultural interaction with the outside world. The international market once again began to affect China's institutional structure. By the 1990s, the international market had become more important to the nation than at any other time in its long history (Lardy 1991, 1). After disappearing for about three decades, a national labor market has been making a return primarily due to the initiation and operation of foreign direct investment (FDI). Private employers followed the lead of foreign investors, and many other employers joined the emerging market to various degrees. In less than two decades, a national labor market developed a visible and substantial presence. By the late 1990s, this new LAP has caused many profound institutional changes.

This chapter addresses this emerging national market as the fourth LAP in contemporary China. We begin with a discussion on the origin of China's labor market, especially the crucial role played by internal-external interactions represented by massive FDI. This discussion is followed by a report on the current situation and operation of the Chinese national labor market. Both foreign-invested employment and Chinese private employment are examined, and some speculation on future prospects is presented. The final section explores the institutional impact the national labor market has had in the PRC.

"Opening" and Foreign Direct Investment: To Import the Market

The question of how a market institution can start to develop in a previously nonmarket economy has captured a central place in the study of comparative and international political economy. It is truly a practical question, especially for nations that are inspired to "catch up" with the developed economies. For policy-related or pure epistemic reasons, the emergence of the market within a nation has been much studied by political scientists, economists, historians, and sociologists. Besides the seemingly superficial but ponderously discussed correlation between a market economy and a political democracy,[2] scholars have devoted remarkable energy and time to explore international conditions, cultural and even religious causes, and other explanations for market development.[3] To a nonmarket nation like China that had been isolated for centuries, international forces may be the decisive factors that halt the self-perpetuation of the traditional institutional structure. As "world system" theorists have argued, a market institution is generally found to be incompatible with centralized political authority, nationally or internationally (Wallerstein 1974, 348). External conditions and influence, under an international political anarchy, appear to be key to the emergence of the market in a nation like China.

Internal-External Interaction: A Mechanism for Changes

Economic development and institutional changes for any nation are hardly isolated events. Tremendous interactions and tensions exist among the nations and between a nation's institutional setting and its outside environment.[4] The internal-external interaction seems to hold fundamental importance to a nation's economic development and institutional changes, especially the development and survival of its market.

The world's international political system, a sovereignty-based nation-states system or an "international political anarchy," causes international economic interactions to be largely market-oriented. The great positive impact of an enduring international market has been the facilitation of domestic markets in every nation, especially those that previously had no market economy. The key to this facilitation is the extensive, lasting interaction between the international market and the institutional system of a nation, as seen through trading, investments, exchange of ideas and cultures, visits, and even migration. But such an interaction hardly takes place automatically, and consequential market introduction and market facilitation are by no means guaranteed. As in any market economy, especially one where there is no central political authority to regulate and mitigate the negatives, exploitative behaviors and inequality of income are inevitable. To many, the international market is thus regarded as confrontational and even adverse to the welfare of latecomer nations by compromising their national political sovereignty and/or by creating a "dependent development" structure. Namely, an integrating world economy based on the market—under international political anarchy—structurally enables rich nations to exploit poor nations.[5] Ideological convictions and observations of this exploitation often complicate the market-facilitating interactions between a nation's internal institutions and the international market. A particular nation's market-based international exchanges are often subject to disruptions and blockages motivated by its and others' noneconomic concerns. Thus, even in an era when the world grows smaller because of the rapid development of technology in transportation and communication, self-imposed international isolation or barriers to internal-external interactions are still commonplace. Many so-called developing nations are especially prone to fear the negatives of the international market. The experience of the NICs (newly industrialized countries), however, has largely proven that, with the proper help of national sovereignty, latecomer nations can take full advantage of the international market in accelerating their economic development. The key role is that of the state in introducing and utilizing the imported market. A survey indicates that bad government is at least as responsible as the unfair international market for economic underdevelopment in many poor nations.[6]

Linking China's Institutional Structure to the International Market

The impact of the international market on a nation's institutional structure can be seen by examining China's emerging labor market facilitated by FDI, which has been flooding the PRC for nearly two decades. Among all the channels through which the international market can affect a nation's institutional structure, FDI is perhaps the most direct, extensive, lasting, and penetrating. The profound entry and operation of FDI has been a fourth shaping and reshaping factor for a nation's LAP. FDI usually leads to the hosting nation's policies of adaptation and adjustment.[7]

FDI is a relatively new market-oriented international economic activity.[8] According to John Dunning (1981), the international transfer of technology and capital started as early as the Industrial Revolution. Yet, very few real multinational corporations (MNCs)— creations of FDI—emerged before the twentieth century. Only after

World War II did the major pattern of foreign investment become direct investment instead of portfolio investment. In essence, FDI means transnational managerial control of business, not just foreign ownership.[9] As a result of FDI, MNCs came into existence as a brand-new form of worldwide economic organization. The development of an international market economy is mainly responsible, Dunning summarized, for the phenomenal development of the MNCs.[10] This development is generally thought to be an irreversible historical trend of the market economy. MNCs and the development of the LDCs (less developed countries) are assumed to have been mutually beneficial and reinforcing.[11]

As a major effort to modernize China, the CCP decided at the end of 1978 to open to the outside. Foreign trade, exchange of personnel and information, and international financial interactions soared. The opening policy transformed China's sagging economy and created a major international trader out of an isolated socialist autarky.[12] Profound and lasting noneconomic impacts resulted from increasing Sino-foreign economic interactions.[13] Under the general policy of "opening," the PRC began to welcome and encourage FDI at the end of the 1970s, viewing it as a major way to participate in the international market and to develop its national economy. As will be demonstrated later, FDI has grown in China at an astonishing speed. Accepting and endeavoring to accommodate FDI reflected Beijing's willingness to take advantage of a world division of labor and/or to explore the benefits of the market mechanism in promoting its economic development program. Since the current worldwide division of labor has a market economy as its operational rule, the Chinese institutional configuration, especially its urban labor allocation patterns, began to confront serious challenges and to experience alternative norms. Those powerful challenges and new norms have, in fact, initiated and facilitated changes in the Chinese LAP, reflecting some fundamental institutional changes, symbolized by the emergence of a national labor market.

Features of a National Labor Market

Domestically, the uniqueness of labor as an economic resource—the difficulty of separating one's working ability as a marketable economic resource from one's physical existence—has made the labor market the most politically and socially distorted of all markets. Compared to community-based labor markets, a national market may achieve apparently higher economic efficiency in the allocation and utilization of the labor resource. Nationwide labor mobility, even if not very thorough, is perhaps the highest achievement of a labor market. Because of the infeasibility of a world market and the political and cultural division of nations, attainment of a single, unified world labor market seems impossible. By the end of the twentieth century, labor mobility beyond national boundaries is, as expected, still very low.[14] Facilitated mainly by the expansion of international economic activities, an international labor market grew alongside the integrating international financial and commodity markets. The now clearly visible but still very limited international labor market is exemplified by the controlled exchange of labor for fixed projects, and by legal and illegal international migrations. The international labor market, highly influential on domestic labor allocation, is largely a supplement to national labor markets and other national LAPs that may not be market oriented.

A national market generally has several institutional features. First, the nation's labor force has achieved a nationwide mobility. Workers are mobile vertically as well as horizontally across boundaries of geography, profession, and industry. Individuals can move from one community to another and change jobs without political or social constraints except for personal or family concerns. Aside from contractual obligations and duties, workers are personally free from their employers. Employers have little control over the lives of their employees beyond the financial sphere. Aside from certain limitations against noncitizens, no legal barriers prevent employers from hiring from every corner of the nation.[15] Institutionalized or de facto national standardization of labor qualifications and performance is largely achieved. As a result, a national labor market, even with varied social and political distortions, tends to have the highest efficiency in allocating and utilizing the national labor resource.

Second, a national labor market, as the largest inclusive LAP, can nonetheless be chaotic, disparate, and even irrational at any given time and place. People with the same qualifications may at different times or in different places be treated or compensated in dramatically diverse ways. The transaction cost of information is responsible for the existence of such disparities. This micro-chaos of the national labor market, just as in the markets for commodities and capital, yields the important advantage of flexibility in competition. The interesting point may be that the labor market tends to have much more of this disparity because it is usually harder to compare two people than to compare two brands or two currencies. It is this natural existence of chaos and disparity that provides the operational basis for the social and even political distortions of the labor market.

Third, pay is determined primarily by the national supply and demand of labor, as interpreted by the employer and the employee. Job information is generally available nationally to job-seekers. Negotiation and bargaining between employer and employee are very important in deciding on working conditions, workload, pay, and promotion. A common distortion of a national labor market is collective bargaining between employers and employees, especially those that are industrial or regionally based.

Fourth, unemployment is a natural result of a national labor market. Completely full employment, no matter how much political or social effort is devoted to promoting it, is impossible. In a mature national labor market, there should be a well-defined and effective national system of unemployment relief, labor insurance, retirement pensions, and job referral services. Underemployment has only an insignificant presence in a functional national labor market.

Fifth, workers' productivity and on-the-job performance are the main criteria for hiring, compensation, and promotion. The selection process is nationally open and competitive. Inside, or secretive, hiring is often deemed illegal or unethical. Personal attributes not directly related to job performance and noneconomic concerns are systematically ruled out of employment decisions. Discrimination based on noneconomic reasons, though a common distortion, has a generally marginal impact in a well-established national labor market. The employer's financial situation is the basis for recruitment and dismissal. Social and political mechanisms have a very limited impact on the employer's employment decisions, especially hiring.

Finally, the labor contract and the above institutional features of a national labor market are protected primarily by the state and accepted by social institutions. Minimum working age, job safety, minimum wages, and maximum working hours are generally nationally enforced regulations. Many of the institutional features of a national market could be just accepted behavioral norms rather than legal rules. For the sake of convenience, therefore, a fairly complete national legal system legitimizing and regulating the labor market can be viewed as the birth of a national labor market.[16]

In reality, naturally, a national labor market tends to carry its own uniqueness imprinted by the nation's overall institutional fabric and its culture. But, even in today's China, the above institutional features are generally considered the basis for any national labor market.[17]

The National Labor Market in Contemporary China

Appearing for less than a century in a very premature form before 1949, a national labor market was reintroduced in the PRC in the 1980s. Its development has been very impressive not only because of its near-zero starting point, but because of the rapid advancement of the market institution and the unprecedented internal-external interactions developed between the Chinese institutional structure and the international market. FDI has played an instrumental role.

Development of a Chinese National Labor Market

The labor market as a national phenomenon has never occurred in China, although a certain market-oriented LAP, the embryonic CLMs (community-based labor markets), may be traced back to as early as the Song dynasty (tenth to thirteenth centuries) in the large cities of southeastern China. The labor market was an alien institution, and a national labor market would be totally incompatible with the family-like Chinese world structure. Once a new dynasty (like the Qing) consolidated its control of the nation, the "sprouts" of a labor market that had shot up during the years of a decaying state would quickly be wiped out. When China was forced to open its doors in the mid-nineteenth century, a market-oriented LAP came along with foreign businesses and gunboats. The Europeans, especially the British and French, set up factories and employed Chinese laborers. A primitive national labor market began to emerge and grow, facilitated primarily by foreign businessmen and the armed forces of their governments. The defeated Chinese state was forced to give the labor market a chance to grow, and the Chinese social institutions centered on the family were in a cyclical decay. Large numbers of released laborers from the declining land-holding peasants (*zigengnong*) became the first people allocated and governed by the emerging Chinese labor market. Gradually, Chinese private employers followed suit, hiring and managing their workers on the same labor market as the foreign businessmen. The surge of Japanese investment in China after the 1895 war blended in Japan's style of a labor market, which was more crude and exploitative. By 1920, more than 2 million Chinese workers were allocated in the primitive Chinese national labor market and about 20 percent were employed by native Chinese businesses (Wang 1987, 9). By 1948, an estimated 8 to 10 million workers, largely concentrated in the major cities of the coastal areas, such as Shanghai and Tianjin, were allocated by the Chinese national labor market (Yue 1989, 20; Wang 1987, 315).

With the establishment of the PRC in 1949, the market-oriented LAP was deliberately and quickly abolished. For nearly three decades (the mid-1950s to the late 1970s), Chinese labor was allocated by the state in an authoritarian state LAP or by local authorities in the collectivized communities. A small and shrinking private economy was allowed in both the rural and urban areas, but private employment of anyone other than immediate family members was strictly prohibited.[18] For a time, China boasted of having no labor market and thus no unemployment, though underemployment in both urban and rural areas was the norm. The labor market, just like the overall market institution, all but disappeared.

After 1978, several reform measures changed the situation and gave rise to a market-oriented LAP in the Chinese economy. First the PRC government began to allow private businesses to grow and employ labor at their own discretion, driven by the pressing need to relieve urban unemployment after the disastrous Cultural Revolution. Then the nationwide decollectivization released huge numbers of surplus rural labor, while restoring the traditional family-based LAP. Those rural laborers gradually and steadily flooded the cities to form the supply pool for a national labor market. Deeply troubled by the inefficiency of the authoritarian state LAP, Beijing launched enterprise reforms starting in 1984, including more autonomy in enterprise management, a certain relaxation of personnel flow control, encouragement of competition among the unit (*danwei*) institutions and workers, and introduction of market mechanisms in labor allocation (such as contract employment and legalization of the status of unemployment under the cover of "waiting-for-job").[19] Finally and perhaps most importantly for the emergence of a national labor market, the CCP regime has been trying desperately to attract FDI since the end of the 1970s.[20] FDI in turn brought in what Beijing wanted, but also institutions and values the Chinese leadership may view as undesirable. A major alternative institution that FDI introduced to China through its active entry and extensive operation has been the market-oriented labor practice.

FDI and Emergence of a National Labor Market

As a Leninist revolutionary party, the CCP understood clearly the negative consequences FDI could bring to its regime and to the overall Chinese institutional structure. Therefore, Chinese policies toward

FDI have gone through phases of "containment" and "experiment" policies, based on an ambivalent attitude of welcome and fear. Beijing tried hard to place the economically desirable FDI in designated areas under central control that was as tight as possible. Location and approval of FDI projects have been strongly influenced by noneconomic considerations. A "special economic zone" scheme was adopted to use and contain FDI and its alien institutions and behaviors. As a result, most FDI enterprises have been concentrated in the coastal areas, in five Special Economic Zones (SEZs), and fourteen other coastal open cities (COCs). Although by the mid-1990s FDI was legally allowed in most of China, strong efforts were still made through economic and administrative means to locate FDI in the SEZs and in certain approved areas of the COCs.[21]

Despite the containment strategy and control policies, FDI snowballed in the PRC. Before 1978, there were only twenty foreign-invested enterprises in China.[22] In 1990, more than 26,500 enterprises were registered as FDI enterprises, with a contracted total investment of US$37.8 billion and an actually invested amount of US$17.7 billion.[23] Fifty-six percent were equity joint ventures, 34 percent were cooperative joint ventures, and 10 percent (about 2,208) were wholly owned FDI enterprises. Half of those FDI enterprises were actually in operation by the end of 1990.[24] Official statistics show that forty-seven foreign countries and areas had direct investment in China in 1990. The biggest contributors of FDI in China are Hong Kong (about 69 percent of the total agreed investment and 81 percent of the total FDI enterprises), the United States, Western Europe, and Taiwan.[25]

Although the Chinese official press has tried diligently to paint an optimistic picture, most of those FDI enterprises are small ventures, with a few notable exceptions such as a coal mining project invested by the Occidental Oil Company and automobile companies invested by Volkswagen. On average, an FDI enterprise in China had only $400,000-500,000 investment from foreign investors in 1990 (this rose to about $950,000 in 1993). A typical foreign investor contributes as little as 30 percent to a joint venture's capital. Only 4 percent of the more than thirteen thousand FDI enterprises in operation in 1990 had advanced technology and only 18 percent had products for export.[26] In short, most of the FDI enterprises were labor intensive and small-scale businesses.

The main purposes of these foreign investors were certainly not helping the Chinese modernization course, as the CCP leadership would like the party members to believe. Rather, their main incentives were to explore a huge and cheap labor force. A survey of 1,066 foreign investors in China concluded that 91.89 percent of them were drawn there by the Chinese labor resource (50.56 percent believed that was their number-one motivation).[27] Data show that Chinese workers in FDI enterprises were paid only 10 to 40 percent of the wages of similar workers in Hong Kong, even with the same productivity.[28] Many workers reportedly were paid even less than 10 percent of the expatriate pay of workers who came from Hong Kong and Taiwan.[29] Another strong incentive, of course, is the age-old dream of benefiting from the great potential of a huge Chinese market.[30] The number-three reason for many foreign investors was favorable PRC policies such as tax breaks.

Almost all foreign investors, especially those who have a say in the management of their enterprises in China, insisted on having independent authority and terms in labor recruitment and management based on market conditions. In spite of finding such requests "foreign," "nonsocialist," and contrary to both the traditional family-based LAP and the authoritarian state LAP, the CCP nonetheless decided to grant them, thus creating a market-oriented LAP in China.

The market-oriented LAP practiced by the FDI enterprises was much more stable and mature than the weak and small Chinese private employment. Seemingly paradoxical, FDI has enjoyed strong political endorsement and support from the PRC state and tremendous popular enthusiasm. All those favorable conditions helped FDI in its bargaining and interactions with the state concerning the development of a national labor market. Step by step, FDI enterprises were granted the rights to hire, pay, promote, and dismiss as they saw economically fit. They soon won the right to hire *anybody* from *anywhere* with little regard to the employees' household registration (*hukou*) or personal dossiers (*dangan*). More important, those new norms and rules were gradually legalized by the state and gained increasing legitimacy. The active FDI employment spilled over and developed a disproportionately profound impact on overall labor allocation in China.

At the same time, previously small private businesses, considered "a supplement to the socialist economy" by the CCP, have had a rapid development. Accompanied by the encouraging propaganda of "getting rich is glorious," "letting part of the people be rich first," and "being a socialist millionaire," private employment grew substantially in the Chinese rural and urban economies. It became commonplace to see people working for private enterprises. Private employers, driven by their market-based rationality, embarked on a clear though crude market-oriented LAP. To gain more legitimacy for their market-oriented behavior, many private enterprises were hiding under the cover (the "red hats") of collective enterprises, or TVEs (township and village enterprises) (Zhang 1994, 100). Some managed to become "FDI enterprises" one way or another. Despite their small size and lack of political support, which meant dealing constantly with harassment by political and social institutions, private enterprises made up the bulk of the emerging national labor market. The joint efforts and prosperity of the FDI enterprises and the private employers have, therefore, made the labor market operational and viable. A national labor market thus emerged in China by around 1988 at the latest, with the initially crucial tolerance by the state, and acceptance by the social institutions. FDI, as the manifestation of foreign influence, has been the chief facilitator of this new LAP. By the late 1990s, a national labor market had become a highly visible presence and significant player in Chinese labor allocation, although it still needed institutionalization and maturing.

Legalization of the National Labor Market

The emerging Chinese national labor market first relied primarily on the spontaneous, voluntary, and competitive mechanisms of the market to allocate and manage the labor force, breaking administrative, geographical, professional, and even communal barriers. The CCP state tried hard to assert its political authority over this new LAP. The SEZ scheme was first implemented for the double purpose of using and containing FDI and its market-oriented LAP. Controlled labor allocation and management naturally led to conflicts and confrontations between the CCP state and foreign investors who wanted to have maximum access to and utilization of Chinese labor. The apparent economic benefits brought in by FDI also quickly caused local leaders in the non-SEZ regions to argue for their share of "utilizing" FDI. The containment strategy could not resist pressures from the inside as well as the outside, so it was scaled back rapidly. In less than a decade (from the end of the 1970s to the late 1980s), FDI and its market-oriented LAP were allowed to operate in almost every corner of the PRC, although a clear policy of preference was still in place aimed at "guiding" the location and operation of FDI. The sometimes tense interactions between the state and the foreign investors—interactions between the Chinese institutional structure and the international market—produced the legalization of the Chinese national labor market at the expense of state and social institutions.

One year after the NPC passed a law recognizing FDI enterprises in July 1979,[31] the PRC adopted its first measure granting legal status to the FDI employment: the Regulation on the Labor and Wages Management in Sino-Foreign Joint Ventures.[32] According to that regulation, local labor bureaus must approve any labor contracts between an FDI employer and its employees. Any new hires of the FDI enterprises must be either recommended or "consented to" by the labor bureaus. The wage level of FDI enterprises was set at 120 to 150 percent of similar state-owned *danwei*s in the same locality (article 8). Thus, the labor bureaus were given authority to control and regulate the labor practices of FDI employers. Aided by the national *hukou* system, the CCP attempted to control the market-oriented FDI employment and thus contain its institutionally erosive force. FDI employers, although granted "autonomous rights" in recruiting and managing labor, were only allowed to hire from local *hukou* holders who were either approved by the labor bureaus to work in FDI enterprises or were unemployed. It was unlawful to hire from outside the local communities or from existing *danwei*s without special permission.

Largely due to persistent demands from foreign investors and local leaders in the unfortunate non-SEZ and non-COC regions, Beijing quickly made numerous retreats.[33] In October 1986, the State Council, led by the reform-minded Zhao Ziyang, issued a Directive on Encouraging FDI in which FDI employers were allowed to hire from existing (but still only local) *danwei*s. They had only to "file," thus report, hiring and dismissal decisions to the local labor bureaus, rather than have those decisions approved (article 15).[34] Cross-province hiring was still subject to approval of the provincial labor bureaus. In less than two years, in May 1988, Beijing adopted a further relaxed regulation jointly proposed by the Labor and Personnel Ministries. Intended "to further implement the autonomous rights of employment of the FDI enterprises," this regulation clearly stated that FDI employers could hire from any *danwei* in the nation, without even asking for approval from the local or provincial labor bureaus. Workers dismissed from the FDI enterprises, however, had to return to their original *danwei*s, LSEs (labor service enterprises), villages, and other communities. *Danwei*s and local governments were ordered not to obstruct labor recruiting and management of the FDI enterprises. Such obstruction could be viewed and punished as a criminal offense.[35]

The harsh language here may well reflect substantial resistance to a national labor market inside the CCP leadership and among the local cadres. This regulation, "correcting" the previous legal barriers to FDI's market-oriented LAP, finally signaled the full legalization of a previously nonexistent national labor market in China (Rong 1990, 148-149). Based on earlier PRC regulations allowing professionals to work in FDI enterprises and local laws granting increased mobility of professionals, the Personnel Ministry in 1990 finally legalized resignation by state employees, including the cadres, thus opening the door nationally for professionals to join the market allocation.[36] A huge surge of FDI thus took place from 1988 to 1990 and again from 1992 to 1994.[37] The local legislation gradually built up a national legal framework for this new LAP. Guangdong and other more open provinces naturally led the way.[38] In the largest city, Shanghai, the municipal government declared in 1990:

Foreign-invested enterprises . . . may self-determine their organization and employment positions. They may recruit their needed labor in this city and may recruit from outside the city as agreed by the municipal labor/personnel departments. The original *danwei* of FDI employees should be supportive and allow its workers to move. If a disagreement arises, the labor/personnel departments shall make the adjudication. All FDI enterprises adopt contract employment. . . . The level and format of salary, bonuses, and awards are up to the FDI employers to decide.[39]

This legal framework—despite the tragedy of 1989, when demonstrations were cracked by the military—was further substantiated and completed in the 1990s. In 1995, the PRC issued a Provisional Regulation on Guiding the Directions of FDI and attached an Industrial Guide List for FDI as its first legal effort to guide the geographic and industrial location of FDI.[40] The legalization of the national labor market, however, does not mean that the market is free from the intervention of the CCP state or social institutions. As will be discussed later, the Chinese national labor market, though legal, is far from a complete or mature LAP.

Similarly, market-oriented native private employment acquired legal status by the late 1980s. As an expedient policy for dealing with urban unemployment and rural underemployment, Beijing first allowed in 1980 each private employer to hire no more than five, then eight unrelated workers. By the mid-1980s, the limit was relaxed to thirty unrelated employees per private business.[41] The thirty-employee limit was soon exceeded by so many private employers that it quickly became irrelevant. Legalization of FDI employment provided strong protection for the politically weak and socially less favored private employers. The fact that many private enterprises were "hiding" among the collective enterprises, TVEs, or even FDI enterprises also helped private employment grow without much political and social repercussion. Less institutionalized and less transparent, the expansion of private employment nonetheless contributed significantly to the legal development of the Chinese national labor market.

Through an amendment to the PRC Constitution in 1988, the CCP finally accepted the massive labor market existing in private enterprises in both rural and urban areas, overcoming substantial political resistance (Liang 1990, 13-14). By the time the PRC adopted its Provisional Regulations on Private Enterprises in 1988, the quantitative limit of private employment disappeared.[42] In that regulation, almost ten years after private enterprises had emerged, their legal status was acknowledged. Regulations on private employment were modeled after the market-oriented LAP practiced by the FDI enterprises. Private employment finally merged with FDI employment to form an emerging national labor market. Legally, unlike FDI employment, private employment was still subject to more monitoring by the state. Among numerous ministries and agencies affecting the operation of private enterprises, the Industrial and Commercial Administration Bureau was tasked to enforce relevant laws and regulations. As a deputy ministry level agency with branch offices down to the township level, this powerful bureau had the authority and responsibility to register, approve, and monitor the operation of every private and FDI enterprise.[43] Every private employer, for example, was required to adopt a contract employment system, and every labor contract had to be filed with the local labor bureau to be monitored.[44] In actuality, however, the labor and commercial administration bureaus have treated the private employment similar to the way FDI employment is treated.

Functional Institutions of the National Labor Market

In a characteristically Chinese way, the institutionalization of the Chinese national market has developed as much outside as inside the formal legal arena. The operation of this new LAP has made the emergence of the Chinese national labor market a self-sustaining process. Such an informal but extremely important institutionalization may be illustrated by an examination of two developments: the declining role of FESCOs (Foreign Enterprise Service Corporations) and the emergence of new institutions such as job referral services and professionals exchange centers. The decline of the former symbolizes the growth of the labor market, and the rise of the latter depicts the operational mechanisms of the Chinese national labor market practiced by the FDI and native private employers.

1. *The FESCOs.* To cope with the first waves of foreign investors in 1979, the PRC government and its local labor bureaus attempted institutionally to "groom" the "alien" FDI employment into the authoritarian state LAP by establishing the so-called Foreign Enterprises Service Corporations. FESCOs were arms of the labor bureaus and the FDI management agencies in major cities like Beijing and Shanghai. Foreign commercial agencies, offices, embassies, and other employers could legally employ Chinese workers only through those state-run job-referral companies. The mission of these services was to provide foreign employers with a qualified and "checked" working force in an orderly fashion. Workers were assigned to various foreign employers and were still considered state employees.[45] The foreign employers paid wages to the FESCO, which paid 50 percent to the workers and used the remaining 50 percent to cover administrative costs, labor insurance, housing, health care, and other benefits for those state employees.[46] To fight the control of the FESCOs and to get and retain the best workers, FDI employers generally paid numerous forms of nonwage compensation such as bonuses, commissions, and fees directly or privately to their employees—to make up for the 50 percent cut the FESCOs took away. Essentially, foreign employers would pay 150 percent of contracted wages to enable the employees to take home their full wages.

FESCOs were present in every major urban area of the PRC, as a major attempt by the CCP to regulate and control the emerging labor market. Very soon, however, they started to fade in terms of employment by FDI enterprises other than pure offices and governmental agencies. Some enterprises, such as the early joint venture hotels in Beijing and Shanghai, were gradually allowed to hire workers through their own channels. By the mid-1990s, FESCOs, with a bad reputation among foreign investors, had come to limit their labor-supply monopoly to exclusively nonenterprise foreign employers. FESCOs were effective only in the major cities, where the political power of the state was fairly strong. In small cities and especially the rural areas, FDI employment has been largely outside FESCO-type control. Many nonenterprise foreign employers, in order to save the additional 50 percent in labor costs, have started to hire people "illegally" from outside the FESCOs. The recently fashionable moonlighting of many highly qualified state employees provided a sufficient pool of such workers.[47] Some FESCOs, in order to supply acceptable workers to their FDI clients, started in the 1990s to try some open and competitive recruiting methods. Legally and officially, the FESCOs remain a major institutional component of the emerging Chinese national labor market. Practically, however, their role and size are being reduced to the point of marginal relevance.

2. *Exchange centers and job referral agencies.* To promote a functional labor market, first within the boundaries of large communities such as provinces and cities, the Talents or Professionals Exchange Centers (*Rencai jiaoliu zhongxin*) and job referral agencies were established in major cities and then in almost every urban community in the 1980s.[48] As with many other institutional changes in China, those centers and agencies developed rather informally without much legal authorization or facilitation from the state for a long time.[49] Many marginalized FESCOs later became such centers as well, just to survive. The centers belonged administratively to the local personnel bureaus while the agencies supposedly belonged to the labor bureaus. The first exchange center was established in Shengyang in 1983. The national exchange center, under the Personnel Ministry, was opened in 1984.[50] By 1991, there were more than eight thousand such nonprofit centers and agencies in the PRC (Zhu and Yao 1991, 315-316) whose mission was to provide a marketplace for employers to meet job-seeking professionals or blue-collar laborers, respectively.

The exchange centers were fairly hierarchically institutionalized, under the National Talents Exchange Center, a bureau-level agency in the Personnel Ministry. The job-seekers, typically local *hukou*-holding professionals, put their applications and credentials in the centers and waited for employers to "find" them and start the process of interviewing. With a proof of local *hukou* and professional credentials, usually a college diploma and an introduction letter from one's old *danwei*, job-seekers could also walk in to check the job listings put out by fee-paying employers. A major function of the centers, besides providing a meeting place and a database, has been the newly acquired role of keeping *dangan*s for market-allocated workers, especially professionals. Because every worker must have his or her *dangan* kept by some *danwei*, the old *dangan* system seriously increased labor immobility. With these new procedures, workers could leave or even resign from their old *danwei* and have their *dangan* "checked" into one of the local centers with a "caretaker's" fee, ranging from 15-200 rmb per month.[51] The FDI or private employers generally did not require a *dangan*. Thus, workers could legally and safely have their *dangan* kept and transferred, gaining a very important freedom from any particular *danwei* boss who previously could use the *dangan* to hold up the workers. The centers could also, based on one's checked *dangan*, issue all-important verifications, identifications, and introductions for such things as applying for a marriage certificate, graduate school, or passport. The old social and political controlling mechanisms of *dangans* and the emerging national labor market somehow acquired a coexistence in the centers, which functioned like surrogate *danweis*.

The type of controls used over those labor market places have depended on the particular local political authority. In some more open areas such as the Shenzhen SEZ, many centers have increasingly become private for-profit enterprises that did not have any legal registration with the local authorities.[52] The CCP's control over the centers, however, still appears to be quite tight in most metropolitan areas. In 1992, for example, I needed the help of a friend, a legitimate "personnel cadre," to get into the Beijing *Rencai jiaoliu zhongxin*, located inside part of the Forbidden City. The Shanghai *Rencai jiaoliu zhongxin* was even more tightly controlled against nonlocal *hukou* holders in 1993. Clearly, in practice, there remained a high barrier based on *hukou* to the mobility of professionals on the emerging national labor market. FDI employers could now legally hire anyone from anyplace, but *hukou* still reduced labor mobility in practical terms. Community-based exclusivity is perhaps more responsible for the power of the *hukou* system than the state's intentions.

The job referral agencies work more like similar institutions in the United States, playing the role of liaison between employers and employees. Unlike the exchange centers, the numerous job referral agencies are much more decentralized and poorly organized. Many have become private enterprises for profit and are much more flexible and more market-oriented than the centers. They generally observe the *hukou* restrictions much less in "selling" their laborers to potential employers. In essence, they have effectively increased labor mobility in the emerging national labor market. Large numbers of rural laborers have been referred by those agencies to work in the urban economy in industries ranging from construction to domestic service. Some even engaged in illicit activities such as selling women and children.[53] Many became so "free" that they did not even bother to register with the local Industrial and Commerce Bureau or Labor Bureau.[54] Some agencies have been controlled by the gangsters for the purpose of extortion and fraud.[55] By the mid-1990s, some American-style "headhunters" started to play an increasing role in the allocation of top managerial and other professional workers.[56]

Attempts have been made to build regional but cross-community professional/talent (*rencai*) markets and labor markets to incorporate the exchange centers and the referral agencies, respectively. The first regional *rencai* market was established in Shengyang in 1994, followed quickly by two others, the Northern Rencai Market (in Tianjin) and the Shanghai Rencai Market the same year. The fourth, the Southern Rencai Market, was formed in the fall of 1995 in Guangzhou, and more are expected.[57] The regional markets were designed to incorporate the more community-based local *rencai* markets, estimated to number more than a thousand by the mid-1990s. By the year 2000, Beijing hopes to have a complete national professional market system based on those state-regulated regional *rencai* markets and the national *rencai* exchange center in Beijing.[58] As a similar step to incorporate the more than fifteen thousand job referral agencies, the first regional labor market was officially formed in Shengyang in October 1995.[59] It was to be followed by more regional labor markets, under the supervision of the Labor Ministry. In some more open areas like the Shenzhen SEZ, labor referral agencies have been substantially incorporated and institutionalized. About a dozen provinces and more than twenty cities/prefectures established supply counters in the main job referral agency in Shenzhen to handle the labor needs in Shenzhen for a small fee. At the same time, many unskilled laborers working for minimum wages in the SEZ came through other, often illegal, channels without any official help or constraints.[60]

Labor Certification and Unemployment Insurance
An important component of a national labor market is national testing and certification of the labor force. Beijing has a certification and promotion system for workers, especially professionals, allocated and managed by the Chinese authoritarian state LAP. The same system is now used as a starting point by most FDI and private employers. Starting in the late 1980s, new measures emerged to address the certification needs of private businessmen or FDI employees who either came from the rural areas or stayed outside state management and routine screening for years. Some local governments have devised a special annual evaluation and certification system for those so-called professional individual households (*getihus*).[61] Currently, numerous colleges, correspondence colleges, and continuing education institutions have offered diplomas and certifications to market-allocated workers. The Personnel Ministry reorganized its existing agencies and established a Personnel Testing Center in 1994 to certify

all professionals in and outside the state sector, according to basically the same system used for state employees. The Labor Ministry also established its Labor Skills Testing Center. Certain private evaluation institutions also emerged by the mid-1990s.[62] More comprehensively, the Labor Ministry planned to complete work before 1998 on the categorization of jobs, ranking of working skills, testing criteria for workers' qualifications, and certification standards and procedures.[63] The important job categorization and skills certification in China, however, as admitted by the labor minister, had not gotten started by 1996.[64]

By the mid-1980s, urban unemployment became a real issue in Chinese reform and began to block the advancement of the market institution, with possible social and political instabilities. Gradually the PRC started to address this natural consequence of the national labor market. Action, however, has been slow and very limited. In 1986, Beijing issued its Provisional Regulation on Waiting-for-Job Relief covering only state employees. It was revised and finalized in 1993. A more comprehensive unemployment relief regulation, the PRC Unemployment Insurance Regulation, is due out before 1998 as called for by the newly enacted PRC Labor Law to institutionalize the unemployment insurance system.

According to official accounts, the new regulation is to cover all urban workers with a network of unemployment insurance and reemployment assistance. Unemployed workers will get 70 to 80 percent of the local legal minimum wages for a maximum of two years. After that, they will be "transferred to the civil administration agencies for social welfare programs."[65] The workers, their employers, and the state will share the financial burden for this plan. The main achievement of this law appears to be a nationalization of the previously existing unemployment insurance of the various *danweis* and localities. Still inadequate (it covers only urban *hukou* holders), the new law nonetheless is likely to promote the institutionalization of the Chinese national labor market. Related to that regulation, a comprehensive pension and social security plan is on the CCP drawing boards as well. Judging by experiments in many local areas, the future PRC national pension plan and social security systems will likely be shared by the state, employers, and employees. They will also cover only the urban-*hukou* holders.[66]

In short, by the end of the 1980s, the emerging Chinese national labor market completed its legalization and started the process of institutionalization.[67] Although there are common features of a labor market such as job-related commercials and job referral agencies, the professional exchange centers are unique. Participating Chinese labor, mainly the highly sought-after professionals and skilled workers, has achieved a realistic though still limited national mobility. The obstacles to national labor mobility, mainly those based on *hukou* and the related rural-urban division, were still important by the late 1990s. Chinese scholars admitted that most exchange centers and job referral agencies have been monopolized by the central and local government agencies or state-owned *danweis,* thus obstructing real national competition and labor mobility beyond the local communities (Ma 1994, 11). The exchange centers and referral agencies, often referred to as talent (*rencai*) markets and labor force *(laodongli)* markets by the Chinese press, have a long way to go before functioning as integrated parts of a national labor market. One study revealed a rather pessimistic picture of their activities: the success rate of the *rencai* markets was only 10 percent in 1994.[68] Labor authorities sometimes still ordered FDI and private employers to accept the same hiring quota as state-owned or CLM employers, restricting the function of the national labor market.[69] Those restrictions, at least, have made the national labor market an incomplete one distorted with many Chinese characteristics. Strong and clear political support for FDI and the national labor market, however, appeared to be on the rise after 1992 when the CCP decided to build a "socialist market economy" as soon as possible.

A Statistical Analysis

The Chinese national labor market, a clear presence by the mid-1990s, was still small and in the process of institutionalization. To the CCP regime, this market has largely been the spontaneous development of a supplement to the socialist economy. Market-allocated labor was mainly in the FDI enterprises and native private businesses. Perhaps motivated by ideological and political reasons, the PRC often calculated the labor working in the FDI enterprises (other than the wholly owned enterprises) as part of the urban workers (*zhigong,* 职工), thus mixing them with the authoritarian state LAP and the societal LAP/CLMs. The widespread collective cover-up of many private enterprises also reduced the accuracy of official statistics regarding the market-allocated labor force. To make things even more difficult, official statistics of the FDI enterprises often cover only those in urban areas and leave out the large number of rural ones. The size of rural private employment has been basically unrecorded and unreported. A very strong bias against private employment and a chronic inadequacy of data collection in the nonstate sectors have systematically underreported private employment in the official statistics.

Size

At the first glance, table 4.1 portrays a rather tumultuous history of the national labor market in modern China. The urban labor force allocated by the labor market, for example, shrank dramatically from more than 35 percent in 1952 (about 40 percent in 1953) to only 1.5 percent by 1970 and to almost extinction (0.16 percent) by 1978 (Yue 1989, 21). Then, with even more dramatic speed, the urban labor market grew by more than eighty-eight-fold in the fifteen years from 1979 to 1994. Such a chaotic history well reflected the turbulent pattern of institutional changes in the PRC from the early fifties to the nineties, centered on the fate of the market institution. By the 1990s, however, the Chinese labor force was allocated by four LAPs in a more complicated framework. Thus, despite the phenomenal growth of the labor market, it still allocated and managed only a small portion of Chinese workers, about 6.2 percent (or perhaps 14 percent—see the analysis below).

Table 4.1 is based on authoritative numbers provided by the PRC's State Statistical Bureau. These numbers, however, may be problematic. Compared to my field findings and even other official sources, the figures appear to have systematically and significantly underreported the actual size of native private employment. For example, the bureau reported 6.72 million urban private employees and businessmen and no rural private workers for 1990. But the official Xinhua News Agency reported in 1991 that there were more than 22.65 million urban private workers and businessmen in 1990, more than three times as many.[70] An internal report by the State Council estimated that, by 1991, there were about 23.9 million private employees in China, and the Chinese private economy grew at a rapid annual pace ranging from 13 percent to 59 percent in the 1980s, significantly higher than that of the whole national economy.[71] Moreover, rural private employees and businessmen, previously not reported at all, were estimated in 1992 to be at nearly 20 million, and they grew by more than 2 million every year after that. The actual size of the total Chinese native private employment by the mid-1990s, therefore, may be safely estimated to be about 75 million, roughly twice the officially reported figures. The technical inadequacy of official statistical information collection and the political, social

Table 4.1. Native Private Employment in China

Year	Size (thousands) urban	rural*	Total†	% of total labor force**	Average income (*rmb*)††	% of urban income	% of state LAP income
1952	8,830	n.a.	8,830	35.5	n.a.		
1955	6,400	n.a.	6,400	22.8	n.a.		
1957	1,040	n.a.	1,040	3.2	n.a.		
1960	1,500	n.a.	1,500	2.5	n.a.		
1965	1,710	n.a.	1,710	3.3	n.a.		
1970	960	n.a.	960	1.5	n.a.		
1975	240	n.a.	240	0.3	n.a.		
1976	190	n.a.	190	0.2	n.a.		
1978	150	n.a.	150	0.2	n.a.		
1979	320	n.a.	320	0.3	n.a.		
1980	810	n.a.	810	0.8	n.a.		
1981	1,130	n.a.	1,130	1.0	n.a.		
1982	1,470	n.a.	1,470	1.3	n.a.		
1983	2,310	n.a.	2,310	2.0	n.a.		
1984	3,390	n.a.	3,390	2.8	1,048	107.6	101.4
1985	4,500	n.a.	4,500	3.5	1,436	125.1	118.4
1986	4,830	n.a.	4,830	3.6	1,629	122.6	115.2
1987	5,690	n.a.	5,690	4.1	1,879	128.8	121.5
1988	6,590	n.a.	6,590	4.6	2,382	136.3	136.3
1989	6,480	n.a.	6,480	4.5	2,707	139.9	131.7
1990	6,710	n.a.	6,710	4.6	2,987	139.6	130.8
1991	7,600	n.a.	7,600	5.0	3,468	148.2	140.0
1992	8,380	19,800	28,180	4.7	3,966	146.3	137.8
1993	11,140	21,950	33,090‡	5.3	4,958	147.3	138.4
1994	13,200	24,380	37,580‡	6.2	6,585	146.1	137.7

Notes: In Chinese official statistics, private employment is categorized as either individual workers (*geti laodongzhe*), or employees of the private enterprises, and individual industrial and commercial households (*geti gongshanhu*).

* There are no systematic statistics about rural private employment before 1992. Judging by 1992-1994 figures, private employment must have been rather sizable in the rural areas in the 1980s.

† Only private employment in the urban areas before 1992.

‡ Estimated figures. *Renmin Ribao-Overseas* reported (May 23, 1995, 2) that by 1995 there were 47 million private workers and employees in China.

** Percent of urban workers before 1992.

†† Only private employment in the urban areas.

Sources: Figures are based on Gao 1993, 581, 621-622; SSB-LM 1991, 7, 29; and *Renmin Ribao-Overseas*, March 2, 1995, 2.

and ideological biases against private employment are perhaps responsible for such significant underreporting. The private businessmen's fear of attracting criticism and the temptation toward tax evasion in a poorly institutionalized taxation system may also help to explain it.

The official PRC statistics on FDI employment are even worse. Major government publications on FDI (for example, Li 1995) rarely mention the size of FDI employment. There are only very unreliable and incomplete national figures on the number of laborers employed by FDI enterprises.[72] Official statistics often greatly contradict each other. The national total of FDI employment is apparently underestimated or underreported. For example, officially there were only 659,392 workers employed by FDI enterprises in 1990 nationwide (SSB-LB 1991, 407). But that same year, the official Xinhua News Agency reported there were more than 2 million workers employed by Hong Kong investors in Guangdong Province alone, and estimated the national total to be nearly 3.6 million.[73] An estimate based on reports about FDI employment in other parts of the PRC led the author to believe that by the early 1990s, at least 4 million Chinese were directly employed by FDI enterprises, roughly five times the officially recorded numbers.[74] The numbers of FDI enterprises and the volume of FDI grew astonishingly, more than eightfold, from 1990 to 1995.[75] Thus, it may be safe to estimate that the 4 million FDI employees at least tripled during the same time. Base on those calculations, FDI employment in the PRC by the mid-1990s may have reached 12 million or more.[76]

By estimating and considering overlapping reports, labor allocated by the emerging national labor market would be around 84 million to 89 million by the mid-1990s, roughly 15 percent of China's total labor force. This figure would make the emerging Chinese national labor market now narrowly the smallest but by far the fastest growing LAP. Based on official figures, market-allocated urban labor grew from a negligible 150,000 (0.2 percent of the urban labor force) in 1978 to more than 13.2 million in 1994 (8.9 percent of the urban labor force)—an eighty-eight-fold increase in fourteen years. The total market-allocated Chinese labor increased more than two hundred and fifty times. If we use the more accurate unofficial estimates, growth of the Chinese national labor market would be greater than five hundred times in those fifteen years. It is indeed an astronomical rate for development of an LAP or the advancement of the market institution. If we take into consideration the vast and also fast-growing CLMs, the two market-oriented LAPs have emerged to allocate and manage more than 241 million Chinese laborers in both rural and urban areas, only slightly smaller than the family-based LAP but much bigger than the authoritarian state LAP;[77] further, they are growing rapidly while the other two are either shrinking or staggering.[78] The future for the four Chinese LAPs may have indeed been written on the wall.

Income

The emerging national labor market consistently offers higher compensation than the other three LAPs. Since 1984, when comparable data became available, native private employees have been paid 25 to 50 percent higher than the average urban workers. They even got 10 to 38 percent more than the "bought-off" state employees. FDI employees generally were paid even higher. In 1990, the average annual income of an FDI employee was 3,260 rmb, about 10 percent higher than native private employees, 53 percent more than the urban average, and 43 percent over state employees (SSB-LB 1991, 409). In Beijing, a typical FDI employee earned two to three times as much as a similarly qualified state employee in 1995. An Apple Computer employee and his FDI-employed wife made ten times as much as they did in the state-owned *danwei* they had left a year earlier.[79]

Furthermore, the recorded and reported wages of private employees often are just the known part of their income, since there are numerous unrecorded bonuses in the private enterprises. The income of the private businessmen, the *getihus*, is even more underestimated and poorly documented by the government. Many of them make several times, even hundreds of times more than an average urban worker. It is a standard practice for foreign bosses to pay their employees substantial additional sums as subsidies and fees, which often amount to more than the reported wages. Therefore, even though the market-allocated laborers generally do not get other state-subsidized benefits such as low-cost housing and health care benefits, they are clearly and indisputably the highest-paid group of labor in the PRC. In places like Shanghai, Beijing, and some inland cities, the author encountered many FDI employees making more than ten times as much as similarly qualified people working in average state-owned *danweis*. Considering the nonmonetary benefits state employees receive, the actual income of market-allocated labor could be at least twice that of state employees. Many "adaptive" foreign investors have learned to provide nonmonetary benefits such as housing and children's schooling to their employees to maintain certain stability of employment. The high pay, according to my field findings and official reports, has been the number-one attraction for the massive number of Chinese, whether employed or unemployed.

Distribution
    Unlike the three LAPs previously examined, the national labor market does not exist in the CCP and state agencies. It has only a negligible presence in the politically sensitive and socially influential professions and industries of education and research, culture, radio and TV, health care, and agriculture. Market-allocated labor has been concentrated in industries like manufacturing, construction, transportation, real estate, and services. The largest portion of the market-allocated labor is in labor-intensive and quick-responding industries like retailing, restaurants, and storage businesses (about 60 to 65 percent) (SSB-LB 1991, 18). Primarily because of FDI employment, the national labor market appears to have a disproportionately large presence in fancy hotels, offices of foreign commercial firms, joint venture firms manufacturing high-tech products such as electronics, and the new service professions like accounting, marketing, and litigation. Finally, there has been a clear and persistent uneven geographic distribution of FDI in China. By the end of 1994, the eighteen provinces in western and central China only had 17 percent (39,363) of the total FDI enterprises and 10 percent ($10.42 billion) of the total FDI.[80]

The National Labor Market in the 1990s

    The emerging Chinese national labor market, while still in the process of institutionalization, continued to grow rapidly in the 1990s. In 1994 alone, FDI grew by over 23 percent.[81] More and more native private enterprises have openly formed the now fashionable corporations issuing their own stocks to private investors, state-owned *danweis,* and even their employees.[82] Many collective enterprises have thus become private-owned corporations practicing more market-oriented labor techniques. The Chinese national labor market is in the process of integration by incorporating both FDI and native private employment, as the FDI employers and the private employers are increasingly recruiting and managing labor in the same way.

FDI and Popularity of Emerging National Labor Market

Laborers allocated by this emerging national labor market are usually China's most productive workers. This is especially true in the FDI enterprises.[83] The high productivity of FDI workers may indicate that they are better educated and managed than their contemporaries in state-owned or collective enterprises.[84] Socially, FDI employees are better respected, though they may have to work harder. It is quite evident empirically that, to urban Chinese youth, working for an FDI enterprise is the second-best choice to moving abroad. The high pay, as mentioned before, is naturally a strong attraction. The fantasy of being associated with foreign wealth and advancement is even more exciting and attractive to the young (Sun et al. 1993). The chance to experience a different value system and authority structure and to control one's destiny through labor mobility are perhaps equally important.[85] Finally, the official press and the CCP propaganda machine have made FDI enterprises symbols of progress and prosperity, and have offered a strong political endorsement to them. Somehow the CCP regime is seen as obsequiously appeasing every foreign investor from anywhere. In a number of unpublicized labor disputes between FDI employers and their Chinese employees, the government appeared to be protecting the employers at the expenses of the workers. This is indeed an irony in a socialist state, where workers are supposed to be the masters. As a result, FDI employment has become the hottest item on the labor market in Beijing. When some two hundred and fifty positions were posted in the spring of 1995, more than twenty thousand qualified professionals applied.[86]

The market-oriented labor practice in FDI enterprises thus became popular socially and politically and evolved into a sort of role model for millions of Chinese workers and managers.[87] In fact FDI enterprises became so popular that quite a few local officials tried everything to attract FDI to their area.[88] Many collective enterprises, TVEs, and private enterprises set up token FDI connections to evade state regulations such as the cyclical "retrenchments" of financial austerity policies and to take advantage of tax credits granted to FDI enterprises.[89] More significantly, some of the huge state-owned *danweis* have created so-called investment-laundry schemes. Large sums of state funds were transferred to offshore branches, mainly in Hong Kong and Macao, of the state-owned giant companies such as Huaren, Huarenchang, Tongda, CITIC (Chinese International Trust and Investment Corporation), and even the Bank of China.[90] These state funds, plus their overseas earnings in foreign currency, were then invested back to the mainland through a variety of channels as "foreign investment," and thus treated as such by the government.[91] Huge tax revenues were lost by the state because of the very favorable tax credits granted to all FDI enterprises. The imported, hence politically protected, market institution advanced with the financial resources of the CCP state, without even changing the state ownership of the property. Some inland local leaders, envious of such behavior, talked more or less openly about establishing a similar investment laundry of their own. As a result, not only many central government agencies but also many provincial governments now have business agencies in Hong Kong and especially in Shenzhen to do just that. In 1993, as an experimental measure of reform, Shenzhen started to allow state-owned enterprises to "have all the rights and benefits granted to FDI enterprises" to ensure "fair competition."[92] A nationwide market allocation of labor became officially condoned and spread to corrode the authoritarian state LAP. The imported authentic market-oriented LAP is unlikely to become the dominant LAP in China soon, but it is indisputably a leading trend.

Table 4.2. Largest Foreign Investors in China (1994)

Country	Overall rank*	1994 ($ billion)	% of FDI (1994)
Hong Kong & Macao	1	20.20	59.8
Taiwan	2	3.29	9.7
U.S.	3	2.49	7.4
Japan	4	2.08	6.2
Singapore	5	1.18	3.5
Korea	6	0.72	2.1
Canada	7	0.22	0.7
Thailand	8	0.23	0.7
U.K.	9	0.69	2.0
Germany	10	0.26	0.8
Total	10	31.36	92.8

Notes: * Out of 150 countries and a total of $303 billion ($95.57 billion used) FDI.

Sources: Statement by Ma Lihong, deputy chief of the FDI Management Bureau of the Chinese Ministry of Foreign Economic and Trade Cooperation (Zhongxin News Agency reported from Hong Kong on June 21, 1995); *Renmin Ribao-Overseas,* April 7, 1995, 1.

Political endorsement and social favors have led to the astonishing growth of FDI in the PRC. The World Bank ranked China in 1994 as the second largest recipient (the largest among the developing nations) of FDI in the world.[93] By 1995, more than 221,777 FDI enterprises were registered and 129,900 were in operation. The contracted FDI exceeded $303.3 billion with $95.6 billion already invested. Seventy-five percent of those FDI projects were industrial ventures, 14.3 percent were in real estate and service businesses, less than 10 percent in infrastructure, and 2.3 percent in agriculture. Among the 150 foreign countries that invested in China, Hong Kong and Macao were by far the largest, followed by Taiwan, the United States, Japan, and Singapore (see table 4.2) The largest wholly owned FDI enterprise by 1995 was Motorola (China) with $200 million assets.[94] Compared to the large Chinese assets abroad[95] and the sizable Chinese foreign currency reserve (over $50 billion by 1995),[96] FDI probably contributes less in capital than in technology, alternative institutions, and management. Contrary to the beliefs of some, FDI has contributed instrumentally to the phenomenal growth of Chinese foreign trade as well as overall Chinese economic development.[97] Statistics show that FDI contributed 10 percent of total Chinese fixed-asset investment, and FDI enterprises produced 14.6 percent of PRC industrial output and 28.7 percent of Chinese exports in 1994.[98]

Features and Adaptations of FDI Employment
FDI employers acquire their employees through three major channels: (1) recruiting through open advertising, examination, and training; (2) selection and provision by their Chinese partners with confirmation from the foreign investors; and (3) governmental allocation or referral through local labor bureaus or FESCOs (Rong 1990, 148-150). Most foreign investors and managers, however, insist on employing their Chinese workers through open recruitment based on competition.[99] Many FDI employees are still considered state employees because they were selected and sent to work in the FDI enterprises by their former state-owned *danwei* bosses. The authoritarian state LAP thus may have some overlap with the national labor market. Many small FDI employers acquire most of their laborers from the local communities, and therefore may actually practice more of the CLMs than a truly *national* labor market. As in other developing countries, FDI enterprises in China use mainly labor-intensive technologies. Young and female workers are the most welcome labor for the primarily assembly-line factories.[100] Many FDI

employers frequently ask their female job applicants to be young, "good-looking," and of a certain height. Photos are often required as part of the application package (Sun et al. 1993, 87-98, 214-216).[101] In Shenzhen, the largest SEZ, a typical FDI enterprise employed six times more young females (less than twenty-five years old and un-married) than males.[102] To foreign investors, a market-oriented labor practice is key to their decision to sink the money into China. An American company manufacturing medical equipment, the West Corporation, decided to terminate its joint venture talks with the Tianjin municipal government in 1991 because the Chinese partner insisted it would take away two-thirds of the $6 per-hour wages (about twenty times the wage level in the Chinese partner) the West Corporation was planning to pay its top Chinese engineers.[103]

As previously mentioned, a cornerstone of the emerging Chinese national labor market has been that FDI employers were given legal rights to hire without regard to a worker's *hukou*. In general, how-ever, the *hukou* remained an effective institutional tool to control internal migration and labor mobility, especially in the major metropolitan areas. Compromises have been made between the "legal" rights of FDI employers and the strong desire to maintain the *hukou* system. In Guangdong Province, for example, the government asked foreign investors to hire workers based on the order of "first local, then outside; first urban, then rural." The rural and outside employees were required to go back to their home place if they were fired.[104] Practically, how much freedom an FDI enterprise can have concerning *hukou* depends heavily on its maneuvering with local officials. Most small FDI enterprises located in rural areas generally have not cared about their employees' *hukou* and *dangan*. But many medium to large FDI enterprises, located mainly in major cities where *hukou* restrictions are tight, have learned to observe the *hukou* restriction, and thus reduce the cost of hiring from outside the locali-ties. For example, "bring the proof of your Shanghai *hukou*" was stated in all eight open recruiting commercials put out by FDI enter-prises in the most important evening newspaper in Shanghai on February 6, 1995.[105] Similar voluntary *hukou* requirements were seen in FDI help-wanted ads in other major cities as well. A key reason has been that it would cost the employer money and time to go through the process of acquiring a temporary residential permit or the more stable but more difficult to obtain transitional *hukou* (like the so-called *blue hukou* in Shanghai or the green card in Pudong).[106] This was seen as too much to risk to a new employee who might leave the enterprise soon, using the job merely as a way to get a legal residence in the major city. Social disapproval of hiring from outside was another observed reason. It was also easier for the FDI employers to verify and control the local-*hukou* holding employees.[107] For important employees, FDI employers would often pay for or fight to overcome the *hukou* restrictions.

FDI employers generally paid even less attention to their workers' previous *dangan*. Gradually, however, they realized the utility of *dangan* in labor management. Plagued by costly turnovers of their employees and the lack of good testing and certification on the emerging national labor market, many FDI employers, especially the well-established MNCs (multinational corporations), began to require their employees to transfer their *dangan* within a few months of hiring. The *dangan* of the employees basically had utility as a string held by the FDI employers. Like the state-owned employers, the foreign bosses learned to use *dangan* to maintain a fairly stable and accountable labor force, since most other employers would require *dangan* to hire a defecting worker. As some Chinese managers and foreign investors commented, this is "to manage the Chinese in a Chinese way" or "a capitalist management with a Chinese character."[108] Here we may see the distortions of the emerging Chinese national labor market by the existing political (the state) and social (the community) institutions with the tools of the *hukou* and *dangan.*

Once hired, a typical FDI enterprise would typically force its employees to work to their full limits. The main incentives available to the managers were monetary. Cash bonuses, reduction of pay, promotions, and other such measures were commonly used. Some FDI managers adapted to their Chinese environment by using honors, family visits, and other nonmonetary rewards to boost their employees' morale.[109] Most FDI enterprises did not have even a company union despite laws requiring them to have one within six months of beginning operation. The CCP organization generally had only minimal existence in FDI enterprises and often became an arm of the management.[110] One FDI enterprise in Shanghai was reported to have refused to hire a CCP member for fear that he might join the two CCP members in the company to form a party group.[111]

Compensation was set in such a way that the immediate supervisors generally had direct means to motivate the workers. In the small assembly line type of FDI enterprises, commonly seen in the Pearl River Delta, piece-rate wages were the norm. There was a huge gap between the wages of Chinese workers and expatriates. Expatriates usually were paid ten to one hundred times more than the Chinese workers and generally housed in hotel-style apartments. Returning

Chinese students from overseas used to be considered expatriates by some FDI employers. But by the early 1990s, only those employees with non-PRC citizenship could be treated as expatriates. The huge difference between the expatriates and the Chinese workers has caused much observable friction and conflict in many FDI enterprises. Interestingly, the Chinese state-controlled press has rarely reported any of these conflicts. Many FDI employers, especially those from Japan, have established a bad reputation of being too demanding and stingy.[112] Weierfu Hotline, a Shanghai-based women's consulting telephone hotline, reported that 50 percent of the female employees in Shanghai's FDI enterprises experienced sexual harassment by their bosses.[113] The often serious problems of pollution, hazardous working conditions, and naked exploitation in FDI enterprises started to draw some attention in the Chinese press after two fires killed about 400 FDI employees in the fall of 1993.[114] Limited state interventions on behalf of the workers have been reported (Li 1995, 192-195).

Native Private Employment: A Crude Labor Market

In the 1990s, the sizable private economy consisted of two parts: one, frequently but not very accurately termed *getihu* economy, was primarily family-owned small enterprises; the other was the private enterprises, often owned by more than one nuclear family and usually bigger industrial enterprises using substantial technology and equipment.[115] In many major cities including Beijing, the *getihus* organized their own associations.[116] Most native private enterprises were small and less capital or technology intensive compared to the FDI enterprises. They were generally in retailing, services, construction or small-scale manufacturing businesses. In the early 1990s, studies showed that on average, a private employer only employed sixteen people. A typical *getihu* employed only 1.5 workers.[117] Less than 1 percent of the native private enterprises employed more than one hundred workers (Liang 1990, 15-16). More recently, however, there have been reports about some large private enterprises having as many as several thousand employees.

In 1995, *Forbes* magazine for the first time included seventeen rich Chinese in its list of the wealthiest people in the world. All were private enterprise bosses who started with privately owned TVEs. The top three each had a net worth of 500-600 million rmb (about $60-72 million), an unheard-of level of personal wealth in the PRC.[118] Almost all had been appointed by the CCP to the various levels of either the Peoples Congress or the People's Political Consultations

Conference, as glorious socialist millionaire cadres joining the united front led by the CCP. Some private businessmen in Fujian Province managed to have annual sales far exceeding $10 million in the early 1990s. One of them, the boss of the Xinya United Bags Company, Wu Xiayun, was establishing branch offices and factories in Germany and Canada and was expecting total export sales of $12 million in 1991.[119] A peasant entrepreneur, Liu Xiaosheng of Shanxi Province, spent 7.3 million rmb in 1993 to buy a bankrupt state-owned steel-making factory, together with its two state cadres, fifteen state employees, and sixty temporary workers.[120] In a town famous for private economy, Shishi city in Fujian Province, private enterprises have established national foundations for journalism and performing arts troupes.[121] An interesting fact is that among the prosperous private employers, many were actually members of the CCP or formerly local cadres in the villages (Liang 1990, 16-17).

Fascinating, glorious, or notorious as they are, Chinese private business people have been facilitating the grassroots transformation in the Chinese LAP and affecting the overall Chinese institutional structure. Profiting from favorable policies toward FDI, the private economy has been de facto encouraged by the Chinese state even after the events of June 4, 1989. "Private economy in China," announced Liu Minxue, the director of the Industrial and Commerce Administration Bureau, "is not overdeveloped at all. On the contrary, it is not enough" since, officially, the private economy had registered assets of only 2.3 percent of the total Chinese assets owned by the state and the collectives, and employed only 4 percent of the Chinese labor force (13 percent of the total urban labor force).[122] Some scholars have argued for the necessity of further privatization of the Chinese economy.[123]

Although not many private employers have used formal labor contracts, their workers have essentially been contracted employees with economic transactions as the main exchange between the employer and the employees. Private employees and businessmen, estimated at nearly 70 million, have typically become market-allocated. They came from local communities as well as distant places. Due to their small scale and strong family and community roots, many private employers employed people based on family connections or referrals. In Wenzhou of Zhejiang Province, a town known for its booming private economy, 50 to 59 percent of private employees were either the relatives or friends of the employers.[124] Many of them came from the rural areas and worked in the cities as "temporary *hukou*" holders or just simply "illegal residents." The millions of "floating people" from the rural areas provided the pool of labor supply. As a result, urban slums and crimes have apparently been on the rise.

Generally, Chinese private employment has been primitive, crude, and even more unfavorable to labor than FDI employment. The income gap between managers and workers could be as large as 120 times (Yao and Murong 1993, 136). One Chinese study concluded that the real income of private employees was lower than that of the state employees due to the longer working hours and lack of labor protection and fringe benefits.[125] Noneconomic exploitation (such as sexual harassment of young female employees at the hands of bosses) and a hazardous lack of labor protection were commonplace, especially in small private enterprises. Many private employers never signed any labor contracts with their employees. Those who did often included anti-labor clauses such as those saying that employees would be completely responsible for their sickness, and on-the-job injuries, accidents, and death.[126] It was common for private employers to force the workers to pay a substantial "working deposit" and "learning fee" subject to the employer's numerous "deductions."[127] Some, allegedly learning from the Taiwanese, regularly fired senior workers right before their retirement to evade financial responsibilities.[128] Deceptive, illegal, or unethical labor practices, just like rampant false representations and "lemon" products, became distinguishing features of many Chinese private enterprises.[129] In fact, many practices of the private economy in China near the end of the twentieth century recalled the history of the early era of the Industrial Revolution in the West. Private employment represented a rather crude version of a national labor market.

Despite their many unsocialist and even un-Chinese behaviors, private employers came to enjoy virtually the same concessions made by the CCP state to the FDI enterprises.[130] The main means available to FDI and private managers were monetary. Employees could leave or be fired, often in a clearly pro-management way. In most FDI and private enterprises, even company unions were almost nonexistent or totally inactive, although by law the businesses should all fund and support company unions.[131] To be politically correct, however, some FDI and private employers allowed and even, occasionally, "wanted" certain CCP local organizations in them.[132]

The first ever "collective contract" signed between a company union and an FDI employer happened in 1995 in a small Qingdao FDI enterprise, although by law collective bargaining and contracts should be the norm. Laborers, therefore, were left in the hands of managers driven by hunger for profits, just as they had earlier been in the hands of managers of state-owned enterprises where, instead of profit, political concerns were more important. The result has been crude market-oriented labor management in these enterprises. Consequently, the turnover rate of the workers has been very high, given the Chinese tradition of lifetime employment. Among the ten thousand or so FDI employees sent by the Beijing FESCO, about 20 percent left their jobs every year in the 1990s.[133] There are no systematic statistics measuring the turnover rate in private enterprises, but empirical observations tend to confirm the extreme lack of job security and labor protection there.[134] Much is still needed to complete the institutionalization of the emerging Chinese national labor market. The PRC Labor Law that formally took effect on New Year's Day in 1995 was hailed as a major step in that direction. But in China, implementing a law is generally regarded more important than passage of a law.[135] Early observation in 1995-1996 failed to point to any significant progress in labor protection on the Chinese national labor market and especially in the private enterprises.

Tales from the Market

Empirical investigations on market-allocated labor have been rather difficult because most FDI and especially private employers are reluctant to talk about their labor practices for fear of being viewed as unsocialist or, worse, un-Chinese. Government-sponsored studies, experiencing the same difficulty in addition to the inadequacy of data collection and the longtime official biases about private employers, have largely produced either propagandist models or unbalanced anecdotes. Besides the commonly total omission of FDI and private employment, published case studies have portrayed either an effective use of FDI and private capital, or an abstract open warning to those who may have illegal labor practices, or a biography of politically and socially correct socialist millionaires.[136] The following four groups of stories, based on the author's field studies, do not claim to represent the great variety of FDI and private employers in China, but they are intended to reflect the basic pattern.

1. *An FDI employer in Shenzhen SEZ.* Heimann Company is a rather typical wholly owned FDI enterprise producing electronic and optical products.[137] Established in 1988 by a group of German, American, and Singaporean investors with a total of 5 million Singapore dollars FDI, it had over 7.9 million rmb assets in 1990 with a reported profit of almost half million rmb. (The actual profit,

known only to the foreign manager and the chief accountant, was believed to be much higher.) At the time of this study, it was owned by an American subsidiary of the German giant Seimens. A majority of its products were for export. In 1992, Heimann had 368 workers and two expatriates (one German manager and a Singaporean chief accountant) (see table 4.3). It is located in a Science and Technology Garden just outside the central city of Shenzhen. It bought its space and rented other facilities from the garden, which was a "management general corporation," a bureau-level state-owned *danwei*. There were twelve FDI enterprises in the garden in 1992. The garden had a complete organization to provide infrastructure, cheap dormitories, basic clinical care, security, and *hukou* and *dangan* services to all employees in the garden. The appropriated state-owned land was the garden's main asset.

Table 4.3. Workers and Wages of the Heimann Company

	Total Employees	Permanent workers*	Contract workers†	Temporary workers‡	Foreign managers
Total	368	11	9	348	2
Male	40	9	1	30	2
Female	328	2	8	318	n.a.
(professional)	56	6	5	45	n.a
(workers)	314	5	4	305	n.a
Wages (,000 rmb)	136.8	4.8	3.3	128.7	80
Average income (rmb/month)**	371.7	436.4	366.6	369.8	40,000
Professional Workers	600-700 300-400				

Notes: * "State employees" with local (Shenzhen) *hukou*.

† Local (Shenzhen) *hukou* holders who joined the labor force after 1982 when all new hires in Shenzhen became contracted workers.

‡ Hired from outside Shenzhen. They had only a "temporary residential permit" subject to their employment and annual re-registration.

** Every employee also got a 100-rmb-per-month benefits fee to cover housing, transportation, health care, and pension needs.

Source: Accounting Office of the Heimann Corporation, May 1992.

Most workers were young unmarried females (eighteen to twenty-four years old). Like most other FDI enterprises in the SEZs, Heimann paid its employees only cash wages with no additional benefits other than the 100 rmb per month benefits fee. Ad hoc cash bonuses and rewards, which could be substantial at times, were not recorded in the company's books. For those who stayed a full year in the company, there was an extra payment in the amount of one month's wages in December. A worker's annual income would be about 6,032 rmb, nearly three times the national average income of urban workers and twice as much as the average worker's income in urban Guangdong the year before.[138] Male employees were paid slightly more than female employees. In the Shenzhen SEZ, however, the wage level at Heimann was considered low. Single employees could live in subsidized company-owned dormitories. The foreign manager, an expatriate from Germany, and the chief accountant with Singaporean citizenship, were paid about 108 times as much as average employees.[139] Their families were housed for free by the company in the Shenzhen Bay Hilton, a four-star modern hotel located by the Seikou Bay. A Heimann car and chauffeur transported them between the company and the hotel. Every month, they got a two-day weekend vacation in nearby Hong Kong. (The workweek in 1992 was six days in China.)

There was no presence of CCP or other mass political organizations like the Women's Association or the Communist Youth League. Enthusiastic members could meet in their spare time in their respective organizations at the garden. There were no unions. One clerk was assigned to take care of all the workers' benefits and complaints. The state employees and the contract workers had their *dangan* checked in to the garden or paid 70-80 rmb per month to have them kept by their original *danweis* under the terms of leaving without pay. The company hired its technical personnel and professionals from all over the nation, but it was very difficult and could be costly to get a permanent local Shenzhen *hukou* for them.[140] For blue-collar workers, the company could hire only from Guangdong Province by the directives and regulations of the Guangdong Labor Bureau. There was a preference for Guangdong villagers since they were considered easier to manage. Many of the company's blue-collar workers were actually formerly peasants in other provinces. They "bought" a rural *hukou* from some remote Guangdong townships or administrative villages for 5,000-7,000 rmb and thus were qualified to search for high-paid jobs in the Shenzhen SEZ.[141] Quite a few blue-collar workers were hired from outside Guangdong (one prefecture in Hunan Province) in the name of "professionals" because they happened to be relatives of the recruiting clerks of the company. Most employees were nonlocal *hukou* holders and thus tended to leave the company fairly easily. The turnover rate was very high. Among the first group of three hundred employees hired in 1988, only seventeen remained in 1992.[142]

Heimann, like most FDI enterprises in the SEZ, used a job application in its hiring, and a simple file to monitor every employee. "Everything is flexible in operation," said a manager. Besides standard personal information, the job application form asked for the applicant's location of *hukou*, original *danwei*, type of previous employment (cadre, state employee, contract worker, urban waiting-for-job youth, or rural waiting-for-job youth), location of *dangan*, why they left the previous *danwei*, family and health information, and "whether they plan to have children." Female workers who answered yes to the last question would be disqualified immediately. The author also witnessed a twenty-six-year-old female applicant being turned away because she was "too old." (The "too old" age for male applicants was twenty-eight.) In practice, the referral of company employees has been important in hiring new workers.

An employee with a good record of referring new workers is appreciated by the company. Dismissal usually came after two weeks' advance notice and with an extra month's pay. To avoid the additional cost, the company tried hard to avoid dismissing workers. Instead of a straightforward firing, numerous visible or invisible pressures and punishments from the supervisors were used very effectively in ridding the firm of unwanted workers. Those who were "squeezed" to resign, like those who resigned voluntarily, did not get any special pay. A very simple resignation procedure form made sure that a leaving employee did not take away any company property. Non-Guangdong people had to get another qualified job in Shenzhen to justify their temporary residential permit or return to their hometowns.

2. *Three joint ventures in Beijing.* These are widely publicized successful cases of large-scale joint ventures between three PRC state-owned companies and two well-known American corporations and a Singapore/Hong Kong/Taiwan investment consortium.

Lido Holiday Inn in Beijing.[143] This hotel and condominium complex, located between the central city and the Capital Airport, was among the oldest (established in 1981), most well-known, fanciest, and largest FDI hotel complexes in China. It was partly owned by a Singaporean company—Yihe Corporation—and managed by Holiday Inn International staffed with Hong Kong, American, Taiwanese, and Japanese expatriates. In 1991-1992, annual sales exceeded US$40 million, with a high profit. In addition to five hundred part-timers (mainly pieceworkers or event workers), the hotel had more than two thousand employees, with about one hundred foreigners as top- and middle-level managers (one American, one Japanese, two Australians, five Germans, thirty Singaporeans, and more than fifty from Hong Kong and Taiwan). The highest salary was for the general manager (a foreigner)—US$5,000 a month. The average monthly wage for foreign employees was US$1,000-1,500 and about US$30-120 for Chinese employees. The Chinese deputy general manager, a senior cadre representing the Chinese partner, All China Tours (a PRC state-owned international travel agency), had a monthly salary of only US$120, roughly 5 to 10 percent of the wages of many of his foreign subordinates. Chinese employees were contract workers with a two-year contract. Most of them were state employees selected and provided by the Chinese partner, in cooperation with the Beijing Labor Bureau. Almost all were Beijing residents in 1992. Only a few workers were hired from outside Beijing as specially contracted workers. Those specially contracted workers and all the single employees lived in cheap dormitories provided by the hotel. The average age of the Chinese employees was twenty-two. Like most other large-scale joint ventures in major cities, Lido had a company union but it was not active.

The Chinese employees were administratively managed by a joint team of Chinese and foreign mangers and supervisors, but politically and socially managed by the fairly complete Chinese managerial offices, including offices for *dangan*, party affairs, and family planning. Nicknamed Lido City, the hotel has been used as the headquarters and training center for the seventeen Holiday Inns in China. Thus, many of its employees came from other provinces, and outstanding employees were later sent to work in other Holiday Inns in other provinces. The foreign management had the right to dismiss workers, with full participation of the Chinese partner in making labor decisions. The foreign managers interviewed believed that Chinese labor was cheap but with low quality—"they don't want to learn!" Another complaint was that the Beijing Labor Bureau closely monitored the hotel's labor recruitment. To avoid political problems, the hotel hired workers largely from the pool of applicants offered by the BFESCO (Beijing FDI Enterprises Service Company). Although the hotel adopted a successful American style of management and English was the official language for internal business, the foreign managers concluded that in order to manage Chinese workers effectively in a joint venture in China, one should avoid using American managers and use ethnic Chinese (from Hong Kong, Taiwan, or Singapore) instead. Strongly praised by the PRC government, the so-called Lido Model is fairly representative of joint ventures in China.[144]

Figure 4.1. Managerial Structure of the Lido Holiday Inn in Beijing

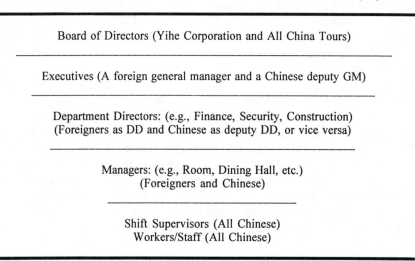

Board of Directors (Yihe Corporation and All China Tours)

Executives (A foreign general manager and a Chinese deputy GM)

Department Directors: (e.g., Finance, Security, Construction)
(Foreigners as DD and Chinese as deputy DD, or vice versa)

Managers: (e.g., Room, Dining Hall, etc.)
(Foreigners and Chinese)

Shift Supervisors (All Chinese)
Workers/Staff (All Chinese)

Beijing Jeep Automobile Company (BJC).[145] This is a case of FDI essentially taking over an existing Chinese enterprise. BJC was the first Sino-foreign equity joint venture in the automobile industry, established on January 15, 1984, between American Motors (now Chrysler Corporation) and Beijing Automobile Factory for a term of twenty years. The initial investment was US$51.03 million, of which American Motors invested 31.35 percent. On September 26, 1985, the first Beijing Cherokee XJ Jeep rolled off the assembly line. The former Beijing Automobile Factory had eleven thousand employees. In four years, more than 65 percent of them were transferred out of the new joint venture, to be reallocated by the Beijing Labor Bureau. The Suanhuan (double ring) Company was established to absorb most of the former employees—similar to a labor service enterprise. The productivity of the BJC workers soared. In 1987, four thousand workers produced 49.6 percent more than the eleven thousand had produced in 1983. Soon after its opening, BJC ran into a serious problem of foreign exchange control, and was viewed as the barometer of the Chinese reform and opening. Thanks to the direct intervention of then premier Zhao Ziyang, BJC passed this difficult time and has been operating quite smoothly. Most of its products have been sold in China as a substitute for imported autos, while some parts were shipped back to Chrysler factories in Mexico and in the United States. It was listed as one of the Top Ten FDI Enterprises every year since 1988.[146] BJC became the second largest joint venture in China with assets of over 1.2 billion rmb, annual sales exceeding 2 billion rmb, and an after-tax profit of 200 million rmb in 1991.[147]

By 1992, the joint venture had about forty-one hundred employees, all of them contracted workers. BJC selected most of its workers from the old Beijing Automobile Factory. Professionals hired from other provinces were all later granted Beijing *hukou* due to the strong clout BJC had in the Beijing municipal government. In 1985, all workers signed a collective contract with the management. Later, individual contracts were used to recruit, promote, or demote workers. Dismissed workers were actually transferred to the LSE of Suanhuan Company to do other jobs or simply to become internal waiting-for-job workers. Heavy labor and some dirty posts were staffed by a relatively small group of temporary workers from the rural areas. The average income for Chinese workers was 200-600 rmb per month plus state-subsidized benefits, including housing. The turnover rate was relatively low because most of the employees were considered state employees at the same time. The productivity of Beijing Jeep workers (9.6 cars per worker a year) was much higher than their Chinese counterparts (less than one car a year) but still significantly lower than that of auto workers in the United States (about sixteen to twenty cars a year at Chrysler factories there). BJC, as a rather typical large industrial joint venture, kept a complete party organization and other organizations and offices. The company union functioned the same as in other state-owned *danweis*. Workers were given limited working time to study party lines. The small group of American expatriates has been active in labor management. The workers they fired, however, were usually transferred to the LSE by the Chinese managers, thus suffering a significant cut in pay but not a total dismissal. There have been stories of clashes between the Chinese managers and the Americans over how to manage the workers effectively in a "Chinese" and "socialist" way.

Beijing Bawei (B&W) Company.[148] This twenty-year joint venture between the American giant boiler maker, Babcock & Wilcox, and the Beijing Boiler Factory illustrates the "one factory, two systems" model. The initial investment was US$36.69 million with equal shares. Unlike many other joint ventures, Beijing B&W did not simply take over the employees of the Chinese partner. Instead, it adopted a policy of one factory, two systems.[149] The southern part of the factory continued to be a state-owned boiler maker, the Beijing Boiler Factory (BBF), while the northern part became a new joint venture called Beijing B&W Company, another boiler maker. The CCP secretary of the BBF was also the chairman of the board of the Beijing B&W. The president of the Beijing B&W, however, was an American, assisted by a Chinese vice president and a team of foreign experts and Chinese managers.

Economically, the Beijing B&W has been very successful. Within one year after its opening in August 1985, Beijing B&W completed its hiring, selecting only two-thirds of the original BBF employees, and doubled economic performance. By 1991, Beijing B&W had a total of 2,474 Chinese employees. All were still considered state employees. Dismissed workers were transferred to the BBF, which was supposedly an independent state-owned enterprise, but which in fact was the labor dumpsite for the more efficient Beijing B&W. Workers had an income level much higher than their former colleagues working at the BBF. But they all shared the same living compound and the same nonmonetary benefits package. Conflicts between Beijing B&W employees and BBF employees occurred rather frequently, and Chinese managers reported lasting headaches in dealing with those conflicts. The internal organization and the income disparity between the expatriates and the Chinese employees were similar to those of the BJC and the Lido Hotel. The Chinese managers reported conflicts between the Chinese and American managers, and some American managers even went on a symbolic strike of several hours.

3. *Two small FDI ventures in Shanghai.* These two firms are examples of small FDI projects that are almost completely outside the control of the Chinese state but operate smoothly, relying on the well-established network of connections (*guanxi*). Their labor practices illustrate well the advancement of the Chinese national labor market.

Wagon, Inc. Wagon is a Taiwanese-invested wholly owned cargo shipping firm representing many famous multinational corporations. Three years after its opening in 1993, it still did not register with the Shanghai Industrial and Commercial Administration Bureau. As an illegal "underground firm," it paid no taxes and was not subject to any Chinese regulations; thus it was very free, as claimed by its manager. Despite its illegal status, it successfully acquired corporate accounts in local banks and rented office space in the center of the financial district of Shanghai, the Bund. It had telephone and fax lines and distributed widely its own corporate letterhead and business descriptions. Because of some unknown good and strong connections in Shanghai, Wagon operated smoothly without any fear of being "detected" by the government. According to its official books, it was losing money in 1995 and 1996, yet the truth appeared to be otherwise. In fact, I was told that there were "hundreds" of such "illegal" and guerrilla type FDI enterprises in Shanghai.[150] By the fall of 1997, however, the company had to relocate to another address and use a slightly different name to avoid being "caught" by the state.

Other than the two managers from Taiwan, there were twelve employees in the firm in the fall of 1996. Most were Shanghai residents who were either waiting-for-job youth or leave-without-pay state employees. A few came from outside Shanghai and were "dark people," because they had no local residential permits or *hukou*. They all came to the firm through referrals of friends and relatives. At least five were recruited by the manager's Shanghai mistress and three were actually CCP members or ex-CCP members. No labor contracts were used, and no filings with the local labor bureau were made. To "save trouble," wages were paid in U.S. dollars rather than Chinese currency. The monthly wages ranged from $140 to $300 while the young Taiwanese managers made $500 a month plus an unknown bonus. Some employees worked part time in the firm, although they still held their full-time jobs in the state-owned local colleges, which had no knowledge of their moonlighting activities.

Gongke Corporation. This is a manufacturing and marketing firm, with most of its investment shares owned by a small U.S.-based company. The real capital, however, came from a few children of some senior cadres (*gaogans*) in Beijing. They earned huge profits through illegal commissions and kickbacks for organizing certain trades (exchanging Chinese pork for Russian trucks) for some state-owned companies in the early 1990s. The funds were then illegally converted into U.S. dollars, transferred to foreign bank accounts, then used to set up a company in the United States; the "wholly-owned FDI enterprise" in Shanghai and Pudong became a subsidiary of that U.S. company.[151] After some setup, Gongke attempted to make and sell pocket-sized plastic cards carrying electronic information for the banking industry.

The two Chinese managers were formerly students in America with permanent residency in the United States. The chief manager was a close relative of one of the real but hidden capital providers. By the fall of 1996, three years after its opening, Gongke had more than ten employees in Shanghai and Pudong. All of the key employees were from one county in Shandong Province, hometown of the chief manager's parents. The reason for such exclusive hiring was that people from that area were known to the relatives of the manager and were considered "honest and easy to manage."[152] Other employees came from job advertisements and by word-of-mouth. The average wage was about 400 rmb (about US$50) a month, and the firm provided basic housing and free lunches for the workers at a very minimum standard. There were no other fringe benefits. The firm finally started to make profits in 1996, but most have been kept in foreign banks. In the official books, Gongke is still struggling to break even. Frustrations have been plentiful, and one of the real capital providers was arrested and prosecuted in Beijing during the summer of 1995. But the managers were confident that they had built an extensive network of connections (*guanxi*) in China and Hong Kong and expected to make "real" profits soon through governmental orders. By the summer of 1997, Gongke made significant profits and started to hire more people.

A native private employer in Hefei of Anhui Province. This high-tech private enterprise was set up to manufacture and market cleaning agents and solutions. Later it began a business of making some electronic components. Thirty-year-old Mr. Liu, owner and boss (the president) of the corporation, earned a master's degree in chemistry from one of the best technology universities in China. After graduation, he refused a state job assignment and stayed in Hefei. He managed to keep his Hefei *hukou* and have his *dangan* checked into the Hefei Professional Exchange Center. First he worked for a year in a TVE in Zhejiang Province. Then he came back and started his own company in 1991. After four years, his company accumulated nearly 600,000 rmb in assets. The company had a total of sixty employees in 1995. It directly employed sixteen people full-time, mainly as office workers, technicians, and marketing agents. About twenty employees worked in two small chemical plants in rural villages outside Hefei city. The rest were basically part-timers on a commission basis. The company was clearly profitable and Liu, though still living a frugal life, decided in 1995 that it might be time for him to "change to a new lifestyle."

To escape from the exclusive tax of 5 percent of total sales imposed on private enterprises, the so-called Industrial and Commercial Tax, Liu attached, or "hung on" (*guakao,* or 挂靠) his company to a major university in the city.[153] The university, a state-owned institution (*shiye danwei*) established an Industrial Center as its for-profit enterprise wing. The center had a group of such "hanging on" private enterprises. Those enterprises paid the center a fixed hanging-on fee and were also expected to voluntarily pay the center a certain percentage of their net profit. The additional payment, however, was often replaced by much smaller bribes to the university cadres who ran the center. In return, the private enterprises got a collective enterprise cover to escape the much larger Industrial and Commercial Tax.[154] The cover had other purposes, some of which were not trivial. Liu recalled that the university, as a state-owned *danwei*, helped him greatly in acquiring his two direct phone lines. Liu, like other private businessmen, declined to discuss the amount of the hanging-on fee and other business expenses, which are estimated to be substantial but "manageable." In private, Liu and other businessmen candidly acknowledged their routine bribes to the officials in the Industrial Center, the Industrial and Commercial Administration Bureau, product registration and approval "experts," and numerous other officials and *danweis* related to sanitation, phone service, taxation, *hukou*, and public security. The reason for spending all that money was that it was "necessary to deal with those difficult officials or offices." It is interesting that most private employers usually did not include the labor bureau in their list of complaints. This may be an indication of the great advance of the national labor market.

The sixteen full-time workers were hired from many places but all were through the "reliable" referral of friends and selected by Liu in his interviews. Many did not have a local Hefei *hukou*. Because most of the sixteen had at least a college degree and were thus considered professionals, or *rencai*, they could move to work in Hefei without much difficulty. With a little payment and effort, private employers like Liu could get a labor permit from the labor bureau for hiring some blue-collar workers from outside Hefei. However, a local Hefei *hukou* was hard to get. Besides the referrals, an employee's security deposit of as much as 5,000 rmb and his or her personal appearance were important. Liu did not care about his employees' *dangan*. He used the personnel exchange centers a few times to search for new workers but relied primarily on the referrals by friends, schoolmates, and employees. Liu described a "rationalization" of his hiring practice, drawing less from friends and relatives and more from "the capable." Still, the two most important company positions were occupied by Liu's relatives: a cousin and a brother-in-law were the chief of staff and the bookkeeper, respectively. Liu himself worked as the accountant, taking care of "the most important job" of finances and cash management.

The sixteen employees all signed labor contracts based on the formality provided by the Hefei Labor Bureau. But the contracts generally did not mean anything, as legal enforcement of all kinds of contracts in China, according to Liu, was "too difficult and too expensive—almost impossible!"[155] Liu fired workers with one week's advance notice and workers resigned at any time, all in disregard for their labor contracts. The wages (roughly 400 rmb per month) were set according to the wage level at the university to which the company was "hung on." But unlike the state employees or the CLM-allocated employees in the university, the company employees did not have any nonmonetary benefits, including the important cheap housing. Commission-like bonuses and rewards were important but often uncertain to most of the company employees. The highest income in the company could be five times as much as the lowest.[156] Large cash awards have been the most important means of managing people, and the turnover rate has been quite high. To avoid the loss of technology and funds caused by these turnovers, Liu has kept a tight guard on company technology and cash.

Liu's manufacturing facilities were in nearby rural villages for several reasons. First was the abundantly cheap labor there. The peasants were "willing to endure the hardest work" with less than half the urban pay. The less restrictive environmental policy substantially reduced costs for Liu's plant, which produced high pollution. Additionally rural taxation was lower on private enterprises. Finally, the peasant workers were easy to manage, and fringe benefits were not needed. The twenty peasants working in the two plants were on piece-rate wages; they worked about ten hours a day in a rented warehouse filled with hazardous chemicals, making cleaning and adhesive agents. Two foremen took care of the plants and no labor contract was used. Liu believed that the poor peasant workers were "the best and the easiest to manage." On average, they could make up to 500-600 rmb per month including overtime for their backbreaking work, if there was an order. Otherwise, they stayed at home with no payment from the company. Other than coverage of directly work-related injuries because this is a "matter of ethics," the peasant workers got no job security, labor protection, or nonwage benefits.

Like increasing numbers of FDI and private employers in Beijing and Shanghai, Liu saw company-subsidized affordable housing as a key to keeping good workers, although it was beyond his ability to provide it at the time of this research. He believed that the current PRC legal system was good for private business, though the enforcement was poor. The ideal white-collar employee, according to Liu, would be a college-educated married male around age thirty to thirty-five. The ideal blue-collar employee would be a young (under twenty-five) unmarried female. He hoped that a joint venture with foreign investors would allow him to expand his business and deal with officials more easily. Local collaborators of this research (two specialists on the province's history and socioeconomic development) commented that the Liu story was rather typical for private employers in that province.

Impact and Prospects of the National Labor Market

The Chinese national labor market is still in the process of shaping itself but has demonstrated a vigor and potential far greater than the family-based LAP or the authoritarian state LAP. More authentic than the socially distorted version of labor market, the CLMs (community-based labor markets), the relatively small national labor market represents the direction and provides the justifications and tools for the CLMs. The existence and operation of the new national labor market reflects the depth and width of the advance of the market institution in China. If the national labor market is generally the last component of a national market institution, then the further institutionalization of China's national labor market may also institutionalize and complete the marketization of the Chinese economy.

Impact of Institutional Changes in the PRC

The emerging national labor market has had a disproportionately profound impact on China's overall institutional framework. Through the direct facilitation of the development of new laws, values, and legal and behavioral norms, it has led directly to the increasing autonomy of the Chinese economy from the institutional confines of the political and social institutions. Second, it created new social classes that are likely to reconfigure those social and political institutions. Finally, some of the basic fabric of the PRC institutional setting has been adjusted and even altered by the emerging national labor market.

The Autonomy of the Economy
The emerging national labor market, practiced by FDI enterprises and indigenous Chinese private employers, has pushed a national

market to be the main economic institution. The advance of this national labor market signals the emergence of the autonomy of the Chinese economy from the traditional sociopolitical complex. The booming private economy of the PRC could not survive without the national labor market. The collective enterprises and even many state-owned enterprises, as described earlier, could not function well without the cheap and flexible peasant workers provided by the national labor market. Both the state-planned socialist economy and the family-based moral economy are shrinking, replaced by the market economy in the allocation and utilization of consumer goods, capital goods, and now labor. The Chinese market economy has yet to mature but the national labor market should be the last jigsaw piece to portray the overall framework and magnitude of a relative autonomous new Chinese economy. Official statistics showed that the PRC state's control of industrial production declined from 70 percent in 1979 to 5 percent in 1995, and control of retail pricing fell from 95 percent in 1979 to less than 6 percent in 1994.[157]

The CCP-ruled Chinese state has almost completely lost its traditional control over the labor force allocated and managed on the emerging national labor market. Even in those joint ventures where many employees may still be considered state employees, the market instead of the political authority of the state has become the institution that allocates and manages labor. This is a significant setback in the state's dominion over the Chinese economy and social life. For perhaps the first time in Chinese history, millions of productive people are allocated and managed by neither the state authority nor the family institution nor the communities. As one FDI employee concluded, "to move from a state-owned *danwei* to an FDI enterprise, you would suddenly find out *nobody* is there to control your life other than your job performance."[158] Those millions, with the personal freedom they acquired from traditional social, political, and even communal confines, have become the active agents of transformation of China's institutional structure and its internalized version, the Confucian culture. If the most important economic resource, the human resource, is to be allocated by the market institution, then the whole Chinese economy is achieving its autonomy versus the state and the social institutions. A great differentiation of the Chinese institutional structure is thus under way.

A New Social Stratification

The operation of the emerging national labor market has directly contributed to a new and consequential social stratification in China in

the past two decades. This restratification is likely to alter the configuration of Chinese social and political institutions and thus affect the
overall institutional structure. An increasingly powerful new bourgeois
class is emerging, almost completely outside traditional CCP control.
This new class consists of private businessmen, foreign agents, professionals, and skilled workers hired by FDI or native private employers. These mobile and highly paid people are estimated to have
numbered somewhere between 12 and 50 million by the late 1990s.
The private employers, who have few direct links to the capitalists of
the pre-PRC era, have formed a special group that is gaining an
increasingly important role in the Chinese economy, society, and
even politics (Zhang 1994). However, a genuine proletarian class is
emerging in the FDI as well as in private enterprises. This new working class is currently in a position similar to the British working class
in the eighteenth and nineteenth centuries and to the American
working class before the New Deal. This genuine working class is also
grossly underrepresented by the CCP.[159]

For more than three decades, under the unified authoritarian state
LAP, the CCP effectively "bought off" the Chinese industrial working
class and distorted it into a privileged group organized in a communist
neotraditional or semi-feudal fashion (Walder 1986). By barring the
majority of the rural labor force from migrating to the cities where
modern life could be found; by providing a socialist welfare and security system at a heavily subsidized price to the urban workers; by implementing tight and direct political and administrative control of the
urban labor; and by crushing the trade unions, the CCP avoided, for
most of its nearly half-century rule, any major confrontation with the
Chinese industrial working class.[160] Another achievement of this
moralistic buying-off strategy was to exclude the working class from
fully participating in the PRC's political process as an independent
group. A significant result, therefore, is that although the PRC is
supposed to be led by the proletarian class, the product of capitalist
development, it is in fact ruled by a revolutionary political and
military party that represents a precapitalist institutional setting.
Ironically, and remarkably, the proletarian class disappeared in the
PRC after 1949.[161]

Over the past two decades, a new and real proletarian class has been
surfacing as the result of the emerging national labor market. The
market-oriented LAP, especially the crude version practiced by
Chinese private employers, is giving rise to a steady formation of
workers who are in real conflict, as a group, with the employers. This
independent working class is emerging outside the buying-off scheme

of the CCP. The CCP lost its ideological appeal to this new class, because it is now a ruling party that resembles the employers rather than the employees. Administratively, the CCP state and the social institutions lost their direct control of this productive working class allocated by the national labor market. The profound political impact of this independent proletarian class is so apparent that we shall soon see the evolution of a bona fide labor movement that may well lead to the growth of genuine trade unions in China. Whether the CCP can capture the political strength of this new proletarian class, as it did before it came to power in 1949, may determine the historical fate of the CCP in the years ahead. Some Chinese scholars have asserted that the increasingly serious labor-capital confrontation will become the focus of China's social problems and a major threat to the political stability of the CCP regime.[162] Most CCP propagandists and officials, however, have yet to act on this new development, either because they have not realized the institutional difference between this new working class and the working class under the authoritarian state LAP, or they are wishfully pretending that somehow the CCP will control it. It is only a matter of time before they wake up to the altered reality.

Institutional Genetic Engineering

Another major impact of the emerging national labor market is an institutional "genetic engineering," transforming the *danwei* as the cells of the China's institutional structure. This has led to substantial separation of the Chinese state not only from China's economy but also from its social life. As discussed earlier, based on concessions made by the CCP leadership, FDI enterprises (and later, quietly, the native private employers) acquired the legal right to recruit and manage their Chinese employees without the restraints of the infamous yet powerful *dangan* and *hukou* systems. As a result, personal mobility of not only the market-allocated labor but also the general populace has reached an unprecedented level in recent history. This grand political compromise has started an institutional genetic engineering effort in China, differentiating the whole Chinese domestic organizational structure at the expense of the authoritarian CCP state.

For more than forty years, *dangan* and *hukou* have been two important tools of the CCP in controlling the Chinese population by continuing the traditional institutional system.[163] Both are responsible for the sharp division of urban China versus rural China. The emerging national labor market, as previously analyzed, has provided the possibility for labor to move with reduced or even no constraints of *hukou* or *dangan*. Allowing FDI employers to hire from anywhere, even from existing state-owned enterprises, started the process of dissolving the institutional barriers among the Chinese.[164] The still limited decline of the role of *dangan* has already produced enough force to restructure the traditional institution of *danweis* as the cells of the Chinese nation.

The once unquestionable authority and comprehensive control over the urban labor force by the CCP, embodied in the mighty role of *dangan*, have been seriously tainted and eroded. In many places, *dangan* have become a formality, and the words put into one's *dangan* bag are now generally much less significant, even irrelevant, to one's career.[165] Such a genetic engineering is bound to have profound impact on people's behavior as well as on the fate of CCP rule. Like *dangan*, the *hukou* system has also been sacrificed by the CCP in its compromising accommodation of FDI. As demonstrated before, FDI employers can hire from anywhere, disregarding *hukou*. Thus, at least legally, both the geographic barrier and the urban-rural separation, hindering labor mobility, have been penetrated. Most private enterprises, many collective enterprises, and even some state-owned enterprises have quickly emulated this practice. A profound consequence is that the populace is substantially liberated and the rural and the urban gap has begun to be bridged. Nearly 80 million surplus rural laborers flooded the cities, and more than 3 million city dwellers have found jobs in the TVEs.[166]

A new development may illustrate those genetic institutional changes. Previously, Chinese citizens relied on their *danwei* ID, *hukou* card, and *danwei* introduction letter as personal identification. Partly because of the decline of the *dangan* system and the insignificance of the *hukou* system, those old identification methods became increasingly confusing, meaningless, and inaccurate. To cope with this situation, Beijing established a computerized national personal ID system. Now everyone is given a photo ID card that carries a lifetime number like the U.S. Social Security number. By 1991, this system had largely replaced those obsolete identification papers.[167] All this may well be only a renovation of the social control method, but nonetheless it is a kind of progress that contributes to greater labor mobility, social liberty, and urban-rural equality, as it is much harder for supervisors or local officials to deny an individual's right of travel and migration. The genetic changes caused by the national labor market are fundamentally altering the institutional fabric of both the Chinese state and family.

Future of the Chinese National Labor Market

The fast-growing Chinese national labor market has clearly been leading the trend of the transformation of Chinese labor allocation. The labor market—national and community-based (CLMs)—appears to be the dominant LAP for the near future. Between the two forms, a national labor market would achieve higher labor mobility in the nation, thus increasing the possibility of more efficient utilization of the labor resource and a more autonomous Chinese economy. But, the CLMs may actually have a better chance to become the dominant LAP rather than the economically superior national labor market. Social and political shocks and dislocations that could be very costly to the legitimacy of the institutional changes would be significantly less in a CLM-dominated LAP. The strong growth and further institutionalization of the Chinese national labor market appears to continue. Judged by the experience of other nations under a similar existing institutional structure, however, a national labor market is likely to be distorted and limited in China in the foreseeable future.

With historical institutional settings similar to China's, most other East Asian nations have achieved a mature and well-developed national labor market. Beijing, like Tokyo and Seoul earlier, realized in the 1980s that it must employ market forces to develop its economy. Therefore, the CCP state began to import and utilize the market, largely through the introduction of FDI. The market gained ground quickly and advanced rapidly. The CCP regime actually has already reaped much economic and political benefit from its market-oriented reform, and, so far, has escaped the fate that descended upon its European and Russian comrades. It is therefore easy to explain why the pragmatic CCP leaders under Deng Xiaoping have embraced the market economy as the savior by the end of the twentieth century. Also like the Japanese, Singaporeans, South Koreans, and Taiwanese, the Chinese have been attempting to distort the originally imported market institution. A brief look at the East Asian style of national labor market may tell us more about the future of the Chinese national labor market.

Multipattern Labor Allocation and Market-Orientation

The current coexistence of four LAPs is not a uniquely Chinese phenomenon. In Hong Kong, Japan, Korea, Singapore, and Taiwan, the family-based LAP is still significant. The famous mom-and-pop stores in Japan and the substantial number of traditional villagers in Korea and Taiwan are good examples. More interestingly, the "advanced" East Asian nations seem to have sizable authoritarian state LAPs and even significant state-owned businesses. Communities also appear to be very important in those nations.[168] The Japanese state has been described as having devised the life-time employment system and seniority-determined pay schedule to control labor mobility, a legacy of the Japanese state-led modernization and the war effort during the Second World War.[169] Multipattern labor allocation may indeed be a common institutional feature in East Asia. Actually, the existence of multipattern labor allocation, to perhaps a lesser extent, can be found in most other nations, since theoretically only a static pre-modern, and ideally "modernized," nation may have just one LAP. What sets the Chinese apart from the rest of East Asia, however, is that the nonmarket LAPs in the advanced East Asian nations tend to be small, insignificant, and even marginalized, whereas in China they still appear to be dominant. In Korea, for example, the decline of the traditional LAPs has been much faster than that in China.[170]

Furthermore, the "nonmarket" LAPs in nations like Japan and South Korea have basically adapted to a strong and clear market orientation. The dominant national labor market and the overall market economy sanction the nonmarket LAPs to function in as market-oriented a fashion as possible. Two similar steel-making complexes in China and Korea, the Baosan Steel Company in Shanghai and the Puhan Steel Complex, were established by the state. They have similarly comprehensive community-based benefits packages and welfare plans. Both have effectively lifetime employment for their workers. Visiting them as a guest, one would feel an almost identical company culture. But there has been an unmistakably strong market orientation in Puhan, and qualitatively much less of one in Baosan. The Puhan Complex was privatized in the early 1990s and is operating on the international market as the third-largest steel maker in the world. But Baosan, with many more employees and much less output, still had to bend to Beijing's political pressure regarding to whom it could sell its products in 1995. Both steel makers provide heavily subsidized housing to their employees. But the Korean company sells the apartments to the workers at a subsidized price as their property, while the Chinese company still basically allocates the apartments at a subsidized rent as a job-related benefit.[171]

The strong existence of the LAPs that are not market-oriented—the family-based traditional LAP and the authoritarian state LAP—

determine the future of the market institution in China. Namely, whether the market-oriented LAP, led by the national labor market, can become the dominant LAP will largely determine whether the Chinese can repeat a successful East Asian style of modernization. If other East Asians can successfully have a market economy with the existence of nonmarket LAPs, the Chinese may do the same. But the critical mass of the national labor market must be reached.[172] The imperative need for further growth and maturing of the Chinese national labor market may be self-evident.

Labor Market with Traces of a Moral Economy
    The imported national labor market has been widely accepted by the Chinese in and out of power. This new, robust LAP is still regarded by many as nothing but a temporary concession to foreign investors. It is legal but not ideal or desirable in the eyes of many CCP leaders. Limitations and controls are often attempted by CCP conservatives, especially on the local level, for the often controversial FDI employment appears to be strongly protected by the central government. Significant distortions of the emerging Chinese national labor market have already developed in the areas of labor protection, community-confined recruitment, and the use of Chinese institutions such as *hukou* and *dangan*. A national labor market with the purity of economic models may never exist in China.
    The appeal of the traditional moral economy is also known to other East Asians. The emphasis on social harmony, unity, and equality is influential to the political leaders and even many employers there. Japanese employers, for example, usually tend to refer to, if not treat, their employees as members of a family, just as many Chinese employers do. Internal unemployment or underemployment is widely used not only by Chinese employers but also by Japanese and Korean employers.[173] The role of the state has been prevalent in all East Asian nations. Independent and effective trade unions were generally suppressed by the states in Korea and Taiwan until very recently.[174] The state has been viewed as a major player in the successful development of elementary and middle education in the NICs that directly contributed to the economic take-off in those nations (World Bank 1993, 199-200).
    A national health insurance program, launched in March 1995, may have signaled the completion of a national labor market in Taiwan. But, among other things, a well-established *hukou* system, which used to be restrictive and powerful in the 1950s and 1960s, still

exists in today's Taiwan to give the authority an effective means of controlling the labor market.[175] The Singaporeans are especially fond of a family-like corporatist national labor "market."[176] In Japan, not only the state but also community-based societal forces exercise tremendous constraints on the market forces.[177] Perhaps only Hong Kong has the most authentic "national" labor market in the whole region. A reading of union publications in Hong Kong, however, may reveal the extensive political and social pressures against labor in Hong Kong under British colonial rule. The years beyond 1997 under the PRC regime may imply more rather than less of such pressures.[178]

This brief comparison that the emerging Chinese national labor market, distorted by its moralistic socioeconomic past and the CCP regime, is not necessarily unique. It may in fact be a necessity for an East Asian style of modernization to succeed. Given the huge, almost unlimited, supply of labor and long history of moral economy, a national labor market with some moralistic distortion may just be a blessing to the Chinese, as it has been to the Japanese and Koreans. Without those necessary distortions and controls, the rapidly advancing labor market could cause too many social and political problems too soon for a smooth and legitimate institutional transformation in contemporary China. The key, however, is how much state distortion is applied to the labor market, how it is done, and how long it lasts. For example, the Korean state, perhaps more pro-business than Beijing, forced employees to work extremely long hours every week even by the end of the 1980s.[179] But the CCP decided in 1994 (arguably prematurely) to let Chinese workers have a forty-four-hour workweek and to reduce that further to forty hours in 1995.[180] The PRC, which is much less developed than Taiwan, leaped forward this time, as Taiwan has kept a forty-four-hour workweek for many years.[181] This may have signaled a faster improvement of quality of life for labor in China, or just a further decline of the central authority of the state.[182] The decline of Beijing's administrative authority in regulating the national labor market could have been compensated by the growth of a good legal system. Yet, the latest figures show that, despite the massive legislation work since 1979,[183] law enforcement in China is still institutionally weak and practically ineffective.[184] Therefore, the Taiwanese merchants reported that, by 1995, they solved 78 percent of their business disputes in China through *guanxi* and only 11 percent through legal means.[185]

In short, the emerging national labor market is likely to grow and mature in China as one of the major LAPs. Judged against the experience of other East Asian nations, where most of the FDI in China came from, however, the Chinese national labor market is likely to be distorted by political and social institutions, especially the state. As a result of a national labor market, labor mobility, labor contracts and bargaining, unemployment, strikes, and genuine trade unions will develop in China. But they are likely to be limited within the existing social and political confines. A well-maintained legal framework for the national labor market, in an era of a declining central administrative ability, may be crucial.

Summary

The young national labor market has led the trend in Chinese labor allocation for the past two decades and is likely to continue its rapid growth and comprehensive institutionalization. Primarily facilitated by FDI, the emergence of the Chinese national labor market demonstrated the strong institutional role of internal-external interactions between the international market and a nation's institutional structure. FDI effectively communicates between a nation's domestic economy, market-oriented or not, and the international market. External influences, therefore, become another major shaping force for a nation's LAP and hence a major avenue for institutional changes in that nation. Practically, in China, FDI provided a legitimate channel and justification for the CCP to accept the labor market despite its extreme sensitivity in PRC politics.[186]

The Chinese national labor market has contributed greatly to the institutional changes in the PRC. The economy is gaining autonomy from the sociopolitical complex, while a separation between the CCP state and Chinese society is occurring. Many Chinese values and norms have been affected by the labor market. We are witnessing in China the rise of a new class of market-oriented, middle-income earners, and a group of rich private property owners. We also see the formation of a genuine working class that is outside the bought-off scheme of the CCP regime and the related (still hidden) trade unions and labor movements. National labor mobility, social liberty, and political participation are likely to continue to increase, facilitated by the national labor market. As a result, the political scene of China is likely to be more colorful and dynamic down the road.

Although the Chinese national labor market is perhaps unlikely to become the dominant LAP in the near future, it is institutionally desirable for it to be a larger and more important LAP than the family-based traditional LAP and the authoritarian state LAP. A dominant LAP of CLMs may effectively sustain a Chinese-style market economy, but the national labor market may create a better bond for the Chinese as a nation in an era of uneven development and regionalism.[187] A nationally based market institution tends to unite a nation powerfully because of its ceaseless expansion and assimilation. The lingering and extensive political and social distortions of the labor market may be necessary and even inevitable in China, just as in other East Asian nations. But the difference is that the nationally based unified distortions of the labor market may increase national unity and curb destructive regionalism and social polarization, while the community-based distortions tend to decrease national unity and fuel regional divisions. Therefore, not only the future of Chinese modernization but also the future of the Chinese nation may rest heavily on the development of the Chinese national labor market.

Notes

1. Basically, except for those who at least tried to unite the nation under one regime, the separatist rulers in Chinese history have been generally viewed as illegitimate and unethical. Any emperor who "reunited" the nation would be praised at least for that act by both traditional records and CCP historians. For examples, see Sima Guang's (司马光) classic *Zizhi tongjian* (资治通鉴), and Fan 1957, 1965, and 1978.

2. Many interesting and profound findings, however, have emerged from studies on this debatable relationship. See, for example, Lindblom 1977 and 1991, and Gabriel Almond, "Capitalism and Democracy" in *PS: Political Science and Politics* (September 1991): 467-474.

3. Famous examples of international conditions include the works on "hegemonic stability theory" and "interdependence theory" and critiques on them in Kindleberger 1973, Gilpin 1987, and Keohane 1984; on dependency theory in Cardoso and Faletto 1979 and Evans 1979; on the development of multinational corporations in Dunning et al. 1974 and Vernon 1972; and the most comprehensive efforts in this regard, in Wallerstein 1974. Well-known examples of other explanations for market development would include Max Weber's classic works.

4. There is indeed an important school of thought in international studies that focuses on the aspect of "international integration" and "international interdependence." (Cf. Keohane 1984, and the summary in Gilpin 1987, etc.)

5. The argument on "dependent development" reflects the fear of loss of control by the state over the assimilating force of the market in developing countries (Cardoso and Faletto 1979; Evans 1979).

6. "Poor Man's Burden: A Survey of the Third World," in *Economist* (London) September 23, 1989.

7. Scholars have explored the aspects of these interactions from many angles and for many purposes. Marxist scholars insist that a global expansion of the capitalist production mode has characterized modern world history (Cox 1987). Wallerstein constructed his world system theory (1974) by emphasizing this expansion of

capitalism as worldwide economic and political socialization and stratification. Peter Gourevitch argued that not only external settings may have an impact on domestic events, but domestic factors may greatly influence the external arrangement as well (Gourevitch 1988).

8. Stephen Kobrin, *Managing Political Risk Assessment.* New York: NYU Press. 1982, 30-31. FDI means the flows of foreign capital, technology, institutions, managerial goals, and skills, as well as cultural values.

9. Dunning 1981, 37-38, and Kobrin 1977, 4.

10. Some neo-Marxist scholars, like Cox (1987) and Wallerstein (1974), have been arguing essentially the same view with different terminology. To them, MNCs represent the worldwide division of labor under the capitalist production mode or a global expansion of the capitalist market economy.

11. Raymond Vernon and his associates are major advocates of these perspectives (Vernon 1971, 1972). Many critics of this belief assert that MNCs are not very beneficial to economic development in host countries since they are mainly exploiters of the cheap labor, resources, and ineffective governments in poor nations. For such critical views, see Biersteker 1978 and Frank 1980.

12. By 1992, China became a top international trader (eleventh in terms of volume). In 1994, China had a total foreign trade volume exceeding $236.7 billion, nearly 21 percent greater than the year before. Foreign trade became more than 45 percent of the Chinese GNP (*Renmin Ribao-Overseas*, January 14, 1995, 1). For a more objective assessment of Chinese foreign trade (about 10 to 20 percent of the total GNP by the end of the 1980s), see Lardy 1991, 150-155.

13. For a general discussion on the foreign influence generated by the international market on the Chinese domestic changes, see Wang 1994.

14. In some regions and at some times, nations may have substantial labor mobility among themselves. A current prototype of such a selective and controlled international labor mobility is the European Union which, if all goes as planned, will become a single state (or nation?) soon.

15. It is here that certain overlapping of a national labor market and the international labor market can develop. Despite powerful political and social concerns, an employer generally is inclined to hire *anybody* who is productive. The issue of illegal immigrants is thus born. Of course, this does not mean that every potential employee everywhere will have equal access to a job. Regionalized or localized employment is common.

16. One, of course, has to distinguish the laws on paper from the actual institutional systems in a nation regarding the labor market. If judged only by the written laws, China would have had a mutual national labor market years ago.

17. For an authoritative and Marxist discussion by Chinese scholars on the concepts of labor market and a Chinese style socialist labor market, see Hu 1993, 638-653. For a list of the features of the labor market offered by the economists from the International Labor Organization, see Simai 1995, 73-76.

18. The PRC never had a socialism as thorough as the former Soviet Bloc. Commune members, for example, were usually allowed to keep tiny but very productive family plots (*ziliudi*) and small-scale family-based sideline businesses. Tiny private vendors existed in the cities as well, even during the peak of the Mao era. This is indeed a big difference in the preexisting institutional conditions for the Chinese. In the former Soviet Union, private ownership of "means of production" was totally illegal until 1990, the eve of the total collapse of the Soviet system. This difference

may help us to understand better the comparative studies attempted by some on the economic reforms in China and Russia (e.g., Shirk 1993).

19. Unemployment finally became a legal concept in the official books in 1994. See the explanation to the *1994 nian guomin jingji he shehui fazhang de tongji baogao* (A statistical communiqué on the national economic and social development in 1994), State Statistical Bureau (Beijing), February 28, 1995.

20. The PRC also tried to utilize a less-strings-attached indirect investment in the form of loans and foreign aid. For example, as the largest recipient of World Bank loans, the PRC in 1994 alone obtained $3 billion from the bank (*Xinhua Daily Telegraph* [Beijing], July 22, 1994).

21. For instance, China set up different tax rates for FDI enterprises in and out of those designated areas in favor of those in the designated areas. See Chinese State Taxation Bureau chief's explanation of Chinese tax laws regarding FDI in China (in *Renmin Ribao,* March 26, 1990, 3).

22. Figures in *Tequ jingji* (Special Zones' economy (Shenzhen), no. 5 (1989): 57.

23. "Three kinds of capital enterprises" (*sanzi qiye*r) refer to the three main types of FDI enterprises in China: Sino-foreign equity joint ventures, Sino-foreign cooperative enterprises, and foreign solely owned enterprises. This book uses the term "FDI enterprises" for all three except where necessary to make a distinction.

24. A speech by Wei Yuming, chairman of the Chinese FDI Enterprises Association on November 8, 1990. As an example of the problematic accuracy of Chinese official statistics, another source claimed that by the end of 1990, only 1,811 wholly owned FDI enterprises were registered in China ("National FDI Enterprise Registration Working Meeting," *Xinhua Daily Telegraph* [Haerbin], March 1, 1991).

25. *Renmin Ribao* (Beijing), August 31, 1990, 5.

26. A speech by Gu Ming, vice chairman of the Legislation Committee of the Standing Committee of the NPC, on May 15, 1990. Also see Chen Xiaoping, "Yanhai jingji jisu kaifaqu" (The coastal economic and technological development areas) in *Yanhai jingji* (Coastal economy) (Nantong, Jiangsu), no. 6 (1990): 27. Nineteen ninety-three figures in *Renmin Ribao-Overseas,* September 15, 1994, 2.

27. SSB report, in *Renmin Ribao-Overseas,* March 28, 1994, 1.

28. Mao En, "Shenzhen tequ yu Pudong kaifa" (Shenzhen Special Zone and Pudong development), in *Tuande shenghuo* (League life) (Shanghai), no. 7 (1990): 27.

29. In *Renmin Ribao-Overseas,* February 9, 1995, 4.

30. The classic British hope of "if everybody in China bought one shoe" is now clearly alive in many minds. The Taiwanese economist Gao Xijuin wrote that the main attractions for Taiwanese investment in the PRC are three: cheap labor (wages are only about one-tenth of those in Taiwan), the low price of land, and tax benefits (in *Tianxia* Magazine [Taipei], March 1990). For an interesting account on the incentives for foreign investors, see Graeme Browning, *If Everybody Bought One Shoe* (New York: Hill and Wang, 1989).

31. The full text of the law, *Zhonghua renmin gongheguo zhongwai hezi jingying qiye fa* (The PRC law on Sino-foreign joint venture enterprises), of July 1, 1979, and revised on April 4, 1990, is in Shenzhen FDI Center, 1991, 28-31.

32. The full text of the regulation, *Zhongwai hezi jingying qiye laodong guangli guiding,* approved by the State Council on July 26, 1980, is in Shenzhen FDI Center, 1991, 245-246.

33. Although the exact stories about the inside political process concerning those retreats have yet to be fully explored, the heated political debate over the

issues of "more opening" and "anti-bourgeois pollution" in 1984-87 may have sufficiently revealed the magnitude of the political struggle inside the CCP leadership.

34. *Guowu yuang guangyu guli waishang touzi de guiding,* issued by the State Council on October 11, 1986, in Shenzhen FDI Center, 1991, 2-4.

35. *Laodongbu, renshibu guangyu jingyibu lushi waishang touzi qiye yongren zizhuquan de yijiang* (The Labor and Personnel Ministries' proposal on further implementation of the autonomous employment rights of the FDI enterprises), Beijing, May 18, 1988. In Shenzhen FDI Center, 1991, 249-250. Also see Li 1995, 171-172.

36. The first such regulation was the 1983 regulation of the State Council calling for "reasonable mobility" for "scientists and technicians"; Wang Chengying, "Zhonguo rencai liudong 15 nian" (Fifteen years of professional mobility), in *Lanzhou xuekan* (Lanzhou journal) (Lanzhou), no. 5 (1994): 21.

37. The first major surge has been widely attributed by the Chinese press to the legalization of the national labor market, whereas the second surge may have been driven by the major market-oriented reform after Deng Xiaoping's famous "Southern Inspection" in early 1992.

38. For example, see the rather detailed local legislation on the emerging labor market in Guangdong Province and Guangzhou city (Shenzhen FDI Center, 1991, 251-267; Guangzhou Labor Bureau 1991, 141-378).

39. "Guangyu guli waishnag zai Shanghai Pudong xinqu touzi de guiding" (Some regulations for encouraging FDI in Pudong new district of Shanghai), Shanghai Municipal Government, September 10, 1990, in *Wenhuibao* (Wenhui daily), September 11, 1990, 3.

40. The guide list publishes the industries where FDI is encouraged, limited, or prohibited. It is subject to regular revisions and updates (*Renmin Ribao-Overseas,* June 28, 1995, 1).

41. For a short history of private employment in the PRC during the 1980s, see Liang 1990, 10-14.

42. The State Council, *Zhonghua renmin gongheguo siying qiye zhanxin tiaoli* (The PRC provisional regulation on private enterprises) (Beijing), June 25, 1988, in State Council 1993, 3-10.

43. The Industrial and Commerce Administration Bureau, *Siying qiye denji chenxu* (Procedures for the registration of the private enterprises), July 1991, in State Council 1993, 211-218.

44. The State Council, *Zhonghua renmin gongheguo siying qiye zhanxin tiaoli* (The PRC provisional regulation on private enterprises), (Beijing), June 25, 1988, articles 27-30.

45. See, for example, the Beijing Municipal Government's *Gonggao* (announcement), April 20, 1986, and Beijing Municipal Government Foreign Affairs Office's *Tongzhi* (notice), April 21, 1986, reconfirming the monopoly by the Beijing FESCO in supplying workers to foreign offices in the capital city. In March of 1995, the Beijing Municipal Government reissued the same directives.

46. Liu Xinfa, deputy manager of the Beijing FESCO's Personnel Department, June 1995.

47. Author's field notes in Beijing and Shanghai, 1993 and 1995. This trend is described by the official media as an "undercurrent" filled with uncertainties and hazards to Chinese employees, as there is no "state *danwei* to manage and protect"

them against the often greedy FDI employers. See Liu Luyan, "Xiayibu zouxian hechu?" (Where's the next step?) in *Renmin Ribao-Overseas*, June 30, 1995, 2.

48. For a brief history on those new institutions, see Hu 1993, 644-648.

49. The Labor Ministry did not issue its administrative directive Provisional Rules on Job Referral until 1990.

50. Liu Jialing, a bureau chief of the Personnel Ministry, "Shinian rencai jiaoliu gongzhu huigu" (A review of professional exchange in the past ten years), in *Zhongguo rencai bao* (Chinese professional daily) (Beijing), January 1, 1991.

51. Many FDI service or promotion centers and even FESCOs also do this job now (Cao et al. 1993, 14-16).

52. For a lengthy report on the numerous "illegal," "greedy," and "cheating" personal exchange centers in Shenzhen, see *Shenzhen wanbao* (Shenzhen evening news) (Shenzhen) December, 16, 1995, 1.

53. See Seth Faison, "Women as Cattle: In China, Slavery Rises," in *New York Times*, September 6, 1995, A1, A4. For some empirical cases of unethical practices of some private referral agencies in an inland province, see *Hefei wanbao* (Hefei evening news) (Hefei), June 10 and 11, 1995, 5.

54. In one city, all forty job referral agencies inspected in 1994 turned out to be illegal, for they had no registration or operation permits. Zhang Zhongying, "Laodongli shichang wenti toushi" (A Look into the problems on the labor market), in *Jingji Ribao* (Economic daily) (Beijing), November 6, 1994, 7.

55. See, for example, the report on the "chaotic" job referral agencies in Shenzhen in *Shenzhen fazhibao* (Shenzhen legal daily) (Shenzhen), December 17, 1995, 1.

56. Official media have expressed doubts about the "rationality and legality" of the "secretive" yet effective operations of the headhunting agencies in causing the "talent drain" from the state *danweis*. See Zhang Yaguang, "Zhongguo rencai shichang toushi" (A look at the Chinese talents market), in *Renmin Ribao-Overseas*, March 19, 1994, 9.

57. *Renmin Riabo*, Beijing, September 15, 1995, 3.

58. See CCP Central Organizational Department and the PRC Personnel Ministry, "Jiakuai peiyu he fazhan woguo rencai shichang de yijian" (On the acceleration of the cultivation and development of rencai market in our nation), in *Shenzhen renshi* (Shenzhen personnel), an internal monthly by the Shenzhen Personnel Bureau (Shenzhen), no. 11-12 (1994): 24-25.

59. *Renmin Ribao-Overseas*, October 21, 1995, 2.

60. Author's interviews at the Shenzhen labor market in 1995. The author found there were a large number of manual workers in Shenzhen who stayed for years without any official permits.

61. Anhui Province started this experiment in September 1993. See *Xinhua Daily Telegraph* (Hefei), March 2, 1994, 2.

62. *Guangmin Ribao* (Guangmin daily) (Beijing), February 18, 1995, 6.

63. Labor Ministry, "1995 nian laodong gongzhu yaodian" (The essentials of labor work in 1995), in *Zhongguo laodong kexue* (Chinese labor science) (Beijing), no. 2 (1995): 18-21.

64. Minister Li Boyong, "Zhiye fengnei—Woguo laodongli gunagli de yixian zhongda gongcheng" (Job categorization—A major project of labor management in our nation), in *Zhongguo laodong bao* (Chinese labor daily) (Beijing) March 14, 1995, 1.

65. *Jingji Ribao* (Economic daily) (Beijing), March 13, 1995, 7.

66. For example, see the description of the pension and social security plan enacted in Shanghai in 1993 *Jiefang Ribao* (Liberation daily), the official newspaper of the Shanghai government, (Shanghai), February 7, 1995, 3. For a general report on the reform and development of the Chinese labor insurance plans, see *Renmin Ribao-Overseas*, December 14, 1995, 1, 4.

67. Of course, this labor market is still far from having "enough legal protection" or a "national standardization" (Ma and Sun ed. 1994, 10-11).

68. *Rencai kaifa* (Development of talents) (Shanghai), no. 2, 1995, 8.

69. For example, Beijing declared that every employer "has the duty" to accept some discharged military personnel (*Xinhua Daily Telegraph* [Beijing], December 12, 1994). The Guangdong provincial government ordered in 1995 that every *danwei* and enterprise, including FDI and native private enterprises, must hire no fewer than 1.5 percent of their workers from among handicapped people. See He Huifei, "Guangdong anbili anpai cangjiren jouye" (Guangdong arranges jobs for the handicapped according to a ratio), in *Renmin Ribao-Overseas*, February 16, 1995, 4.

70. *Xinhua Daily Telegraph* (Beijing), March 9, 1991. Cited in UPI and other foreign media.

71. *Jingji tizhi gaige naican* (Internal reference on economic system reform), an internal publication by the State Council (Beijing), no. 2 (1992): 37-39.

72. For many reasons, some of them obviously political, such as weakening critics, the official and semi-official publications on FDI enterprises in China tend to underreport and even neglect information on FDI employment in China. Important journals covering FDI like *Shanghai xiangang jingji jikan* (The Shanghai Hong Kong economic quarterly) list and report many details about FDI enterprises in the PRC but with almost no information about their employees.

73. *Xinhua Daily Telegraph* (Guangzhou), November 21, 1991. This figure was used widely by other Chinese media and was confirmed by a field trip of mine to Guangdong in 1992.

74. For such reports see, for example, *Renmin Ribao-Overseas*, June 28, 1990, 3; August 31, 1990, 5; and November 15, 1990, 3.

75. Ma Xuohong, deputy chief of the FDI Management Bureau of the Chinese Ministry of Foreign Economic and Trade Cooperation, told this to the Zhongxin News Agency in Hong Kong in June of 1995. In *Renmin Ribao-Overseas*, June 22, 1995, 5.

76. An official report estimated that the FDI enterprises employed about 10 million to 12.6 million people in 1995 (*Renmin Ribao-Overseas*, April 27, 1995, 1, and July 4, 1995, 2).

77. Some Chinese scholars estimated that by 1992, there were more than 46.04 million urban workers allocated by either the national labor market or the CLMs, roughly 30.15 percent of the total urban labor force (Hu 1993, 649).

78. An important qualification must be noted here. The actual combined size of the national labor market and the CLMs may be significantly smaller than 241 million because there could be considerable double counting due to the fact that many private employers are also CLM-based collective employers. What is more, many FDI employees in joint ventures may still be state employees under the authoritarian state LAP.

79. Liu Luyang, "Renshe ziwo" (Understanding oneself), in *Renmin Ribao-Overseas*, June 6, 1995, 2, and Ji Xiaobi, "Rensheng jizhuangwan" (Sharp turns of life), in *Renmin Ribao-Overseas*, July 20, 1995, 2. The Apple employee and his wife,

however, suffered considerably from having no stable housing, as they could not afford to buy an apartment yet. They gave up their apartment when they had to leave their old *danwei* because their moonlighting plan of one family, two systems was scorned by the *danwei* boss, who insisted that they both stay or leave—meaning giving up their *danwei*-related benefits, including the important housing allocation.

80. Statement by Ma Lihong, deputy chief of the FDI Management Bureau of the Chinese Ministry of Foreign Economic and Trade Cooperation, in Hong Kong (reported by Zhongxin News Agency, June 22, 1995).

81. *Renmin Ribao-Overseas*, April 7, 1995, 1.

82. As one case illustrated, however, coming out of hiding may be a great disadvantage, even a disaster for private enterprise. A very successful private enterprise with fourteen hundred employees and assets of over 20 million rmb hid under the collective cover for three years. In 1988, the owner (Shi Sanning) attempted to reveal the true identity of the enterprise, according to the requirement of a new law issued that year. Local government (Haerbin, the provincial capital city of Helonjian Province) felt that 20 million in assets was "too big to be a private enterprise." Shi's license was suspended and he lost 15 million rmb. After some three years of nationwide debate, and thanks to direct intervention from Beijing, Shi finally had his private enterprise licenses reissued in 1992. For a good summary and discussion on this case, see *Zhongguo jingji tizhi gaige* (China economic system reform) (Beijing), no. 5 (1992): 56-58.

83. Chinese official media have been filled with reports on the significantly higher productivity in FDI enterprises. For example, the Beijing government acknowledged that the average per-worker productivity in the FDI industrial enterprise, including the Chrysler-invested Beijing Jeep Automobile Company, was four to six times as high as the average productivity of Beijing workers (Beijing Municipal Economic Commission 1990, 9, and 1992, 2 , 109).

84. Almost every foreign manager I interviewed asserted that his Chinese employees were productive and good, while expressing a general depreciation of the quality of the Chinese labor force at large. Market-oriented management may be important. But perhaps, as one foreign manager commented, FDI employers tend to "get the cream of the Chinese labor force" (field notes in Guangdong, Shanghai, and Beijing, 1992).

85. The workers apparently tend to overly enjoy their newly acquired freedom. In FDI enterprises in the SEZs, the employee turnover rate is, often "unnecessarily," very high. See, for example, Mao En, "Shenzhen tequ yu Pudong kaifa" (Shenzhen Special Zone and the Pudong development), *Tuande shenghuo* (League's life) (Shanghai), no. 7 (1990): 26.

86. Liu Luyan, "Xiayibu zouxian hechu?" (Where's the next step?) in *Renmin Ribao-Overseas*, June 30, 1995, 2.

87. However, "illegal" and "immoral" labor management in those FDI enterprises was common and was generally overlooked by state authorities. Besides the extremely exploitative wage level and the slumlike living conditions, many young female employees in the FDI enterprises in the SEZs could not get married without risking being fired (Mao En, "Shenzhen tequ yu Pudong kaifa" (Shenzhen Special Zone and the Pudong development), *Tuande shenghuo* (League's life) (Shanghai) no. 7 (1990): 27. Interestingly enough, the national press is generally inhibited in report-ing any negative stories about FDI enterprises. The major source of complaints and even criticisms is naturally in some small local publications in non-SEZ areas, such as the

above article, and Liu Yu's article on the environmental devastation in the SEZs in *Xinshidai luntan* (New era forum) (Chendu, Sichuan), no. 2 (1990): 29-31; and Wang Maoling's article criticizing FDI employers in *Jingji wenti* (Economic issues) (Taiyuan, Shanxi), no. 7 (1990): 2-9.

88. Some measures used by local leaders have become so disgusting that people began to use words like "foreigner's slave" or "foreigner's walking dogs" in private (author's field notes, 1992, 1993, and 1995).

89. This kind of illegal practice has developed to such an alarming extent that the government now forcefully emphasizes the necessity of verifying the existence of foreign investment before issuing a license to an FDI enterprise. Numerous cases of fake FDI enterprises have been revealed in the Chinese press lately. In Guangxi Province, the government at one time voided the licenses of 309 phony FDI enterprises (*Renmin Ribao-Overseas*, June 19, 1995, 2). Nationwide, Beijing shut down more than seventy-five fake FDI enterprises by 1994 and reported about 40 percent of the total FDI enterprises (more than twelve thousand) were in name only (*Renmin Ribao-Overseas*, April 27, 1994, 2).

90. By the end of 1994, for example, there were 1,658 PRC-owned enterprises in Hong Kong alone with total assets over $44 billion (*Renmin Ribao-Overseas*, November 21, 1994, 6, and December 14, 1994, 5).

91. Several such cases were officially reported in praising tones (*Renmin Ribao-Overseas* April 29, 1991, 1; May 18, 1991, 3; May 25, 1991, 3; and June 28, 1995, 5). Foreign observers also have noticed such an "investment laundry" phenomenon (see news analysis column in *The China Business Review* [Washington], spring and summer issues, 1992).

92. *Xinhua Daily Telegraph* (Shenzhen), March 4, 1993, 2.

93. The largest recipient was the United States. See World Bank, *World Investment Report 1994*, Washington, 1994.

94. *Renmin Ribao-Overseas*. March 24, 1995, 5.

95. Due to the incompetence of state management and rampant corruption, there was significant capital flight from the PRC in the 1980s and 1990s. Officially, by the end of 1994, Chinese overseas assets exceeded 1,000 ventures in 120 countries with a total value of 2 trillion rmb (about $240 billion) (*Renmin Ribao-Overseas*, November 2, 1994, 1). The real size could be much larger. See Richard Hornik's "Bursting China's Bubble" in *Foreign Affairs* (May-June 1940): 28-42. The horrendous mismanagement has prompted Beijing to call for strong actions "to stop the draining of our overseas assets," in *Jingji Ribao* (Economic daily) (Beijing), November 19, 1994, 1.

96. *Xinhua Daily Telegraph* (Beijing), January 27, 1997.

97. It may underestimate the role of FDI to say that it is not sufficient or necessary to the development of Chinese foreign trade (Lardy 1991, 15). In 1994, for example, FDI enterprises alone constituted 37 percent of China's total foreign trade (*Renmin Ribao-Overseas*, January 14, 1995, 1).

98. Chinese foreign trade grew very rapidly in the past two decades, from $20.64 billion in 1978 to $236.7 billion in 1994—a nearly 11.5-fold increase. (The Chinese GDP increased 3.76-fold during the same period.) See *China in Brief: Factors Fueling China's Rapid Economic Development* (Beijing: New Star Publishers, 1995), 3, 11-12; and SSB, *1994 gnomon jingji he shehui fazhang de tongji gongbao* (1994 SSB statistical communiqué on the national economy and social development) (Beijing), February 28, 1995, item 6.

99. An impression from my field studies. This is especially the case in the SEZs and in designated areas of the COCs where the labor market is better developed. The Taiwanese investors were told before going to the Mainland that they should recruit as many workers as possible from the labor market. See Xiao Xinyong, "Ruhe zhaomu yu shenghe dangdi zhigong?" (How to recruit and check the local workers), in *Touzi Zhongguo* (Invest in China) (Taipei) (December 1995): 92-93.

100. A comparative study on FDI in developing countries concluded that labor-intensive and female employment are two features of FDI enterprises in Hong Kong (Chen 1983, 207).

101. The author collected several FDI recruiting ads containing such requirements. For example, see the ads in *Changzhou Ribao* (Changzhou daily) (Changzhou) August 12, 1995, 1; *Shenzhen laodon shibao* (Shenzhen labor times) (Shenzhen), every issue of August 1995; and *Xinmin wanbao* (Xinmin evening news) (Shanghai), every day in August 1995.

102. Mao En, "Shenzhen Tequ yu Pudong kaifa" (Shenzhen Special Zone and Pudong development), *Tuande shenghuo* (League's life) (Shanghai), no. 7 (1990): 27.

103. Author's interview with a West Corp. managerial employee in Philadelphia, January 1991.

104. Guangdong Provincial Government, *Guangdongsheng gunagyu weishan touzi qiye yonggong de guiding* (Regulations of Guangdong Province on FDI enterprises' labor management) (Guangzhou) April 10, 1989, articles 6 and 8.

105. There were a total of sixteen help-wanted ads in the newspaper of *Xinmin wanbao* (Xinmin evening news) (Shanghai), February 6, 1995.

106. This transitional and quasi-*hukou* was a major reform of the *hukou* system in Shanghai—one of the most tightly controlled urban areas. Beyond the temporary residential permit (the so-called *jijuzheng*), an employer could apply for a *blue hukou* for its non-Shanghai employees who had more than a high school education, had worked in the enterprise for at least three years, and had a fixed place to live. With an annual fee, the *blue hukou* allows its holder to enjoy basically all the community-based benefits and rights except participating in the local college entrance exam and the community-based local labor reallocation. After five more years, a qualified *blue hukou* holder may apply for a formal Shanghai *hukou* with a substantial payment as the so-called urban construction fee. *Blue hukou* is also available to "investment immigrants." See Shanghai Municipal Government, *Shanghais nanying hukou guangli zhanxin guiding* (Provisional regulations on the management of the blue *hukou* in Shanghai) (Shanghai), February 1, 1994, 21 articles.

107. In some cases, an FDI employer may even physically hold the *hukou* proof of his employees, in addition to some cash deposit, to prevent costly turnovers (author's field notes in Guangdong and Jiangsu, 1989, 1992, 1993, and 1995).

108. Author's interviews in Beijing, Guangdong, Jinagsu, and Shanghai in 1993 and 1995.

109. For example, see the column of "Experiences of Management in FDI Enterprises" on the front page of the *Renmin Ribao-Overseas* in 1991-1992.

110. For stories about how some CCP organizations "helped" the management and a CCP branch secretary served well as an "assistant to the general manager," see *Renmin Ribao*, May 23, 1995, 3.

111. The CCP Constitution requires any three members in one place to organize a party group or branch. The story is in *Xinan wanbao* (Xinan evening news), Hefei, August 1, 1995, 6.

112. For example, 65 percent of the 6,478 surveyed Chinese workers "were un-happy" with their Japanese bosses in 1992 (in *Renmin Ribao-Overseas*, February 9, 1995, 4). Foreign media reported this much earlier. See "Chinese Unhappy at Japanese Ventures" in *The Korea Times* (Seoul), May 17, 1992, 9.

113. *Xinmin wanbao* (Xinmin evening news) (Shanghai), February 20, 1995.

114. See *Yanhai xinchao* (New tides) (Shantou), no. 2 (1995): 10-12. In Guang-dong, 70 to 80 percent of 657 FDI enterprises failed labor protection inspections in 1992 (*Renmin Ribao-Overseas*, February 8, 1993, 2). In local media, complaints of labor abuse by FDI employers are more common. For example, see the cases listed against FDI employers in *Shenzhen laodong shibao* (Shenzhen labor times), Shenzhen, August 22, 1995, 1.

115. Typical *getihus* also practice family-based traditional LAP in nonagri-cultural industries. Many of them have hired or are to hire from the emerging national labor market (Liang 1990, 14). Here we have an interesting overlapping of the family-based LAP and the national labor market.

116. Press conferences by the Beijing *Getihu* Association, reported by *Renmin Ribao*, April 4, 1990, 2, and April 16, 1990, 3.

117. *Jingji tizhi gaige naican* (Internal reference on economic system reform), an internal publication by the State Council (Beijing), no. 2 (1992): 37.

118. There are clearly many more such millionaires in today's PRC. See *Zhong-hua zhoubao* (China news weekly) (Philadelphia), no. 171 (April 7-13, 1995): 1. A caution here. Some of those private entrepreneurs may actually be heads of some pros-perous community-based collective enterprises or TVEs. For example, see the detailed story about one of those *Forbes* millionaires, Zhang Guoxi, in Yao and Qiu 1993, 169-180.

119. *Renmin Ribao*, September 25, 1990, 5, and January 5, 1991, 2. Because of Wu's donation to the local communities and government-sponsored events, and his help in promoting China's exports, he was granted numerous honors and titles.

120. "Liu Xiaosheng maixia guoying gangtichang" (Liu Xiaosheng bought a state-owned steel factory), in *Renmin Ribao-Overseas*, April 12, 1993, 2.

121. Lin Zhuwu, "Shishi yongdong minying qiye wenhuachao" (The cultural waves of the private enterprises in Shishi), in *Renmin Ribao-Overseas*, May 11, 1995, 3.

122. *Zhongguo gongshang shibao* (Chinese industrial and commerce times) (Bei-jing), March 11, 1991, 1.

123. Liu Yingqou: "Zhongguo jingji minyinghua de biyaoxin he xianshixin fengxi" (An analysis of the necessity and feasibility of privatization of the Chinese economy), in *Jingji yanjou* (Economic research) (Beijing), no. 6 (1994): 48-55.

124. Liang 1990, 17. Liang, a top PRC official in charge of managing private enterprises, believed that such a family-based recruitment may have contributed to the harmonious stability of the Chinese private employment.

125. Song Linfei, "Zhongguo siyou jingji de xianzhuan yu fazhan qushi" (The current situation and prospect of the Chinese private economy), in *Nanjin shehui kexue* (Nanjin social sciences) (Nanjin), no. 5 (1994): 52-58.

126. Zhang Zhongying: "Laodongli shichang wenti toushi" (A look into prob-lems on the labor market), in *Jingji Ribao* (Economic daily) (Beijing), November 6, 1994, 7.

127. See the cases reported in *Xinan wanbao* (Xinan evening news) (Hefei), June 15 and 16, 1995, 2.

128. For example, see the cases reported in *Shenzhen laodong shibao* (Shenzhen labor times) (Shenzhen), August 1, 1995, 1.

129. Author's field notes in Anhui, Beijing, Guangdong, Jiangsu, and Shanghai in 1993, 1995, and 1996.

130. For a recent report and comment on private employment, see Zhang Houyi, "Woguo siying qiye zhongde laozi guangxi" (Labor relations in the private enterprises in our nation), in *Gongren Ribao* (Worker's Daily) (Beijing), February 24 , and March 3, 1995, 8.

131. For a rare case of an effective and active company union in a major FDI enterprise, see Beijing Municipal Economic Commission 1990, 113-125.

132. There was a propagandist story about how a very successful private entrepreneur who is not a party member in Liaoning Province "looked" for and benefited greatly from the presence of CCP branches in his group corporation. See Zhang Shuzheng, "Ma zongcai zhao dang" (President Ma looked for the party), in *Renmin Ribao*, January 20, 1994, 3.

133. Older Chinese employees who value a stable and lasting job are said to generally prefer Japanese employers to European and American employers even though the Japanese firms generally pay less and demand more. Liu Luyan, "Xiayibu zouxian hechu?" (Where's the next step?) in *Renmin Ribao-Overseas*, June 30, 1995, 2.

134. Author's field notes in Anhui, Guangdong and Jiangsu Provinces in 1992 and 1995.

135. Many FDI employers simply ignore the PRC labor laws. In 1995, for example, many foreign managers in Liaoning province were found forcing employees to work much longer than the legal working hours with no additional pay. The same investigation also revealed that many foreign managers, mostly from Korea and Taiwan, even physically punished workers for using rest rooms. Shengyang Trade Union, "Shengyangshi sanzi qiye labodong guangxi zhuankuan diaocha" (An investigation on the labor relations in FDI enterprises in Shengyang city), in *Lilun yu shijian* (Theory and practice) (Shengyang), no. 3 (1995): 16-17.

136. See, for example, Beijing Municipal Economic Commission 1990, 17-131, and 1992, 10-100; Yao and Murong 1993, 131-138, 169-269.

137. Actually the Chinese partner, the state-owned Shenzhen Electronic Corporation, owns about 15 percent of Heimann's shares.

138. Ma et al. 1993, 621; SSB-LB 1991, 175.

139. In another neighboring joint venture between an Australian company and a Chinese cable-making factory, the one foreign manager from Hong Kong and two foreign technicians from the United States were paid sixty to eighty times as much as the average employees.

140. Joint ventures usually have a better chance because the Chinese partner, typically a state-owned *danwei*, can mange to get some scarce local *hukou* quotas from the Shenzhen municipal and Guangdong provincial governments.

141. Such a commercialization of *hukou* has been clearly evident in the PRC since the 1960s. Usually, people just legally swap their *hukous,* with one side paying the other in private. Semi-legal activities such as bribing *hukou* authorities were more common. The formal sale of *hukou*, however, is still considered illegal and is seen mainly in remote rural areas.

142. In a Sino-Australian joint venture enterprise in the same garden, fewer than eighty of the first group of nearly six hundred employees remained after two years.

143. Author's interviews with foreign managers in the hotel in 1992.

144. For example, see the whole page devoted to the hotel in *Renmin Ribao,* July 20, 1991, 2, and May 31, 1991, 8.

145. Based on Beijing Municipal Economic Commission 1990, 22-41, and 1992, 10-16, 60-64.

146. The Chinese government has sponsored such a national appraisal annually since 1988. The main criteria are scale of net investment, profitability, total sales, exports, and the degree of technology. In 1990, each of the Top Ten had FDI of $41 million to $200 million; profitability up to 82.4 percent; per-worker productivity up to 455,000 rmb; and export ratio up to 64 percent. See *Jingji Ribao* (Economic daily) (Beijing), August 1, 1990, 1. By 1995, the Top Ten evaluation evolved into four categories: ten largest exporters, ten largest sales, ten highest per-employee profit/taxes, and fifty "best" FDI hotels (*Renmin Ribao-Overseas,* July 4, 1995, 2).

147. *Touzi shibao* (Investment times), Shenzhen, March 18, 1992, 3. According to this newspaper, there are now sixty-two FDI enterprises in China that have over 100 million rmb assets. Among the 506 largest industrial enterprises of the PRC, thirty-one are FDI enterprises (6.1 percent).

148. Based on the author's interviews and Beijing Municipal Economic Commission 1990, 43-59, and 1992, 22-33, 65-72.

149. Words of the manager of Beijing B&W, Cao Nong, in Beijing Municipal Economic Commission 1990, 42.

150. Those firms generally maintain as few as possible assets inside China so, in case they were unlucky enough to be busted by the authority, they could quickly restart by using a different name in a modern-day guerrilla style of business activities.

151. This kind of illegal capital flight from China and money laundering started in the 1980s and became very large and alarmingly common by the mid-1990s. Most of such "private" capital was embezzled state funds, bribes, illegal kickbacks, and insider-trading profits from corrupt officials and managers of state-owned enterprises.

152. Some larger FDI enterprises also practice such hiring. A major Taiwanese firm in China hires exclusively from two counties in Shandong for its plants in five Chinese cities. A smaller Taiwanese firm in Guangdong hires exclusively from a county in Henan Province (author's field notes in Taipei, April 1995). The heavy reliance on referral may explain this phenomenon.

153. This tax is collected by the mighty Industrial and Commercial Administration Bureau, which is the most important authority controlling the private enterprises. It only applies to private enterprises. Unlike other income taxes collected by the Taxation Bureau, this special tax is based on 5 percent of total sales rather than the net income or profit, and thus is harder to evade. This tax alone may have been the reason that massive numbers of private enterprises, like Liu's company, hid under the cover of collective enterprises in a variety of ways.

154. Tax evasion has been a major problem in the Chinese private economy. One investigation concluded that virtually all private enterprises studied in the Wuhan area reported less than half of their sales and income to the taxation authority. See *Nankai xuekang* (Nankai journal) (Tianjin), no. 2 (1992): 52. The state is estimated to have collected only 10 to 30 percent of the taxes the private enterprises owe. This is due partially to the shortage of cadres monitoring the private businessmen. On average, one cadre from the Industrial and Commercial Bureau has to take care of four hundred to one thousand *getihus* and private enterprises. See *Jingji tizhi gaige naican* (Internal reference on economic system reform), an internal publication by the State Council (Beijing), no. 2 (1992): 38-39.

155. To collect debt, as Liu described, one usually has to mobilize tremendous social and political connections. Going to court is considered ineffective, expensive, and "bad for business."

156. This may be an underreported figure. One study shows, for instance, that in Hubei Province, a relatively less open and less developed province, private employers normally pay themselves seventy to three hundred times more than they pay their employees. See *Nankai xuekang* (Nankai journal) (Tianjin), no. 2 (1991): 52.

157. *Xinhua Daily Telegraph* (Beijing), September 25, 1995, 1.

158. Cited in Ji Xiaobi, "Rensheng jizhuangwan" (Sharp turns of life), *Renmin Ribao-Overseas*, July 20, 1995, 2. Emphasis added.

159. For a recent report on the declined position of Chinese workers in China's "sweatshop socialism," see Anita Chan and Robert Senser, "China's Troubled Workers," in *Foreign Affairs* 76, no. 2 (March/April 1997): 104-117.

160. See Wang Jianchu, "Lun jianguohe gongren yundong de sanci cuozhe" (On the three setbacks of the union movement after the establishment of the PRC), in *Shiling* (The field of history) (Shanghai), no. 4 (1994): 36-42.

161. This unique history of "reversing the clock" obviously demands much further study by China scholars as well as comparative political scientists.

162. Yang Fan, "Laozi maodun jianchengwei woguo shehui maodun de jiaodian" (The capital-labor confrontation will become the focus of our nation's social conflicts), in *Yanhai xinchao* (New tides) (Shantou), no. 2 (1995): 10-12.

163. For a description of these two Chinese institutions in the 1990s, see Ogden 1995, 176-180.

164. Because this policy is considered subversive politically by CCP hardliners, there was a move in the spring of 1991 by Beijing to "quietly" limit the negative effect caused by such actions of the FDIs. The CCP issued internal directives aimed at capping the wages of FDI employees, with the hope that it might reduce the attractiveness of FDI enterprises to top-quality Chinese workers in state-owned enterprises. (See the reports in *The China Business Review* [Washington] [January-February 1991]: 8-12.) Very soon—by 1992—this effort turned out to be a complete failure. The new PRC Labor Law of 1995 stipulated that employers who hired workers from existing *danweis* should pay for the possible "damages" the old *danwei* might suffer from the sudden leave of its employees. But practically, the employers have generally avoided such payment by hiring full-time moonlighting workers.

165. Author's field notes from the late 1980s to mid-1990s, demonstrating a rather clear trend of decline of the significance of *dangan* in the eyes of the Chinese.

166. *Renmin Ribao-Overseas*, January 4, 1993, 1. Foreign media reported that more than 150 million rural people moved to the cities in the 1980s. See *The Far Eastern Economic Review*, June 9, 1994, 22.

167. To experiment with new means of social control, the PRC in 1995 established an "IC" system first in Shanghai. Every *danwei* including state agencies and foreign-invested firms must apply for an identification card containing electronic information about the name, address, type of business, and registered assets, etc., of the holder. The IC card is required for services ranging from opening bank accounts, taxation, social insurance, and labor management to public security (author's field notes in Shanghai, August 1995). Also see *Jiefang Ribao* (Liberation daily), the official daily of the Shanghai Municipal Government, July 3, 1995, 1.

168. For some firsthand information about labor allocation in those East Asian nations, see Jiang Shuji et al., *Dao zhiyu jingji zhilu* (The road to a free economy) (Taipei), Chung Hwa Institute for Economic Research, 1991, 245-292; Korean Ministry of Labor, *Labor Law of Korea* (Seoul) (1992): 3-38, 121-154; and *Labor Administration* (Seoul) (1992): 11-73.

169. Yukio Noguchi, *The 1940 System*, summarized in Gale Eisenstod, "Confucius or Marx?" in *Forbes*, December 4, 1995, 76, 80.

170. Kim Chong-Je (金钟吉), "The Experience of Korean Economic Development and its Lessons for China," Chinese translation in *Caijing luntan* (Financial and economic forum) (Dalian), no. 5/6 (1994): 19-20.

171. Author's field notes in Puhan, Korea, 1992, and in Shanghai 1993, 1995, and 1996. For an interesting report on the labor management system in Baosan Steel Company, see *Zhongguo jingji tizhi gaige* (Chinese economic system reform), no. 5 (1992): 34-37, 40.

172. Some officials have realized that small size is among the current major problems of the Chinese national labor market. See Xin Renzhou, "Problems in China's Labor Market and Their Causes" in *Keji daobao* (Science and Technology Herald) (Beijing), no. 2 (1995): 62-64.

173. This is especially true in the massive number of small enterprises outside the major metropolitan areas like Tokyo and Osaka (author's field notes in Japan in 1992 and 1993). Apparently, even during the painful and unprecedented institutional changes of the Japanese economy in the 1990s, internal employment and reemployment, the so-called hidden unemployment, which was estimated to be higher than the official unemployment rate of 2.5 percent in 1995, were still very important to the major Japanese employers such as Toshiba, NTT, Nippon Steel, and Kawasaki Steel. (See Kazuki Tezuka, "The Japanese Labor Market Today," in Hax et al. 1996, 45-51.)

174. For a discussion on the strong role of the state in keeping down the true wages and suppressing the unions during the "crucial years" of economic development in the NICs and especially in Korea, see Colin Kirkpatrick, "Export-Oriented Industrialization and Income Distribution in the Asian Newly Industrialized Countries" in Meine P. van Dijk and Henrik S. Marcussen, eds., *Industrialization in the Third World: The Need for Alternative Strategies* (London: Frank Case, 1990).

175. Author's conversation with Yu Zongyuan (于宗元), the director of the Chung Hwa Institute for Economic Research of Taiwan, Taipei, April 12, 1995. Perhaps more intrusive than the PRC *hukou* or personal ID, every Taiwanese is required to carry a personal ID card that also contains the residential information of his or her spouse and parents.

176. For an official statement on this corporatist market-oriented LAP, see Singaporean Government, *Singapore: The Next Lap* (Singapore: Times Editions, 1991), 61.

177. The CEO of Canon Japan, for example, told his American audience in 1992 that a good company should be a part of the community and should not overlook the community's welfare for the sake of its own profits.

178. Author's interviews with union leaders in Hong Kong, 1995. Also see Li Zhuren (李卓人), "Tunji yiqe, yingzhang weilai" (United to fight in the future), in *CTU in Solidarity*, Hong Kong Confederation of Trade Unions, no. 12 (July 1994): 1-2.

179. In 1988, the Korean workers still had a fifty-two- to fifty-three-hour work-week (Korean Labor Institute, *Labor and Wages Statistics* [Seoul 1993]), whereas the Chinese had a forty-eight-hour workweek.

180. According to the decree of Premier Li Peng (李鹏), all Chinese employers were to start to adopt the forty-hour workweek on May 1, 1995. The *shiye danweis* (institutions) were to complete the adoption by May 1, 1996, while the *qiye danweis* (enterprises) could wait until May 1, 1997. In *Guowuyuan gongbao* (State Council bulletin) (Beijing), March 25, 1995. For the detailed implementation measures, see *Xinhua Daily Telegraph* (Beijing), March 26, 1995, 2.

181. The author found some Taiwanese investors already starting to complain about this "leap forward" policy for increasing their labor costs (field notes in Taipei and Guangdong, 1995).

182. Some speculated that this was a politically motivated decision to appease workers at a precarious time of political succession. Other suggested that by reducing the workweek, more than 1 million new jobs could be made available for the massive surplus labor (figures from the spokesmen of the Ministries of Labor and Personnel, in *Renmin Ribao* [Beijing], March 26, 1995, 3).

183. According to Tian Jiyun (田纪云), a top CCP leader, the PRC passed two hundred eighty laws and procedural laws, more than seven hundred regulations, and more than forty-two hundred local laws since 1979. In *Xinhua Daily Telegraph* (Fuzhou), January 12, 1996.

184. According to Xiao Yang (肖扬), the PRC Minister of Justice, there were only eighty-nine thousand professional lawyers and fifty-seven foreign legal offices in China by 1996. *Renmin Ribao-Overseas* (Beijing), January 15, 1996, 4. As a comparison, the United States (about one-fifth of China's population) had about 850,000 lawyers in 1995 (*Time* magazine, January 29, 1996, 43).

185. Wei Xue (韦旭), "Toushi gongguangyi 2" (Review public relations business II), in *Touzi Zhonggu* (Invest in China) (Taipei) (December 1995): 44.

186. As late as in 1994, Beijing apparently still felt the political and social sensitivity of the labor market. See State Planning Commission, "Peiyue he fazhan woguo laodongli shichang de duice yangjou" (A study on the policy for cultivating and developing the labor market in our nation), in *Gaige yu lilun* (Reform and theory) (Beijing), no. 7 (1994): 28-32, and no. 8 (1994): 39-43.

187. For an overview on the problem of regionalism in the PRC, see Brugger and Reglar 1994, 86-88.

Conclusion: China at the Institutional Crossroads

We have proposed and used labor allocation patterns (LAPs) as the indicators in our inquiry into the institutional continuities and changes in contemporary China. A brief review of LAPs in China's two-thousand-year history and a more in-depth examination of LAPs in contemporary China have brought us to the point of conclusion. In this final section, we summarize several findings about China's transforming institutional structure, as reflected by our study of China's LAPs.

Continuity of China's Institutional Structure

A traditional institutional structure has existed in China for centuries, reinforced by Confucian culture and by natural and self-imposed international isolation. For most of Chinese history, basically one dominant LAP, the family-based traditional LAP, has prevailed. From the landholding peasants (*zigengnongs*) in the Qin and Han dynasties (second century B.C. to second century A.D.) to the peasants in today's PRC, the family-based traditional LAP has allocated and governed the majority of the Chinese. As a result, a family-like societal institutional framework became *the* institution, upon which China's entire institutional structure has been built and maintained. Consequently, China acquired a remarkable institutional stability and cultural cohesion. Reproduction-centered social values and family-centered social institutions dominated people's political and economic behaviors. Great social harmony was achieved as long as the institutional structure could withstand the strains. However, the accumulated institutional strains, demonstrated by the decay and collapse of the family-based traditional LAP over time, led to periodic institutional explosions or implosions, but did not do much to generate new institutions. The repetition of dynastic cycles and the alternation of political unity versus division have made the history of China—the longest continuous civilization—colorful and dramatic but also paradoxically stale and dull.

Most of China's institutional structure and its internalized version, the Confucian culture, with a legalist core, were established some two thousand years ago. The basic values, institutions, means of ruling, and modes of production experienced very limited change over the next two millennium, during which time the brilliance and diligence of the Chinese people produced some of the world's best artifacts, scientific findings, workmanship, and literature.[1] These achievements, however, failed to alter the traditional institutional structure beyond often trivial and temporary repairs. The numerous rebellions, revolutions, and wars—some of them among the bloodiest in human history—were classic examples of human tragedy in the sense that they seldom changed much institutionally even though they were terribly destructive of property and lives. Over time, the stable Chinese institutional system was mythologized to become the fatalistic belief in the elusive "mandate of the heaven."[2]

The unparalleled stability and continuity of China's institutional structure was perpetuated with a heavy price. After its peak of performance in the mid-Tang dynasty (eighth century), it started a continuous decline caused primarily by a simple but powerful factor—population growth. New knowledge and innovations were discouraged. At least by the early thirteenth century when the North Song dynasty collapsed, as the institutional framework became increasingly rigid, centralized, and internationally isolated. The Chinese people experienced centuries of technological and economic stagnation, brutal imperial despotism covered and legitimized with the family institutions and values, declines in living standards, bloody wars and rebellions, as well as decay of ethics in general. Chinese politics were generally painted with sweet "family values" but carried out with ruthless violence and vicious plots. A legitimized separation of words from deeds and of titles from contents thus became an infamous but influential informal institution governing Chinese behavior.[3] This deep philosophical and ethical tradition led to pragmatism, but often also led to the destruction of legal systems and the rise of personal rule and the infamously crucial role of personal connections (*guanxi*) in daily life.

Society was negatively affected as well. After the thirteenth century, China economically degenerated into a poor, stagnant, and even malnourished nation. Nutritional intake declined chronically as per capita grain production declined after the Tang dynasty and rarely returned to that high level. As a result, the highest value of the family-centered institutional structure, to reproduce more people, was greatly compromised and twisted. Hence, tens of millions of people lost their lives at an accelerated pace in wars and famines; many needs of the majority were systematically suppressed, and many more desires were denied. Institutionally speaking, despite the horrifying sacrifices that China made, the nation was static for millennia; it is this stagnation that is considered to be the origin of China's backwardness.

The Institutional Mixture and Transition in Today's PRC

This study has identified and examined four coexisting patterns of labor allocation in the PRC in the 1980s-1990s. The basic information and characteristics of these four LAPs are summarized in table C.1 as a substantiated and expanded version of table I.1.

The coexistence of four major LAPs in today's PRC demonstrate that China's institutional configuration is a mixed and transitional one. The family-based traditional LAP is currently the largest but is experiencing a steady decline. The authoritarian state LAP is still the most important LAP politically and economically but is stagnant and under pressure to change. The community-based labor markets (CLMs) are growing very rapidly, with the likelihood of becoming the future dominant LAP in China, but represent a social or communal distortion of the labor market. Finally, a national labor market is emerging, but its maturation has yet to take place.

By the late 1990s, the four LAPs appeared to have carved up the Chinese labor force. This unique phenomenon determines much of Chinese politics, economic development, and social life. We see the powerful, still dominant presence of the CCP state in Chinese politics, economy, and social life as reflected in the still-dominant authoritarian state LAP. A revitalization of the local- or region-centered Chinese institutional framework is on the rise, as the rapid development of CLMs shows. The restored family-based traditional LAP reestablished much of the pre-modern institutional structure in the rural areas. The rapid emergence of the national labor market convincingly illustrates the increasing autonomy of China's economy

Table C.1. Labor Allocation Patterns in the PRC

	Authoritarian state LAP (ASLAP)	Family-based LAP (FLAP)	Community-based labor markets (CLMs)	National labor market (NLM)
Size (millions)	114 (1994)	480 (1993)	158 (1993)	85-89 (1995)
Rank	third	largest	second	smallest
Growth	slow	declining	rapid	very rapid
Institutional foundation	the state (polity)	family (social life)	community & market	the market (economy)
Historical origin	royal shops & *guanshang*	*zigengnong & diannong*	villages & CBEs	FDI & *getihou*
Birth date	mid-1950s	restored in late 1970s	mid-1950s, CLMs in 1980s	late 1980s
Age	four decades	centuries	two decades	one decade
Location	urban	rural	urban/rural	urban/rural
Industries	nonagri-culture	agriculture, handicrafts	nonagri-culture	nonagri-culture
Overlaps with	CLMs & NLM	CLMs & NLM	ASLAP, NLM & FBLAP	ASLAP, CLMs & FBLAP
Economic significance*	largest	third	second	smallest
Political status	highest	lowest	third	second
Social status	second	lowest	third	highest
Main implication	authoritarian "socialism"	Chinese pre-modernity	distorted & localized markets	autonomy of national economy
Prospect	diminishing transforming	reduced existence	new dominant LAP?	increased size & role

Notes: Due to overlapping, the total of the four LAPs may exceed the total of China's labor force, estimated by the Labor Ministry to be 825 million in 1994.[4]
* Measured in current shares of the Chinese gross domestic product.

from the sociopolitical complex. Statistically, the Chinese labor force and thus the whole population have acquired progressively higher mobility in the past two decades.[5] But compared to labor market–dominated nations such as the United States and even Japan (whose national labor market is known for distortions), the mobility of Chinese labor is still rather limited, precisely because of the existence of the major nonmarket LAPs.[6]

Each of the four LAPs has historical origins that can be traced back at least to the nineteenth century. The largest (family-based) and the second largest (the CLMs) are organized along family and community lines. Therefore, each has easily gained substantial institutional legitimacy because of their deep historical roots. A drastic differentiation of the Chinese economy from the sociopolitical complex is under way, as revealed by the rapid growth of the market-oriented LAP—a national labor market and the CLMs. Many laborers are now allocated and managed by the advancing market institution, signaling that the final stage of the marketization of China's economy has arrived.[7] But the strong presence of the nonmarket LAPs—the largest family-based LAP—and the dominant authoritarian state LAP, is powerfully resisting and distorting the emerging market institution and greatly complicating the process of Chinese modernization. The state, still resembling a giant patriarchal structure, has been leaving its imprint on the formation and development of the Chinese LAPs. However, some LAPs, especially those market-oriented ones, may have already reached the critical mass to grow out of the control of the CCP state.

The grand Chinese institutional changes could have several outcomes with varied implications for other nations. As analyzed in chapter 3, the dominant Chinese LAP in the near future appears to be the CLMs. If that becomes reality, would we see some regionalized Chinese politics and economies? Would a polity of federalism be possible? Or will China split? If the authoritarian state LAP continues its domination, the powerful central government of the CCP state may continue its traditional role in China's institutional system. The rapid changes of the LAPs thus offer a reliable yet convenient way to see the future of China.

Source of Changes

Other than the four forces responsible for shaping and reshaping the LAPs, as presented in the introduction, two findings of our study further demonstrate the source of changes of Chinese LAPs and the functionality of the continuities of China's institutional structure.

First, besides the importance of the preexisting institutions, we see the crucial role played by foreign influence in general and foreign direct investment (FDI) in particular. Because investors from Hong Kong, Taiwan, and other overseas Chinese communities have made up the overwhelming majority of FDI in China, the institutional changes in the PRC are likely to follow what happened in those Chinese "nations," as the market-oriented LAP practiced by FDI employers in the PRC exemplified (see chapter 4). Those "Chinese foreigners" have brought much of their "modern" but Sinicized institutions to China through their labor practice. Despite the fact that FDI employment is still treated by the CCP state as a temporary "concession," the impact of those foreign and modern but still essentially very "Chinese" institutions has been immense and lasting.

The "digested" market-oriented LAP from those overseas Chinese nations seems to fit into the Chinese climate better than those coming directly from the West. Hong Kong, which has over 60 percent of total FDI in China, legally became part of China in 1997. Will the Hong Kong FDI still be treated with temporary or expedient measures as that of other foreign investors? Or will the Hong Kong style of the market institution become a permanent part of the changing Chinese institutional structure? Either way, the market institution is likely to be much more important in the PRC. Conceivably, if the Chinese can successfully complete their economic development program, the PRC may just have an institutional system like that of today's Korea, Singapore, or Taiwan and perhaps yesterday's Japan.[8] What would that imply for the rest of the world? The active role of an authoritarian but nonetheless effective state in encouraging, protecting, and "utilizing" FDI has been a key to the development of the market in general and a national labor market in particular in the PRC. This is in strong contrast to economic reform in another heavily populated old nation—India.[9] Unlike the Indian case, there were very few open attacks on FDI initially, and after nearly two decades the benefits of FDI have earned it a deep institutional legitimacy in China.

Second, a few uniquely Chinese institutions, primarily the household or residential registration (*hukou*) system, continued in the PRC in the reform years and have apparently functioned to smooth out and even facilitate the changes represented by the emergence of the market economy. The most important impact of those institutions has been their effective provision of special controlling mechanisms for the segmentation of the Chinese population by temporarily excluding or shielding many from the new but often painful institutional changes. As part of the preexisting institutions, the *hukou* system, the unit (*danwei*) institution, and the dossier (*dangan*) mechanisms have all played important roles in the institutional changes concerning labor allocation currently unfolding in the PRC. Even by the late 1990s, when a national labor market has emerged and the CLMs are growing rapidly, those institutions still effectively separate the massive rural labor force from the urban economy and limit the internal migration of people.[10] Furthermore, they are still important tools by which the state and all other types of employers in general can exercise ultra-economic controls over the workers and the population at large. These Chinese institutions have significantly smoothed the advancement of the market institution through their powerful functions of social control and exclusion, even though they created significant social injustice and regional differentiation among the Chinese.

The CCP, relying especially on the *hukou* system, managed to control social mobility or dislocation caused by the advancing market economy, and contain much of the "negatives" of the market into separate, thus easily manageable, areas. The political stability of the CCP regime, compared to many other communist regimes in reform, may be due largely to the function of this uniquely Chinese *hukou* system. Similar systems in places like Taiwan and even Japan provided similar functions in their history.[11] Indeed, social/political distortion of the emerging and imported market institutions has been a leading feature of the institutional changes in the PRC. The profound but perhaps ethically questionable issue of exclusion or discrimination in a nation's modernization process may actually have been instrumental to these changes.

Although the role of the *hukou, danwei,* and *dangan* may be declining (perhaps an indicator of the pace of the institutional changes), they will need to be in place for some time simply because the more than 200 million surplus laborers in China still must be institutionally stabilized and even excluded in order for a viable market economy to be established. This finding is likely to have wide application in other heavily populated developing nations. Naive calls from some Chinese economists or radical demands from "democracy fighters" to amend or even eliminate the *hukou* in the near future imply a great peril to Chinese modernization.[12] A minority of scholars, however, has argued bluntly for a "strengthening" of the social control role of the *hukou* system while "trimming" its resource reallocation functions (Chen 1995, 140).

Recent changes in the *hukou* system may enable it to continue its function in a Chinese-style market economy.[13] The most important developments have been the adoption of two special types of residential registration to make the *hukou* system more accommodating to the rising needs of the Chinese labor market—to allow increased labor mobility while maintaining the state's social and political control of the people. The first type of residential registration is the so-called temporary residential permit (*zanjuzheng*). The other is the so-called blue-stamp *hukou,* or blue card. Those transitional and quasi-*hukou* systems have been adopted by most Chinese cities, mainly in the economically most prosperous urban metropolises like Beijing, Shanghai, and Shenzhen.[14] Other reform ideas have been debated but have yet to be tried on a large scale.[15]

These two special types of legal residence require the holder to be a cadre or talent (professional), pay a one-time and then an annual registration fee, have valid local jobs, and be reviewed annually. The difference is that the blue card (or stamp) *hukou* requires the sponsoring employer to be a major enterprise (in Shenzhen, the government set one blue *hukou* sponsorship per 1 million rmb investment or 100,000 rmb annual tax payment). If not a cadre or talent with a college degree or more, one must first be employed with a *zanjuzheng* for three years before becoming eligible to apply for a blue *hukou.* The blue *hukou* functions more like the regular *hukou,* and its holders are allowed to enjoy basically all the community-based benefits and rights except participating in the local college entrance exam and community-based local labor reallocation. They can have the same local wages, resident tuition for elementary and middle schools, and political rights, and most important, the chance to get a regular *hukou* in two to five years. They can also, like local residents, rent or purchase apartments and own private businesses. But they must pay a high annual fee, which was set at 2,000 rmb in Shenzhen in 1995-1996.[16] Once they are ready to apply for a regular local *hukou*, they have to pay a substantial "urban enlargement fee," or "urban construction fee," which was set in Shanghai in the late 1990s at 20,000-100,000 rmb—roughly four to ten years' average wages.[17] Those two temporary *hukou* cards, however, only covered the nonstate-planned migrating urban population and left the larger number of floating peasants out until the mid-1990s. In the summer of 1995, to cope with the estimated 80 million floating peasants who were causing tremendous social and political problems, the PRC Public Security Ministry expanded the *zanjuzheng* system to cover all nonurban *hukou* holders.[18] Since then, anyone who works outside his or her hometown for longer than one month must register for a *zanjuzheng*. Any job applicant must have a personal identification card *and* a local *hukou* card or blue *hukou* card or *zanjuzheng*. Employers and employees would be punished if nonlocal residents were found working without a *zanjuzheng*. Whether the PRC state will be able to implement this reformed *hukou* effectively seems to be a profound test of its ability to continue its leadership in the Chinese institutional transformation.

The Dragon Enters the Nets

Our study of Chinese institutional continuities and changes by examining LAPs has confirmed the belief that China has gone through so much change that it is now departing from its long and glorious historical position as the stable but stagnant "center" of the world. As the current Chinese LAPs and their changes demonstrate, despite all odds, China appears to have irreversibly entered a double net on its way to modernity: domestically, the dragon of the Chinese state has entered the net of the market economy. Externally, the dragon of China has entered the net of the existing nation-state system based on international political anarchy and the international market economy.

In primarily the past two decades, the family-like Chinese state, as the center of the traditional institutional structure, has entered the net of a differentiating institutional structure featuring a rapidly advancing market institution. The decline of the authoritarian state LAP and its associated institutions like the *hukou* illustrate the autonomy of the economy, and even social institutions have been on the rise. This is an unprecedented development in China's long history, and the Chinese state—finding the net often uncomfortable and "degenerating"—naturally kicks and screams all the way. Our analysis of the PRC LAPs, however, unmistakably points to the conclusion that the Chinese state is losing its traditional ability to be an almighty dragon versus other Chinese institutions such as the market, family, and social groups. The state itself, as already shown by changes in the authoritarian state LAP, has become more susceptible to economic and social forces. Widespread corruption and crimes,[19] and the continued and even increased importance of *guanxi,*[20] vividly illustrate the much-reduced status of the Chinese state.

As the already disproportionate presence and effect of the foreign influence continue to grow rapidly, China has gingerly but irreversibly entered the net of the international market and international politics. The great institutional transformation, reflected by the emergence and development of market-oriented LAPs in the PRC, demonstrates the crucial and lasting role of foreign influence, especially FDI. The unsocialist and even un-Chinese labor market has now gained deep legitimacy, even among the CCP leaders. By making profound institutional changes to have market-oriented LAPs and thus a market-oriented economy, the Chinese appear to have wholeheartedly embraced the international market as the norm for their economic activities. After about one hundred years, they have finally and legitimately accepted the traditional institutional structure as just one form of a national institutional structure, not a way of life for everyone on earth. Other than the traditional leading but diminishing role of the state, international competition and the domestic market appear to be the two new major driving forces for the continuation of the Chinese institutional changes.

Notes

1. For a conceptual reconstruction of Chinese political thought that was basically formed in the Qin and Han dynasties, see Ames 1994.

2. The power of belief in this notion in Chinese politics was discussed by some as recently as the early 1990s. See, for example, Liu 1990 and Fang 1991.

3. The separation of *"ming"* (名, statement, name, title or words) from *"shi"* (实, reality, deeds, facts, or contents) has been a foundation of Chinese pragmatism since the Warring States era (fifth to third centuries B.C.). The CCP, especially under Mao, utilized this tradition to its greatest advantage. Famous examples include the inventions of terms such as "people's democratic dictatorship" and "workers are the masters and the CCP officials are the servants."

4. Labor Ministry's 1994 Annual Report, cited in *Renmin Ribao* (Beijing), May 11, 1995, 1. In the introduction of this book, we calculated this figure in 1993, based on official figures from the SSB, to be 705.49 million. This unusually big one-year increase of the Chinese labor force is perhaps another example of the problematic accuracy of Chinese official statistics.

5. In the 1950s-1970s, domestic migration was controlled tightly by the PRC central government. Starting in the 1980s, people began to move at an accelerated pace outside the administrative reallocation. From the early 1980s to the early 1990s, internal migration increased 290 percent. In five major cities, migration grew 114 percent in just four years in the late 1980s. See Cheng Xi, "Woguo renkou chianyi

fengxi" (An analysis of migration in our country), in *Tongji yangjou* (Statistical studies) (Beijing), no. 6 (1994): 56-60.

6. One Chinese study estimated that the mobility rate of Chinese urban laborers in 1992 was only 2.7 percent, while the same rate for the American manufacturing industry was already 12 to 36 percent in the early 1980s; for the Japanese labor force the rate was 13 percent in 1985. See Wang Aiwen, "Woguo laodongli shichang fayue pingu" (An estimate on the development of labor market in our country), in *Zhongguo laodong kexue* (Chinese labor science) (Beijing), no. 6 (1994).

7. On the one hand, a labor market usually is the last part of a national market economy to be established. On the other hand, by the mid-1990s, the commodity, real estate, information, and even the financial markets were being developed to be the dominant ways of allocating and utilizing those economic resources in the PRC. For a description of the current development of those markets in China, see Hu 1993, 475-637, 653-714.

8. As an "industrialized" nation, as so termed by the OECD (Organization for Eco-nomic Cooperation and Development), Singapore remained to have much of the tight social and information control measures Beijing has been working hard to enforce in China. For example, the Singaporean control of cable and satellite TV and "porno-graphic materials" was very similar to that seen in China. But unlike the much more traditional regime in Beijing, the pragmatic Singaporean government did recognize the "need" for maintaining a government-inspected legal "red-light zone" (author's fields notes in Singapore, 1995).

9. For a report on the difficulties caused by the various nationalist groups who used Indian "democratic processes" to oppose FDI in that nation, see "India's Eco-nomic Nationalists," in *Economist* (London), August 12, 1995, 27-28. The Chinese press also noticed such an "Indian resistance to opening." See the three articles in the full-page *"Haiwai liaowang"* (Overseas observation) column of the *Wenhui Bao* (Wenhui daily) (Shanghai), August 16, 1995, 9.

10. A "reportage" published in 1995 vividly demonstrated the effectiveness of the *hukou* institution in social and especially migration control. It described how a rural *hukou* policy branch in Hunan Province "worried" about and investigated a newly arrived Buddhist monk who joined a local temple but had a problematic *hukou* identification. See Cao Jiangping, ed., *Zhongda anjian zhenpou jishi (B)* (Reports on the resolution of major cases, Vol. B.) (Xining: Qinghai Renmin Press, 1995), 43-51.

11. Chapter 4 had a brief mention of the *hukou* system in Taiwan. In other East Asian nations, noticeably pre–World War II Japan, similar systems functioned at times to fulfill much-needed social control roles.

12. For example, some Beijing-based economists argue that the *hukou* system needs to be phased out through "reform" to increase labor mobility. See Ma et al. 1994, 312. For radical criticisms on the *hukou* system, see *China Focus*, a Princeton-based periodical edited by Liu Binyan. Other Chinese scholars, like the chairman of the Economic Department at Shenzhen University, however, criticize such views and believe that the *hukou* system needs to be strengthened in places like the prosperous Shenzhen SEZ to control labor mobility. See Zhang Mingru, "Yangge kongzhi renkou de zhengzhang" (Tightly control population growth), in Liu 1991, 349-353.

13. For some representative discussions on the reform and continuation of the *hukou* system, see Chen Hongbing et al., "Lun shichang jingji tizhixiade hujizhidu

gaige" (On the reform of the *hukou* system under a market economic institution), in *Jingji jingwei* (Economic fabrics) (Zhengzhou), no. 1 (1995): 78-81.

14. For the Shenzhen "blue-stamp *hukou*," see *Zhongguo qingnianbao* (Chinese youth daily) (Beijing), March 16, 1995, 1.

15. For example, a repeated idea on reforming *hukou* has been to open *hukou* control on the levels below counties, i.e., to have free migration in the townships and county-seat cities. See State Planning Commission, "Peiyue he fazhan woguo laodongli shichang de duice yangjou" (A study on the policy for cultivating and developing the labor market in our nation), in *Gaige yu lilun* (Reform and theory) (Beijing), no. 8 (1994): 39-43.

16. See *Shenzhen renshi* (Shenzhen personnel), an internal monthly by the Shenzhen Personnel Bureau (Shenzhen), no. 11-12 (1994): 3, and no. 6 (1995): 22-24.

17. See Shanghai municipal government, "Shanghais nanying hukou guangli zhanxin guiding" (Provisional regulations on the management of the blue *hukou* in Shanghai), 21 articles, Shanghai government's public notice, February 1, 1994. In Wuxi, a prosperous metropolis in southern Jiangsu Province, this fee was 16,000 rmb in 1994 while in the suburban Xishan city of Wuxi, the same fee was 3,000 rmb in 1995 (author's interviews in Sunan, August 1995).

18. "Gonganbu bangbu zanjuzheng shengning bangfa" (The public security ministry issued rules on applying for a temporary residential permit), in *Guangmin Ribao* (Guangmin daily) (Beijing), August 3, 1995, 4.

19. The rise of crime in China has been clear and steady. The government indirectly admitted that there was a 19.75 percent increase of criminal cases in 1994 over 1993 (*Renmin Ribao-Overseas*, March 17, 1995, 1). Yet a widespread sharp sense of insecurity and a justified "overreaction" by people who were used to security under the tight political control worsened people's faith in the authority of the state.

20. The statistical bureau in Shandong Province in 1994 surveyed two thousand urban households in twenty-five cities/counties and concluded that the fees for human feelings, i.e., for connections (mainly gifts) on average rose fourteenfold in thirteen years to be 5.6 percent (2.4 percent in 1981) of total household expenditures in *Xinan wanbao* (Xinan evening news) (Hefei), June 15, 1995, 6.

Appendixes

1. Landmarks of Labor Allocation in the PRC

1949	The PRC was created by the CCP.
1949-1951	Land reform restored the family-based traditional LAP.
1955-1957	The establishment of the authoritarian state LAP in the cities and collectivization replaced the family-based LAP in the countryside.
mid-1950s	The urban societal LAP began to develop in the "collective enterprises."
1958-1961	The Great Leap Forward.
early 1960s	The rural societal LAP began to emerge in the "commune-brigade enterprises" (CBEs).
1966-1976	The Great Cultural Revolution.
1978	The Third Plenary Meeting of the Eleventh CCP Central Committee. Reform and opening began.
late 1970s	Decollectivization restored the family-based traditional LAP.
early 1980s	Private economy began to develop beyond the scope of the family—the getihous began to hire workers. The township-village enterprises (TVEs) began to replace the CBEs to develop the community-based labor markets (CLMs).
1980	The State Council proclaimed its Regulations on Labor and Wages Management in the Sino-Foreign Joint-Venture Enterprises. The market-oriented LAP was "imported."

1984	Reform of the state-owned economy started in the urban areas.
1986	Labor reform started in the state-owned enterprises; certain market mechanisms were used to improve the authoritarian state LAP.
1988	A national labor market was legally formed with the facilitation of foreign direct investors.
1989	The "June 4th Incident."
1992	Deng Xiaoping's "Southern Inspection" started a new wave of reform and opening. A national labor market became operational.
1993	A constitutional amendment about "the state practices a socialist market economy" was adopted.
1994	Shanghai and other cities began to use a "blue *hukou*" system.
1995	The PRC Labor Law took effect. The state started to allow a substantial portion of college graduates to look for jobs on the labor markets.
1996-97	The completion of all the basic laws for a socialist market economy, including a national labor insurance system, took place. All state-owned enterprises are to adopt the 100 percent "contract" employment system.
1997-98	A new effort by the CCP, under the leadership of Jiang Zemin and Zhu Rongji, aiming at "solving" the financial problems of the state-owned enterprises, are to produce massive urban unemployed (*xiagang*) workers.

2. Locational Profile of Individuals Interviewed

This book has benefited from data collected through interviews with a few hundred individuals and visits to many *danwei*s (units) and places during my five field trips to China in 1992, 1993, 1995, and 1996. The selection of individuals and *danwei*s was by no means completely random, thus no effort to draw generalized statistical conclusions from those interviews solely was attempted. Rather, the information from these sources has largely been used as illustrative and confirming anecdotes. We acquired important background information, crucial leads, and a vital "feel" through those interviews and field visits.

In addition to the sources indicated in the preceding chapters, we report here very briefly the jobs and locational characteristics of people interviewed. A small number of them were interviewed by phone or correspondence.

Anhui Province (Anqin, Feixi, Hefei, Hanshan, Wuhu, Yuexi)

A mayor and party secretaries, senior CCP and government officials, cadres and clerks; journalists; scholars; professors; policemen.

Senior managers and cadres of state-owned enterprises and collective enterprises; village cadres and TVE (township and village enterprises) managers; private employers and managers of foreign-invested enterprises.

Employees in state-owned enterprises, institutions, and the military; workers in collective enterprises, including labor service enterprises; joint venture employees; *getihu*s (individual households); college and graduate students; unemployed; retired; villagers; and *manglius* (floating people).

Beijing

Senior CCP and government officials, cadres and clerks; journalists; scholars; professors; policemen.

Senior managers and cadres of state-owned enterprises and collective enterprises; managers of foreign-invested enterprises; foreign investors and businessmen.

Employees in state-owned enterprises, institutions, and the military; workers in collective enterprises, including labor service enterprises; employees of foreign-invested enterprises; *getihu*s; college and graduate students; retired; unemployed; *manglius*.

Chongqing

Government officials, cadres and clerks; state employees; villagers; *manglius*.

Guangdong Province (Baoan, Dongguan, Guangzhou, Shenzhen)

Senior CCP and government officials, cadres and clerks; cadres representing other provinces; scholars; policemen.

Managers and cadres of state-owned enterprises and collective enterprises; private employers and managers of foreign-invested enterprises; foreign investors and businessmen.

Employees in state-owned enterprises, institutions, and the military; workers in collective enterprises, including labor service enterprises; employees of foreign-invested enterprises; *getihus* and multimillionaires; college and graduate students; unemployed; *manglius*.

Guangxi (Guiling)

A journalist; *manglius*.

Guizhou Province (Guiyang)

A journalist; cadres of state-owned enterprises; a worker in a labor service enterprise; *manglius*.

Hebei Province (Zhuozhou)

A military officer.

Heinongjiang Province (Jiamusi)

A multimillionaire private employer, his family and three employees.

Hubei Province (Shiyan, Wuhan)

Managers and cadres of state-owned enterprises; college and graduate students; *manglius*.

Hunan Province (Zhuzhou)

Cadres of state-owned enterprises; an employee in a state-owned enterprise; college and graduate students; *manglius*.

Inner Mongolia (Baotou)

A cadre and an employee of a state-owned enterprise.

Jiangsu Province (Nanjing, Changzhou, Wujiang, Wuxi)

Mayors and party secretaries, government officials, cadres and clerks; a journalist; senior managers and cadres of state-owned enterprises and collective enterprises; village cadres and TVE managers; private employers and managers of foreign-invested enterprises.

Employees in state-owned enterprises, institutions, and the military; workers in collective enterprises, including labor service enterprises; joint venture employees; *getihu*s and millionaires; college and graduate students; unemployed; villagers; *manglius*.

Liaoning Province (Dalian)
A cadre of a state-owned institution.

Shanghai Municipality
Senior government officials and advisors, cadres and clerks; journalists; scholars; professors; policemen.

Senior managers and cadres of state-owned enterprises and collective enterprises; private employers and managers of foreign-invested enterprises; foreign investors and businessmen.

Employees in state-owned enterprises, institutions, and the military; workers in collective enterprises, including labor service enterprises; employees of foreign-invested enterprises; *getihu*s; college and graduate students; unemployed; *manglius*.

Sichuan Province (Chendu)
Government officials, cadres and clerks; senior managers and cadres of state-owned enterprises; employees in state-owned institutions; villagers; *manglius*.

Xinjiang (Urumiqi, Yili)
A senior government official; employees in state-owned institutions.

Zhejiang Province (Deqin, Shaoxin)
A journalist; village cadres and TVE managers; an employee in a state-owned enterprise; a joint venture employee.

Hong Kong
Senior government officials, advisors, legislators; journalists; scholars; professors.

Managers of PRC state-owned enterprises and institutions.

Foreign investors and businessmen; independent union leaders; foreign workers.

Employees of foreign-invested enterprises; private business owners.

Taiwan (Taipei, Taichun)

Senior GMD and government officials, advisors, cadres and clerks; journalists; professors; scholars.

Senior managers and cadres of state-owned and private enterprises; union leaders; labor training officials.

State and private employees; employees of foreign-invested enterprises; college and graduate students; businessmen; foreign workers; farmers.

Bibliography

Ames, Roger T. *The Art of Rulership: A Study of Ancient Chinese Political Thought.* Albany, N.Y.: SUNY Press, 1994.

Arrow, Kenneth J.: "The Division of Labor in the Economy, the Polity, and Society" in O'Driscoll Jr., Gerald ed.: *Adam Smith and Modern Political Economy.* Ames, Iowa: The Iowa State University Press. 1979.

Bachman, David. *Bureaucracy, Economy, and Leadership in China.* New York: Cambridge University Press, 1991.

Barnett, Robert W. *Wandering Knights: China Legacies, Lived and Recalled.* Armonk, N.Y.: M. E. Sharpe, 1990.

Bauzon, Kenneth, ed. *Development and Democratization in the Third World.* Bristol, Pa.: Crane Russak, 1992.

Becker, Gary Stanley. *The Economic Approach To Human Behavior.* Chicago: University of Chicago Press, 1976.

————. *A Treatise on the Family.* Cambridge, Mass.: Harvard University Press, 1981.

Beijing Municipal Economic Commission. *Waishang touzi gongye qiye jingying guanli chutan* (An initial exploration on the management experiences of the FDI industrial enterprises). Beijing, 1990.

————. *Waishang touzi gongye qiye jingying guanli chutanzhier* (An initial exploration on the management experiences of the FDI industrial enterprises-II). Beijing, 1992.

Beijing Foreign Investment Service Centre, ed. *Collection of Laws and Regulations for Foreign Investment in China.* 1988, 1989, 1990.

————. *A Directory of Organizations Associated with Foreign Economic and Trade Affairs in Beijing.* 1989.

Beijing Jeep Company. A Provisional Regulation on the Labor Contract System. 1988.

Berliner, Joseph. *Factory and Manager in the U.S.S.R..* Cambridge, Mass.: Harvard University Press, 1957.

Bhalla, A. S. *Economic Transition in Hunan and Southern China.* New York: St. Martin's Press, 1984.

Bian, Yanjie. *Work and Inequality in Urban China.* Albany: N.Y.: SUNY Press, 1994.

Bianco, Lucien. *The Origins of the Chinese Revolution,* Stanford, Calif.: Stanford University Press, 1967, 1971.

BIAP (Business International Asia/Pacific Ltd.). *Asias Labor Market Tapping the Regions Greatest Resource.* Hong Kong: BIAP, 1979.

Biersteker, Thomas. *Distortion or Development? Contending Perspectives on the Multinational Corporations.* Cambridge, Mass.: MIT, 1978.

Booth, Anne, and R. M. Sundrum. *Labor Absorption in Agriculture.* Delhi, India: Oxford University Press, 1984.

Botwinick, Howard. *Persistent Inequalities: Wage Disparity under Capitalist Competition.* Princeton, N.J.: Princeton University Press, 1993.

Breuilly, John. *Nationalism and the State.* Chicago: University of Chicago Press, 1982.

Brugger, Bill, and David Kelly. *Chinese Marxism in the Post-Mao Era.* Stanford, Calif.: Stanford University Press, 1990.

Brugger, Bill, and Stephen Reglar. *Politics, Economy, and Society in Contemporary China.* Stanford, Calif.: Stanford University Press, 1994.

Brunner, Karl, and Allan H. Meltzer, eds. *Stabilization Policies and Labor Markets.* Amsterdam: North-Holland, 1988.

Burton, Charles. *Political and Social Change in China Since 1978.* Westport, Conn.: Greenwood Press, 1990.

Byrd, William A., and Lin Quinsong. *China's Rural Industry: Structure, Development, and Reform.* New York: Oxford University Press, 1990.

Cai, Shenglin (蔡胜林) et al. *Zhongguo xiangzhen qiye nianjian 1994* (The yearbook of Chinese township and village enterprises, 1994). Beijing: Zhongguo Nongye Press, 1994.

Cambell, Nigel. *A Strategic Guide to Equity Joint Venture in China.* New York: Pergamon Press, 1989.

Cao, Rongxin (曹荣新) et al. *Shenzhen rencai shichang* (Shenzhen professionals market). Shenzhen: Haitian Press, 1993.

Cardoso, F. H., and Enzo Faletto. *Dependency and Development in Latin America.* Berkeley: University of California Press, 1979.

Casati, Christine. Satisfying Labor Laws and Needs. *China Business Review* (July-August 1991): 16-22.

Chan, Anita et al. *Chen Village, Under Mao and Deng,* Berkeley: University of California Press, 1992.

Chen, Edward K.Y. *Multinational Corporations, Technology and Employment.* New York: St. Martin's Press, 1983.

Chen, Ji (陈骥). *Zhongguo gonghui 15 nian* (Fifteen years of the Chinese trade union) Beijing: Gongren Press, 1993.

Chen, Jiaji (陈家骥) et al. *Enterprise Management Style in China.* Beijing: Chinese Economy Press, 1988.

Chen, Junjie (陈俊杰). Jiazhu chuantong yu nongcun qiye de jiazhuhua (Family tradition and the familization of the rural enterprises). *Shehuixue yu shehui diaocha* (Sociology and social investigation) (Beijing) no. 2 (1994): 57-59.

Chen, Kongming, and Hu Henian, eds. *Utilizing Foreign Capital in Practice.* Beijing: Chinese Peoples University Press, 1986.

Chen, Naixing, and Yang Yuexing. *Personnel Management in Modern Industrial Enterprises.* Beijing: Economic Management Press, 1988.

Chen, Tianren (陈天任). *Qiye laodong zhidu gaige yu shijian* (The reform and practice of the enterprise labor system). Beijing: Wenjin Press, 1992.

Chen, Yingying (陈婴婴). *Zhiye jiegou yu liudong* (Structure and mobility of the professions). Beijing: Renshi Press, 1995.

China News Digest (CND). *Huaxia wenzhe* (China news digest), an Internet Weekly established in June 1991. Web site: http://www.cnd.org or ftp: cnd.org/pub/hxwz.

(CNDC) Chinese News Development Corporation, ed. *Zhongguo zhengfu jiegou* (The structure of the Chinese government). 2 vols. Beijing: Xinghua Press, 1989.

Cho, Soon. *The Dynamics of Korean Economic Development.* Washington, D.C.: Institute for International Economics, 1994.

Clark, Hugh. *Community, Trade, and Networks: Southern Fujian Province from the Third to the Thirteenth Century.* New York: Cambridge University Press, 1991.

Cole, Robert E. *Work, Mobility, and Participation: A Comparative Study of American and Japanese Industry.* Berkeley: University of California Press, 1979.

———. *Japanese Blue Collar: The Changing Tradition.* Berkeley: University of California Press, 1971.

Coleman, Kenneth E., and Daniel N. Nelson. *State Capitalism, State Socialism and the Politicization of Workers.* The Carl Beck Papers, University of Pittsburgh, 1984.

Cook, Linda. *The Soviet Social Contract and Why It Failed: Welfare Policy and Workers Politics from Brezhnev to Yeltsin.* Cambridge, Mass.: Harvard University Press, 1993.

Cox, Robert W. *Production, Power, and World Order.* New York: Columbia University Press, 1987.

Cui, Zhiyuan (崔之元). Market Incompleteness, Innovation, and Reform. *Politics and Society* (March 1991).

———. *Di erci shixian jiefang yu zhidu chuanxin* (Second liberation of thinking and institutional innovation). Hong Kong: Oxford University Press, 1995.

Davidson, Laurie, and Laura K. Gordon. *The Sociology of Gender*, Chicago: Rand McNally College Publishing, 1979.

Davis, Deborah, and Steven Harrell. *Chinese Families in the Post-Mao Era.* Berkeley: University of California Press, 1993.

De Bary, William Theodore et al. *Sources of Chinese Tradition.* 2 vols. New York: Columbia University Press, 1960.

De Neubourg, Chris: *Unemployment, Labor Slack and Labor Market Accounting: Theory, Evidence and Policy*. Amsterdam: North-Holland, 1988.

Deng, Xiaoping (邓小平). *Deng Xiaoping wenxun* (Selected works of Deng Xiaoping). Vols. 1 and 2. Beijing: Renmin Press, 1985, 1992.

Deng Yunte (邓云特). *Zhongguo jouhuang shi* (Chinese history of famine relief), Shanghai: Shanghai Books, (1937) 1984.

Deyo, F., ed. *The Political Economy of the New Asian Industrialism*. Ithaca, N.Y.: Cornell University Press, 1987.

Dittmer, Lowell, *China Under Reform: A Preliminary Reassessment*. Boulder, Colo.: Westview Press, 1993A.

————. & Samuel Kim eds. *China's Quest for a National Identity*. Ithaca, N.Y.: Cornell University Press, 1993B.

Domenach, Jean-Luc. *The Origins of the Great Leap Forward: The Case of One Chinese Province*. Boulder, Colo.: Westview, 1995.

Duara, Prasenjit. *Culture, Power and the State: Rural Society in North China, 1900-1942*. Stanford, Calif.: Stanford University Press, 1988.

Dunning, John. *International Production and the Multinational Enterprises*, London: Allan and Unwin, 1981.

————. et al. *Economic Analysis and the Multinational Enterprise*. London: Blackwell, 1974.

Ebrey, Patricia Buckley, and James L. Watson, eds. *Kinship Organization in Late Imperial China, 1000-1940*. Berkeley: University of California Press, 1986.

Eckstein, Alexander. *Communist Chinas Economic Growth and Foreign Trade*. New York: McGraw-Hill, 1966.

Emerson, John Philip. *Administrative and Technical Manpower in the Peoples Republic of China*. International Populations Reports Series P-95, No. 72. U.S. Department of Commerce, 1973.

Epner, Paul. Managing Chinese Employees. *China Business Review* (July-August 1991).

Epstein, Edward C., ed. *Labor Autonomy and the State in Latin America*. Boston: Unwin Hyman, 1989.

Esherick, Joseph W., and Mary B. Rankin, eds. *Chinese Local Elites and Patterns of Dominance*. Berkeley: University of California Press, 1990.

Evans, Peter. *Dependent Development, the Alliance of Multinational, State and Local Capital in Brazil*. Princeton, N.J.: Princeton University Press, 1979.

Fairbank, John K., and Kwang-Ching Liu, eds. *The Cambridge History of China, Vol. 10, Late Ching 1800-1911, Part I*. New York: Cambridge University Press, 1978.

————. *The Cambridge History of China, Vol. 11, Late Ching 1800-1911, Part II*. New York, Cambridge University Press, 1980.

Fan, Gang (樊纲). *Gongyouzhi hongguan jingji lilun dagang* (A theoretical outline for the macroeconomics of the public-owned economy). Shanghai: Shanghai Press, 1990.

Fan, Wenlan (范文澜). *Zhongguo tongshi jianbian* (Brief history of China). Beijing: Renmin Press. Vols. 1 and 2 1957, Vol. 3 1965, and the rest 1978.

Fang, Lizhi. *Bringing Down the Great Wall.* New York: Random House, 1991.

Fei, Xiaotong (费孝通). *Xiao chengzhen siji* (Four records of small towns). Beijing: Xinhua Press, 1985.

Feinerman, James V. *The Rule of Law Imposed from Outside: Chinas Foreign-Oriented Economic and Legal Reforms.* A paper presented to the Forty-third annual meeting of the AAS, New Orleans La., 1990.

Fewsmith, Joseph. Special Economic Zones in the PRC. *Problems of Communism* (November-December 1986).

Fong, Pang Eng, ed. *Labor Market Developments and Structural Change: The Experience of ASEAN and Australia.* Singapore: Singapore University Press, 1988.

Forbath, William. *Law and the Shaping of the American Labor Movement.* Cambridge, Mass.: Harvard University Press, 1991.

Frank, Isaiah. *Foreign Enterprise in Developing Countries.* Baltimore: Johns Hopkins University Press, 1980.

Freeman, John. R. *Democracy and Markets: The Politics of Mixed Economies.* Ithaca, N.Y.: Cornell University Press, 1992.

Friedman, David. *The Misunderstood Miracle: Industrial Development and Political Change in Japan.* Ithaca, N.Y.: Cornell University Press, 1990.

Friedman, Edward et al. *Chinese Village, Socialist State.* New Haven, Conn.: Yale University Press, 1991.

Fu, Yunlong (傅云龙) et al. *Shehui zhuyi shichang jingji yu chuantong wenhua* (Socialist market economy and traditional culture). Beijing: Central CCP School Press, 1995.

Gai, Jun (盖军). *Zhongguo gongren yundong shi jiaocai, 1919-1949* (Textbook on the Chinese labor movement, 1919-1949). Shanghai: Huadong Shida Press, 1988.

Gao, Kelin (高克林). *Explaining Planned Commodity Economy.* Huhhot, China: Inner-Mongolia People's Press, 1985.

Gao, Shangquan (高尚全) et al. *1993 zhongguo jingji tizhi gaige nianjian* (Yearbook of economic reform in China, 1993). Beijing: Gaige Press, 1993.

Gates, Hill. *Chinas Motor: A Thousand Years of Petty Capitalism.* Ithaca, N.Y.: Cornell University Press, 1996.

Ge, Xiangxian (葛象贤), and Qu Weiying. *Zhonghuo mingong chao* (The tides of Chinese peasant labor). Beijing: Zhongguo Guoji Guangbo Press, 1990.

Gerschenkron, Alexander. *Economic Backwardness in Historical Perspectives.* Cambridge, Mass: Harvard University Press, 1964.

Gilpin, Robert. *The Political Economy of International Relations.* Princeton, N.J.: Princeton University Press, 1987.

Gold, Thomas B. *State and Society in Taiwan Miracle.* Armonk, N.Y.: M. E. Sharpe, 1986.

———. After Comradeship: Personal Relations in China Since the Cultural Revolution. *The China Quarterly* (December 1985).

Goldstein, Avery. *From Band-Wagon to Balance of Power.* Stanford, Calif.: Stanford University Press, 1990.

Gordon, Andrew. *The Evolution of Labor Relations in Japan, 1853-1955.* Cambridge, Mass.: Harvard University Press, 1985.

———. *Labor and Imperial Democracy in Prewar Japan.* Berkeley: University of California Press, 1991.

Gourevitch, Peter A. *Politics in Hard Times Comparative Responses to International Economic Crises.* Ithaca, N.Y.: Cornell University Press, 1988.

Greenfield, Liah. *Nationalism: Five Roads to Modernity.* Cambridge, Mass.: Harvard University Press, 1992.

Griffin, Keith. *Institutional Reform and Economic Development in the Chinese Countryside.* Armonk, N.Y.: M. E. Sharpe, 1984.

Grove, Linda, and Christian Daniels, eds. *State and Society in China Japanese Perspective on Ming-Qing Social and Economic History.* Tokyo: University of Tokyo Press, 1984.

Guangzhou Labor Bureau. *Laodong zhengce fagui huibian* (Collection of labor laws and regulations). Guangzhou, 1991.

Guo, Moruo (郭沫若) et al. *Zhongguo nuli zhi yu fengjianzhi fenqi wenti nengwen xuanji* (Collections of the timing of slavery and feudal systems in China). Beijing: Sanlian Press, 1956.

Gupta, Kanhaya L. *Industrialization and Employment in Developing Countries: A Comparative Study.* London: Routledge, 1989.

Hadenius, Axel: *Democracy and Development.* New York: Cambridge University Press. 1992.

Haggard, Stephan. *Pathways from the Periphery The Politics of Growth in the Newly Industrialized Countries.* Ithaca, N.Y.: Cornell University Press, 1990.

Hall, Peter. *Governing the Economy: The Politics of State Intervention in Britain and France.* New York: Oxford University Press, 1986.

Hannan, Kate, and Ma Hong. *China, Modernisation and the Goal of Prosperity: Government Administration and Economic Policy in the Late 1980s.* Cambridge, N.Y.: Cambridge University Press, 1995.

Harding, Harry. *Chinas Second Revolution.* Washington, D.C: Brookings Institution, 1987.

Harrod, Jeffrey. *Power, Production, and the Unprotected Worker.* New York: Columbia University Press, 1987.

Hartland-Thunberg, Penelope. *China, Hong Kong, Taiwan, and the World Trading System.* New York: St. Martin's Press, 1988.

Hax, Herbert et al. *Economic Transformation in Eastern Europe and East Asian: A challenge for Japan and Germany.* Berlin: Springer, 1996.

He, Xin (何新). *Zhongguo wenhuashi xinlun* (New thought on Chinese cultural history). Beijing: Renmin Press, 1990.

Herzberg, Frederick et al. *The Motivation to Work.* 2d ed. New York: John Wiley and Sons, 1959.

Hoffmann, Charles. *The Chinese Worker.* Albany, N.Y.: SUNY Press, 1974.

Howard, Pat. *Breaking the Iron Rice Bowl*. Armonk, N.Y.: M. E. Sharpe, 1988.

Howe, Christopher, and Kenneth Walker. *The Foundations of the Chinese Planned Economy*. Houndmills, U.K.: Macmillan, 1989.

Howell, Jude. *China Opens its Doors: The Politics of Economic Transition*. Boulder, Colo.: Lynne Rienner Publishers, 1993.

Hsü, Immanuel C.Y. *The Rise of Modern China*. 5th ed. New York: Oxford University Press, 1995.

Hu, Angang (胡鞍钢). *Tiaozhan Zhongguo: Denghou zhongnanhai mianning de jiyu yu xuangzhi* (Challenge China: Opportunities and options for the post-Deng CCP leadership). Taipei: Xinxinwen Press, 1995.

Hu, Ping (胡平) et al. *Zhongguo shichang jingji quanshu* (The comprehensive book on the Chinese market economy). Beijing: Huaxia Press, 1993.

Hu, Rulei (胡如雷). *Zhongguo fengjian shehui xintai yanjiu* (A study on the structure of the Chinese feudal society). Beijing: Sanlian Press, 1979.

Hua, Shan (华山). *Songshi lunji* (On the history of Song). Jinan: Qilu Books, 1982.

Huang, Daoxia (黄道霞) et al. *Zhonghua remin gongheguo dashiji 1949-1989* (The chronicle of the PRC). Beijing: Guangming Daily Press, 1989.

Huang, Philip C.C. *The Peasant Family and Rural Development in the Yangzi Delta, 1350-1988*, Stanford, Calif.: Stanford University Press, 1990.

Huang, Shu-min. *The Spiral Road: Changes in a Chinese Village*. Boulder, Colo.: Westview Press, 1989.

Huang, Xiyuan (黄希源). *Zhongguo jinxiandai nongye jingji shi* (Modern history of agriculture in China). Zhengzhou: Henan Renmin Press, 1986.

Huntington, Samuel. *Political Order in Changing Societies*. New Haven, Conn.: Yale University Press, 1970.

International Labor Office (ILO). *World Labor Report, 1-2*. London: Oxford University Press, 1987.

———. *Thirteenth International Conference of Labor Statistics: Report of the Conference*. Geneva, 1982.

Jacobson, Harold, and Michael Oksenberg. *Toward a Global Economic Order: Chinas Participation in the IMF, the World Bank, and GATT*. Boulder, Colo.: Westview Press, 1989.

Jian, Bezan. *Qinghang shi* (The history of Qing and Hang). Hong Kong: China Books Press, 1984.

Jiang, Zemin (江泽民). *Zhonggong shisida zhengzhi baogao* (The political report to the Fourteenth National Congress of the CCP). Beijing: Renmin Press, 1992.

———. *Zhonggong shiwuda zhengzhi baogao* (The political report to the Fifteenth National Congress of the CCP). Beijing: Renmin Press, 1997.

Jin, Guangtao (金观涛). *Zhongguo de chao wendingxin jiegou* (The Chinese super-stability structure). Beijing: Dabeiku Press, 1987.

Johnson, Chalmers. *Peasant Nationalism and Communist Power*. Stanford, Calif.: Stanford University Press, 1962.

Keleinberg, Robert. *Chinas Opening to the Outside World: The Experiment with Capitalism.* Boulder, Colo.: Westview Press, 1990.

Kelliher, Daniel. *Peasant Power in China: The Era of Reform, 1979-1989.* New Haven, Conn.: Yale University Press, 1992.

Keohane, Robert. *After Hegemony.* Princeton, N.J.: Princeton University Press, 1984.

Kindleberger, Charles. *The World in Depression 1929-1939.* Berkeley: University of California Press, 1973.

Knox, F. *Labor Supply in Economic Development.* Westmead, U.K.: Saxon House, 1979.

Kornai, Janos. *The Economics of Shortage.* Amsterdam: North-Holland, 1980. *The Road to a Free Economy.* New York: Norton, 1990.

———. *The Political Economy of Socialist Systems.* Princeton, N.J.: Princeton University Press, 1992.

Korzec, Michael. *Labor and the Failure of Reform in China.* London: Macmillan, 1992.

Kratochwil, K. V. *Rules, Norms and Decisions.* Cambridge, U.K.: Cambridge University Press, 1989.

Kraus, Willy. *Economic Development and Social Change in the Peoples Republic of China.* New York: Springer-Verlag, 1982.

Kumar, K. *Transnational Enterprises: Their Impact on Third World Societies and Cultures.* Boulder, Colo.: Westview Press, 1980.

Labor Ministry. *Xuanli de gaige zhi huaQiye laodong gongzi shehui baoxian zhidu gaige dianxin jingyan xunbian* (Bright flowers of reform: Selected cases of reforms on labor, wages, and social insurance in the enterprises). Beijing: Labor Press, 1991.

———. *Quanyuan laodong hetongzhi gongzuo zhinan* (Working guide to the total labor contract system). Beijing: Labor Press, 1992.

Lardy, Nicholas. *Foreign Trade and Economic Reform in China.* New York: Cambridge University Press, 1991.

Lawson, Key. *The Human Polity: A Comparative Introduction to Political Science.* 3d ed. Boston: Houghton Mifflin, 1993.

Lee, Hong Yung. *From Revolutionary Cadres to Party Technocrats in Socialist China.* New Haven, Conn.: Yale University Press, 1990.

Legters, Lyman et al. *Critical Perspectives on Democracy.* Lanham, Md.: University Press of America, 1994.

Lehmbruch, Gerhard, Corporation and the Structure of Corporatist Networks. In *Order and Conflict in Contemporary Capitalism,* edited by John Goldthorpe. London: Clarendon Press, 1985.

Levitan, A. et al. *Human Resources and Labor Market. Labor and Manpower in the American Economy.* New York: Harper and Row, 1972.

Li, Chenggui (李成贵). Chuantong nongcun shehui zhongfa zhidu de lixin shengshi (A rational examination of the patriarchy system in traditional rural society). *Minshou yanjiu* (Folklore studies) (Jinan) (1994): 1-4, 38.

Li, Lanqing (李岚清). ed. *Zhongguo liyong waizi jichu zhishi* (Basic knowledge on using foreign investment). Preface by Jiang Zemin Beijing. Beijing: CCP Central School Press, 1995.

Li, Mengbai (李梦白) et al. *Liudong renkou dui dachengshi fazhang de yingxiang ji duice* (The influence of the floating people on the development of the big cities and the relevant policies). Beijing: Ribao Press, 1991.

Li, Qiang (李强), *Dangdai Zhongguo shehui fenchen yu liudong* (Social stratification and mobility in contemporary China). Beijing: Zhongguo Jingji Press, 1993.

Liang, Chuanyun (梁传运), ed. *The Guidebook for Managing Private Enterprises in China.* Beijing: Beijing University Press, 1990.

Lieberthal, Kenneth, and David M. Lampton, eds. *Bureaucracy, Politics, and Decision Making in Post-Mao China.* Berkeley: University of California Press, 1991.

Lieberthal, Kenneth, and Michal Oksenberg. *Policy Making in China: Leaders, Structures, and Process.* New Haven, Conn.: Yale University Press, 1990.

Lin, Ganquan (林甘泉). On the Economic Basis of Feudal Absolutism in Qin and Han. In *Qinhan shi lunchong* (On the history of Qin and Han). Xian: Shangxi Renmin Press, 1983.

Lin, Yifu (林毅夫). Guanyu zhidu bianqian de lilun (On the theory of institutional changes) in *Caichang quanli yu zhidu bianqian* (Property rights and institutional changes). Shanghai: Sanlian Press, 1992.

———. *Zhidu, jishu yu Zhongguo nongye fazhan* (Institution, technology, and the agricultural development in China). Shanghai: Sanlian Press, 1994.

Lindblom, Charles E. *Politics and Markets: The Worlds Political-Economic Systems.* New York: Basic Books, 1977.

———, ed. *Democracy and Market System.* New York: Oxford University Press, 1991.

Ling, Zhu. *Rural Reform and Peasant Income in China.* New York: St. Martin's Press, 1991.

Lishisuo (The Institute of History, Chinese Social Science Academy), ed. *Zhongguo ziben zhuyi mengya wenti lunwen ji* (On the sprouts of Chinese capitalism). 3 vols. Beijing: Renmin Press, 1963-1965.

Little, Daniel. *Understanding Peasant China.* New Haven, Conn.: Yale University Press, 1989.

Liu, Alan P. L. *Phoenix and the Lame Lion: Modernization in Taiwan and Mainland China, 1950-1980.* Stanford, Calif.: Hoover Press, 1987.

Liu, Binyan, *Chinas Crisis, Chinas Hope.* Cambridge, Mass.: Harvard University Press, 1990.

Liu, Ying (刘英) et al. *Dangdai Zhongguo nongcun jiating* (The rural families in contemporary China: An investigation in fourteen provinces). Beijing: Shehui Kexue Wenxian Press, 1993.

Liu, Zongxiu (刘宗秀), ed. *Baiwei xuezhe dui shenzhen de sikao* (The thoughts on Shenzhen from a hundred famous scholars). Shenzhen: Haitian Press, 1991.

Local Government Documents and Regulations on Labor Management in Foreign Enterprises. A. Darning city, 1987; B. Shenzhen SEZ, 1987 and 1989; C. Guangdong Province, 1989.

Loveridge, R., and A. L. Mok. *Theories of Labor Market Segmentation: A Critique.* The Hague: Martin Nijhof, 1979.

Lu, Simian (吕思勉). *Qinhan shi* (The history of Qin and Han). Shanghai: Kaiming Books, 1947.

Ma, Hong (马洪). *New Strategy for Chinese Economy.* Beijing: New World Press, 1983.

———, and Sun Shangqing, eds: *1993-1994 Zhongguo jingji xingshi yu zhanwang* (Economic situation and prospect of China, 1993-1994). Beijing: Zhongguo Fazhang Press, 1994.

Mao, Zedong (毛泽东). *Mao Zedong xuanji 1949-1966* (Selected works of Mao Zedong, 1949-1966). Vols. 1-5. Beijing: Renmin Press, 1973-1978.

Marx, Karl, and F. Engels. *Selected Works.* London: Lawrence and Wishart, 1968.

Maxwell Communication Corp. *The China Directory of Industry and Commerce 1989.* Hong Kong: Maxwell Communication Corp., 1989.

McCormick, Barrett L. *Political Reform in Post-Mao China Democracy and Bureaucracy in a Leninist Sate.* Berkeley: University of California Press, 1990.

Meier, Gerald M. *Emerging from Poverty.* New York: Oxford University Press, 1984.

Migdal, Joel S. *Strong Societies and Weak States: State-Society Relations and State Capabilities in the Third World.* Princeton, N.J.: Princeton University Press, 1988.

Miles, Robert. *Capitalism and Unfree Labor.* London and New York: Tavistock Publications, 1987.

Moore, Barrington. *Social Origins of Dictatorship and Democracy.* Boston: Beacon, 1967, 1993.

Moors, Hein, and Rossella Palomba, eds. *Population, Family, and Welfare A Comparative Survey of European Attitudes.* New York: Oxford University Press, 1995.

Murphy, James. *The Moral Economy of Labor Aristotelian Themes in Economic Theory.* New Haven, Conn.: Yale University Press, 1993.

Nam, Charles B. et al. *International Handbook on Internal Migration.* Westport, Conn.: Greenwood Press, 1990.

Nee, Victor, and David Mozingo, eds. *State and Society in Contemporary China.* Ithaca, N.Y.: Cornell University Press, 1983.

Needham, Joseph. *Science and Civilization in China.* Vols. 1-4. Cambridge, N.Y.: Cambridge University Press, 1954-1995.

Nimkoff, M. F., and Russell Middleton. Types of Family and Types of Economy. *The American Journal of Sociology* 66, no. 3 (1960): 215-225.

Niu Renliang (牛仁亮). *Laoli: Yongyuan shiye yu qiye xiaoli* (Labor force: Underemployment, unemployment, and enterprise efficiency). Beijing: Zhongguo Caijing Press, 1993.

Noer, David M. *Multinational People Management.* Washington, D.C.: Bureau of National Affairs, 1975.

Nolan, Peter et al. Towards an Appraisal of the Impact of Rural Reform in China. *Cambridge Journal of Economics* (March 1986).

Nolan, Peter, and Dong Fureng, eds. *Market Forces in China: Competition and Small Business.* London and New Jersey: Zed Books, 1989.

North, Douglass, *Structure and Change in Economic History.* Norton: New York, 1981.

————. *Institutions, Institutional Change and Economic Performance.* New York: Cambridge University Press, 1990.

Nove, Alec. *The Soviet Economic System.* London: George Allen and Unwin, 1977.

————. *Socialism, Economics and Development.* London: George Allen and Unwin, 1986.

Office of State Council Leading Group for Foreign Investments: *Provisions of the State Council of the PRC for the Encouragement of Foreign-Invested Enterprises and the Supplement.* Beijing, 1987 and 1989.

Ogden, Suzanne. *Chinas Unresolved Issues: Politics, Development, and Culture.* Englewood Cliffs, N.J.: Prentice Hall, 1995.

Oi, Jean C. *State and Peasant in Contemporary China: The Political Economy of Village Government.* New Haven, Conn.: Yale University Press, 1989.

————. Communism and Clientelism: Rural Politics in China. *World Politics* (January 1985).

Orren, Karen. The Primacy of Labor in American Constitutional Development. *American Political Science Review* 89, no. 2 (June 1995).

Paauw, D. S., and J.C.H. Fei. *The Transition in Open Dualism Economies.* New Haven, Conn.: Yale University Press, 1973.

Packenham, Robert. *The Dependency Movement: Scholarship and Politics in Development Studies.* Cambridge, Mass.: Harvard University Press, 1992.

Parish, William L., ed. *Chinese Rural Development: The Great Transformation.* Armonk, N.Y.: M. E. Sharpe, 1985.

Parnell, Martin. *The German Tradition of Organized Capitalism: Self-Government in the Cola Industry.* Oxford, U.K.: Blackwell, 1994.

Parsons, Talcott. *The Social System.* New York: Free Press, 1951A.

————. *Toward a General Theory of Action.* Cambridge, Mass.: Harvard University Press, 1951B.

————. *Social Structure and Personality.* New York: Free Press, 1964.

————. *Sociological Theory and Modern Society.* New York: Free Press, 1967.

Patterson, Perry, ed. *Capitalist Goals, Socialist Past: The Rise of the Private Sector in Command Economies.* Boulder, Colo.: Westview Press, 1993.

Peng, Huei En. *Taiwan fazhande zhengzi jingji fenxi* (The political economy of Taiwans development). Taipei, Taiwan: Fengyun Luntang Press, 1995.

Perkins, Dwight H. *Agricultural Development in China, 1368-1968.* Chicago: Aldine, 1969.

———. *China, Asias Next Economic Giant?* Seattle: University of Washington Press, 1986.

Perry, Elizabeth. State and Society in Contemporary China. *World Politics* (July 1989).

Perry, Elizabeth, and Wong, C. *The Political Economy of Reform in Post-Mao China.* Cambridge, N.Y.: Harvard University Press, 1985.

Picchio, Antonella. *Social Reproduction: The Political Economy of the Labor Market.* New York: Cambridge University Press, 1992.

Poggi, Gianfranco. *The State: Its Nature, Development, and Prospect.* Stanford,Calif.: Stanford University Press, 1991.

Polanyi, Karl. *The Great Transformation: The Political and Economic Origins of Our Time.* Boston: Beacon Press, 1957.

Pomeranz, Kenneth. *The Making of a Hinterland: State, Society, and Economy in Inland North China, 1853-1937.* Berkeley: University of California Press, 1993.

Popkin, Samuel. *The Rational Peasant: The Political Economy of Rural Society in Vietnam.* Berkeley: University of California Press, 1979.

Powell, Simon G. *Agricultural Reform in China.* New York: St. Martin's Press, 1991.

Przeworski, Adam. Could We Feed Everyone? The Irrationality of Capitalism and the Infeasibility of Socialism. *Politics and Society* (March 1991).

———. *Democracy and the Market: Political and Economic Reforms in East Europe and Latin America.* New York: Cambridge University Press, 1991.

Putterman, Louis, ed. *Continuity and Change in China's Rural Development.* New York: Oxford University Press, 1993.

Pye, Lucian. *The Dynamics of Chinese Politics.* Boston, Mass.: GH Inc., 1981.

Qi, Lan (齐兰). *Woguo xianjieduan jibeng gongzi wenti yanjiu* (A study on the basic wages issue in current China). Beijing: Zhongguo Caizheng Jinji Press, 1993.

Qian, Qizhi (钱其智) et al. *Jigou gaige yu bianzhi guanli zhengce fagui wenda* (Rules and policies on institutional reform and staffing management). Beijing: Renshi Press, 1990.

Qiao, Lijun (乔立君) et al. *Zhongguo buneng luan* (China can not afford chaos). Beijing: Central CCP School Press, 1994.

Rawski, Thomas G. *Economic Growth and Employment in China.* New York: The World Bank and Oxford University Press, 1979.

Reich, M, D., M. Gordon, and R. C. Edwards. A Theory of Labor Market Segmentation. *American Economic Review* 63, no. 2 (1973).

Renshibu (Personnel Ministry), ed. *Guojia gongwuyuan zhanxing tiaoli shiyi* (Explanation of the state provisional regulation of civil servants). Beijing: Renmin Press, 1993.

Renshibu and Zhongzhubu (Personnel Ministry and CCP Central Organization Department), eds. *Xianzhen ganbu pingyongzhi guanli jingyan yu zhengce huibian* (Policies and lessons in the management of the appointed xianzhen cadres). Changsha: Hunan Keji Press, 1993.

Ri, Shan (日山), ed. *Zhuming xuezhe lun shichang jingji* (Famous scholars on the market economy). Beijing: Renmin Press, 1993.

Rima, Ingrid H. *Labor Market in a Global Economy.* Philadelphia: Temple University Press, 1996.

Robinson, Thomas W. *Democracy and Development in the East Asia.* Lanham, Md.: University Press of America, 1990.

Rong, Zhonghua. *Waishang touzi qiye de chuangban yu gunali* (The establishment and management of foreign-invested enterprises). Beijing: Zhigong Jiaoyue Press, 1990.

Rostow, W. W. *The Stages of Economic Growth: A Non-Communist Manifesto.* Cambridge, U.K.: Cambridge University Press, 1969.

Rowan, Richard, ed. *Readings in Labor Economics and Labor Relations.* Homewood, Ill.: Richard Irwin, 1980.

Saith, Ashwani, ed. *The Re-emergence of the Chinese Peasantry Aspects of Rural Decollectivisation.* London and New York: Croom Helm, 1987.

Sassen, Saskin. *The Mobility of Labor and Capital: A Study in International Investment and Labor Flow.* New York: Cambridge University Press, 1990.

Schmitter, Philippe. Neo-corporatism and the State. In *The Political Economy of Corporatism,* edited by Wyn Grant. New York: St. Martin's Press, 1986.

Schmitz, Hubert. *Technology and Employment Practices in Developing Countries.* London: Croom Helm, 1985.

Schwartz, Pedro, and Ramon Febrero, eds. *The Essence of Becker.* Stanford, Calif.: Hoover Institution Press, 1996.

Scott, James. *The Moral Economy of the Peasants.* New Haven, Conn.: Yale University Press. 1976.

Sell, Ralph R. Market and Direct Allocation of Labor Through Migration. *Sociological Quarter* (Washington, D.C.) (winter 1983).

Sen, Amartya. *Employment, Technology and Development: A Study for the International Labor Office.* Oxford, U.K.: Clarendon Press, 1975.

———. *On Economic Inequality.* New York: Oxford University Press, 1993.

Shenzhen FDI Center. *Touzi fali fagui xuanbian* (Selected laws and regulations on investment), Shenzhen, Shenzhen Touzi Chujing Zhongxin (Shenzhen FDI Promotion Center), 1991.

Shirk, Susan. Recent Chinese Labor Policies and the Transformation of Industrial Organization in China. *China Quarterly* (December 1981).

———. *Competitive Comrades: Career Incentives and Student Strategies in China.* Berkeley: University of California Press, 1982.

———. *The Political Logic of Economic Reform in China,* Berkeley: University of California Press, 1993.

Shoji, Shiba. *A Cross-National Comparison of Labor Management with Reference to Technology Transfer.* Tokyo: Institute of Developing Economies, 1973.

Shue, Vivienne. *The Reach of the State: Sketches of the Chinese Body Politic.* Stanford, Calif.: Stanford University Press, 1988.

———. *Peasant China in Transition: The Dynamics of Development toward Socialism, 1949-1956.* Berkeley: University of California Press, 1980.

Sima, Qian (司马迁). *Shiji* (History). Beijing: Renmin Press, 1984.

Simai, Mihly, ed. *Global Employment: An International Investigation into the Future of Work.* Tokyo: United Nations University Press, 1995.

Skocpol, Theda. *State and Social Revolutions.* New York: Cambridge University Press, 1979.

Slomp, Hans. *Labor Relations in EuropeA History of Issues and Developments.* Westport, Conn.: Greenwood Press, 1990.

Smith, James P. *Female Labor Supply: Theory and Estimation.* Princeton, N.J.: Princeton University Press, 1980.

Solinger, D. *Chinese Business Under Socialism.* Berkeley: University of California Press, 1984.

Southall, Roger, ed. *Labor and Unions in Asia and Africa.* New York: St. Martin's Press, 1988.

Spence, Jonathan. *The Search for Modern China.* New York: Norton, 1990.

Squire, Lyn. *Employment Policy in Developing Countries: A Survey of Issues and Evidence.* New York: The World Bank and Oxford University Press, 1981.

SSB (State Statistics Bureau), ed. *Zhongguo tongji zhaiyao 1992* (A statistical survey of China 1992). Beijing: Zhongguo Tongji Press, 1992.

———. *Zhongguo tongji zhaiyao 1993* (A statistical survey of China 1993). Beijing: Zhongguo Tongji Press, 1993.

SSB-LM (State Statistics Bureau and Labor Ministry), ed. *1990 Chinese Labor and Wage Yearbook.* Beijing: Zhongguo Tongji Press, 1990.

SSB-LM (State Statistics Bureau and Labor Ministry), ed. *Zhongguo laodong tongji nianjian 1991* (Labor statistical yearbook of China 1991). Beijing: Zhongguo Laodong Press, 1991.

SSB-PB (State Statistics Bureau, Population Bureau), ed. *Zhongguo renkou tongji nianjian 1993* (China population statistics yearbook 1993). Beijing: Zhongguo Laodong Press, 1993.

SSB-RB (State Statistics Bureau, Rural Bureau), ed. *Zhongguo nongchun tongji nianjian 1992* (China rural statistics yearbook 1992). Beijing: Zhongguo Tongji Press, 1992.

Standing, Guy, ed. *Labor Circulation and the Labor Process.* London: Croom Helm, 1985.

State Council Legal Bureau. *Jiti, geti, siying jingji kaiye jingying zhengce fagui xunbian* (Selected policies and laws on the opening and operation of the collective, household, and private economy). Beijing: Zhongguo Minzhu Fazi Press, 1993.

Sun, Weichuan (孙慰川) et al. *Sanzi qiye yingpinouzhe zhinan* (guidebook on finding jobs in the FDI enterprises). Nanjing: Hehai University Press, 1993.

Sun, Zhumin (孙祚民). *Zhongguo nongmin zhanzheng wenti tangso* (A study on the issues of Chinese peasant wars). Shanghai: Xing Zhishi Press, 1956.

Tang, Yijie (汤一介), ed. *Zhongguo zongjiao: Guoqu yu xianzai* (Chinese religion: Past and current). Beijing: Beijing University Press, 1992.

Tarling, Roger, ed. *Flexibility in Labor Markets*. London: Academic Press, 1987.

Taylor, Jeffrey. Rural Employment Trends and the Legacy of Surplus Labor, 1978-86. *The China Quarterly* (December 1988): 732-766.

Thomas, S. Bernard. *Labor and the Chinese Revolution*. Ann Arbor, Mich.: Center for Chinese Studies, The University of Michigan, 1983.

Timmer, Peter. *Agriculture and the State: Growth, Employment, and Poverty in Developing Countries*. Ithaca, N.Y.: Cornell University Press, 1991.

Tomlins, Christopher. *The State and the Unions: Labor Relations, Law, and the Organized Labor Movement in America, 1890-1960*. New York: Cambridge University Press, 1985.

Turner, Lowell. *Democracy at Work: Changing World Markets and the Future of Labor Unions*. Ithaca, N.Y.: Cornell University Press, 1991.

Twitchett, Denis, ed. *The Cambridge History of China, Vol. 3, Sui and Tang China, 589-906*. New York: Cambridge University Press, 1979.

Twitchett, Denis, and Michael Loewe, eds. *The Cambridge History of China, Vol. 1, The Chin and Han Empires, 221 B.C.-A.D. 220*. New York: Cambridge University Press, 1986.

Ullerich, Curtis. *Rural Employment and Manpower Problems in China*. Armonk, N.Y.: M. E. Sharpe, 1979.

Unger, Jonathan. *Education under Mao: Class and Competition in Canton Schools, 1960-1980*. New York: Cambridge University Press, 1982.

Van Ness, Peter, ed. *Market Reforms in Socialist Societies: Comparing China and Hungary*. Boulder and London: Lynne Rienner Publishers, 1989.

———. and David Stark, eds: *Remaking the Economic Institutions of Socialism: China and East Europe*. Stanford, Calif.: Stanford University Press, 1990.

Vernon, Raymond. *Sovereignty at Bay: The Multinational Spread of U.S. Enterprise*. New York: Basic Books, 1971.

———. *Economic and Political Consequences of Multinational Enterprise*. Cambridge, Mass.: Harvard University Press. 1972.

Wade, Robert. *Governing the Market: Economic Theory and the Role of Government in East Asian Industrialization*. New Haven, Conn.: Yale University Press, 1990.

Walder, Andrew G. *Communist Neo-Traditionalism: Work and Authority in Chinese Industry*. New Haven, Conn.: Yale University Press, 1986.

———. Factory and Managers in an Era of Reform. *The China Quarterly* (June 1989): 242-264.

Wallerstein, Immanuel. *The Modern World-System: Capitalist Agriculture and the Origins of the European World-Economy in the Sixteenth Century*. New York: Academic Press, 1974.

Wang, Baoshu (王保树). *Economic Law.* Chengdu, China: Sichuan Peoples Press, 1988.

Wang, Dingding (汪丁丁). Zhidu bianqian de yiban lilun (General theory of institutional changes). *Jingji yanjou* (Economic studies) (Beijing), no. 5 (1992).

Wang, Fei-Ling. *Institutions and Institutional Change in China: Premodernity and Modernization.* London and New York: Macmillian Press, 1998.

———. Floaters, Moonlighters, and the Underemployed: A National Labor Market with Chinese Characteristics. *Journal of Contemporary China* (Oxford, U.K.), forthcoming.

———. To Distort the Market: The Role of Society in Chinese Modernization. *Chinese Journal of Political Science (CJPS)* (Los Angeles) 1, no. 1 (May 1995A).

———. Four Cheers for International Political Anarchy. *Journal of Chinese Political Science* (Knoxville, Tenn.) 2, no. 1 (winter 1995B).

———. International Market and Domestic Changes: The Case of China. *In Depth* (Washington, D.C.) 4, no. 1 (winter 1994).

Wang, Guichen (王贵宸) et al. *Zhongguo nongchun jingji xue* (Rural economics of China). Beijing: Renmin University Press, 1988.

Wang, Haibo (汪海波) et al. *Xinzhongguo gongyi jianshi* (A short history of industry in the new China). Beijing: Jingji Guangli Press, 1986.

Wang, Huning (王沪宁). *Dangdai Zhongguo cunlou jiazhu wenhua: Dui Zhongguo shehui xiandaihua de yixian tansuo* (Village and clan culture in contemporary China: An exploration of China's social modernization). Shanghai: Shanghai Renmin Press, 1991.

Wang, Jianchu (王建初) et al. *Zhongguo gongren yundong shi* (The history of the Chinese labor movement). Shengyan: Liaoning Renmin Press, 1987.

Wang, N.T. *Chinas Modernization and Transnational Corporations.* Lexington, Mass.: Lexington Books, 1984.

———. *Transnational Corporations and Chinas Open Door Policy.* Lexington, Mass.: Lexington Books, 1988.

Wang, Shan (王山). *Disanzhi yanjing kan Zhongguo* (Look at China through the third eye). Taiwan Edition. Taipei: Zhouzji Wenhua, 1994. (Originally published as a translated work by a fictitious German scholar in Beijing in 1992/1993).

Wang, Shaoguang (王绍光), and Hu Angang. *Zhongguo guojia nengli baogao* (An analytical report on the capacity of the Chinese state). Shenyang: Liaonong Renmin Press, 1993, and Hong Kong: Oxford University Press (China), 1994.

Wang, Weili (王维礼). *Zhongguo xiandai shi* (Contemporary history of China). Shengyang: Liaoning Renmin Press, 1984.

Wang, Xiaoyi (王晓毅). Nongcun shehuixe zii Zhongguo de fazan (The development of rural sociology in China). *Nongcun jingji yu shehui* (Rural economy and society) (Beijing) no. 4 (1994)

Wang, Ying (王颖) et al. *Shehui zhongjian cheng: Gaige yu Zhongguo de shetuan zhuzhi* (The media of the society: reform and the Chinese social associations). Beijing: Zhongguo Fazhang Press, 1993.

Wang, Yu (王余), and Li Yuehong. *Dier zhiye chongye zhinan* (Guidebook on working on second jobs). Beijing: Dangan Press, 1992.

Watson, James L., ed. *Class and Social Stratification in Post-Revolution China*. Berkeley: University of California Press, 1984.

Weber, Max. *Economy and Society*. Berkeley: University of California Press, 1978.

White, Gordon, ed. *Developmental States in East Asia*. New York: St. Martin's Press, 1988.

White III, Lynn T. *Careers in Shanghai: The Social Guidance of Personal Energies in a Developing Chinese City, 1949-1966*. Berkeley: University of California Press, 1978.

Wilkinson, Endymion. *The History of Imperial China*. Cambridge, Mass.: Harvard University Press, 1991.

Woetzel, Jonathan. *China's Economic Opening to the Outside World: The Politics of Empowerment*. New York: Praeger Publishers, 1989.

Womack, Brantly. *Contemporary Chinese Politics in Historical Perspective*. New York: Cambridge University Press, 1991.

Woo, Jung-En. *Race to the Swift: State and Finance in Korean Industrialization*. New York: Columbia University Press, 1990.

Xia, Jizhi (夏积智), and Dang Ziaoji, eds. *Zhongguo de jiuye yu shiye* (Employment and unemployment in China). Beijing: Laodong Press, 1991.

Xin, Changxing (信长星). *Jiuye shiye* (Employment and unemployment). Beijing: Renmin University Press, 1992.

Xue, Muqiao (薛暮桥). *China's Socialist Economy*. Beijing: Foreign Language Publisher, 1981.

Yan, Ruizhen (严瑞珍), ed. *Zhongguo nongcun jingji xue* (Chinese rural economics). Beijing: Zhongguo Jingji Press, 1994.

Yang, Chuntang et al. *Legal Advisor to Economic Management in Enterprises*. Changchun, China: Northeast University Press, 1986.

Yang, Hongshan (杨宏山). Wandong nongcun Jidujiao de diaocha yu sikao (An investigation and reflection on the Christianity Craze in rural east Anhui). *Jianghuai luntang* (Jianghuai forum) (Hefei) no. 4 (1994).

Yang, Mayfair M. *Gifts, Favors, and Banquets: The Art of Social Relationship in China*. Ithaca: Cornell University Press, 1994.

Yao, Wei (姚维), and Murong Qiu (慕容秋). *Chaoji fuhao* (Super rich). Beijing: Tuanji Press, 1993.

Ye, Yaojun (叶尧军). *Zhongguo dushi fazhan shi* (The history of Chinese capitals). Xian: Shangxi Renmin Press, 1988.

Yue, Guangzhao (悦光昭), ed. *Labor Policy and System in China*. Beijing: Economic Management Press, 1989.

Yuan, Fang (袁方). The Current Labor and Employment Issues in China. *Beijing University Journal*, no. 4, (1990).

Yuan, Lunqu (袁伦渠), ed. *Xinzhongguo laodong jingji shi* (The labor history of new China). Beijing: Laodong Renshi Press, 1987.

Yuan, Shouqi (袁守启) et al. *Laodongfa quanshu* (The complete book on labor laws). Beijing: Yuhang Press, 1994.

Zagoria, Donald. China's Quiet Revolution. *Foreign Affairs* (spring 1984).

———, and Li Chang. *The Nature of Mainland Chinese Economic Structure*. New York: Columbia University Press, 1972.

Zeng, Fanhua (曾繁华). *Tiefanwan, heifanwan, jinfanwan* (Iron rice bowl, black rice bowl, gold rice bowl). Zhenzhou: Henan Renmin Press, 1993.

Zhang, Hongyan (张鸿雁). *Minzu pianjian yu wenhua pianjian* (National prejudice and cultural prejudice). Shengyang: Liaoning Education Press, 1993.

Zhang, Houyi (张厚义). Siying qiyezhu jiecheng zaiwoguo shehui jiegou zhongde diwei (The social status of the private employers in our country). *Zhongguo shehui kexue* (Beijing), no. 6 (1994): 100-116.

Zhang, Jin (张晋) et al. *Laodong renshi guanli cidian* (The dictionary of labor and personnel management). Chendu: Sichuan Keji Press, 1987.

Zhang, Mingyuan (张铭远). *Huangse wenming: Zhongguo wenhua de gongneng yu moshi* (Yellow civilization: The function and models of Chinese culture). Shanghai: Shanghai Wenyi Press, 1990).

Zhang, Sai (张塞) et al. *1992 Zhongguo fazhan baogao* (China development report 1992). Beijing: Statistics Press, 1992.

Zhang, Siqian (张思骞) et al. *Zhongguo nongye fazhan zhanlue wenti yanjiu* (A study on the strategic issues in Chinese agricultural development). Beijing: Zhongguo Shehui Kexue Press, 1988.

Zhang, Yanzhong (张言中) et al. *Santou tequde laodong gongzi yu laodong baoxian* (Labor, wages, and labor insurance in Santou Special Zone). Beijing: Renmin Press, 1990.

Zhang, Yuyan (张宇燕). *Jingji fazhan yu zhidu xuanze* (Economic development and institutional selection). Beijing: Renmin University Press, 1992.

Zhao, Renwei (赵人伟) et al. *Zhongguo jumin shouru fenpei yangiu* (A study on Chinese income distribution). Beijing: Shehui Kexue Press, 1994.

Zhong, Nian (钟年). Zhongguo xiangcun shehui kongzi de bianqian (The evolution of social control in Chinese villages). *Shehuixue yanjou* (Sociology studies) (Beijing), no. 3 (1994): 90-99.

Zhou, Kuizhen (周奎真) et al. *How to Correctly Carry Out Enterprise Law: A Collection of the Newest Practical Laws and Regulations.* Beijing: New Times Press, 1988.

Zhu, Cishou (祝慈寿). *Zhongguo gudai gongye shi* (Industrial history of ancient China). Shanghai: Xueling Press, 1988.

Zhu, Qizhen (朱启臻), and Yao Yuqun, eds. *Qiuzhi shouce* (Handbook on job-searching). Beijing: Zhonghuo Cajing Press, 1991.

Index

About the Author

FEI-LING WANG is Assistant Professor at the Sam Nunn School of International Affairs, Georgia Institute of Technology. Born in China, he graduated from the University of Pennsylvania in 1992 with a Ph.D. degree and taught at the University of Pennsylvania and the United States Military Academy (West Point). His research interests are comparative and international political economy, world politics and international relations, East Asia and China studies. He has published several works in these areas in English and Chinese languages.